"TAKING IT APART"

Chapter 1

Happy New Year

For me, 1974 ended at a party near the Country Club in Kilkerry, Indiana. Whenever holidays loomed on the horizon, I dreaded the trip back from school to Kilkerry. North Central Indiana is flat and relatively featureless. Kilkerry lies at the area's heart.

One of Joe Rivers's friends from Purdue was having a party while her parents were away. I was drinking Miller's out of quart bottles. The house was a modern style from the 1950s. The living room was a sunken affair and gave the impression that the ceiling was lower than it actually was. A huge fireplace of Bedford stone took up one wall, with a mantle and several small ledges, all consisting of slabs of stone, jutted out from the fireplace.

The TV was on and showed the ball coming down the pole on Times Square in New York. There were about 25 or 30 of us, all home from several colleges. We greeted 1975 with cheers. Not long afterwards, I felt my knees go wobbly and realized I should go to the Farm and go to sleep.

I have a vague recollection of hitting on Rivers's friend, our hostess. I cannot recall her name or what she looked like. I just remember that she wasn't offended by my efforts, only amused. I said goodbye to several people, put on my coat, and braved the out-of-doors.

The January air of the new year was just as cold as the December air had been a few minutes earlier. I shoved my hands into my jacket pockets and began to walk the two or three blocks to where I'd parked. I'd used one of my Uncle Adolf's construction company trucks, an old Ford with Adolf's name, followed by "Inc.," on the door on each side. ("Adolf" was not really my uncle's name. That was just an endearing term, a nickname by which I referred to him to friends and in my mind, never to his face. "Adolf" as in the guy with the funny mustache who killed all those people and started World War II.) When I got to the truck, I had problems fitting the key into the lock. But finally I got it in. The engine turned over a couple of times slowly, then fired up. It was then that I noticed that the windshield was covered with snow and ice. But I was drunk and tired and wanted to get back to the Farm to get some sleep. I rolled down the window, stuck my head out, turned on the lights and took off, ducking my head in from time to time to keep warm.

Several minutes later, I walked up to the front door of the house where we'd just been partying. Several people turned and said hello. Rivers asked me what I was doing back.

"Got the truck stuck," I replied. There were a few groans, people realizing that there would have to be a group effort to push me out wherever it was that I was stuck. Then somebody asked where and I said, "Drove it into the country club swimming pool."

Suddenly everyone was looking at me. I think they thought I was joking. "Gotta get it out," I said. "Adolf'll kill me."

Rivers was laughing. "How're we gonna get it out of a fucking swimming pool!?" he asked. I tried to explain my theory, but the words didn't come out too clearly. Rivers said something to Warren, a friend, everyone seemed to agree with something that Ottinger, another friend, said, and soon I was being propelled out the door and down the street towards the country club, the arms of several of the dozen or so people around giving me support and direction.

The back entrance runs along a ridge overlooking Fairland Park. That entrance was a way of shooting between Lincoln Road and Deffenbaugh, two of the main streets in Kilkerry. Since then the country club has closed off the driveway to through traffic. The golf course at the club was nice, by Kilkerry standards. There were only two courses in the entire town. The pool was average, sort of what you'd find at a Holiday Inn, and the other facilities were fairly average as well. Several of my friends' parents were members. Warren's folks were; Hennings's parents were real golf freaks, so they were members, too. Eva and Adolf weren't members, though. They viewed expenditures for anything pleasurable as being frivolous and on the verge of sinfulness.

Eva was my nickname for Adolf's wife, my aunt. And it's not that she shared any traits with Eva Braun. Eva Braun was apparently a polite, clueless, mousy person who smiled a lot and liked little kids. The aunt was a real bitch, a lot like the woman who ran the Treblinka death camp and had lamp shades fashioned from the skin of her victims. But at the time that I had re-christened the aunt my freshman year of college, I had not read these particular facts from history, or else I would have found out the first name of the woman at Treblinka and bestowed that upon the aunt as a nom de guerre. But then, I would have had to explain repeatedly the terms. Eva and Adolf were readily identifiable by friends, acquaintances and total strangers.

The lights were on in the country club and the parking lot was full, but nobody seemed to have seen the truck. But there it was. I'd driven down a hillside, smashed over a chain-link fence, and come to rest against the stainless-steel railings of the back of the diving tower.

Rivers jumped behind the wheel and started it up. I was only allowed to watch, but everyone else was as drunk, or nearly as drunk, as I was. He backed it over the fence and started it up the slope, but the snow made the ground slick and the right rear tire started spinning after only four or five feet up the hillside. A bunch of guys got around to the front of the truck and started pushing it. Rivers used their help to start rocking the truck. They would push the truck as Rivers gave it gas, then quickly back away as he hit the clutch. The effort became really focused on the rocking of clutch, gear, clutch, gear. With each rocking motion, the truck seemed to move just a bit farther up the grade. After a while, with a final push from the guys, it broke the crest of the hillside. By then the de-icer had gotten really hot and melted all the ice and snow from the windshield. Rivers shoved me back behind the wheel. He was laughing now that the work was done.

I looked back and saw that the hillside behind the diving board was all fucked up. There were huge ruts leading up to and then across the chain link fence. The fence was leaning over, only a foot or two from the ground. I expected someone from inside to come running out, and cops pulling up to bust us. But no—the party inside seemed not to have let up in the least, and no one had even come out. I shrugged, closed the door, and waved goodbye to everyone as I pulled away.

As I started for the Farm, I relaxed a bit. The drive was five miles, roughly, over straight, flat roads laid out in squares on the rural countryside, once I got out of the town limits. But about a half-mile down the road, just shy of the limits, I remembered that I was out of cigarettes. There was a convenience store right there, and so I hit the brakes and veered into the parking lot.

I did my best to enunciate the brand of cigarettes I wanted. I must have passed the scrutiny of the clerk because she shoved a pack of Vantage Menthols across the counter. As I left the store, I nearly ran into three or four kids from my high school.

They were a couple of years behind me. One was a girl whose brother had been a classmate of mine. He and I had started kindergarten together. We'd gone to the same schools all our lives the way in which kids who are born and raised in rural areas grow up and live there forever. I started talking with them. I'd not hung out with them when I'd been in high school. Besides age difference, there was also the gap between me as a future "leader" and them. These kids weren't in the "accepted" group in high school. They were kids who were just wanting to get out of high school and get on with their lives.

But then, I got into the car with them. I don't know why. We ended up driving around for a couple of hours. I was plastered, but they weren't—they hadn't even been drinking. But I didn't really want to go back to the Farm, and the crisis with the truck and the swimming pool and being out in the open air had given me a second wind. We were all just shooting the shit. Then they took me back to the truck. Right about then I got the idea that they were looking down on me, that they were getting a satisfied feeling that after all of this time, that I was on the skids, a person who had been such a hot shit in high school. And that at least they weren't as pathetic as me. If I hadn't been drunk, I would've said something. Put them down. But hell, if I hadn't been drunk, I wouldn't've gotten into their car in the first place, or spoken to them as I came out of the convenience store. I didn't have anything in common with these people. They were going to spend the rest of their lives running like rats on some exercise wheel in this mid-North Indiana cage. I didn't like them any more than they liked me.

I got into the truck and drove it about two miles. That's about as far as I got because then the stupid thing stopped dead. Like came to a crawling stop with the motor running. I tried to get it going, but it wouldn't move. The gears wouldn't engage. I tried and tried, but it wouldn't work.

I didn't want to leave it parked in the middle of the road with no lights on so that some poor bastard would drive along and hit it. Somebody could get hurt that way. Especially if they were as drunk as me. I mean, I was, after all, a conscientious drunk. So I left the truck there, with the motor running so the battery wouldn't die, and the lights on, so that any moron could see the damn thing. I figured there was no risk of somebody stealing it— even thieves had to take off and get drunk on New Year's and, besides, it wouldn't move. And the truck was an old rusting hulk, anyways.

I started walking and hadn't gotten a couple of hundred yards in the pitch-black tundra of that night before car lights flooded me, and I heard someone pulling over. I walked the few yards back and the guy rolled down his electric window and wanted to know if I wanted a ride: another drunken soul who was charitable in the holiday season. He was going the same direction I was. As we took off he asked me about the truck back there and I told him it was mine—well, not really, but I didn't qualify the technicalities of legal title at that time. He asked me what had happened with it, and I described the symptoms. He told me straight-off that the clutch was fried and asked me if anyone had been riding the clutch. I thought back to the rocking of the truck in the effort to get it up that hillside and realized the source of the vehicle's demise but just told the guy, "No."

It was then that we arrived at the end of Eva and Adolf's quarter-mile long driveway. I thanked the dude and walked up the gravel lane, as I had when I was seven years old and getting off the bus from school. I carefully worked the key into the lock of the front French doors, eased them shut behind me, and made my way upstairs. I then got into bed and passed into the arms of Morpheus.

It was about the eighth or ninth time that Eva yelled at me that I woke up.

"Joe Rivers is on the phone," she said. "Where's the truck?"

My head hurt. I could feel tiny grains of sand gouging into the surfaces of my eyeballs. "What time is it?"

"Seven. What did you do to the truck?"

Not "with" or "where is it" but "what did you do to it."

"Clutch dropped," I replied as I pulled on my pants. I started for the other room to get the phone.

"You smell like liquor," she said as I passed her.

"I don't know how that would be," I said, yawning. "You know I'm underage."

I got to the phone and said hello.

"Just wanted to call you," Rivers said. "We were driving around and found your truck."

Eva was standing about six feet away, trying to listen to every word. Of course she couldn't hear Rivers, but she was trying to make me believe she could.

"Yeah, the truck got fried."

"No kidding," Rivers laughed. "We found it running with the lights on and just pushed it over to the side of the road. Warren has your keys."

"Thanks."

"Sure thing. Hey—you going back to school today?"

"I only wish," I replied. The day was going to be dreadful for me here today in Kilkerry, hung over, and getting bombarded with guilt over the truck not being returned.

"A bunch of us are going to meet later at the bar at Howard Johnson's. Watch some bowl games. Want us to pick you up?"

Only in Kilkerry could a Howard Johnson's bar sound like a wild and crazy place. Besides, going to a bar in Indiana was always a hassle for me. Getting carded and having to leave sucked. But I glanced at Eva and weighed my options.

"Sure," I said, and we agreed that someone would be out to get me at noon.

I said goodbye and hung up. The phone that was next to Eva and Adolf's bed was an ancient thing that weighed a ton and had a rotary dialer. When Eva had gone through her decorating period a couple of years before, she had painted anything that didn't move gold, then used a rag or something to wipe the gold finish with a stain that was supposed to give the item an antique look—that was what the "look" was called in the magazine that she was using as a guide. The phone in the bedroom was no exception, but within a couple of weeks the paint on the handset had worn off and the phone now had a black band between the earphone and the mouthpiece.

"You aren't going anyplace," Eva said. "The roads are awful and they're telling people to drive only if they absolutely have to."

I glanced past her out the window, and saw clear skies and a bright sun pouring light down on modest snows. There was no use in arguing with her. So I shrugged and walked past her to the bathroom.

The bathroom was rotting away, like the rest of the house. But it was a really good gauge of the overall decay of things. It was like Dorian Gray's portrait, a thing hidden away from visitors, and yet the true mirror of everything. I stretched and yawned, then reached into the shower/tub to start the water. I made sure not to touch anything unless I really had to. And I knew that there would be plenty of hot water because Eva, Adolf and the Cousin (I hadn't mentioned him before) only took showers in the evening, before they went to bed. They viewed my taking a shower in the morning as peculiar.

Eva and Adolf had bought the Farm at the end of World War II, during Adolf's First Great Period of Affluence. He had been, after all, a white middle-aged male back home in the States, thanks to 4-F status, while the rest of the world was at war. In various ways reminiscent of Mr. Haney in Green Acres, Adolf had, during the war, hatched various money-making schemes through which he had made out like a bandit. The forty acres, house and various out-buildings hadn't been cheap, but he'd had the cash to swing the deal. The land was covered mostly with hills and woods, but also had two small fields and a modest pasture. The driveway snaked for a quarter-mile from the county road up to the top of the hill where the house stood. From the road, the house was quite imperious with its white pillars on the front porch making the structure look like a mansion. Inside, though, the house was not all that big, even though it had four bedrooms and a bath upstairs and three rooms downstairs.

During Adolf's Second Great Period of Affluence, roughly 1962-63, he'd remodeled much of the interior of the house, including the bathroom. But he would save a penny here or there. "Take care of the pennies and the dollars will take care of themselves," was his oft-stated philosophy—and the remodeling work was no exception. He had paneled the bathroom, including the walls of the shower/tub, with imitation dark green marble that was actually a plastic surface backed by some sort of cardboard. Within a year after the paneling was installed, the walls began to buckle and crack. To make matters worse, Adolf had viewed the purchase of a water softener as being as much of a wasteful indulgence as membership in the country club. The iron content of the water was extremely high. Consequently, the walls of the shower/tub, the tub itself, and its sliding glass door were now orange with over a dozen years' coating of iron.

As the water ran, I walked over to the toilet. I really had to go and couldn't wait. I looked down to make sure the seat was up, then began to piss and tried not to smell or breathe. I wanted to spare myself looking down unless absolutely necessary. The toilet didn't flush correctly. The pipes running out of the house and onto the hillside behind the house had been installed at the turn of the century, when the indoor plumbing had been installed. By this time there were half-a-dozen really good-sized trees growing along the pipe's route from house to hillside. There were bunches of roots that had, no doubt, grown into the pipe to block it. But replacing the pipe would have cost money, and Eva, Adolf and the Cousin forming such a cohesive family unit, didn't care if the toilet flushed properly. There was, thus, a coagulation of shit in the toilet that only flushed partially out after each use. And I don't mean that there were one or two small turds afloat in there. I mean that it was solid and oozing with pieces of toilet paper here and there. No one said anything about it, but then again, it was part of the reason that they never had any visitors. They hadn't for years. What would they do if someone needed to use the head?

As I finished showering, I felt the rumble under my feet of the Cousin's stereo. As I dressed, I did my best to ignore Frank Sinatra belting out hits of the 1940s and 1950s at loud volume. Frank, Lanie Kazan and Johnny Mathis were about the only musical artists the Cousin listened to these days, and he always listened to them at top volume during breakfast.

There were so many reasons why, when we had breaks at school, I was always the last person in the fraternity to leave and the first person to return.

The three rooms downstairs were the kitchen, a rather oddly-shaped living room, and a room that had once been a dining room. But Adolf and Eva had never had guests to dinner at any time, and so a dining room was useless. So, during the 1962 renovations, when the dining room was carpeted and paneled, Eva re-christened it the TV Lounge. Why she decided to do that, I never figured out. There were, at any given time, four or five TV sets in the room. None of them worked. Whenever the television set in the living room would fry out—and that was pretty much an annual affair as Adolf was never one to shell out the money necessary to obtain a good set that would last several years, he simply bought cheap ones that wouldn't last too long—the set in the living room would be moved to the TV Lounge. Adolf would then go into Kilkerry and buy a new set, bring it home, and set it in the place formerly occupied by the other set, and the sets before it. I guess Adolf couldn't bear the thought of throwing away something he'd paid a couple of hundred bucks for only a year before, even if it was useless. Hence, the TV Lounge had become sort of an elephants' graveyard for TVs. In addition to the dead sets, the TV Lounge also contained several dust-laden bookcases, the shelves of which were filled with old hardbacks and an ever-growing collection of Reader's Digest condensed books that Eva was amassing to read one day when she and Adolf retired. I had read Love Story that way. I had wondered, at the time, why everyone else thought that it was risque. It was only when I got a chance to compare the version out in paperback with the condensed version that I realized that the people had condensed the original in large part by cutting out the obscenities and racy passages.

Finally, in addition to mounds of dirty laundry lying here and there, the TV Lounge was also home to the Cousin's stereo, a console model that he'd bought used at some sale. Not only did it have a turntable, amp and speakers, it also had a tuner and—appropriately enough—in the same polished wooden housing, a 25-inch color TV that, of course, was fried out and didn't work.

As I came down the stairs into the TV Lounge, I hit the floor as hard as I could and the needle on the album jumped from Frank, mid-note, to the orchestral bridge of whatever song he was performing.

"Good morning," I said to the Cousin, and moved quickly past him before he could react.

I walked into the kitchen where Eva and Adolf sat at table. The table and chairs were from Adolf's Fourth Great Period of Affluence—1969, when he'd obtained and completed good-sized contracts on one of the factories in Kilkerry. The set was surprisingly nice, a colonial design by Ethan Allen. The refrigerator, too, had been a surprising purchase of good quality. It was a modern-looking thing and had replaced a Coldspot that had been rooted to the asphalt tiles of the kitchen since the days when dinosaurs walked the Earth.

One of the few bright spots in the design and construction of the house was the varnished knotty pine that paneled the kitchen. It was the real thing, tongue-in-groove nailed up long ago, probably when the Coldspot refrigerator had been purchased. Whenever I looked at the kitchen paneling I was always reminded of when I was six or seven years old. Eva and Adolf had wakened me. It seemed as though they'd wakened me in the middle of the night, although it was probably more like 10 p.m. The Cousin had returned from the county fair, all agog. He'd won a ribbon for the Suffolk ewe he'd shown in the sheep competition. That was the reason for Eva's and Adolf's excitement. I mean, the Cousin never won anything on the up-and-up. He only won when he cheated. This, however, was one of those rare occasions of victory for him. The ribbon was for third place in a competition of three sheep. There weren't very many Suffolks being raised in our county at that time. But the Cousin was excited about something else—he'd heard this new group called the Beach Boys. I remember sitting on Eva's lap, listening to the Cousin bubbling on about the music, and I stared sleepily at the knotty pine walls.

I sat down at the table. Adolf looked at me sullenly. Eva set a plate with two fried egg sandwiches on it in front of me. That was my breakfast of choice when I was at the Farm in those days.

"What happened to the goddamn truck?" Adolf demanded.

I started to explain when the Cousin came in and started bitching about how I'd made his album skip. "He's ruining my albums," he complained to Adolf.

"I'm sure that leaving them out of their sleeves lying on the floor all the time in there like you do hasn't hurt them any," I said and smiled, then tilted up my plate so that the Cousin could see the eggs. For whatever reason, the sight of eggs had an emetic effect on the Cousin. The Cousin became violently ill at the mere sight of eggs. That was why I loved eggs for breakfast there at the Farm every goddamn day.

As I ate, I related an expurgated version of the previous evening's events worthy of the Reader's Digest condensed books. Basically, I said that the clutch in the truck had dropped just out of the blue. Adolf grumbled about the "goddamn men" who worked for him riding the clutch, and the topic of the truck was safely closed for the day.

"He thinks he's going to town," Eva said, nodding her head in my direction.

"Can't," Adolf stated flatly. "The roads are treacherous."

Adolf always said that the roads were "treacherous." Dew on the ground made the roads "treacherous."

"Don't forget to feed the livestock," Eva reminded me. The end of her sentence was punctuated by a muffled howl from the basement.

That's another thing that was always strange—the weird relationship that Adolf, Eva and the Cousin had with animals. The Cousin would acquire animals, and once the novelty of that particular beast wore off, abandon the animal for me to care for. The "livestock" constituted just such a case. The Cousin had purchased a couple of head of cattle two years before, with the idea of raising them on the pasture that grew, unused, over a relatively large portion of the farm. He bought them in the early part of spring. The plan was to take them to the butcher in early autumn, keep a good portion of the meat in the freezer out on the breezeway behind the kitchen, and sell the rest. However, doing that involved work, and the Cousin grew disinterested in the idea as the cattle fattened and summer turned to autumn, then winter set in. The front field, down the hill from the house, was harvested a couple of times a summer for hay anyways, and Adolf would divert part of this to the Cousin's cattle. Those cattle were now probably amongst the safest creatures in the world. They would not end up on anyone's plate.

Then there were the sheep. Every two or three years the Cousin would revisit his youth and memories of his competing in 4-H, where he won that third-place ribbon so long ago, and he would purchase sheep, purportedly to raise for wool. He wouldn't buy them completely on his own. Rather, he would talk Adolf into going halfsies on them. Of course, the Cousin never sheered the damn things. That involved work that he was loath to perform. So the ten or twelve sheep that he bought would become the wooliest on the planet as their coats grew and grew. But there is an interesting aspect to raising sheep.

They attract dogs. Not the friendly little dogs such as those that helped Scottish farmers herd their flocks. No. All around the farm in the early 1960s a couple of developers had built pre-fabricated housing into which various families of hilljacks, people one generation or less removed from the hills of Kentucky and Tennessee, had moved. Some had even seen work in the movies, getting onscreen time as extras in the making of *Deliverance*. Upon moving to the country, these people had promptly let their pet dogs loose to run. The dogs were strange hybrids of Doberman Pinschers, pit bulls, German shepherds and rabid wolverines. The good folks moving to the country didn't realize that faithful Rover had tens of thousands of years of carnivore imprinted in his genes. Adolf couldn't complain too much about the exodus of hilljacks. His company was, after all, doing work on the houses. That work was part of the reason for his Third Great Period of Affluence. But at night, after their masters were asleep, the dogs would congregate in packs, then enter the pasture to kill the Cousin's sheep. The dogs weren't killing the sheep for food—most of the dogs were as overfed as their corpulent owners. No, the dogs killed out of a lust for blood. Once they fell upon the flock of sheep, they would mow through it, killing in a frenzy. The sheep were defenseless. Worse, while evolution had instilled a hilljack type of viciousness into the doggies, farmers had somehow bred resistance out of the sheep. A sheep could get simply knocked over and die from fear. Adolf would become angered at the dogs. The sheep cost anywhere from a hundred to three hundred dollars. There was a county fund for livestock killed by dogs—go figure—but the fund only paid up to twenty-five bucks a head for dead animals. This gave rise to Adolf and the Cousin keeping on the lookout for dogs. Their constant vigilance resulted in sprints to the bottom of the stairway to the stack of rifles and shotguns that just sat there for ready use. They would then shoot at the dogs, and usually they hit one or two. This ongoing war did not bode well for good relations with the neighbors. In fact, Adolf and the Cousin were roundly hated as being dog killers by most of the people in the area. There was an irony to all of this, though, and that was Adolf's, Eva's and the Cousin's professed love for animals, especially dogs, even though I began to suspect that the Cousin kept sheep for the plausible excuse of killing dogs.

The Cousin's love for canines was so great that three years before, he had purchased an old English sheep dog. The "plan" that the Cousin had envisioned included building some sort of kennel outside, and training and raising the dog, for show. There the Cousin could win a ribbon, much like his third-place ribbon at the county fair long ago in his youth, and be roundly admired for all to see. Then he could breed puppies and sell them. Unfortunately for the dog that the Cousin bought, these dreams involved work by the Cousin—work that he was loath to perform. So it was that the dog went to the basement. The basement in Adolf's and Eva's house was really only a room for the furnace, water heater and tank for the heating oil for the furnace. Also, it was a room through which ran the sewage and other effluent from the bathroom. So the dog lived down there in filth and solitude, short visits from persons spent only feeding it. That was the howl that I now heard.

That seemed to conclude matters in the minds of Eva and Adolf. Then they ignored me and went on to discuss the more pressing matters in their lives—the latest vicious gossip that had been circulated by the neighborhood sewer of such matters, a woman named Delores Pottman who lived only a half-mile or so away. In the world of Mrs. Pottman, everyone was a suspect—except herself, her family, and the person with whom she was talking at the moment. From Delores, Eva would find out the latest person who'd been diagnosed with a fatal illness and the current roster of persons engaged in extramarital affairs. To listen to Delores tell it, the neighborhood around the Farm was peopled by those either fucking or dying. Well—maybe there's a deeper truth to that. Maybe that's all that people do anyway. But the gossip that Delores spread was bitter. It was mean and meant to hurt the subject of it. And most of it was so extraordinary that one couldn't believe it on its face. A couple of years before, Delores said that the woman who lived two doors down from her wasn't expected to live out the week. But when I drove into town, that woman was on her riding lawn mower and smiled and waved to me as I passed by. Eva refused to believe that Delores may have misled her on that one. But then Eva believed that everything that was printed in *The National Enquirer* was true and that big-time championship wrestling was real, unscripted sport. Her intellectual world revolved around gossip, the *Enquirer* and the various cheap books about the latest peccadilloes of the Kennedy family. All of her reading material was stacked in a coal scuttle next to her chair in the living room. And she rarely left the house.

Meanwhile, I soon finished breakfast and went back upstairs to lie down and wait for someone to come out and pick me up to go to the bar at HoJos. I also would try to shut out the music of Frank Sinatra by putting a pillow over my head.

I used to wonder about how I'd gotten here. Early on in life Eva told me that she had explained everything to me once and that that was enough. I had no recollection of any such explanation. I was forced to put together bits and pieces as I found them.

I was an only child of parents killed when I was an infant. That my parents were college graduates I knew from snide comments that Eva and Adolf had made every once in a while about college graduates—that the two that they knew were dead, how much did their degrees get them, ha ha ha. My parents had taken a post-partem trip out of state and left me with Eva and Adolf until they got back. My parents died on that trip. It's confusing as to whether their deaths were in a car wreck or a plane crash. No one ever told me the precise incident. I had given up asking any questions years before. I was not even sure on what side of the family Eva and Adolf fell—paternal or maternal. I knew only that my dead parents were people of whom Eva and Adolf disapproved. For that reason alone, I figured that I would have gotten along fine with my parents.

I lay on the bed, glancing occasionally at the clock on the night stand between my and the Cousin's bed. Even though there were four bedrooms on the second floor of the house, I was forced to share a room with the Cousin. Until I was 13 or 14, I'd had a room of my own. I had been evicted and moved in with the Cousin so that Eva could use my room for storage. Almost immediately upon my relocation my former room was filled, floor-to-ceiling, with various items that Eva was storing for the eventual move to her dream home, a place to be built in the future somewhere on the Farm. Adolf's ways with money being what they were, I truly doubted that the "dream home" would ever be more than just a dream. In the meantime, the existence of that dream allowed Eva to rationalize tolerance of existence in the decaying homestead.

The other bedroom was uninhabitable. Its door was nailed shut. Four or five years before, squirrels had gnawed their way through the walls of the dormer that jutted up from the roof. Adolf, rather than expending the time, energy and—to him, most importantly—money to effect repairs, had simply nailed shut the door. After all, there were plenty of bedrooms for the number of people living in the house.

I glanced again at the clock. I'd been this way for years, waiting for people to come out and get me. During high school, I'd agonized over the passage of time, wishing it to elapse to the day I would leave the Farm and go to college. College stood for freedom in my life. Even though I enjoyed certain types of success during the years leading up to high school graduation, there were things missing from my life. I mean, I was the kid who was always elected to student council, but who was never invited to a party. I was out of touch with a lot of the aspects of culture within my age group. Sure, I listened to music on the radio—well, for a while there, I quit even that when my transistor radio fried out and I couldn't get WLS, the big Chicago station, anymore. FM was just coming into its own. I remember during my junior year, I took journalism, and most of the rest of the class consisted of seniors. I felt like an outsider when they would talk about groups like the James Gang, Jethro Tull and Grand Funk Railroad. I wanted to get beyond where I was.

My quest for rationality had started early, around second semester of seventh grade or thereabouts. I began reading materials from "the other side." I began to question things like America's involvement in Vietnam.

Next to Eva and Adolf's house was a small house, with an exterior made of concrete block that had been cut or molded to look like rock. The house had two ten-by-ten rooms connected by a swinging barroom door. The place reeked of fertilizer that had been stored there years before. At some point prior to Eva's and Adolf's acquisition of the Farm, the little house had been used as servants' quarters. Since the last servants to use the place had been Japanese, Eva and Adolf called it the Japanese house. There were even a couple of ginko trees growing behind it. In the mid-1960s, when the Cousin was in his period of "radicalism"—he grew a moustache, objected to American involvement in Vietnam and successfully dodged the draft—he had cleaned out the Japanese house, painted the concrete walls, and added furniture and a wood-burning stove. It was out there that he and his friends would gather to listen to Bob Dylan and Phil Ochs, discuss the great questions of the day, and consume modest quantities of various concoctions of alcohol. When I was about 11 or 12, I would sneak into the Japanese house and pick up the books and magazines that were on brick-and-board shelves, or just lying around. I read Zinn and Berkeley and Bertrand Russell. I'd grab any copy of Ramparts magazine I could get my hands on. And by that time, whenever I read a newspaper, there was some mention of any of the day's demonstrations or student revolts. While the Cousin was into the political end of it, he wasn't into revolution on the cultural front. His hair was always short. He wore the standard clothes of the day. And I remember one time around Christmas, in 1967, I rode into town with him on an errand for Eva, picking up something at the grocery. I was humming along to "Hello, Goodbye," by the Beatles, and he was putting it down. "That music has no deep meaning. It's not something you'll be listening to ten years from now."

In 1968, Eva and Adolf took one of their rare vacations. Apparently they knew someone who had a cabin at a lodge in Wisconsin. I never met the people, and I don't remember what the connection was, but Adolf got one week in the cabin for free, and so we went to Wisconsin on vacation in late August. It would not have mattered the destination—it was free, and that settled matters for Adolf. The Cousin stayed at the Farm.

On our return, we drove around Chicago on I-294. The weather was scorching. Adolf had not yet purchased a car with the frivolous luxury of air-conditioning. That trip changed his mind. In the meantime, we drove through hundred degree weather in heavy traffic. It was just before the Democratic National Convention. I saw scores of military vehicles driving around in preparation for the riots. When we got back, I had to start school almost immediately. At night I was glued to the TV, watching the riots and the weirdness. I remember William Buckley and Gore Vidal getting into it in their roles as moderators. Vidal called Buckley a cryptofascist and Buckley called Vidal a faggot. They promptly sued each other. In the meantime, I was going to school each day, and there were interesting discussions of what was transpiring only 150 miles away. I was the only one who was wondering about why the police were doing this to people who were only exercising their rights to free expression. Everybody else in the class—and I mean everyone—wondered why the cops were acting with such restraint.

The next fall, I wore an armband in support of the October 15 moratorium against the war. My armband wasn't one of the official armbands distributed nationwide, black with a white dove. I just grabbed one of Eva's black, elastic hairbands. I was the only person in school who wore an armband that day. In the afternoon I got jumped by four guys who were wearing Wallace buttons—their way of showing support for the military and racism in one, fell swoop. They tried to pull the armband off, pulling on it and dragging me down the hall. Two pickup trucks could have pulled on that armband looped around their trailer hitches and not snapped the goddamn thing. But these guys didn't care. They slammed my head into lockers as they tried to unbend my arm and pry open my fingers. They finally gave up.

Here I was, a member of student council, class vice-president, member of the speech and debate teams, jumped by hoods whose main extracurricular activity was theft. When I was seated in the principal's office, crying, the principal's only comment was that I shouldn't be causing trouble in school. Of course, my high school is the same high school that, years later, expelled a little kid for having AIDS. Great place, really "progressive." It always has been and, if I know the people there, always will be. Of the four guys who beat me up, one was killed in a motorcycle wreck shortly after dropping out from high school, and the other three have, on and off, been provided free room and board by the state's Department of Correction. The spring following the moratorium, the morning after the shootings at Kent and Jackson State, a show of hands in one of my classes indicated that 34 of the 35 people there, including the teacher, thought that the shootings were good—not just "defensible," but good. As in let's go out and shoot a few dozen more. And this wasn't a view fostered by some Marxian dialectic. Mine was the only vote in the class that the shootings were murder or, at the very least, unfortunate for everyone in that there was a loss of human life. There were people in that school who were actually giddy over the Kent State shootings.

It was at about this time that the Cousin's anti-war fervor took a pragmatic twist. He'd worked in the McCarthy campaign in Kilkerry and was even mentioned, though not by name, in James Simon Kunen's Strawberry Statement. Student deferments had been abolished and the Cousin's number was up. The Army wanted him. It was time for him to serve his country.

The night before the Cousin was to be inducted, he fell down two flights of stairs at Indiana University at Kilkerry, or "IUK." Well—nobody actually saw him fall. And he didn't have any cuts, bruises or abrasions consistent with a fall. He said that he had fallen, several people found him lying on the floor with his books strewn around him, and he was moaning in pain. He spent the night in the hospital and was given a doctor's excuse to stay home from the war. Eva and Adolf eventually hired two neurosurgeons to verify the injuries the Cousin had suffered and to attest to the "fact" that the Cousin was impaired sufficiently, under applicable regulations of the United States Army, that he was unable to die for his country. Over the course of a year the Cousin made seven trips to the Selective Service Center in Indianapolis. He was labeled a "malingerer" by the good doctors there and was forced to undergo several batteries of tests and physical examinations, all the while wearing a backbrace and using a cane. But eventually perseverance, and his uncanny knack for falling in the correct direction and manner when he closed his eyes and leaned back his head attempting to touch his nose with his index fingers—and the thousands of dollars that Eva and Adolf paid for expert testimony from their neurosurgeons—won out over military intelligence.

The Cousin's efforts were well-rewarded. Not only was he spared a trip to Southeast Asia, but he bought a new car with the proceeds of settlement that he reached with IU-K over their defective stairs. Somehow, the Cousin contended, one of the poured concrete steps became "loose" and caused his fall. The day after the threat of the draft had passed, the Cousin was miraculously cured of his back problems. He chucked the back brace and the cane. Neither Eva nor Adolf commented on the Cousin's recovery from a physical condition that had been, until recently, a dominant theme of evening conversation at the family supper table. Eva and Adolf squelched any mention of it from me. And the Cousin had then transformed from a slightly-left-of-center asshole, to a right-wing asshole. Now he was even espousing the virtues of Rhodesia.

As time passed, I craved leaving that place to go to college. You see, my parents had left a trust fund for my education. Eva and Adolf had been silly enough to mention its existence to me when I was in junior high. They had used it to threaten me. "If you don't blah blah blah like we tell you, you won't get to use that trust fund for school."

I'd always been a good student. In grade school and junior high, I'd always made the various honor rolls and received certificates of achievement in each of my subjects at the end of the school year. The existence of the trust fund and the prospects of going away to college had given me hope. Those prospects had made the then-present in Kilkerry seem bearable.

I succeeded at a lot of things. By senior year I was a state finalist in debate and speech, vice-president of the Honor Society, president of the Student Council, president of the Dramatics Club, and member and officer of a whole bunch more. I was in the top ten percent of my class. I was building the resume for my college application.

One day during my freshman year, I'd sat down in the high school library with The College Handbook, that really thick sucker that lists every college and university in the United States. I sent away for bulletins from about 20 schools that first time. As time wore on, I would go back to the book and browse through descriptions of schools. If anything about a school struck my fancy—its location, its curriculum, anything—I sent away for a bulletin. After all, this was in the days when schools sent such materials, free of charge, to anyone who requested them. By the end of my freshman year, I had a shelf full. I was ready to narrow the field.

One of the few friends I had in high school, who was a year ahead of me, went to DeForrest, a small private liberal arts college about a hundred miles from Kilkerry. I had written for materials from there and reviewed them. The school had an excellent reputation. Some writers had referred to it as part of Indiana's "Ivy League." I'd heard people refer to it as the "Harvard of the Midwest." Funny thing—I'd never heard anyone refer to Harvard as the "DeForrest of the East." Anyways, at the end of the summer before my senior year, the admissions office invited a bunch of seniors-to-be who had shown interest in the school to come down to campus and visit for a weekend—stay in the dorms, hear lectures from real professors, etc. I had jumped at the chance—it was, after all, a weekend away from the Farm. Once I got there, I realized that I wouldn't get to see "real college life." DeForrest didn't have a summer school, and the campus was deserted. Mainly we saw films, and we listened to a couple of profs give sample lectures. I ended up staying up all night talking with two guys from the suburbs of Chicago. Talking with two people who lived so close to a major city was wild enough as it was, but then they started telling tales of getting high and doing other drugs, as though such things were everyday parts of life. I bought a bumper sticker the next day that had the DeForrest seal and the name of the school in gold and black. When I got back to the Farm, I attached it to the steel double file I used for evidence cards at debate tournaments. Part of the reason for my having done that was to have a university sticker on my debate files as I'd seen other debaters do. As the year moved along, the pull to DeForrest was even stronger.

When my SAT results came back, and put me in a really small percentile at the top, I received solicitations from schools that had obtained my name and address from the SAT people. DeForrest wrote to me, a follow-up that said that they really wanted me and that I should come down for another weekend. This time there would be real, live students walking around. I did that.

I was assigned the fraternity as a place to stay for the weekend. I ended up getting totally buzzed all weekend and the admissions office offered me scholarship money, but not a full tuition scholarship.

I still was receiving bulletins. When I would get home from school, I'd immediately check the mail. On Saturdays I would run down to the mailbox about mid-morning and wait for the mail to arrive. Once in a while, amidst all the bills and bank statements, would be items for me from DeForrest or the other schools I'd written.

What was weird about the bank statements was the appearance of envelopes from the other of the two main banks in Kilkerry. Adolf insisted on banking at United Bank, as that was the bank that always employed him for various construction projects. The "other" bank, Federal Bank, was the "enemy." I didn't know why he and Eva would be doing business there.

Soon the shelf in the Japanese House wasn't big enough to hold all the bulletins I was receiving. Each week at least one or two more items would arrive. There were always pictures in the bulletins, most showing students strolling on sunny days across beautiful lawns, books under arms, or students sitting in the union building or in dorms. I would look at these pictures and imagine myself being there. Living that existence. Away from Eva and Adolf and the Cousin and the Farm and Kilkerry. The move to college would not be simply geographical and physical—it would be existential as well. Just as importantly, in my mind, I would change there. From who I was, the geek academic, to something—else.

When I got back to the Farm, after my weekend at DeForrest during the regular school year, the first weekday evening back, the four of us were at the supper table when Adolf brought up the subject of school.

"Have you decided where it is you want to go?" he asked between bites of fried round steak.

I told him about the places I had applied: Harvard—not likely that they would accept a non-valedictorian from a high school in the backwaters of society; DeForrest—a place I really liked that had a good reputation; and Indiana State. Indiana State had offered me a debate scholarship worth about $400.00. Not a lot. And the reputation of the school was the worst of the four state-owned schools—the others being I.U., Purdue, and Ball State University. I had no intention of going to a state-owned school. And I was adamant—although I didn't say so to Eva and Adolf—about going away to school.

"What are you going to do for money?" Adolf asked.

Now this conversation was taking place half-way through the second semester of my senior year of high school. No one had ever mentioned anything about my having to obtain money for college. There had been references to the trust fund, but not for a long time.

"I assumed that the trust fund would take care of it."

"Not for a place as expensive as that place," Eva said curtly.

"Well," I said, "How expensive of a place is it that the trust can afford?"

Eva ignored my question. For that matter, she ignored me, and spoke as if I was not there. "I don't see why he has to go away to school. IU-K is a perfectly good school." (She pronounced it letter-by-letter of the acronym—I-U-K. I pronounced it "yuck.") "After all, it was good enough for our son."

She gestured towards the Cousin, who just nodded in agreement.

"You could live here and go to school," Adolf said to me. "That would save a lot of the money."

"For what?" I asked.

Adolf cleared his throat and gestured towards the Cousin. "Your Cousin is having problems with his business. He needs the money."

I felt the blood drain from my head a bit. All of my life the Cousin had gotten whatever he wanted. Now they were going to give him my ticket out of here? I thought "Bullshit."

"I'd like to know more about the trust," I said. "I want to know how much money is available."

"You don't need to know any such thing," Eva snorted. She had a tendency to snort a lot, especially in conversations in which I was a party or a topic.

"I have every right to know," I said, my voice quivering a bit.

"You'll know what we want to tell you," Adolf ruled.

I got up from the table and walked outside. I walked across the lawn, and climbed over the fence and walked across the pasture. I walked on, to the treeline at the far side of the pasture, and down to the creek there. I threw rocks into the water. I was angry, but I didn't know what I could do. I had no knowledge of the financial aid available to students. The trust fund was there for me, and I had assumed—bad idea—that it would cover everything. If I had known sooner, I would have tried to learn about the system. But over those several years, as the bulletins had come in, Eva and Adolf had just watched the materials come in and not said a single thing. They must have chuckled a lot to themselves, pondering the day that I would realize the futility of my efforts.

The next day, I sent a simple letter to the director of admissions at DeForrest. In it, I said that I would really love to attend the school, but that their offer of financial aid was insufficient and that I couldn't afford the place, and I thanked him. Then at school, in the blank on the form for the commencement programs, naming the college that I would attend the next Fall, I wrote Indiana State. Maybe I couldn't go to the school of my choice, but there was no fucking way that I was going to go to IU-K.

I called the ISU debate coach and told her that I would be accepting her scholarship offer. She was happy. I certainly was not. During one of my last classes in high school, I was paged over the intercom to report to the principal's office. That was not unusual, being president of so many things as I was. But when I got there, one of the secretaries told me that I had a phone call and that I could take it in a side office. When I picked up the receiver, the DeForrest director of admissions greeted me cheerfully.

"I received your letter," he said. "And I'm sitting here with the director of financial aid. We can increase the scholarship money and arrange a student loan for the rest. If we did that, could you come here to school?"

I heard myself saying yes and thank you and this was wonderful.

Well, that was how I'd ended up at DeForrest.

I looked at the clock on the nightstand between my and the Cousin's beds. The hands of the clock seemed to have barely moved. The hangover was beginning to creep up on me. It was seeping into every pore in my body. It had also found a chink in my psyche and was spreading through my central nervous system. I was getting depressed and jittery.

As was so often the case, I sat up and looked out the window, hoping that whoever was coming to pick me up would hurry so I could be out of there. I looked at the stretch of road that ran from the south, wound past the end of the lane, under a railroad trestle then past our neighbors' house, and on to the north. It would be at least another hour until my ride appeared. What was ironic was that my existence at the Farm was so shitty that even going into Kilkerry was preferable. Kilkerry was a word that was one "k" short of containing the acronym that was really at the heart of the town. I shook my head, lay back on the bed, and closed my eyes.

Even though my views in high school regarding politics were beginning to get radical, my lifestyle wasn't. Sure I was elected to a lot of things, but I was never invited to any parties by anyone in my high school class. When the others were wearing jeans and cotton shirts, until the second semester of my senior year, I was wearing double-knit slacks from some sort of mix-and-match collection at Sears.

Second semester of my senior year in high school was epochal for me. It marked the first time I got high. Actually, the first time I got high was the second time I had ever smoked pot. The first time I smoked, I hadn't gotten off. The friend of mine who had gone to DeForrest came back to visit for a weekend and he had brought a couple of his friends from school with him. His parents were in Jamaica or some place and he and his friends had come up to party, and to pig out on the food in his parents' freezer and pantry and to make fun of the natives. I had gone over to just hang out, ask questions about college, etc. When they asked me if I wanted to get high, my eyes nearly bugged out, but I was ready. I'd given the notion of trying pot a lot of thought since the conversations with the guys from Chicago. I was really paranoid about it. I ran around to make sure all of the blinds were drawn on the windows of the room where we were going to smoke. That was laughable—the house was a good half-mile from that of the nearest neighbor, and the view of my friend's parents' house from the road was obscured by trees. Nonetheless, they humored me and let me close the drapes. One of the guys ended up rolling some homegrown in notebook paper because nobody had any rolling papers. I didn't get off, even with the chemicals of the notebook paper filling my lungs. It was not until later that I realized that quality of pot was not constant, but varied greatly.

The first time I really got high was about three weeks later. A girl who had just moved into our school district from Milwaukee was extremely pretty. All of the jocks in our school were asking her out, but she had said no. She and I started talking one day in French class, and the next thing I knew, we were set for a date that night to get high—and she had the weed.

I drove a van at the time. It was a 1963 Ford Econoline with white, oxidized paint, a rusted-out body, and the name of Adolf's company fading on one side where he'd hired a drunk painter to do the work about ten years before. The van had sat unused at the Farm for a couple of years. Then I had claimed it shortly after I'd received my driver's license. The interior of the van wasn't much better, but I'd tried to fix things up. I'd painted the

19

walls flat black, added a cheap shag rug, and hung beads from behind the seats. She and I drove down back roads in the country, smoking from a pipe she had and listening to music on the 8-track. I got extremely high. Driving seemed to be a real hassle. The van moved very slowly. But there wasn't any traffic and the music was really good. I'd never heard music sound like that before. It was the album Fragile by Yes. When I took her home, I thanked her. I knew then that my life had changed forever. I had experienced a different type of awareness.

By the time my freshman year of college started, I smoked a lot. And I augmented my intoxication on pot with alcohol. I took speed, especially to pull an all-nighter for a paper or an exam. I even tripped once. I was kicking out of my anal-retentive, student council mindset. I could think on a level different from the one I'd been confined to previously. Drugs aren't necessarily the only means of breaking out of such a mold, but I can't think of what else it could have been, during that crucial time of my life, that could have had effects even approaching the effects of drugs. I was too locked in to my old ways, focused on too narrow a slice of reality. Getting high jarred me loose from that.

Through it all, although DeForrest was actually a relatively conservative place, my limited contacts with it had consisted of counter-cultural activities and lifestyle. Hell, given the area in which I had been raised, anything would have seemed "hip." DeForrest represented a place of refuge, a spot of light at the end of my tunnel out of high school, where, at the end of my senior year, I was voted Most Radical in my class. It was not difficult to be considered a radical in my old high school.

I actually dozed off for a little while. It was one of those weird daytime/hangover naps that doesn't really impart rest but simply allows one to pass by a few more minutes on the planet. I awoke to the yelling of Eva at the bottom of the stairway that Warren was there. With Eva yelling at me—wondering when I was going to feed the livestock and where did I think I was going—and Frank still singing at 9 on the stereo volume, I ran out the front door and jumped into Warren's VW V-9, the square-backed mini station wagon that seemed ever-popular on campuses and among my college friends. When I got in I pulled out my Navy pilots glasses—really cool shades—and put them on. We took off, Warren peeling out and throwing gravel.

A lot had changed since high school. All of my friends "back home" these days were from other high schools in our county. They were people who'd graduated from the nearly-all-white suburban high school on the south side of Kilkerry.

Warren said we had to pick up Henning, and that was a little bit of a detour, but not much of one. Henning's parents lived in the town's oldest subdivision. I'd never been to their house before, but he and Warren had grown up together, so when we got out of the car, Warren just went in through the door of the garage next to the overhead without bothering to knock. When we got into the garage, it was obvious that Henning had set up his room in there—complete with roll-out couch and an easy chair.

"I'll tell Don and Rachel I'm leaving," Henning said. "Be back in a second."

I'd never before heard someone call their parents by their first names. It seemed odd.

When we pulled into the parking lot at HoJos, I did a quick count of vehicles in the parking lot. I had developed a rule of thumb in my brief span of frequenting bars—always be wary of a bar where the parking lot has more pickup trucks than the sum of the other vehicles combined. The pickup trucks were a sure sign of hilljacks, and that meant trouble. Fortunately, a great number of people had decided to kill their hangovers with a little bit of the hair of the dog and so the parking lot was full. The pickup trucks projected a strong presence, but they did not make up the dreaded majority.

I didn't know what I would do if we got carded. I hated the idea of going back to the Farm, but my worry quickly passed as the waitress took our order for a pitcher as we sat down at the tables our friends had shoved together.

One of the football games was on, on the first big-screen TV that I had ever seen—about four feet wide and tall, but the picture was really weird. You had to be sitting at the correct angle or else it was all blurry. Nobody at our table was paying much attention to the game, though. Instead, everyone was getting shit-faced and talking about the party the night before. I caught a bunch of good-natured shit about the incident with the truck and the swimming pool. The incident was fairly extreme and everyone liked it for a story that they could tell once they got back to school after break.

We sat that way, becoming blissfully sedated, through the afternoon. Somebody said something about Oklahoma having won the national championship. At another point, several of us went out to huddle in the parking lot and take a break from drinking in order to get high. Eventually, people started excusing themselves and leaving.

Warren and I decided we needed to change bars. We didn't realize there were very few bars open in Kilkerry on this holiday. We drove over to South Washington Street, the main north-south artery of Kilkerry, and headed north to the downtown area. We passed IU-K, then crested a hill. My view down South Washington Street was unobstructed for a mile or so, all the way to where the street jogged at its intersection with Markland Avenue, one of the town's primary east-west thoroughfares. And all the way down there, written in huge, red illuminated letters, I saw HELL. The Shell station that was located there had old, huge letters on the roof of the house behind it. But the lights inside the "S" had blown out. So there, beckoning us in three-foot letters, was HELL. I chuckled at the beauty of that, at how accurate it was.

We never found another bar that was open, and it got late, so we left town for the countryside and the Farm.

I walked in and said hello to Eva and Adolf. The Cousin was gone someplace. I got bitched at for having gone into town. I ignored the comments and went upstairs to crash.

I had endured the last full day at the Farm. Tomorrow I'd be going back to my true home—college.

Chapter 2 - End of Break

I woke up to the blaring of Frank Sinatra. The hangover wasn't all that bad—the day before I hadn't done any shots or anything similarly stupid. But two days' partying had left me a little short of energy. Then with the Big Band sound thundering up the stairway and through the hardwood floors, I was not pleased. After a few moments, I realized I would be going back to college that day, so I steeled myself for the bathroom. I pissed and tried not to look or inhale. I always avoided taking a crap at the Farm. If I was in town, I would use the facilities at a restaurant. Even the bathroom in a really filthy gas station was preferable.

I jumped into the shower, then quickly dressed and went downstairs where I stomped through the TV Lounge, causing the needle to jump not once, but several times, like the last few skips of a stone on water. The Cousin's cursing made me happy. As I sat down at the table, Eva was setting my plate, with the usual two fried egg sandwiches, in front of me. Adolf just stared at me.

"Your uncle is taking you back to school this morning," Eva said. That made me very happy — not "afternoon" but morning. "You'll need to be ready in a few minutes..

I said, "No problem," and wolfed down the sandwiches. Ten minutes later I was back downstairs with a big duffel bag I had purloined from the United States Postal Service. The mailman had left it at the fraternity at the end of fall break when the mail of several days had accumulated. There were two reasons I had taken it. First, I needed a big canvas bag like that for my laundry. Second, the date that the bag had been made was stenciled on the side, and the day and month were my birthday. It was fate that determined that I was to exercise dominion over that item of Federal property stitched together, in all likelihood, by a Federal inmate somewhere. Anyways, the sucker held a lot. I didn't own that many clothes, and everything that I had was either on me or in the bag. I also had packed a few albums that either I had received for Christmas or removed from the Cousin's forgotten collection of 1960s music that was rotting in the Japanese House. He had abandoned that musical taste when he no longer could be drafted and his political views had veered sharply to the right.

I really wasn't looking forward to two hours of riding back to school in the car with Adolf. We rarely spoke. Well, we rarely conversed. He would inform me of things, and attempt to dictate to me things I should be doing. He would never enter into any kind of meaningful conversation. That was true of him, Eva and the Cousin. The only time Adolf had ever really tried to "talk" to me was the day before I left for college. I had done all of my shopping. My things were all packed. I was ready to get the fuck out of there. I was finally escaping. Eva stopped me as I was going out the door. Her tone was somber. I thought, Fuck! She found the bottle of gin that I had hidden in my clothes! Instead, she said, "Your uncle will be home any minute. He wants to talk with you." She added, "Don't laugh at him."

That had been a beautiful late summer afternoon and when Adolf arrived, I got into his car and he drove to another farm he owned, a few miles away, where I had engaged in an abortive attempt to raise money for tuition by raising crops. We rode mostly in silence. I figured I would let him initiate things. We got to the farm, got out of the car, and started walking one of the fence lines.

"I know you're not very religious," he said. That was about as close as he could come to acknowledging that I was an atheist. "When you get down to school, though, you might find that being the member of a church will have benefits—like finding a part-time job or getting a meal when you otherwise wouldn't have one."

I thought, what a bunch of horseshit. If you only act like you believe, you can manipulate the situation and enjoy material benefits. I said nothing, and that threw him off a little. After a few moments of walking along, I could tell that he was getting back to the outline he had in mind for this "man-to-man talk."

"Another thing," he said, thoughtfully. "Do you know how they'll assign roommates there?"

"They'll just assign them," I said with a shrug.

"Well, if they assign you one of those funny ones, you ask for a new assignment then and there!"

I realized that he meant gay people. I decided to have a little fun and make him squirm a little bit. "But I've always liked people with a sense of humor," I said.

"That's not what I mean!" he said quickly and sharply. I could see he was flustered. His face was turning red. "Funny ones. You know what I mean." Then, without waiting for me to say "yea" or "nay," he continued to the final points of this man-to-man talk. "And remember this—avoid three topics and you'll never worry about losing friends. Never talk about sex, politics, or religion."

I thought about his espousal of this little kernel of wisdom. He had, after all, no friends. The world was divided into three categories of people for him: immediate family—Eva and the Cousin; business acquaintances; and Everyone Else. I didn't know where I fit in. Also, discussing important topics was one of the main reasons I was looking forward to college. "What else is there to discuss?" I asked.

Adolf stammered. He hadn't expected such a blunt question. I think he felt that he had an obligation to lecture me, and that he would get the lecture done quickly, and be done with it. "Well," he began, " there are lots of things to talk about . . . like . . . uh, well, there's . . ."

Rather than stand there all day listening to him sputter, I suggested, "Sports?"

His expression bore relief. "Yes—there you go. Sports. Yeah. You can always talk to other fellas about sports. But try not to get anybody angry with you."

With that we went back to the Farm, his one and only man-to-man talk thankfully over.

I sat down in the living room in Eva's chair. Next to it was the brass coal scuttle Eva had converted into a sort of library. It held a stack, about a foot-and-a-half high, of magazines, tabloids and books. Eva subscribed to *The National Enquirer*, and believed every word printed in it. She also was a devout follower of the trials, tribulations and exploits of the Kennedy family. Whenever a book was published concerning the activities of members of that family—dead or alive —Eva would buy it and consume its words as gospel. The more tawdry the activities, the more intensely she read. The Kennedys were icons for her. She was, after all, devoutly Roman Catholic. She said the rosary every morning for an hour or more.

Ah yes, the second of the three topics Adolf viewed as being taboo: Religion. I've already described my political "birth." Now for the "genesis" of my religious beliefs—or, rather, my beliefs about religion. Eva went to church every week, and took confession just as often. Each of the family's cars had a medal of St. Christopher—the patron saint of travelers—pinned to the fabric just above the rear-view mirror. In contrast, Adolf had talked, on occasion, of being raised as a Baptist. From his and Eva's conversations, I knew he had been a Methodist at the time they were married. These days, he went to a Lutheran church every week because it was expected of him. I don't think that he really cared about denominational nuances. His concerns were more materialistic than spiritual—he had obtained a lot of contract work for his construction company from other members of the flock. He might have been just as happy being a Catholic, but for the fact that when he and Eva had married in the 1940s, the Catholic Church had frowned upon its members marrying outside the Faith. Adolf had been forced to sign an agreement that all of the children of the union would be raised Catholic. That had rankled Adolf. Had the local priests just offered him a contract or two, he probably would have gladly converted. Instead, although the Cousin had been baptized in the Catholic Church, that had been Adolf's only concession to the agreement and the Pope. The Cousin had been raised Lutheran. I never saw that much of a difference between the two churches. The Lutherans didn't use as much Latin in their services. And Lutheran ministers were officially allowed to marry and fuck.

I was, for some reason, also baptized as a Roman Catholic—but it was a late baptism, after my parents had died. I mean, I can remember the baptism. So I guess that I was four or five years old at the time. Then I was promptly raised as a Lutheran. When I was about eight years old, all of the other kids in the church who were my age started taking catechism classes on Saturday mornings. That was an entire course of study that qualified them to take communion at the age of 12. Adolf didn't object when I turned down the pleasure of that course of study. I wanted to stay home and watch the Three Stooges. He wanted to save the few pennies on gas that driving me into town to the church would have cost. But then, after classmates of mine in Sunday school started talking about the history of the Lutheran church, I grew curious and started reading books and articles about Martin Luther, the church, and about Christianity. On top of that, when things got slow in Sunday school class, I'd flip open a bible and read passages. I mean, fuck off in school by reading something other than that which is directly before the class and you get admonished. Fuck off in Sunday school by reading the bible, and they can't get pissed off. By the time that everyone was getting ready to take communion for the first time, I was pretty well-read on the related subjects. On the Big Sunday when everyone—except me— would be taking their first communion after Sunday school let out, we had a substitute for our regular teacher. He was the father of one of the other kids in my class. He asked everyone for their reactions to taking communion for the first time. When he got to me, I said that I'd chosen not to take communion. He said that I was being immature. I just looked at him and said that I really didn't think I was able—at the age of 12—to commit myself to something as a belief system for life, especially with all the undertones of cannibalism in the rite of communion itself—eating flesh and drinking blood. He left me alone after that. Damn. And right before I was going to tell him how Martin Luther's constipation and his desire to wed shaped the Reformation more than his thoughts on the subject of a god. In other words, Martin Luther's asshole and dick won out over his brain.

Of course, I was also bombarded at school with religion. Even though ours was a public school and supposedly free from such matters, our area of the country was a place where people ignored inconvenient mandates from the Supreme Court. I remember one class in which the fable of Adam and Eve and the Fall arose. People in the class were talking about the Garden of Eden as though it had been an actual place and Adam and Eve had been actual people. I stopped a bunch of them by saying, "Now wait a minute. There are a lot of contradictions there. Like Cain slaying Abel and fleeing to the land of Nod, East of Eden, and taking a wife." "So?" somebody asked. "Well, where did those people come from? There's no mention of more people pouring out of Eden." There were a few moments of silence, until one of my classmates, whose father was a fire-and-brimstone preacher, said with a condescending smile, "The Bible doesn't say that God stopped making people." Ooh! I could see a couple of smug smiles and sense the acclaim of Good Point! for her comment. But then I asked, "Do you believe in original sin?" She replied that she did. "Then what about the descendants of all those new people over in Nod, created outside the lineage of Adam and Eve? They never committed original sin, and they aren't descended from anyone who did. What about them?" There are two outcomes possible in an argument with a born-again. Either they win (although that has never been an event in one of my discussions with a born-again), in which event they talk about how their belief is reasonable, or they cop out by saying, "Well, we cannot always understand the Lord, so we must believe it on faith." And blah-blah-blah. The latter is what she did then.

The Cousin eventually stopped going to Adolf's church in the mid-sixties. The Cousin was in classes at IU-K. A part-time instructor at IU-K at that time was a priest. The guy wore a leather jacket, rode a motorcycle, and preached a sort of hip ministry. The Cousin had been among the priest's several young converts to Catholicism although, given the fact of the Cousin's baptism, he had always been a Catholic—at least according to the people in Rome who keep official tallies of such things. Nonetheless, the Cousin took catechism classes and memorized a bunch of stuff about the church. Eventually he'd taken communion—the whole nine yards. But then the hip priest had quit his job, rejected his vows, and turned around and married a nun. That was it for the Cousin's days of religion. He soon lapsed. His Sunday mornings had become periods of hangover recovery, sitting in a reclining chair out on the east lawn, a huge tumbler of iced tea beside him and a book, open and face down, lying on the ground beside him.

My own religious "development" took a different turn. By my sophomore year of high school, I viewed myself as being an agnostic. I then decided that if there was a supreme deity, that it deserved to have its ass kicked. I mean, look at the story of Job. The poor guy is doing everything his god wants him to do. God and Satan get bored one day. They're crowing back and forth about how great they are. God says something about how Job will stay faithful no matter what the deity does to him. The two make a bet. God wipes out Job's family, his possessions, and gives him boils on top of it. And for what? A bet. What kind of asshole is that? Every day I went to school, the born-again mind-set dominated everything. I couldn't stand it. Then on Sundays, one of my two days away from the born-again environment of my school, I was forced to go to church. It blew out an entire morning during which I could have been doing something worthwhile. But I couldn't just stop going to Adolf's church. Such intellectual honesty would have resulted in little else but a more concentrated effort to save my heathen soul. So for about a year I went to church, at the little Methodist church in the hamlet a mile or so away from the Farm, with the Cliffords, whose three kids were all around my age. I went every week for a few months. Then I would miss a week here and there. By the end of my junior year in high school, I was staying at the Farm nearly every Sunday, working on debate or reading.

The crowning point of my confrontation with the world of Christian intolerance that dominated my high school came one day during my English class, first semester of my senior year. I was in the accelerated class for people going on to college. I had the same teacher I had the year before for advanced English, and she had taught my Latin class freshman year. I had always received an A in her classes. One day, at the start of class, she asked us what the most indisputable fact in history was. My classmates looked at one another with quizzical expressions. I raised my hand. Now at that point of my life, I had never heard of nihilistic solipsists—people who believe that nothing exists outside of themselves. Had I known about such beliefs, I would have said that there are no indisputable facts. Instead, what I said was: "Lincoln is dead." I mean, that seemed to be empirically true. The teacher's expression softened slightly, as though she pitied this young heathen dumbass. "No," she said. "The most indisputable fact in history is that Jesus Christ is the Son of God and died for our sins . . ." and blah-blah-blah. My classmates all nodded and smiled. Most of them agreed with the teacher. The other few were already learning the skill that is so handy in padding one's grade-point in college—kissing the ass of anyone who holds the power to grade. After class, I went up to the teacher at her desk and explained that her little sermon was a violation of my constitutional rights and that she couldn't preach in school. I never got another A in her class after that day, although I worked just as hard as I had worked before, and the quality of my work was the same. Oh well, I guess I was just being smited.

I was shaken back to the present by a harsh voice.

"Where's all of your underwear?" Eva demanded as I prepared to go out the door to put my duffel bag in Adolf's car.

"I threw it all away," I replied without a thought.

"Why did you do that!?"

"I don't wear it anymore."

She looked at me as if I was from another planet. But the truth was that a couple of months before, I had discarded all of my jockey shorts in the spirit of my person cultural revolution.

I stowed the duffel bag in the trunk of Adolf's car and tossed my copy of *The Teachings of Don Juan* by Carlos Castaneda, onto the front seat. Warren had turned me on to the book. It sounded fairly interesting. An anthropology grad student had gotten fucked up on peyote and mushrooms for a couple of years in the Sonora Desert with an old Yaqui medicine man. Not only did the book interest me, but reading it would give me reason to not talk with Adolf for the 100-mile, two-hour trip back to DeForrest.

I carted everything out to Adolf's huge Buick Electra Limited.

That was one thing about the family. They might have been living in decrepit housing, but Eva, Adolf and the Cousin sure drove nice cars.

When I was really young, the unwritten rule was that Eva got a new Chevy every even-numbered year, and Adolf got a new Ford every odd-numbered year. Then Adolf hit his Third Great Period of Affluence. On Palm Sunday in 1965, a huge storm front moved through the midwest. It hit the area we lived in rather hard, wiping out Germantown and pulverizing big sections of Kilkerry. Adolf's construction business went ape-shit after that. Eva got a new Oldsmobile every year after that and Adolf got a new Pontiac or Buick. When that particular period of decadence was over, and the recession of 1970 had set in, they couldn't revert to their old ways. But that was when Adolf figured out that, during a recession, all the factory workers would have their cars repoed during layoffs. So, still, Eva and Adolf bought nearly new cars every year, hardly used and very cheap.

The Electra Limited that Adolf drove now was designed for America's interstate highway system—the car had a gigantic 455 cubic inch engine, a long wheel base and the weight of a small tank. Sitting in the plush interior, I always felt like we were cruising along in a living-room-on-wheels.

The Cousin had a Limited, too. But then the Cousin had, over the course of a decade, bought and sold more cars than a modest-sized Buy Here/Pay Here lot. He was the "only" child in the eyes of Eva and Adolf and, consequently, very spoiled. If he wanted a car, then by god he'd get a car. Before he graduated from high school, he'd had a 1953 Plymouth roadster (totaled), a 1959 Sprite (totaled), a 1961 Chevy Impala (totaled) and, for his graduation from high school, in 1963, a brand-new Chevy Impala Super Sport that was destroyed by a tree that fell on it during the Palm Sunday tornado. After high school, at different times, he had a Jaguar (re-poed) , a Lincoln (re-poed), a Mercury Marquis (re-poed), a Catalina station wagon (totaled), a Delta Royale (re-poed), a Pontiac Catalina sedan (re-poed), and a Toyota Land Cruiser, that he still had.

The Cousin was spoiled in other ways as well. In fact, the term "spoiled rotten" constituted an understatement. I always thought he had been born rotten and that his environment and experiences merely constituted refinement of that quality. As the last male to carry on the family surname, and as Adolf's only child, the Cousin had gotten anything he had ever asked for. As a result, the Cousin had been thoroughly hated by his class mates in school. He'd been thrown out of Little League for throwing bean balls at opposing batters. When he had been in band and demoted from first trumpet, he had refused to give up the seat and parroted to the band instructor Adolf's enlightened opinion that any male who taught music was a faggot. That got the Cousin one of his many trips to the principal's office. Whenever the Cousin played any kind of game, he took more pleasure in cheating and winning than in working at winning on the merits.

He taught me how to play chess when I was six. When I started beating him, he informed me that my pieces were allowed to move only one space at a time—queen, rooks, and bishops as well as pawns. When I started beating him even with these restrictions, he quit playing me in chess altogether. And not that I was any young Bobby Fischer.

The Cousin's inability to acquire social skills in high school culminated near the end of his sophomore year with his hitting another student in the middle of the forehead with a foot-long piece of rubber hose that was filled with lead shot and taped at both ends. The kid he hit had required stitches, and later became a deputy sheriff. The Cousin was expelled. Adolf promptly hired a lawyer who found a loophole that allowed the Cousin to transfer to another school in the county, even though Adolf wasn't a taxpayer, and we didn't reside, in that school district. Cash dollars exchanged hands along the way somewhere. When the Cousin had started getting into problems there—the first day of classes—even Adolf had to put his foot down. The Cousin mellowed out a bit at school then. He entered choir—the only extracurricular activity in which he participated that did not involve some sort of felonious conduct—and eventually graduated with close to a C average. He'd then been accepted at IU-K. Of course Indiana statutes then required the state's public colleges to accept any graduate of an Indiana public high school, so the Cousin's acceptance was no sort of miracle. Over the years, the Cousin would take out his frustrations, when he got home, by beating me up. And I mean beating up. I'd be left with bruises, rug burns, all sorts of nice stuff. Adolf and Eva would laugh about it as it occurred in front of them, as though this were some sort of rough-and-tumble family joke. I had no gauge for comparison. I, too, thought that it was some sort of joke that was standard conduct in other families.

Adolf spoiled the Cousin, even into adulthood. The Cousin started a company that sealcoated residential driveways. The big paving company in Kilkerry had encouraged the Cousin to start his little business shortly after he finished his degree at IU-K. The residential work was too labor-intensive for them to show a profit. So the Cousin had hired some ex-convicts through the unemployment office in Kilkerry and paid them extremely low wages. Well, the "wages" were payments in cash for which the Cousin did not expend the energy of withholding taxes, and for which he was later to have problems with the IRS. His little company did pretty well. The paving company even let him do the contract work on a couple of small business parking lots. The Cousin started reading Fortune about that time and wearing a pinkie ring. He cooked up a plan for taking big contracts away from the paving company. The Cousin floated a "campaign contribution" to a senator and got an SBA loan to finance his scheme. It was about that time that the senator told the paving company what the Cousin was doing. The paving company then gave the senator an even larger campaign contribution, and shut down the Cousin's business.

The Cousin used the SBA loan to buy two speedboats, another nice car, a trip to New Orleans where, he later bragged, he met one of the stars of the television series "The High Chapparell," and to pay the retainer for the attorney and other fees related to the personal and corporate bankruptcies that he was forced to file. Oh, and because he had obtained an SBA loan, a company that sold space in vanity printings contacted him by "official letter" and invited him to send them his biographical material as being one of the Top Ten Thousand Young Business Leaders of America. Of course, his bio would be included in their volume for the small fee of One Hundred Fifty Dollars ($150.00), but in return he would also receive his very own gold-embossed copy of this little "Who's Who." I'd received several such solicitations for "Young Leaders of Tomorrow" when I'd been president of all the things in high school. But the Cousin and Eva and Adolf took the damn thing about the business leaders seriously, even as the Cousin was going down the tubes and Adolf was pumping money to the Cousin so that the Cousin could avoid tax evasion/fraud charges and a stretch as one of those Federal inmates stitching together United States Postal Service duffel bags. I figured that Adolf went down a good fifty grand after the thing was over. But that goddamn little "Who's Who" sat there on the coffee table in the living room as proof to the three of them and the visitors, that they never had, that the Cousin was really a smart cookie in the realm of business, regardless of what the creditors of his business and the bankruptcy trustee said. After the collapse of the Cousin's business, Adolf decided the Cousin had managed matters so well—and, after all, the Cousin was without employment and had never degraded himself by working for another person— that he should move into the second-in-command position of Adolf's company and prepare for the day when Adolf stepped aside and retired. At that point, the business would belong to the Cousin and all would be right with the world.

Meanwhile, I had read David Copperfield, and a couple of other depressing novels by Dickens when I was in junior high and high school, but during that time I didn't see my situation at the Farm as being all that bad. As I said, I didn't have any perspective. I thought that everyone's life was like mine. I knew I wanted to go away to college and escape, but until I had been away, I didn't know just how bad things were at the Farm. I had three meals a day, a nice warm place to sleep and my clothes bought for me. By the time I reached high school, I had a bunch of activities that kept me away from the Farm. When I was forced to be at the Farm because I had nothing else to do, I simply went upstairs after supper, to the room that I shared with the Cousin, and read until I went to bed at about nine or nine thirty. Then sleep would envelop me as I was transported to another day.

All of this was going through my mind as I sat in the car as Adolf got in.

Eva didn't speak to me as we left. The Cousin didn't speak, either.

"We're going to the Shop, first," Adolf said as we turned towards Kilkerry.

I sighed with relief as we left the Farm, safe in the idea that I would not have to return there for another couple of months at least.

The Shop was the focus of Adolf's life. It was where he made his money. It consisted of four buildings that had been patched together, and was the home of Adolf's Construction Company. The drive from the Farm to the Shop was only five miles and took only a few minutes.

We motored past the homes of people I'd known during my childhood and was trying fast to forget. Mitch Shipman's house passed by. He had been a bully in my school. During his senior, my sophomore, year of high school, he'd told me that he would kill me one day. Nice guy. The principal had even responded to that one, and had come to my defense. It was after the wrestling season was over and Shipman's contributions to the school's team would no longer be important.

As we passed the houses, I thought about all of the thousands of factory workers who lived there. Kilkerry's entire economy was based on the auto industry, with two huge plants employing lots of union workers who made inflated wages and then centered their lives around acquiring consumer goods on installment payment plans.

It was barely after 7 when we got to the Shop. No one else had arrived as yet. I walked through the building, to the front, and went outside to grab *The Indianapolis Star* Adolf had delivered to the Shop each weekday. I was used to reading that paper, even though it was extremely right-wing. I flipped through it, killing time, anxious to get on the road and back to school. I also hoped we would be on the road long before eight o'clock, when Adolf's secretary would arrive. She was a real bitch. The men who worked for Adolf called her the Barracuda. The moniker stuck, although no one dared call her that to her face. Her face possibly bore a similarity to that predator, and her disposition was very much in line with that of the vicious fish. However, I thought that with her skinniness she looked like a crane or stork. I easily could imagine her, perched on one skinny leg in shallow, mucky water, poised to spear a small amphibian or other life form with her sharp beak.

The company was in sheet metal. It manufactured and installed air ducts for commercial and industrial enterprises. The men were members of the sheet metal workers' union. The work demanded highly skilled people. Consequently, the men were making damn good wages. When times were tight and construction was down, there were a lot of men who were laid off, but those times did not occur very often.

Adolf hated unions. This is an understatement. He cringed at the idea of having to pay for anything, and labor was one of those things. Once, when the union had been on strike and the men drew strike pay by picketing, in a polite way, the various union companies around the State, Adolf had nearly run down a picketer whom he claimed was blocking his parking spot. In fact, there were no reserved parking spots, as such, but the statement had sounded plausible to Adolf. Since the Cousin's business had folded, and since the Cousin viewed himself as having managed well the ex-convicts who had worked for him in his sealcoating company, the Cousin was trying to act as an intermediary between the company and the men. The Cousin was trying to "create a new image for the business, that of a progressive company moving to adapt to the changes of a modern world, etc."

Fortunately, Adolf didn't have all that much to do before we left. I read the paper nearly the entire time. The shop foreman came in just before 7:30. His name was Jim Stevens, and he'd been working for Adolf, except during times of temporary lay-offs, for over ten years. The men were always polite to me, and Jim was no exception. He said good morning and asked if I was going back to school. I said yeah, and then Adolf called Jim into his office to leave the orders for the day. Jim was the shop foreman, as opposed to being foreman of a job out in the field. He was too big to be out in the field, unless they were in a real pinch. He was huge, at least three hundred pounds. Since so much of the work involved working up in the air on scaffolds, Jim stayed in the Shop and fabricated the ducts that would be transported to the job sites for installation. Not only was it difficult for Jim to climb scaffolds, but when he was on the scaffolds, and the other men were on them, too, his weight would cause the structures to sway with each of his movements. He was really big, and his first wife had been, too. They had been so big, in fact, that, before his first wife's death from obesity-induced coronary, Jim had come to the Shop one day and ordered angle iron and concrete blocks from one of Adolf's suppliers. Adolf had agreed to that, with Jim reimbursing Adolf. Jim had needed the materials to build a new bed, as his and his wife's bed had collapsed under their weight.

Usually Adolf visited job sites for most of his work day. The sites were scattered around the State: Lafayette, Marion, Muncie, New Castle, Peru, Monticello—all scattered about the flat expanses of mid-North Indiana, and each town bearing a strong resemblance to the other. Today, though, he had to go to Indianapolis to see an engineer in a firm there. That meant that he would take me to school, then conduct his business on the way back. I would be back at school no later than 10:30.

We headed out of Kilkerry, South on U.S. 31, towards Indianapolis. The day had that gray sky of mid-winter that is so prevalent in Indiana. Traffic was light as we sped along. Fortunately Adolf chose not to force conversation. I was into reading Castaneda. The land we were rolling past was some of the best farm ground on the planet. The dirt was black in the furrows when it was plowed, rich in minerals. When we got to the north side of Indianapolis, Adolf took I-465 West, on around to U.S. 40, where we got off and continued west.

U.S. 40 had once been a major highway in the United States. It was the old "National" highway, four lanes of concrete and asphalt that ran coast-to-coast in rough description of the 40th parallel. When Interstate 70 had been built, though, 40 had lost both traffic and grandeur. The various states through which it passed had also lost considerable funding for repairs and maintenance to 40. The old mom-and-pop motels that stood every half-dozen miles or so were no longer doing the kind of business they once had enjoyed. Most now were either closed completely or renting by the week to hilljacks and other transients who couldn't afford real apartments. The signs still stood—MOTEL—with the name of the place above or below those letters, but the paint was faded and peeling. Most travelers were over on the interstate, doing their business with the corporations—Holiday Inn and Ramada and so on—that fed on the interstate and the traffic of its on and off ramps. So the old motels on 40 sat and rotted.

The Teachings of Don Juan was really a trip. I'd heard a lot about it, but reading it was a different kind of experience. Castaneda was a sorcerer's apprentice. He was hanging out with this old guy, taking peyote and mescaline, and smoking datura. In one passage, he talked about tripping while a lizard was with him, and Don Juan had sewn the eyes of the lizard shut. Weird stuff, out-of-body experiences. And the old man's philosophy, as Castaneda described it, seemed close to my own of the past two years, that importance of the plants, to Don Juan, was their ability to produce episodes of peculiar perception, and that such incidents of nonordinary reality were the only means of acquiring knowledge.

Adolf had been, thankfully, quiet the entire way down from Kilkerry. When we pulled off U.S. 40 to a narrow, two-lane state highway, we were only a few miles away from campus.

DeForrest was in a small town, Glendale, that was, in turn, in the south central part of the state. The area around Glendale was a pleasant contrast to the area around Kilkerry. Here there were still flat fields, but there were also hills and wooded areas. There were very few factories in this part of the state, so the industrial rot that constituted the fabric of the area around Kilkerry and its sister towns was markedly absent here.

As we were only a couple of miles out, Adolf broke the silence. "Find out about your grades from last semester as soon as possible. We want to know."

"Okay," I grunted. We'd almost made it a hundred miles without talking.

"There's no sense in wasting money down here if we don't have to."

I looked at him. I didn't know how to react. The money in the trust was for my education. Period. How things usually transpired for payment of my tuition was that Adolf would give incorrect dates to the bank. He would tell them tuition was due at a date later than that by which it was actually due. I would receive several notices from the university, then a notice of cancellation of registration. Then I would frantically make calls to the bank. At the last minute, the check would arrive. I hoped to have circumvented the problem this semester by having sent a letter a couple of weeks earlier to the trust officer at the bank informing him of a deadline for payment of tuition that was a couple of weeks earlier than the real deadline. The only reason Adolf did that thing with the tuition was just meanness. I sighed with relief as we crossed the city limits of Glendale. He slowed the car as we passed Eastside Liquors, where much of my spare change went, and then we were on the street where the frat was located. When we pulled into the driveway, I knew I would be free in only a few moments.

Now you have to understand that here, by saying "fraternity," I mean the physical plant, the structure of the house itself. The national fraternity had "traveling secretaries." They were young Nazi/former jocks who had belonged to one chapter or another of the fraternity across the country and had never grown out of the communal experience or gotten a life. One traveling secretary had made this distinction the semester before during a visit to our chapter house. In what I am sure the traveling secretary thought of as a heavy, deep insight into existence, he distinguished between the physical plant—the physical structure of the house itself—and the membership or brotherhood or whatever you want to call it of the fraternity as organization and "thing." When he made the pronouncement, I thought it would soon be followed by a wink and a laugh and we would all see that he was only joking. Unfortunately, he was not joking. He maintained this serious look on his face and launched into something else. In talking to a couple of upperclassmen later, I learned that the people who visited from national always made that distinction. It sounded absurd to me, but hey—it was their house and their nomenclature.

To my pleasant surprise, there was a car in the parking lot. Clancey, a psych major and a member of my class, had gotten here first. I got out of the car and walked to the back door. It was unlocked. I went back to the car and heard the trunk lid pop open. I got out my duffel bag and hefted it around to the side of the car. Adolf rolled down his window.

"Here," he said gruffly and handed me a twenty. "Like I said. We want to know about your grades." With that, his window rolled up and he pulled away.

Goodbyes with members of the family were always so poignant.

Chapter 3 - Back To School

I was dragging the duffel bag on the ground behind me as I walked into the house, and I kept dragging it up the stairs and into the hallway of Second Old.

The fraternity had been built back in the twenties. A new wing had been added around 1968. There were a main or first floor, a basement, and then two stories above. So you described where you were or where you wanted to go in the house, for example, by saying Second Old—where my room was this semester—or Third New, etc. The new section of the house had the sterile feel of institutional architecture of the 1950s and 1960s. It was very functional. The old section of the house was different. As I came out of the stairway and into the old section, I felt at home. The carpet on the floor was of a soft reddish/orangish mix of fiber, and its nap was deep and old and soft. The walls were paneled with dark woods in good, thick sheets that had been there a long time and were of good enough quality to last a long time more.

I got to the door of my new room and tried the key in the lock. The key worked, but not without some difficulty. The doorknob and lock looked as if they had been installed when the old section of the house had been built. Once I got in, I shoved the duffel bag into the closet and drew a big breath.

Just before finals the previous semester, everyone in the house had gone through room preferences. The seniors all went first, each drawing from a deck of cards and the high card among them going first. Each person chose a room that way, with corner rooms, for example, going pretty quickly, since those had two windows. I was in my second year at DeForrest, but since I'd spent my freshman year living in the dorm, I wasn't very high in seniority. Nonetheless, I had gotten a single in Second Old for a couple of reasons. First, the house was only at two-thirds capacity. Second, when I had drawn during room prefs, I'd gotten the second-highest card in my pledge class. The room I'd gotten was only ten-by-ten with a three-by-four closet immediately to the right as one walked in. And it had an old style window, facing out onto the parking lot in the back of the house. The ancient plaster-and-lath walls needed painting. Right after I was done with finals, and just before I'd left for break, I'd moved everything I'd had in my room with Criminal Phil and stacked it in the middle of my new room. Everything was sitting there now, as I'd left it. The only "organization" that I'd done before I'd left was to lay out my rug—a spiffy royal blue thing that the Cousin had actually given me as a Christmas present the previous year—set up my stereo, plug in the little refrigerator I had, and toss a mattress on the floor. There was still a lot of work to be done, but I had no intention of doing it right then. I went in search of Clancey to party.

Clancey's two brothers were doctors in a family that placed a lot of expectations upon its children. Consequently, Clancey felt a lot of stress to succeed. He was a psych major, and wanted to become a shrink. He was very coherent, too, until about two-thirds of the way through a semester. Then he became a little unhinged. After finals the year before, he'd taken off to Oregon and worked there as a lumberjack. That had been a big surprise to his family, who had thought that he was going to stay at home in a nice Detroit suburb and work as an orderly in a hospital there. But when he'd come back, he was one hell of a lot calmer than when he'd left. He'd obviously made the right choice for summer work. At the end of the previous semester, he'd again been uptight. But when I walked down the hallway in Second New, I heard his stereo and knew he'd be relaxed and ready to party.

I knocked on the door and he yelled to come on in. He smiled when he saw it was me.

"I beat ya back," he said with a chuckle.

"Fuck you," I said. "Got any beer?"

He gestured toward the refrigerator. "I got two cases of Stroh's."

"Wanta sell one?"

We agreed on a price, and I took the case down to my room and put the cans in my refrigerator. I stuck a couple in the tiny freezer portion, and took a warm one with me back to Clancey's room. I popped it open and sat down. It really didn't bother me that it was warm. I just wanted to catch a buzz, being back at home.

It was weird being in the frat when only a couple of people were there. It was kind of eerie. I expected one or another of the "brothers" to come around a corner with a beer in hand, or to see a game of hallway frisbee in progress, or to hear someone paging someone else on the intercom. There was nearly always a stereo blaring away some place, and the scent of incense and pot floating in the hallways. But now the hallways were empty, with a musty smell tinged with odor of open, partially-full beer cans lying about and fermenting. At the end of a semester, people's thoughts were focused on relieving stress and getting drunk, not with niceties of cleaning up after themselves.

Then again, the month of January was not a month for a hell of a lot of work.

In the 1960s, the university had instituted a new academic calendar—a 4-1-4. There were two, typical four-month semesters. But these semesters sandwiched January, and January was "Winter Term." The concept sounded really neat. There were no grades, for one thing. All of the classes were "pass-fail." Each student was required to have four Winter Terms completed in order to graduate. Furthermore, each student only took one class during Winter Term. And the classes were completely different from what was standard fare. One could take photography, or electric trains, or go off-campus to another city, state or country—and probably a third of the students did that. For most students, Winter Term meant—parties. The academic demands were light, and besides, there was nothing else to do in Glendale in the dead of winter, so parties were a natural consequence of the environment. I was signed up for the same Winter Term course I had taken the previous year. I had checked with both the registrar and my debate coach, and both authorities had said I could do so: varsity debate. In other words, I was getting academic credit to go to the same tournaments and do the same work had there been no Winter Term. I was definitely free to party.

Clancey had put on Stevie Miller's "Joker" album, and I had retrieved my aluminum film cannister of pot, along with my small hash pipe. We got high and started swapping stories of what had happened to us over break.

Over the course of the afternoon and into the early evening, more people arrived. The first day or so after a break was festive. Most of the people were glad to be back, away from home and the prying eyes of restrictive parental units. Clancey and I ordered a pizza and inhaled it. At one point, Jennings stuck his head in the door, having scented the pot smoke in the air, and sat down for a while. He'd brought a couple of cases of Little Kings back from Ohio. Little Kings were seven ounce bottles of cream ale. Indiana didn't sell them at that time. So having them—or any beer or other alcoholic beverage not sold in Indiana—was something of a delicacy. Plus, since they were cream ale and not simply beer, they carried about twice the punch of the Stroh's I was drinking. Symington came in at some point after that, I think when we were playing air guitar to Uriah Heep's "Magician's Birthday." Symington took one of Jennings's Little Kings and told us about a newt he had acquired as a pet over break. It was along in there that Clancey and I were talking about the bottle of 151 rum that he had on his desk, and the motorcycle, a picture of which was tacked to his wall, that he'd decided he wanted to buy one day. That was how we came up with the idea for the T-1000.

Quite simply, the T-1000 was a boilermaker, consisting of 151 rum as both the shot and about half of the contents of the mug into which the shot was dropped. The rest of the mug was cream ale purloined from Jennings. We each did one. I was pretty wasted then, but the T-1000 sort of rocketed me out. Symington did three of the goddamn things. One of the last things I remember of the evening was walking down the hallway in Second New, heading to my room to crash out, trying to avoid Symington as he jumped into the walls and the ceiling of the hallway attempting to catch flies for his pet newt. Of course, since it was January in Indiana, there were no flies. But for some reason, his brain was getting the impression that there were hundreds of them flying about.

I made it back to my room, hassled with the doorknob, got the door open, and fell down, unconscious, on my mattress.

I hadn't forgotten about that third taboo matter in Adolf's little lecture as I left for college—sex. As I lay there in my room, my mind dawdled with some sort of fantasy involving breasts and nudity and such things.

You see, I was 19 years old and I had never had sex. I was a virgin. That was a fact not widely known about a male my age at that point of the 1970s. The assumption was that one had lost one's virginity in high school. I had never actually told the truth to anyone. And certainly that "assumption" was an assumption because a lot of people wanted everyone else to think not only that they had gotten laid at least once in life, but that they got laid on a regular basis. As to the application of the assumption to me, I had never corrected anyone if they implied it.

Not only was I a virgin, but I was terribly inexperienced sexually. Like twice I had seen—live and not just in photographs or on film—female breasts. Twice. My knowledge of sex had been acquired in that healthy, all-American way—dirty jokes, Playboy, and guesses based on anatomy charts. I mean, I had only a vague idea of what sexual intercourse was. I only minimally knew the mechanics. I didn't fully understand about penetration, in other words.

Sex was not something Eva and Adolf discussed. I couldn't imagine them as ever having had sex. The whole notion seemed to be too intimate to fit into their angular lives. I would have thought that the Cousin was a product of immaculate conception, but for the fact that he was such an evil shithead. But I never got the little lecture from either Eva or Adolf about "the birds and the bees." I was never given a pamphlet, like my girlfriend senior year of high school was by her mother, and told to "read it." I got nothing.

Back in my freshman year of high school I had helped Eva and Adolf one evening by sweeping and mopping the floors at the Shop while they performed other cleaning tasks—thus saving ten bucks or whatever for a cleaning service. For some reason, I cannot remember now, the back seat of Adolf's car was full and I had to sit between Eva and Adolf in the front seat. On the way back to the Farm, as we pulled up to a stop light on some side street heading out of the beautiful town of Kilkerry, right around the area where the defunct steel mill had left mountains of slag heaps, I glanced to the right at a car parked in the curb lane. There were what appeared to be two guys with a woman, and the woman was bent over the front seat facing the rear of the car, and one of the guys was pounding away behind her. That's all that I saw, catching only a glimpse of the ancient activity, before Eva slapped my face and told me to look straight ahead. I didn't dare say anything about the incident the rest of the evening but, the next day at school, I told a couple of the guys what I had seen and we all exchanged chuckles.

One of the scariest events of my early life was my first wet dream. Again, this happened during my freshman year of high school, when the hormones were first coursing through my young body, causing my voice to change, my height to increase abruptly, and hair to appear where it had never appeared before. I awoke in the middle of the night from a very interesting dream, but I had to go to the bathroom. When I got into the bathroom, I looked down at myself. It looked as if pus was coming out of the head of my dick. Goddamn! I thought that maybe I had VD or something—I only knew that such diseases existed, but did not know specifics about how they were acquired. I mean, at that point of my life, having been bombarded by the born-agains in my environment and with the constant presence of a Calvinistic, punishing asshole of a supreme deity overlooking everything in the Kilkerry area, subliminally I guess I thought that it was possible to get VD from impure thoughts combined with air-borne spores. Regardless of the paucity of my knowledge concerning the mechanics of sex, I had a whole passel of impure thoughts about sex every day. Over the next few months I kept the strange malady from which I seemed to suffer every week or so a secret. Thankfully, someone's dirty joke one day, and the lyrics of the Beatles' "I Got a Feeling," made me aware that I did not have VD, but an average libidinal drive.

I had assumed that, upon reaching college, the loss of my virginity would be nearly immediate. At this point of my sophomore year, however, that loss had yet to occur. I didn't know how to bridge the gap from polite conversation with a woman, to "mashing"– i.e., making out—to removal of articles of clothing, and onward after that. I was very uptight. There was no release from this tension. I didn't entertain the thought of masturbating. I'd been raised in Kilkerry to believe that masturbation is sick.

So I kind of rattled on, going out on occasional dates, and fantasizing with certain crucial junctures of those fantasies missing. My face was always breaking out and the pile of back copies of Playboy grew on one of the shelves in my room. By now I was not confident that all of this would change one day. I wasn't confident of anything. There had to be some sort of magic formula that would make me sufficiently attractive to a female that she would say "yes" and my quest would be at an end.

I sank deeper into my mattress, nice sexual patterns developing as I slipped into unconsciousness. I might have been caught in the frenzy of raging hormones, but there was one thing of which I was certain.

Ah yes, it was good to be back home!

Chapter 4 - Getting Organized

I was first aware of being conscious. My eyelids felt as though they were lined with rough grains of sand gouging tracks into the tissue. I groaned and started to lift my head, but then a pounding from my temples resonated through my whole body. Finally, I forced my eyes open. I was in my room at the frat. It all came back to me: the 151 rum, the newt, the beers, everything. I eased to a sitting position. I knew from past experience that this hangover would be bad at first but then, over the next couple of hours, would abate. Rum hangovers are not so extreme. The worst are tequila hangovers. They make one feel as if the previous evening had been spent tripping. Next are whiskey hangovers. Whiskey has adulterating flavor substances that fuck up the capillaries in the brain. A close third is red wine, a pleasant enough high, but a really devastating low the next day. Whiskey and wine can be real creepers as hangovers. You wake up feeling great but then, a couple of hours later, time slows to a crawl. As far as other hard booze goes, gin and vodka are fairly innocuous—distilled substances fairly free of any sediment that could sink into the blood vessels and fester. Finally comes beer.

I'd learned my freshman year about dodging hangovers. The first, and least desirable, way is not to drink in the first place. Wrong choice! That wouldn't be any fun. Another other way is to not get drunk on an empty stomach—eat! And that's what we had done having inhaled a pizza. Eating helps to pump up the blood sugar. Next is to take an aspirin before retiring for the evening, something I had failed to do. Drinking a lot of water during the day and keeping a big glass next to one's bed are important to offset the dehydration. I usually kept a big tumbler next to my mattress, but had neglected to do so the previous night. However, I had wakened a couple of times and walked down the hallway to the water fountain and drunk like a camel before crossing the Sahara. Finally, I took vitamins. Alcohol burns through vitamins like crazy.

I put on my ratty-ass robe, a terrycloth garment I'd had since I'd been in the hospital with mono after graduating from high school. I grabbed my soap, shampoo and toothpaste and wandered down the hall to the showers. Nobody was up yet, although the big hand on the clock was at 12; the little hand was telling everyone to sleep in.

I cranked the hot water and enjoyed the way it seemed to rinse away the grime of the hangover. I got dressed, the clean jeans feeling great against my skin. I hassled with all the crap in my duffel bag and came up with the hiking boots Eva and Adolf had bought me for Christmas. I'd really wanted hiking boots. They were practical for getting around, especially considering the fact that I did not have a car or a bicycle. I had hoped for a pair with Vibram soles and a suede finish that I could treat for water protection with mink oil. I mean, I wanted bona fide hiking boots. As was so often the case, however, Eva had opted for buying the cheapest boots she could find. They were dark blue with sort of a velour finish. When I put them on, I felt as if they were pinching the insteps of my feet, slightly behind the big toes. I stood up and walked a pace or two back and forth, to see if maybe they would settle a little differently with weight on them. But no—I still felt the pinch. And I didn't have any other shoes for this kind of weather.

I went downstairs and through the huge dining room to the kitchen. On every weekday except Tuesdays, when the earliest class on campus wasn't until ten o'clock for some reason, we had an ancient lady who fixed breakfast made-to-order: eggs, bacon, sausage, hash browns, just about anything that you'd want, except any good sources of fiber or whole fruit. The ancient lady also made these round rolls that consisted of dough dropped into the deep fryer. Outside of her presence (of course) the people in the frat referred to these rolls as enemas, because of their effect on the gastrointestinal system. But really everything tasted pretty good that she made. I pigged out as I read the *Star*, marveling, as I always did, at what had to be the last vestiges of journalistic reactionary philosophy in the United States.

As I was about finished, Jimmy Carson, the president of the house, came into the dining room. He'd been elected just before the end of the semester. He'd barely edged out Kyle Edwards, and there were some hard feelings between the two of them and their friends. Carson took the whole frat thing pretty seriously. His father had been in the frat, and his father before him. Kinda weird. I mean, the reasons I had pledged the frat the previous spring were to get out of the dorm—we couldn't have kegs, and there was a big risk of getting busted there. Well, there were reasons for the risk of getting busted in the dorms.

The social structure of the campus revolved around the fraternity/sorority, or Greek, system. The commonly-held myth was that DeForrest had the highest percentage of Greek students, 85 percent, in the United States. While the former part of that myth might have been true, the reality of the percentage was more like an even half. But even with that, the Greek system dominated the campus. The university's administration did its best to perpetuate the system. Two reasons were fairly persuasive: the Greek alums gave a lot of money to the school, and, if the Greek system faltered at all, then the university would have to build more dormitories to house the refugees. There were several repercussions from this system. First was that the dorms were directly under the control of the university, and so big parties involving alcohol were difficult to bring off. Alcohol, technically, was illegal at DeForrest. As late as the early 1960s, a group of students who met at a different bar every week (and there were six bars), and who called themselves the Black Friars, had been busted for drinking and promptly expelled. Around the same time, a DeForrest student had the misfortune of having his face shown in a newscast clip in a story about the annual

Spring Break pilgrimage to Daytona Beach. He wore the traditional Old Gold shirt with black, block letters that read "DeForrest" while holding a can of Budweiser. When the student arrived back at DeForrest at the end of break, he had been expelled. The university was quick to point out that, once a person becomes a student of DeForrest, s/he is under the control of the university, 24 hours a day, 365 days a year, until that student graduates or otherwise matriculates.

Things had eased up since the 1960s. Kegs sat outside the kitchen doors of several of the frats each weekend, and no one was written up by the dean. It wasn't uncommon, even with as small of a campus and a student body as DeForrest had, for a frat, or two or three frats combined, to host a party with seven or eight kegs. DeForrest really developed its alcoholics early, handling its freshmen like major league baseball teams handle rookies in spring training. In future years, many of the alums would have to function well at business meetings or gala cocktail parties or any of a number of types of receptions, at any of which the refusal to consume alcohol would be deemed as impolite, perhaps even suspect. DeForrest also boasted one of the highest rates of marriage among its students. People met at DeForrest, graduated from DeForrest, and married shortly after commencement. There was a very high divorce rate among these alums and alcohol, no doubt, helped them cope with their marriages' demise. Thus, most students drank, and many drank heavily.

Second, students in the Greek living units, as dorms and Greek houses were referred to at DeForrest, were much much much much less likely to be busted—for anything: booze, drugs, you name it. The students who lived in the dorms, and alums from the dorms, were not as cohesive as the alums of the frats and sororities. Plus, the Greek alums gave a lot more money. The result was that the only busts for drugs that had occurred in the last few years had been of students either living in one of the dorms or one of the handful of students living off-campus in apartments. This was called living O.I.T., for "out in town." Quaint, huh?

Consequently, with so much emphasis on the Greek system, the campus was extremely split, sociologically. There was very little interaction within the classrooms. People went to lectures, had occasional discussions, then went back to the house, and that was that. Even though the campus was small, it was possible to arrive as a freshman, get caught up in the Greek system, and then not emerge until four years later, down at the bars during senior week.

With such a large percentage of the students living in the Greek system, though, the "rah rah" factor—the mindless following of the doctrines of a frat or sorority—was greatly watered-down. Although on other campuses all or nearly all of the Greeks were atavistic, at DeForrest only three or four of the houses had such an attitude. That was a reflection, too, of students' attitudes, in the aftermath of the late 1960s.

I took my dishes back to the kitchen and set them on the aluminum table next to the sink, went back upstairs to grab my notebook and a couple of books and headed down to campus.

My grades second semester were important. They determined whether I would stay in school. I'd had four classes at the start of the previous semester. I'd dropped one, nearly aced a second, gotten a solid "hook," or C, in a third, and was perilously close to flunking the fourth. If I only could have passed that last one, with even the lowest of Ds, then I would have been okay. The last class was taught by a real prick. I'd bagged half of the classes in his course. And really, that was pretty good attendance for me. He'd bitched about it, though, and on the two exams going into the final I'd had a solid D on the first, and barely flunked the second. It didn't help that his exams involved, increasingly, materials from his lectures. He was becoming more of a Nazi towards students since the school newspaper had named him the worst prof on campus. Finally, I should have done well on the final but for one minor problem. We'd gotten a bad batch of mescaline near the end of the previous semester. It was so bad that all it was good for was to use as speed. I mean, there were no visuals with it, no nothing. Since speed was scarce at the end of the previous semester, and since I needed it in my two weeks of studying for the final in his class, I'd popped a couple of hits every day leading up to his exam. I was fine. I was really absorbing the materials. His final was my last final of the semester. I popped two hits after breakfast that morning and took a last look-see at my notes. As I walked down to campus later, I could feel the first rushes of tripping. Out of a couple of hundred hits that had arrived on campus, I got the only two that were worth a shit, and I took them that morning. I had a rough time focusing on the pages of the blue book as I tried to write. Even with all that, I felt I had a chance to pass.

Once I got into the second semester, I could really fly. My schedule looked to be pretty cool. Educational psychology was supposed to be a pud course, pretty easy. It was really difficult to overcome the inertia of the multiple choice tests and escape a C, but it was also difficult to get less than a C. It was taught by one of the older, distinguished profs on campus. Speech pathology was a required course for the double major I was trying to cultivate. The reviews on it were that if you studied past tests, you'd be okay. Constitutional law interested me because it was the study of cases involving civil rights and liberties according to the University Bulletin. Con law was taught by Doctor Fredrick, a kinda quiet guy, but one who was supposed to be really cool as a prof. I'd heard that the class was for people on a track to go to law school and was taught in the Socratic method, the method most favored by law schools. I wasn't all that sure I wanted to go to law school— that was, after all, the path meant for me—but the mix of students that I had heard were signed up for the class sounded interesting. There were a lot of poly sci jocks—political science majors—in the class. A lot of juniors and seniors. Several of the handful of conservatives on campus were in the class, as well as a few of the radical majority. It might be interesting, I thought, just to listen to people getting pissed off at one another. Finally, political and social philosophy sounded like it would be my favorite course. It was taught by Professor Thomas Gleason. He was a pretty weird guy. His hair looked as if he never washed it, and he chain-smoked Pall Mall straights in class. I'd walked by a booth in the student union one time where he was sitting with another prof and several students, and it was difficult to miss the heavily jaundiced discoloration of the fingers on his hand. He was really intense, and I had heard some good things about his class.

For my classes the upcoming semester, I had also designed a method of positive reinforcement for attendance. I decided to work on that later, when I would try to get my room into shape.

There was a light dusting of snow everywhere, and a few flakes were coming down. I headed towards the Faculty Annex, an old house that stood next to the Academic Quad that housed the professors of lesser seniority. I found Gleason's office, upstairs and around a tight corner. He had the syllabus for each of his classes in big, brown envelopes taped to his shut door, so I grabbed one and scanned it. Then I walked across the alley, into Wesleyan Hall, where the poly sci department was located. I said hello to the secretary and asked her about the syllabus for con law. She sort of abruptly jerked one out of the stack of syllabi that rested on a shelf behind her without saying anything. I smiled and walked out. Nearly all the readings for the course were Supreme Court cases, and I knew where all of those were in the stacks of the library, where I headed next. For a school with such a hotshot reputation for academic excellence as DeForrest, the library was pretty anemic. It was three stories high with a basement. I went to the card catalogue and looked up the authors and titles for my philosophy class. I was really pleased to see that each of the four or five books on the list—Thomas Hobbes's Leviathan, Jean-Jacques Rousseau's Discourses, John Locke's Second Treatise of Government, and a couple of others— were all in our library's collection. I got the call numbers, went up into the stacks, and grabbed them. I filled out the cards and checked out the books, then walked over to the Student Union Building, or the UB as it was commonly called, to get a coke. The place was pretty deserted. I wasn't surprised. This was first day back and a lot of the people wouldn't be getting out just yet. The grill/fountain in the UB was called the Hub, and there were half a dozen janitors from various parts of campus taking a break there. I got a coke and got out of there.

I walked down the street and turned the corner at the place where the ruins of the U Shop and the bakery stood. The U Shop was a little store that was like a drug store without the pharmacy. It was a place where students could buy various little shit and cash checks. The bakery was next door and had had really odd hours. It was a place to get caffeine and various forms of refined sugar during breaks in the middle of all-nighters. It was rumored that the university had been trying for years to buy the building, but to no avail. The owner was said to have hated the university and loved the notion of the building being an eyesore against the backdrop of modern campus living. The owner had died and, weirdly enough, the next day the buildings had caught fire. Firefighters rushed to the scene and attempted to stop the blaze in very odd ways. One of the reporters for the student newspaper took pictures of a fireman pointing his firehose at one of the two electrical breaker boxes that were on the back wall of the building. The thing exploded and knocked the firefighter on his ass. The firefighter had then stood up and pointed his hose at the other breaker box. As the reporter took pictures of this scene unfolding, one of Glendale's Finest, a patrolman on the police force, walked over and grabbed the kid's camera, then pulled out the film, exposing it. Two days later, the university negotiated the purchase of the ruins and the lot it had stood on. The matter had then gone to court, however, when the heirs started arguing over who would get what cut.

I walked over to the apartment of some friends of mine, Austin Taylor and Michelle Morrison. Apartments, and the people who lived O.I.T., posed a danger to DeForrest, as an institution. Not only did they pose a financial danger, as described earlier, but they posed an even greater threat to the "society" of DeForrest. The president of D.F.U. had labeled as "asocial non-persons" those who lived off-campus. Of course, just because those persons had matured and grown intellectually to a point where they were alienated by the puerile bullshit games of Greek living, did not deter the University from waging its war.

As a DeForrest student, one was required to live in either a dorm, or a sorority or fraternity. Students were allowed to go O.I.T. only under exceptional circumstances. Although there were a couple of hundred students actually living O.I.T., the university's official count was something like 48. The typical reason was dietary/health: a hometown doctor someplace wrote an excuse for Tommy or Susie to live in an apartment. I never was told the specifics of any one such excuse. If the reason was that the food in the particular living unit posed a threat to the health of the student in question, then that was a legitimate excuse for nearly everyone on campus—college food sucks, is chock-full of starch and grease, and has the nutritional value (and flavor) of cardboard.

The next most popular reason went like this. A student went to a local business person and got a letter from her/him stating that the student had to live off-campus for work-related reasons. But what did that mean? There were no coal mines where one would slog at odd hours, waking up others on the pristine campus. Nonetheless, students obtained such letters, usually from their prospective landlord, and they were then "official." A landlord's letter usually "cost" in the form of higher rent and a long-term lease.

My favorite reason available for going O.I.T. was religion. If one's religion was such that his/her lifestyle was incompatible with others in the "living unit," one could go O.I.T. I never heard of anyone citing this reason. The campus was too heavily WASP. Sure, a few Catholics were thrown in there, and a couple of members of the Hebrew religion. And the campus had a couple of dozen token blacks. Regardless of the mix of persons on campus, "religion" was there in the student handbook, of this nominally Methodist school, as a reason listed for going O.I.T. I wanted to approach the dean with a letter stating that I had converted to Tantric Buddhism and, as such, believed that the enthrallment of my senses was the only means by which I could attain true enlightenment; that orgies, drugfests, extreme intoxication on any available substances, and total degradation of my body and soul were the only means by which I could achieve one-ness with the Universe. I'm sure that if I had done so, one of the old ladies who worked as a secretary there would have listened to me in a bewildered manner, and then promptly croaked of a coronary.

Of course, what the great majority of those students who lived O.I.T. did, especially their senior year, was to have a room in a living unit, and have Mommy and Daddy (or Mommy or Daddy, since so many of the parents, especially if they were DeForrest alums, were divorced) pay for an apartment at the same time. The university was happy—one of the living units was getting the money. The living units were happy. The individual students were happy. And the reputation of the university for conspicuous affluence and hypocrisy was maintained at the highest levels.

I first met Austin and Michelle our freshman year, and we'd been good friends ever since. Austin was a poor boy from southern Indiana. During high school he had lived with his grandmother and been something of a hood. But his grades had always been good, and then he took this little test called the SAT and DeForrest offered him a full-tuition scholarship. Thus it was that he escaped Upper Appalachia. Michelle's parents, on the other hand, were wealthy and had an oceanfront home—an estate, really—back east. Despite her background—the type of background that shaped the world-view of most DeForrest students—she was not a snob at all. She also would not put up with Austin's bullshit when we'd sit around and argue about anything in particular. In fact, quiet as she normally was, she would not put up with anyone's bullshit.

Austin and Michelle lived behind the student health center in a small house that had been divided into three apartments. They had just moved into the place at the end of finals. Austin had been living in an apartment with Pete Farris. But Austin and Michelle had wanted more privacy. Even though they'd gotten along fine with Farris, the situation was still a little uncomfortable—Austin and Michelle were a couple and so it was difficult for them to live with someone else. Part of the reason that the situation had seemed good at the start of the previous semester was that the apartment that Austin and Farris had gotten was directly across Anderson Street from the sorority in which Michelle was a member. But after a semester, Michelle had decided to drop any pretense. Her parents now paid her room-and-board at the sorority and, reluctantly, her half of the rent at this new place. Farris had found somebody else with sufficient health problems or work-related needs, split the apartment, and so Austin and Michelle had moved into this place. From the street, even with the foliage missing from the trees, one could hardly see it. I could make out the rear end of Austin's beat-up Impala station wagon parked in the narrow driveway. The front porch was tiny, but it was really cool, edged in black, wrought-iron with matching wrought-iron table and two or three chairs. Everything was rusting slightly.

I banged on the door and saw some movement inside. It was cold standing on the front porch, even though I was bundled up in wool. Austin opened the door, smiled when he saw that it was me, and invited me in.

"How was Christmas?" I asked.

"Fine," Austin shrugged, smiling. "Saw some friends from the old days. That was about it. You?"

"Not much. Oh, well—almost put one of Adolf's company trucks into a swimming pool."

Austin grinned, then chuckled. "Wanta get high?" he asked as he started rolling a joint.

"Sure," I said, and started chucking my coat and muffler.

There were still things in boxes, but for the most part the two of them had unpacked. Picasso's Blue Man hung on a narrow piece of ancient plaster wall between the doors to the kitchen and the bathroom. The furniture in the place had been obtained from other students who had left an item or two behind in previous years: old and over-stuffed chairs, a couch with vinyl cushions and back, and making up shelves and the legs of a coffee table were plastic milk crates ripped off from the campus living units. The walls were covered in old, musty wallpaper of a faded pattern, and the carpet on the floor left a sort of film on one's fingers after a brief touch. There were only two windows, and those were in the south wall, but the drapes—old things that probably had not been drycleaned since they were purchased at some unknown rummage sale somewhere back in time— were always drawn. There were a couple of lamps, and a ceiling light fixture that Austin and Michelle never used. The kitchen was small and old, but the walls were covered in real tiles, green and grouted. The bathroom was tiny, and the tub had been jerry-rigged with a makeshift shower.

"Where's Michelle?" I asked.

"Over at the sorority, picking up a couple of things she has over there. The housemother's been . . ."

"Yeah, I know," I said, cutting him off. Michelle's sorority's housemother was like many of the housemothers on campus. She was a widowed grandmother whose own children had grown up and moved away. Her residence in the sorority was probably her third or fourth such experience. She moved every few years to another campus in the midwest to fulfill a similar role. She was advanced in years and the past decade-and-a-half had passed her in a blur. She was still confused by the notion that a male and female could co-habitate without benefit of marriage. That one of her "girls" was only nominally residing in the sorority both shocked and offended her. But she would keep plodding on, a living symbol of parenthood present in the campus setting. Michelle had told us that the housemother, on those few occasions when Michelle had eaten meals at the house, commented on Michelle's residential status. It wasn't that Michelle was unique in her residential situation—every sorority had at least one or two women doing the same. Others before Michelle, from the late 1960s on, had suffered from the same ugly tongue, either of this housemother or one of the others on campus. The difference was that at dinner one evening the semester before, Michelle had told the woman to fuck off.

"They're gonna fire Farina," Austin commented as he fired up the joint. He coughed a little as he inhaled, then handed it over to me.

Farina was an anthropology prof who was a major pain to the administration. He'd been voted Professor of the Year for three years running. He "related" to his students, dressing in jeans, growing his hair long, and occasionally cussing in his classes. He "told it like it was." In other words, he expressed his world view in an iconoclastic method that was compatible to the cynicism that was incipient to undergrads. And the university was trying to get rid of him. It wasn't that he had failed to publish in his discipline. He had. It wasn't that he lacked credentials—he had all the credentials in the world. They were impeccable. His mistake was that he was more highly qualified than the head of his department—who did NOT have a Ph.D.—and, departmental infighting being what it is, Farina had become rather vocal about the shortcomings of his bureaucratic superior. His superior had subsequently voiced his displeasure to the rulers of the university. So the previous spring, Farina had been denied tenure. This spring was the denouement.

I'd never had Farina for a course. I'd never even met the man. The student newspaper—The Daily DeForrest—a newspaper that was, appropriately enough, published twice a week, on Tuesday and Friday—had been keeping track of every development in the controversy. The paper had expressed its support for the professor, but things were looking sort of dim right then. Eva subscribed to it, having it mailed, twice a week, to the Farm. It was one more example of Eva wanting to monitor my activities.

I agreed with Austin that Farina was going to be fired. "But there sure will be some pissed off people," I observed.

"We have him for magic and religion next semester," Austin commented.

"You both signed up?" I asked, but then realized how silly my question was. Ever since they'd met, Austin and Michelle took the same courses together.

"Yeah. We've been reading some Zen lately, that sort of stuff," he said as he ashed the doobie.

Just then, the door to the apartment opened and Michelle walked in. When she saw me she said hi and sat down next to Austin on the couch and reached for what was left of the joint.

"How're things over at the house?" Austin asked in a mocking tone.

"Figure this one," Michelle said, exhaling smoke. "The president of the house doesn't think that they should 'cover' for me living off-campus. I said it's my business where I sleep. I mean, I'm paying full house bill."

"What, they want you to stay there even if you don't want to?"

"Got me," she said. "I mean, we had a big fucking discussion of it. Fortunately my 'roommate' was behind me a hundred percent."

"Why wouldn't she be?" Austin asked. "She gets a single that way."

"Yeah. They had a vote on it. A vote. Go figure," she said and finished off what was left of the joint.

Austin asked me if I wanted any wine, and I said sure. He came out with a big bottle of Yago Sangria and glasses from the jars of cheap brands of jelly. He poured and we toasted Winter Term.

"What are you taking for Winter Term?" he asked.

"Debate."

"Same as last year?" Michelle asked and I nodded. "I didn't know you could take the same Winter Term twice.

"I checked it out and it's legit. What are you guys taking?"

Austin walked over to the stereo and turned on the FM. "We're doing a thing for sociology. Studying an urban commune in Washington, D.C."

I was stoned so it took a couple of minutes for that to sink in. "Are you guys gonna have to go out there?"

"Yeah," Michelle replied. "We'll stay out there for a week, week after next."

"We'll get to sleep on floors and work with the People," Austin stated. "We'll get to find our ways around the Nation's Capital for the day when the Revolution comes." The last part of the statement was shaped with that same mocking tone.

The radio station that was playing was the only cool station that we could get in Glendale. Well, the student radio station played some pretty cool stuff, but the signal was mono. So everyone listened to WNAP, the radio station in Indianapolis that had staked its claim to hip culture as it existed in central Indiana.

I don't know why I'd missed the brand-new TV. Austin saw my reaction, and before I could say anything, he explained, "Michelle's folks got us that. It's a brand-new Sony Trinitron. Remote control and everything." With that he grabbed the little box and turned the thing on. After a few moments, the picture flared on.

"Man, the color is really good," I exclaimed after a minute or two. The color was good. I was accustomed to the Zeniths that Eva and Adolf had owned and the Zenith that was in the informal living room at the frat. The colors on those sets were too vivid to be real. Tones blew the eyes. College bowl games were always a gas with the colors of the field and the uniforms and everything. But the colors on the Trinitron were real.

"You gonna try to get cable?" I asked. Cable had only arrived in Glendale the previous fall. The frats and sororities had been hooked up and then some private residences. The rest of the places in town—and back in Kilkerry for me, for that matter—were still dependent on aerial reception. That meant that even though Austin and Michelle got great color, they would only be getting it on 4, 6, 8, and 13 out of Indy, and 2 and 10 out of Terre Haute.

"Fat chance," Austin said with a chuckle. Yeah, it was inconceivable that the university would allow any type of cultural development in the town that would provide some sort of advantage to the people living O.I.T. "You have to see what else we got," Austin said, and seemed to hassle with some crap on the shelf below the TV. What he brought up were two boxes with wires that seemed to be connected to the back of the TV. Each box had a dial on it. Austin hit the remote control, and the screen on the TV went blank. Then he hit another button and lines appeared on the screen—one line about two inches wide on each side of the screen, and a dotted line that ran straight down the middle of the screen.

"What the fuck's this?" I asked, still staring and trying to make sense of what I saw.

"It's a game," he replied.

"They're real big on the coast," Michelle added. "My parents got us one and my brother one."

"It's video ping pong," Austin continued. "It's called Pong."

The game was extremely primitive by our standards today. Austin took all of ten seconds to show me how to play. I've always considered myself to be a gamester. And I really got into Pong. I found that by twisting the dial a certain way, I could put English or spin on the video "dot" that constituted the ball, just like on a real ping pong table. The thing really sucked us in. We killed one bottle of Sangria and another joint. We did a round-robin tournament with best-of-five matches. I told them about the book by Castaneda I was reading.

"You know," Austin said, "I heard that UCLA expelled him from its doctorate program."

"Where'd you read that?" I asked.

"Seems to me like it was in Rolling Stone."

"Do you remember when?"

"Not right off hand, no."

"We could ask Farina," Michelle said. "He might know. It's in his discipline."

"I'd appreciate that," I said. "I mean, nobody seems to know anything about him."

"Oh, hey!" Austin said quickly. "What time is it?"

I looked at my watch. "Almost two," I said, surprised at how time had flown.

"We have to go by his office sometime today," Austin said.

"You'd better go now," I advised. "I mean—it's getting late and it's Winter Term and all."

And just like that I was saying goodbye and heading back out into the cold toward the frat. The air was crisp. It felt good to be out again and moving around in it.

The walk was only a couple of blocks. I went in the front door of the fraternity— and by "fraternity," I mean the physical plant—and stomped off my boots. The damn things were really digging into my feet now. I looked down at them and swore. Not only did they wear badly—they were extremely cheap-looking as well. And inside I could feel dampness. My feet were hot and they couldn't breathe. So they were sweating, until the moisture from outside began soaking in. Then the sweat started turning really clammy. I shook my head and went upstairs to my room. It took me about a minute of messing with the lock and the key before the door finally opened and I got in. Once I was in my room I took off those fucking shoes, then the wet socks, and moved my toes.

I was just standing there like that when Criminal Phil stuck his head around the corner and asked me if I wanted to go to Indy to the airport. "Ridgeway's coming in," Phil told me. "We meet him at his plane in about an hour."

I said sure, and sat down to put on the tennis shoes I'd brought from the Farm.

"Nice Pro Keds," Criminal Phil observed as I laced on the high tops.

"I ripped them off my cousin right before I left. Goddamn but I'm glad I did." The shoes were pliable but heavy. They felt like they could last forever. "Got anything to drink?" I asked as I stood up and grabbed my coat.

Criminal Phil said he had a 12-pack, and we went by his room and grabbed it and his coat, then went on out to the parking lot.

Criminal Phil's old man, a building contractor in suburban Chicago, was always dropping money on him and his brother. Anything that they wanted, they basically got. This break, Criminal Phil had been given a new Chevy Impala convertible.

"Nice wheels," I said as I got in on the passenger's side.

"The old man got this for the old lady last month and she didn't like it, so I got to bring it back. My brother gets it next month."

We rocketed out of the frat parking lot and onto the street, then we hit the highway and were gone. The beer was Stroh's, and once I'd gotten past the first one—quite a contrast between the taste of the Sangria and now the beer—it really tasted pretty good. I tossed my empties into the back, and Criminal Phil and I shot the shit about break and all sorts of good shit like that. The stereo was pretty cool and was dialed into WNAP. BTO started cranking, and Criminal Phil turned up the volume as he lit a bowl of pot.

By the time that we got to the airport, we were pretty crispy. I knew my eyes were probably bloodshot as hell, but I didn't have anything illegal on me and I wasn't driving, so I wasn't too worried. As we walked into the terminal, I felt anxious to travel. It's weird to be in an airport and not traveling. People were going every which way and the announcements were crackling over the PA, announcing this or that flight.

We checked the manifest for Ridgeway's American Airlines flight, then approached the metal detector for the right concourse. I walked through the thing with Criminal Phil right behind me and, as I did, the beeper went off. The air marshal asked me to step over to the side, and then ran the hand unit over me. He got no response, but then eyed me suspiciously before he said I could move along.

"I wonder what set that off," I said to Criminal Phil as we moved down the concourse.

"Shit," he said. "I think that it was me, not you. I still got the hash pipe in my pocket."

"Oh fuck!" I exclaimed.

We got to Ridgeway's gate just as his plane was taxiing to a stop. He was right at the front of the group coming off the plane and greeted us as he walked past us toward the baggage area.

"I hope you guys have some beers, because I am thirsty," he said as we hurried to keep in step with him. "Can you believe it? They fucking carded me on board the fucking flight!"

That seemed like a particularly callous thing to do to Ridgeway, who always had a beer in hand.

"You bring any beer back with you?" Criminal Phil asked.

Ridgeway grinned. "A case of Genessee Cream Ale. You'll love it."

We got onto the escalator and went to the luggage carousel. I kept a lookout for any drug-sniffing airport dogs that might sit up and take notice as we walked by, but we were fortunate. It wasn't long before we had Ridgeway's bags and were ensconced in the Chevy headed out to the interstate. The late afternoon sun shone in our eyes. Ridgeway told us about some of the bars he had hit back home in the New York suburb where his parents lived. His father was a broker at the New York Stock Exchange, and Ridgeway's stories seemed to be about life on another planet. The Chevy rolled along quite smoothly over the pavement. The beers tasted good.

"Dig that sign," Ridgeway said from the back seat, and I looked over at a huge billboard that read, in red white and blue, "God, guns, guts made America great—Let's keep all three!"

"Yeah, right," I said. "It should be Sex, drugs and—what?" I couldn't think of an appropriate third part.

The trip went quickly. It was almost suppertime by the time that we got back. And we were almost out of beer. I dimly remember eating ham and cheese sandwiches and tater tots and washing everything down with milk. The next thing I knew, it was morning and I was waking up sober.

Chapter 5 - This Room Is For Men Only

I awoke on the mattress in my room. The different concoctions of alcohol I had consumed the day before had done a number on my head. But I was only 19 and my body didn't necessarily know any better. I stretched and sat there for a few minutes. I was hungry, needed to piss, and I felt kind of gritty, so I got up.

I stood and stretched and looked at the centerfold, taped to the wall, from a recent issue of Playboy. I felt my dick become tumescent. I wasn't sure that there really were women who looked like the centerfolds. I had heard that the photographs were airbrushed of any blemishes. At that moment, I really didn't care.

Saturday mornings meant housework. Each member of the frat was assigned a task. All the other frats on campus assigned the various chores to be done to their pledges—the underclassmen who'd just joined. Two years before, though, according to the fraternity archives, our house had passed a rule that everybody shared in the work equally. It was a rule that still stuck in the craw of the national fraternity. But hey—it was our house, not the national's. I went down the hall where the assignments had been posted by the House Manager. I'd been assigned to sweep the carpet in Second Old and dump the trash. Those tasks took me all of maybe 20 minutes. I went in search of the House Manager to have him inspect my work and scratch me off the sheet. Our House Manager was Dan Benson, a sophomore who was not well-liked. But he was the only person who had volunteered for the job. He had just gotten up when I found him in Third New. He came down, took a look at the rug and trash cans—now empty—and crossed me off the list. I then went downstairs and wolfed down breakfast, and walked back up to the Informal Living Room. Activity was just beginning to pick up, as people got up and cussed about having to do any work on Saturday. I got to my room and shoved every item that I had there to the middle and away from the walls. I ran downstairs to the storage room in the basement—a room that was called the Womb, for some unknown reason—and grabbed a paint brush, a roller and a can of paint that held the better part of a gallon of latex.

The flat white paint went on thick and even. I used the brush at the places where the roller wouldn't reach. Then I used the roller. The room being as small as it was, I was done in less than an hour. I took the remnants of the paint and the roller and brush downstairs and cleaned everything up. I was so neat about it all that I hadn't even gotten any paint on me. I kicked back in the Informal, waiting for lunch to be called while the paint in my room dried.

While I watched Bugs Bunny and Friends, people walked through going about their Saturday housework. "Doc" Rudolf, a Junior, came in sipping coffee and just stood there for a minute, staring at the TV and trying to wake up. Sometimes nicknames made sense. Once in a while the logic of a nickname was quite convoluted, but existed nonetheless. With Doc you might have expected him to be pre-med or something similar, but there was nothing. I still have no idea why he was called Doc. Dan Benson came into the Informal just then.

"Rudolf," Benson intoned. "Have you finished your housework?"

"Fuck off," Rudolf replied, not taking his eyes off the TV.

Benson blanched at that. Repartee in the frat could be cold and callous. What pissed Benson off was that he was doing his job and he was catching shit for it. This only happened a couple of dozen times every week, but it still got to him.

"Do the work now," Benson ordered.

"And I said fuck off."

Benson flew out of the Informal and into the stairwell. Rudolf continued sipping his coffee and staring at the TV.

It's amazing that we had opted to endure the bullshit of fraternity life. The coming months would be the worst of it. I'd joined the frat to both escape the dorms and to live in this specific house. I hadn't felt like I fit in the previous semester. The other people in my class had a year's experience under their belts of living in the house. The music that I had been into—fairly hard rock, like Black Sabbath, Uriah Heep, BTO—wasn't "in." People were listening a lot to the Allman Brothers and Marshall Tucker and the Who. I progressed musically, but not very willingly. And a lot of the posters and shit I'd had in my room freshman year were long since gone. They were too wild or blatantly drug-oriented. Tastes in the frat went more to subtlety, by comparison. Anyways, it's important to understand the dynamics of fraternity life at the time.

At the time, fraternities were struggling with the aftermath of the 1960s. They were being inundated by hippies or, at the very least, people who were leaning towards hippie tendencies. The pictures of the people in the chapter composites of the time show the hair getting longer with each year. There were big splits in the houses between these people and people who were at the opposite end of the social spectrum. The rift could be characterized as one between pot smokers and beer drinkers. And that's not entirely accurate, either, because nearly everyone who smoked pot also drank beer. The two groups would divide over a question of rah-rah and adherence to ritual, on one hand, and pursuit of a wild sort of individualism reflective of the hedonism of the times, on the other. What happened was that the number of pot smokers in a frat would grow, members of the fraternity would seriously question all the horseshit that was attendant upon being in such a communal living situation, alumni relations would go to hell, finances would then dry up, and the house would either fold, or the national frat would come in and start all over again, usually taking the side of the beer drinkers, who were usually rah-rah, i.e., strongly into the Greek system. Everyone else, especially people who smoked pot or used other drugs, would be kicked out. Alcohol posed less of a threat to the social order than did other drugs. Breaking shit and getting into fights was, if not behavior acceptable to the old alums, at least behavior that could be understood among red-blooded American young males and, therefore, tolerated. To the alums with the money i.e., the alums in their 50s and 60s and 70s—long hair, beat-up jeans, weird music, and other odd patterns of behavior represented life, not so much from another time, as from another planet.

In our house, however, there was no clear gauge of what constituted the sides people were on. There were pot smokers on both sides, and right wingers as well. In our situation the schism had more to do with other personality traits. And it was such a waste of time. I think a lot of us would have leapt at alternatives that did not exist at DeForrest, e.g., co-ed dorms or reasonably-priced apartments not run by slum-lords. In the end, the more rational people in the house went O.I.T. instead of putting up with the bullshit In the meantime, certain people naturally hung around with one another—a situation that the national frat termed as "cliquishness," as though employing choice in one's friends is pathological.

And so what later would be recognized as having been the opening shot of the fraternity civil war was fired that morning as I sat in the Informal watching Bugs Bunny and waiting for paint to dry.

It took only a few moments for the president of the house to come down with Benson. Carson didn't like Rudolf. For that matter, Carson had a grudge against a lot of the people in the house. His likes and dislikes hadn't had much of an effect in the past. But Carson had never been the president of the house before. He ordered Rudolf to start his housework "right fucking now." There was shouting, and a lot of cussing. A few other people drifted into the room, watching. Edwards appeared vindicated, having lost the election to someone who was power-hungry. I got disgusted and went upstairs. Besides, not only had I seen that particular episode of the Roadrunner—the episode where Wiley

Coyote buys the Acme darts and attaches a stick of dynamite to each one—but I figured that, by now, my paint was dry.

I bought a Pepsi for a quarter in the stairwell pop machine and went back to my room. I flipped on the light and examined the paint job for any spots that I'd missed. I was surprised at the nice, even job I'd done. I placed things around the perimeter of the room and I set up my stereo on short planks for shelves and bricks.

My stereo was not all that expensive. Eva and Adolf had told me they would buy a stereo for me for graduating from high school. My girlfriend at the time knew a place where they had great deals on discontinued models. The Hitachi I got never died. Well, the tuner and the amp never died, but the 8-track tape deck had fried out the previous semester from playing way too many bootleg tapes way too many hours every day. I'd pitched the tapes. I'd blown the original speakers the first week of freshman year, and during the summer I'd picked up used speakers for thirty bucks at a Kilkerry stereo shop. The previous owner had upholstered the cabinets. They were 24 inches tall and looked impressive. And somewhere along the way I acquired a truly cheap turntable. The platter for the records wasn't even the full size of an LP. Of course, I didn't take that good a care of my albums. A really good turntable would have been a waste. The music popped and cracked as the needle worked its way over old divots and made new ones. Occasionally a beer would get spilled on an album lying on the floor. But the stereo was functional.

Once the stereo was connected, I turned on WNAP and assembled the rest of the room. I put books on the the shelves, then tossed the mattress against one wall. In the alcove created by the imposition of the closet in one corner, I built my "desk." It was a piece of plywood two feet wide by a foot-and-a-half deep set on two stacks of bricks with an old Stroh's beer box serving as a sort of drawer for pens and bullshit. I had salvaged three or four cushions from ancient couches that had been discarded by the house. I tossed these on the floor in place of chairs for guests. Above the desk I drew my schedule of classes for the week in the coming semester, with a magic marker, with hour-long blocks marked by subject. I had decided to motivate myself by keeping score of my class attendance. I figured that attendance was the only thing that was keeping me from good grades. By the time I was done it was time for lunch.

People were standing around in the Informal, waiting for the dining room officially to open so we could be seated and fed. The housebitch was chatting with two or three of her little favorites. .

There were several aspects of frat life that made no sense to me, and the presence of a housemother was one. The university (supposedly) required Greek living units to have housemothers. The dorms had resident counselors who were usually from the small group of DeForrest graduate students. The housebitch that we had was a real bitch. She had emigrated from Romania at the end of World War II. The joke in the house was that she'd slept her away across the Atlantic on a troop ship, entertaining the couple of thousand soldiers on board as fare. Her accent was thick and she had tremendously awful tastes in clothes. She was extremely prejudiced. In descending order she hated: Black people, people from any country in which the predominant language spoken was Spanish, Jewish people, the Irish, and Italians. Most of all, she hated guys in the house who did not take her seriously, were openly contemptuous of her, or who didn't show her the degree of respect she thought was her due. One would have thought that having emigrated from Europe at the end of World War II, she would not have liked Germans, but she went to great pains when the subject arose to emphasize to whomever would listen that Hitler had done good things for the German people. And she played favorites among the guys in the house. It was the same as having Eva or one of her minions there. This day the housebitch was blathering about manners. Her comments were loud. Then Carson came downstairs, and I connected everything. The housebitch was talking about Rudolf and what had transpired the short while before after I had gone back up to my room. Then the waiters yelled up the stairs that lunch was ready.

When I had lived in the dorm the previous year, there was no ceremony to meals. The doors to the dining room opened at a certain time, meals were served. Serving stopped at a certain time. If you missed the meal, too bad. While you were there, you behaved as you would in any restaurant. In the frat, there was a sort of ceremony to lunch and dinner. Consistent with that unwritten ceremony, the housebitch was escorted by Carson to her seat at the head of what was considered the main table. Everyone else in the house followed them and took up places as they wished. When everyone had chosen a place to sit they remained standing until the person at the other end of the housebitch's table said a prayer. As an atheist, I found the whole thing to be rather offensive. As a sentient creature, I also didn't particularly care to show any respect to the housebitch.

The housebitch was in a snit, mortally offended over having heard Rudolf yelling the word "fuck" several times. Guys on either side of the split were pissed. The house chaplain—yes, we had one, a theology major who actually believed that there was a supreme deity—sat at the housebitch's table and asked everyone to bow their heads for prayer. Now that was a new one. I'd never heard that request for bowed heads. There might have been a prayer at meal time, but there was also a healthy respect that culminated in not requiring everyone to participate. I just stood there, as I usually did, politely quiet. I looked over and saw that Carson was taking a head count of people who weren't bowing their heads. I wondered if he was going to write a letter to god about it. I wondered if Carson would count himself as not having bowed his head since he had to have his head raised high to see everybody around the huge diningroom whose heads weren't bowed. Our food dutifully blessed, we were allowed to sit and eat.

Edwards and his buddies, Tom Buchanan and Dennis Jones, were seated at the table next to mine. They were all in the same year, had pledged together, and hung around all the time with each other. They also generally ran for house offices at the same time and were euphemistically called the Triumphirate. Rudolph was with them.

"Nobody can order anybody else around in a house. I mean, this isn't a police state," Rudolf said loudly.

Edwards started talking. I cringed, waiting for Edwards to try and toss a long word into the next sentence. His vocabulary was rife with malapropisms, the result of his trying to sound as though he was from anyplace other than the Indiana side of the Ohio River, looking straight across at Kentucky. Fortunately, he simply prattled on about despotism and our present situation in one and two syllable words..

The dining room was quiet, glances shot at the housebitch's table. Carson's face turned from pink to red to a deep umber tinged with bile as his anger rose. I imagined Nixon's reactions when Watergate first went down. The moments of tension passed. We continued our meal.

Another custom was that, when one finished one's meal, that person rose and requested the housebitch's permission to leave the dining room. Rudolf and the others stood up, en masse, and left the room without so much as a goodbye to the housebitch. Oops—major league breach of etiquette. It took a few moments for the incident to sink in at the housebitch's table. When it did, she very curtly tossed down her napkin. Carson ran around to her chair and helped her to her feet and the whole table escorted her fat ass out of the dining room.

There were laughs and uneasy sounds around the room. I pushed away from the table and went on upstairs. I wanted to survey my room and put a few final touches on it. I stood there hassling with the lock on the door. Just then Ridgeway yelled at me from down the hall that I had a phone call.

I walked the ten yards or so to the recessed area that held the phone in Second Old and grabbed the received from Ridgeway. "Line two," he said, and I hit the flashing button and said hello.

"Your grades just came in the mail," Eva said. Two days since I'd heard that voice. I'd been so happy. Then I realized her tone. Sort of amused and happy and peppy. Then she said, "Don't you want to know what you got?"

"Sure," I stammered. Then there was another pause, and I said, "Tell me what they are."

"You don't have to snap at me," she replied. "One B," which would be political theory—so the bastard hadn't given me an A—"One C" which would be psych, and that was what I had anticipated—"And an F."

I felt my shoulders sag. I'd never received a grade that low in my entire life. I felt like such a shit. Eva was prattling on about what a waste all of this was, and why didn't I just quit now and maybe I could do the Cousin some good because he could use the money from the trust and so on. I was numb and mumbled goodbye and hung up. I leaned back against the paneled wall and stared at the thick nap of the hallway carpet.

Buchanan walked by just then and said something about making a run to Eastside Liquors. I reached into my pocket and fished out three bucks and told him I wanted a quart of vodka. I didn't specify brands, but I didn't have to. For that price I would get whatever was the cheapest, rot-gut brand on the shelf. I went back to my room and put on an album, "The Beatles—1965," and looked out the window at the grayness of the day. I didn't know what the fuck I was going to do. At least I was still enrolled for Winter Term and for the next semester.

Fortunately, there was a knock on the door, and I turned around and Cindy McCormick and Jillian Jones walked in.

Cindy and Jillian were each a year ahead of me—more than that, now, since my grades from the previous semester had been officially imposed upon me. I'd met Jillian my freshman year, but hadn't gotten to know her well until March. I'd met Cindy the previous semester. They both lived in Starr Hall, the only dorm on campus that housed upper-class women. That dorm had been built like only in 1970 and was an object of pride for the university. The building appeared annually in the live-action photos for the university Bulletin. That was ironic. Campus social life was so Greek that upper-class women who weren't in sororities were viewed by the hard-core Greeks as being rejects. And yet the living unit where the upper-class women lived appeared on the front cover of the university Bulletin for all the world—and incoming freshmen—to see. Of course, anyone who didn't live in one of the in houses was viewed by the hard-core Greeks as being a reject, too, but in their eyes at least we were nominally Greeks. We were bending our knees and paying homage to their gods. In our eyes they—the people in the in houses—were all still douche bags. Anyways, it wasn't the new buildings but the old, brick buildings, ivy clinging to their sides, that really gave the campus its charm. Starr and the Science Temple were simply ugly boxes by comparison.

Starr had been dropped onto an area of ground adjacent to the Dells. The Dells consisted of a main "valley"—not very large, perhaps two hundred yards long and a hundred yards wide, but a valley by the standards of flatland Indiana—into which fed two or three ravines. The area was covered with lush grass and trees. For some reason that natural beauty offended the officials of the university. Those officials were always trying to hack more of it away in favor of some shit like Starr. Starr was clear on the other side of campus from the frat, so it was a long walk.

When I'd first met Jillian, she had just started going out with a guy in the dorm. For some reason, she'd never dated much in high school, if at all. She was a tad bit big-boned, but not in a distracting way. Up close her face bore the slight scars of a teenage bout with acne, but you had to be really close to be able to tell that. She had long, medium-brown hair, and a funny way of laughing that could be either mirthful or malicious, depending on her intent. She was also brilliant. The previous semester she had hardly studied. She drank heavily, smoked pot constantly, and did a bunch of other drugs, notably the acid that had hit the campus like a tidal wave. Yet she still came out with a four-point. As in all A's. She was also a bit twisted.

She'd been a virgin when she'd arrived at DeForrest, she was fond of telling anyone who would listen. A guy in the dorm had been the first guy she'd had sex with, and she'd fallen in love. Unfortunately, he had not fallen in love with her and did not care to continue the relationship. Jillian had apparently been devastated. I don't know. That was a part of the story. She could be extremely mean at times, and the root of that was probably way back in her childhood, but her break-up with her first true "love" contributed to it. She'd kept to herself for a while after that but then, after the past summer, when she'd returned from spending three months at her parents,' she'd begun partying really heavily. She was a philosophy major, but for some reason Farina was her adviser. She had taken every course that he taught, and she was now working on some sort of project that required her to write a paper. She laughed about her "anthro" research. I thought it was another facet of her cynicism.

Starr was comprised of suites—four or five tiny bedrooms formed a perimeter around a living room that served as a common area. Jillian shared her suite with Cindy, and also Patricia and Ruth.

Cindy was Jillian's closest friend. She had long, dirty-blond hair that was usually dirty. She was loud, wore thick glasses, had complexion similar to Jillian's, and was fat. I never saw her wear anything but flannel shirts, fatigue pants, and Earth shoes. She could drink guys under the table. She had little concern for what others thought of her actions or conduct, and this honesty was her most appealing quality. She would sooner tell a rah-rah frat rat to fuck off as look at him. She was also a poly sci major.

The walk from Starr was such a long one, and the weather out bad enough, that it was surprising that they had walked over all that way without calling. I imagine if I hadn't been there for some reason, that they would have worked their way back to Starr, partying from frat to apartment to dorm.

"Got anything to drink?" Cindy asked.

"Got any pot?" Jillian asked almost at the same time.

I was jolted from my momentary depression over grades. I figured this was as good a way as any to get over the shock. I would deal with the reality in the morning. I explained about the liquor run, and Jillian said something about mixer and got up to go to the pop machine in the stairwell. I sat down next to the stereo and pulled out "Crosby, Stills and Nash"—their first album, on the cover of which they and two of their band members are sitting on a couch—an album I'd gotten for Xmas. In fact, it was still in the plastic that I peeled off. The texture of the cover was coarse. When I put the record on the turntable, there were no snaps or crackles or pops, as there would be in a few days.

Jillian returned with four or five Sprites, and I pulled out the handy dandy film cannister, the contents of which were dwindling.

Jillian sniffed the air and looked at the walls. "Just paint your room?"

"Yeah, this afternoon. Here," I said, and handed her the bowl.

"How creative. Flat white," she observed and took a hit.

"Well, it's just a start," I replied and poured our drinks into glasses.

Cindy said, "Did you hear the latest about Farina?"

"What," I asked, looking up and passing glasses to the two of them.

"There was some sort of secret faculty committee that reviewed the denial of his tenure."

"Farina doesn't even know who was on the committee," Jillian said.

"I gotta take a piss," Cindy said suddenly, and stood up.

I refilled the bowl and handed it to Jillian. I sipped my drink, and then flipped the album over. I looked at the album cover, then opened it, to the picture of Crosby, Stills and Nash standing somewhere in heavy coats, furs, and everything looking cold, and wondering what drugs they were on when the picture was taken.

Cindy came back and grabbed her drink. "Your fraternity brothers are weird," she said.

"Yeah," I agreed. I mean, so what? What she was saying was a given.

A few moments later, there was a knock at my door. Edwards and Buchanan were standing there, and they signaled me to come out into the hallway. I closed the door behind me, figuring that another battle in the Frat Civil War was being fought. They were looking at each other, then they looked at me. Buchanan tried to look past me, into the room. Edwards seemed a bit ticked off. "You gotta do something about your friends," he said.

Buchanan said, "The large one. What's her name?"

"Cindy."

"Yeah. Right. Her. She came into the bathroom a minute ago when I was taking a crap." His tone hinted that his statement was self-explanatory in setting forth the description of a "problem."

"Okay. She was in the bathroom."

"The women's bathroom is on the first floor."

"I know where it is. What—it bummed you out that she used the same restroom as you?"

They looked at me as though I were dense about this whole thing. "Yeah," Edwards said. "That's exactly the point. The women's restroom is on the first floor."

Indeed, there was a women's restroom on the first floor. Whereas the restrooms upstairs were rather utilitarian and functional—I guess that was a symbol of our maleness—the women's restroom was decorated in frills, etc. The cleaning of that room was assigned as housework each week, so it wasn't a mystery what it looked like behind the door. However, the women's restroom was a hell of a lot farther away from some rooms, like mine, than the communal restroom just down the hall.

"If you guys are so sensitive about it," I said, "I mean—they're just bathrooms. There's not much privacy as it is. Maybe we should have our own, private bathrooms in each room here."

Buchanan seemed offended. "But she walked past the stall I was in and asked how I was doing."

I said, "You could have closed the door to the stall." I shook my head and went back inside.

"What was that all about?" Cindy asked, nodding towards the door.

"A couple of the brothers were upset that you're using the bathroom up here."

"Fuck them. I'm not walking all the way downstairs when there's a fucking bathroom up here."

"It's not like you wouldn't expect them to get pissed off," Jillian said to Cindy. "In every frat that you've done that, the guys have gotten pissed off about it."

I shrugged and loaded another bowl. I didn't see the big deal, either. Fuck it. I sipped my drink and took a hit. Yeah, I realized, if it had been a woman other than Cindy— if it had been one of the girls that Buchanan dated, he would probably have been laughing about it. But because it was a woman who would never be the Homecoming Queen, he was pissed off.

Getting drunk on hard liquor is a lot different than getting loaded on beer or wine. Beer isn't nearly as concentrated, so, unless you're "shooting" beers, drinking the beer through a straw (and thus, somehow, magnifying its effects), or drinking on an empty stomach, your intoxication is gradual. Wine has a lot of sugars in it, and those sugars buffer the effects of the alcohol and help delay the feeling of intoxication. Of course, the sugars also ensure that, once that level of intoxication is reached, it is a plateau that is a longer buzz. But hard booze has the ability to really rocket a person into a drunken stupor. I was doing nicely in that regard with the vodka and Sprite at this point. Things became unhinged for me at some point in there. I remember that Sid, probably my best friend in the house, arrived back from break late in there somewhere, and he sat down with us for a while. And I remember "TV" Snyder wandering in. As the rays of the late afternoon winter sun slanted through the window, I vaguely remember talking Jillian and Cindy into buying more vodka when somebody announced that they were going on a liquor "run." I went downstairs to dinner and wolfed down some sort of food substance. And then it was evening, and we were listening to an album by Abbie Hoffman, entitled "Wake Up, America!" and we played rock and roll, and then these fuzzy red disks rolled across the windows of my consciousness, and I was lost.

Chapter 6 - The Week Should Be Shortened By A Day

I had always hated Sundays. They are flavored by the Christian bloodletting of communion and crucifixion. When I was a child, I was required to go to church every Sunday morning. Even later, when I had successfully skirted the requirement of church attendance, Sundays were not very much fun. The World was dead—few businesses were open, nearly everybody else was either sleeping in, hungover, or involved in some sort of worship service. Large meals at noon collapsed into afternoons of bad sugar buzzes or long naps on uncomfortable couches. Sundays in the frat were no different.

I woke up at about 6:30, a bit hungover, but not all that badly. Vodka, as I noted earlier, is a rather clean buzz. It is distilled and clear, as compared with whiskey, which sits around for years in rotting wood absorbing all the biological crud there; or as compared to tequila, the product of cacti, the decomposed components of which give the microbes material to shit and piss. Then we promptly drink that microbial sewage. On top of the fact that vodka is so clean, we had been mixing it with Sprite. That had pumped a lot of sugar into my bloodstream. I'd been taking multiple vitamins, too; not a lot—just the generic for One-a-Days. Well, this was before the concept of "generic." They were called "off-brand," or something similarly indicative of second-rate. But those second-rate vitamins were better than nothing at all. I looked around the room, and it wasn't too trashed. There were albums lying about, and some empty plastic cups.

I walked down the hallway to the can. Even though the bathrooms were communal, they were so much better than the Farm. My body rid itself of wastes. Then I went back to the room and started studying. I had promised myself I would be ahead of things second semester. The house was quiet, with everyone asleep. I needed the quiet. I was reading Thomas Hobbes for my philosophy class. The Leviathan was written in the 1600s, so the language was really archaic. Spellings back then weren't standardized. The same word could appear in a couple of different ways. The message was bleak, too. Hobbes was writing during a time in which the king was thought to be chosen by god. If one disagreed, the consequences were severe—imprisonment, torture and/or death. Out of all of this, Hobbes described the state of nature as being a war of all against all, and emphasized that humans were unique in that the weakest amongst us could kill the strongest. Really optimistic shit. I could envision the streets of London, rat-infested and the gutters filled with human waste; the stink of death everywhere, and people living to their early thirties at best. Who would want to live longer than that? I worked on Hobbes until about 9:00. By then my stomach was really growling, and the kitchen would be just opening for breakfast.

On Sundays we had a different breakfast cook than the one who came in during the week, but the concept was the same. We could go down to the kitchen and get whatever, individually and made-to-order. That sounds somewhat spoiled or pampered, but some of the houses on campus, especially the sororities, were worse. One sorority had a breakfast buffet for lunch, with frat boys as waiters wearing white serving jackets and gloves. I got a big plate of eggs and sausage and potatoes and toast, and a glass of orange juice to wash it all down. A couple of other guys were down there. Rudolf was giving Edwards flak about the bars the night before. That was another aspect of Sunday mornings—standing around in bathrobes or sweats, swapping stories of the night before. The guys who were old enough, or those who had fake IDs, or those just lucky and got in, would talk about the events at the bars the night before. Or if we had a party in the house, tales would be traded. Oftentimes, guys would kid somebody about getting laid, and the object of the joking would smile and deny that any such thing had happened—which was usually the truth, but everyone acted like something had.

I carried my plate and glass up to the Informal where several people were already sitting around, parts of the Sunday *Star* spread out on the huge table in front of the couches. I grabbed a section and went over the lastest news from the World as, on TV, the credits for the movie on "World War II Theatre" came on. Every week, we vegged out and stuffed ourselves, reading the paper, and watching Hollywood heroes blast each other for god and country. That week's movie was pretty good. I got sucked into it and three hours of my life passed by. *The Caine Mutiny* is really cool, with Humphrey Bogart as a crazy ship's captain, and Fred MacMurray as a bad guy. The ending is really great, with Jose Ferrer throwing a drink in MacMurray's face, and MacMurray agreeing that he—MacMurray—is a scumbag. Here in the fraternity, during the spring months, the TV would usually go to college basketball then, later, baseball or other movies. In the fall, or during the winter before the Super Bowl, the afternoon would be occupied with pro football. After a while, I ran upstairs to shower and dress. By the end of the movie, the Informal was full. People awaited the meal. Sunday dinner was a big thing. We marched in behind the housebitch and whomever she'd picked as her escort. Fortunately, I had always been successful in avoiding that particular chore.

Many years ago, some college bureaucrat somewhere discovered that a lot of money could be saved if college students were fed as much starch as possible. Consequently, instant mashed potatoes, in particular, occupy a dominant place in the menus of dorms and Greek "living units." That was an irony, in our situation, in as much as we wasted so much money in the frat on custom-made breakfasts. Hell, if we simply had eliminated the sausage and bacon from the breakfast menu, we would have saved a bundle. But that didn't occur to anyone as a means of saving money. We were sort of like the family in the Phyllis Diller series in the nineteen sixties, a series that lasted all of thirteen weeks. In it, she and her family were multimillionaires who woke up one morning broke, but who continued to live—at the graces of a bankruptcy trustee or some loophole in the law—in the mansion that had been their home. But they were eating, like, mac and cheese or something. They didn't understand that certain things had changed in their lifestyles. The show was a sit-com rip-off of Chekov's *The Cherry Orchard*, which I'd had to read freshman year. Anyways, we had roast beef on the table. Only one nice slice per person. Then tons of mashed potatoes and as many rolls as we could cram down our throats. The meal passed without event, the war of the fraternity in a lull for the moment.

There were other aspects to Sundays that were a bit different, one of which was why I did my best to stuff myself at noon. On Sunday evenings, no living unit served a meal. Whether that was meant as a measure to save money (on a campus where students drove Mercedes Benzes and Jensen Interceptors, etc.) or what, I don't know. But we were on our own for supper. If I stuffed myself enough at dinner, I could forestall the pangs of hunger until the next morning and, in the process, save money for more worthwhile pursuits—largely biochemical. Also, at that time in the State of Indiana there were no liquor sales. None. No carryout, no bars. No nice restaurants serving wine with dinner. No booze. Period. The 1800s bornagain ministers in their black clothing had obtained the blessing of the State Legislature to decree that alcohol was not to be sold on the day of their lord. That meant that certain people in the living units on campus were popular on Sundays—the people who had had the foresight to stock up on alcohol in anticipation of Sunday. By mid-afternoon they would be sought out and found. Some whine and wheedle and grovel in order to obtain a half-pint or a six-pack. On Saturday, I had blissfully disregarded the coming 24-hour period of prohibition, and so I spent Sunday afternoon ensconced before the TV watching college hoops. I.U. was on a real run that season, unbeaten to date. Kentucky appeared to be their closest competitors for the national championship. And I.U. had already dispatched Kentucky earlier in the season, in the game of their perennial rivalry.

Early evening arrived and, with it, "60 Minutes." This was back in the "old days" when Mike Wallace was old, but not ancient. It was such sport, to watch the reporters on that show skewer somebody. After "60 Minutes" came the weekly Bond movie.

I wasn't all that inspired to watch spies that night, so I wandered up to my room. I was just sitting down to put on an album when there was a knock at the door and Sid came in. I vaguely recalled shooting the shit with him the night before.

"Wanta get high?"

Ah yes—the eternal question. I said "sure," and Sid sat down on one of the throw pillows and pulled out the rolled-up baggie in his shirt pocket. While he loaded a bowl, we discussed our respective Christmas breaks. He was impressed with my country club escapade. I was growing fond of the story and of people's reaction to it..

Sid had turned me on to The Who the previous semester. Weird as it may seem, until that time I had never listened to their music. He was disappointed that I didn't have any of their albums. The question of his going back to his room and getting a Who album never arose. His stereo system was high-end, with albums that never made noise except for music. His uncle owned a stereo consulting company, and designed and installed stereo systems for rich hippies. His uncle had given Sid what the uncle looked upon as being castoffs—twin column Infinity speakers that stood four feet tall; a Marantz amp with a Sony pre-amp; a Thorens turntable with this weird arm by Ramco that slid across on a titanium bar; and a Tandberg twin cassette deck. My needle, with nothing else, would have butchered one of his albums. But I had CSN, so I put that on.

"I've been working on my room," he said, gesturing toward the room catty-corner from mine.

"Oh—yeah," I replied, realizing we were going to be neighbors for the semester. He had preferenced the room that had belonged to a guy, Clifton, who had transferred in to DeForrest the fall semester, then had promptly transferred back out. Clifton had been weird. He had long hair but didn't smoke pot, or even drink. As a junior, he had gotten a corner room as a single. "But at least you have that cool barn paneling," I said. DeForrest students were paneling their rooms with the weathered boards from the exteriors of barns. It looked pretty cool to do a room that way. I was a tad naive about it all, though. It wasn't until I saw the twentieth or thirtieth barn out in the country missing sections of siding that it hit me that the DeForrest students weren't just going out to farms where the owners were tearing down their barns. I mean, there weren't enough barns being torn down in the entire state to supply the needs of DeForrest students for this particular commodity.

"Not as much," Sid replied, with a note of irritation.

"What do you mean?"

"Jennings came in while we were at break and tore about a third of it off my wall. Clifton told him he could do it. Gave him that much paneling."

"Huh? This I gotta see."

So we finished smoking the bowl and walked across to Sid's room. Paneling ran around two of the three walls. The closet took up the fourth wall. What was left was several feet of exposed plaster with big white holes where the nails had been.

"What the fuck did Jennings do with it?"

Sid shrugged. "Got me. He's got a room in Second New—used it for the wall above the desks."

All the rooms in the new section of the house were identical. Each had two closets on one wall opposite a counter/desk that ran the length of the room, over which was a shelf. Above that was about four feet of drywall up to the ceiling. Yeah, it would have been about that much that Jennings needed.

I commiserated with Sid's woes, but then he suggested that, since we were in his room anyway, we might as well listen to his stereo. That suggestion made sense. He had a couple of easy chairs and a couch. The furniture had been in the fraternity, passed around person-to-person for years. He put on "A Nice Pair," by Pink Floyd, and pulled out the house bong after the music started up.

The house bong was ancient-looking, although it could have been no more than five or six years old. It was made of glazed pottery, and was a dirty brown color. It stood a little over a foot tall, and looked like the kind of thing paleolithic villagers would have used to smoke ceremonial ghanja around huge bonfires in the jungle night. The bowl was a single construction of wood, a cylinder about five or six inches long and an inch or so in diameter that fit like a plug at an angle into the base, which was flared out and formed a globe of sorts about eight or nine inches in diameter. The water inside the thing tasted as though it had never been changed.

We sat, smoking and listening to tunes, then Sid changed albums to The Who, "Live at Leeds." He said something about recording a new album later in the evening. Every Sunday at midnight, WNAP played an album in its entire length without interruption so people could record it. Sid said it was Dylan's new album.

That sounded weird. "Dylan? He hasn't put out a new album in years. I mean—Bob Dylan?"

"That's what they said on NAP, that they were going to play the new Dylan album."

I shook my head and did another bong. I walked back across the hallway. I was ready to just lie there for a while and meditate on things. But there was a knock at the door.

There was a giggle or two as the door opened, and Candace walked in with her friend Brenda. They belonged to the same sorority, just a half a block or so away. Candace and I were on the debate team, and were the de facto captains of it, really, but we were only now beginning to speak to one another again after having been partners at a tournament the previous January.

"We thought we'd come over and see if you had any pot," Candace said as Brenda closed the door.

I didn't want to seem as if I was not a gracious host. Besides, I'd had a crush on Brenda since freshman year. "Okay," I said. "Have a seat." With that I grabbed the film cannister and my pipe and loaded up.

Brenda was screwing around with my tuner. "Have you heard the new program on NAP?" she asked.

"You mean the Dylan album that they're playing tonight?" I thought that maybe she was using the wrong words to express what she meant. New album, new program— could be that she meant the same thing.

"Dylan has a new album?" Candace asked as I handed her the bowl.

"It's been hyped all day on NAP," Brenda said to Candace, by way of a mild admonition. "No, that's on at midnight. I meant Dr. Demento—have you heard it yet?"

I told her I had heard the ads for it but that I had not heard the show itself.

"It's coming on in a minute or so. Mind?"

"Not at all," I said as Candace coughed on the hit that she had taken and handed the bowl to Brenda.

It was a comedy-type show, featuring humorous songs and shticks from radio and live performances and studio recordings. The host had a high-pitched funny-sounding voice and intro'd each bit in a laughing/laughable way. The songs were a riot. "Friendly Neighborhood Narco Agent." "Junk Food Junkie." Two or three Tom Lehrer songs. Some stuff by Spike Jones. In between was the host's patter. By the end, I was surprised that an hour had passed so quickly. Dylan's album started to play. Dr. Demento became a fixture of my Sunday evenings.

Once Dylan was on, Candace started talking about the latest gossip from their sorority, all of which I sort of blew off. I was ready to crash. She and Brenda finally sensed that, and said good night. I closed the door after them and pulled off my clothes. I started to get a hard-on thinking about Brenda. As I fell asleep, pornographic reels played through my head, although I still was not sure of the specific mechanics of sexual intercourse.

Chapter 7 - The Windowpanes Were Clear To See Through

Life's epochal moments seemed to occur on a daily basis. Everything was Earth-shattering. One of those moments had been the year before when I'd tried acid for the first time. It was really a very mild form of purple microdot, but I saw things differently. By the previous fall, I was ready to try some more. I tried different forms of the stuff. Each time I had taken it, though varying in intensity, the acid had been pretty mellow. Part of what I wanted to do, though, was to push myself, and see things as weirdly as they could be seen. Stories from the campus underground were about things people had seen and done when tripping radically, including actually hallucinating. I was ready to explore my brain. The brain is the ultimate toy. I wanted to play with mine as much as I could. On the fringes out there lurked something else. It was strange, but I had to get near it.

Someone loaned me *The Electric Kool-Aid Acid Test*, by Tom Wolfe, about Ken Kesey and the Merry Pranksters. It was at the start of Winter Term. Some of us were getting loaded and telling drug stories, and after we had talked about acid for a while, the person handed me the book and told me that I'd like it. I had set it on my bookshelf and not yet picked it up.

There were three basic forms of acid. One type was blotter—small squares of paper onto each of which a drop of acid had been applied. There were different types of blotter, each distinguished by the cartoon character that was stamped on the paper. The most popular that year had been Mr. Natural, with R. Crumb's famous character walking across the paper with one hand in the air. The Mr. Natural had been pretty mellow, really. Blotter could vary in strength. I'd heard of a type called Berkeley White that had been around a couple of years before that was supposed to have been pretty heavy, leaving the psyches of several people in its wake, but blotter was usually pretty mellow. Another type of acid consisted of variations of compressed powder into which the acid had been absorbed. The powder was compressed into tiny pieces—microdot—or into larger cylinders–barrel. The powder differed in color, too, so that there was purple microdot, orange barrel, purple barrel, and so on. Most of this stuff was also pretty mellow.

Finally, there was windowpane. This consisted of tiny sheets of gelatin onto which the acid had attached itself. The sheets were then cut into smaller pieces. I had never done the stuff and never even seen it. I'd only heard about it. Acid is a pretty strong drug, and not much is necessary to get a person off. As I said before, the other forms of acid varied in intensity. I'd taken blotter that seemed as if it had been drained of its strength while being carried around in someone's wallet for a year—LSD breaks down when exposed to heat, light and air. One thing about windowpane that I'd heard was that it came in two intensities—strong and stronger.

I had gotten the rhythm down for doing acid. I would do it in the late afternoon of a day following which I had nothing to do. Coming down from acid was always interesting, but it was tough getting to sleep, and the hangover the next day was a hassle. Dealing with people had a twist to it. It was tough to focus on certain tasks, especially studying. I had tried getting high the day after one time the previous semester, and the pot had had no effect on me. But getting drunk had brought about the sought-for effects of ridding my system of the effects of the acid, so that was what I did anymore on the day after—got drunk.

Winter Term was Winter Term. I didn't have a whole shitload to do. One day I got another check from the bank for the next installment of textbooks that I wouldn't buy. The check—never for more than $25.00, the bookstore's limit—was for $23.48. I went to the bookstore, cashed it, bought a coke in the Hub, and walked back through the chill January air. When I got back I went to Criminal Phil's room, up in Third Old. Sid was up there, too, and we were just sitting around, trying to think of something to do, when there was a knock at the door.

I'd seen the guy at a party OIT the year before. He was called The Captain. He had blond hair that fell straight and well past his shoulders. A scruffy beard covered his face. He always wore a buckskin jacket like in an old cowboy movie, with fringe on the sleeves and going across the back. He even wore an earring—quite controversial in Indiana in those days. He could not have been more conspicuous in Glendale if he had walked around with a neon sign above him that said DRUG DEALER. He seemed to just pop up at places where drugs seemed to be in vogue—an apartment, a few rooms in the dorms, various people's rooms in half a dozen or so of the frats on campus—and then he would disappear. Only a few people seemed to have encountered him. Nobody really "knew" him. I knew he wasn't from our area. I doubted he was even from Bloomington and its huge population of hippies. He just didn't seem to fit in with the environs of Indiana. I figured he was probably from Chicago or Madison, Wisconsin.

He was polite in saying hello as I explained to Sid and Phil who he was. The Captain set a small tackle box down on the floor and opened it. We all peered into the thing. Each compartment, that would usually hold a fishing lure, contained, instead, various kinds of pills. The Captain explained rapidly, but clearly, what each was. Then he showed us a couple of bags of pot that he had in the large cargo area in the bottom where you usually store a couple of reels and some spools of fishing line. Finally, he held up the windowpane.

At that point, I still had pot, and I wasn't awash in money, so I passed on the bags. I bought a gram of hash, though, and then asked about the windowpane. I ended up buying one-and-a-half of what he called "four-ways" for eight bucks. Sid and Phil were low on money and so they split a four-way. The Captain thanked us, and he was on his way, disappearing into the cultural wilderness that is Indiana.

It was three in the afternoon. I didn't have any classes to worry about. I was way ahead on my studies for the semester yet to come. So I took the acid I had in my hand. I bit down on the gelatin pieces and caught that awful acid taste. I had always heard that in order to maximize the effects of acid, bite down on the hits. Sid and Phil took theirs. Then Sid asked me how many hits had I done. When I told him, his eyes grew wide.

"Do you realize how much of that shit you just did?"

I shrugged, but I got the idea that Sid was warning me. Then he laughed a bit, as if to blow it all off. It was then that I clicked over the total number of hits that I had done. I hadn't done just one-and-a-half hits. I had done one-and-a-half four-ways. That was the method of counting hits of windowpane, I realized. So I had done six hits of acid. That was quite a bit—and of a type of acid that, legend had it, was quite strong. I shrugged and smiled back at Sid. The look that I got back had some humor in it, but also trepidation. Like—okay, you've gone and done it now. A whole shitload of acid. Careful not to freak out.There wasn't much that I could do or say. The acid was already starting to dissolve in my stomach on its quick trip to my central nervous system. I could only kick back and enjoy the visuals.

That had been a major concern of mine when I had first tripped, freaking out. I had this vision of stepping out onto a window sill and doing a swan dive onto concrete from 12 stories up. Or screaming and withdrawing into a fetal position while somebody called the police, an ambulance, and Eva and Adolf, and I would be carted off to some mental ward. There was so much propaganda floating around out there. Shit had been drilled into us in various presentations starting in grade school and working all the way up through high school about the evils of drugs. And all of the TV shows had been programmed that way— Joe Friday and "Go Ask Alice," and a bunch of other media crap. On that fateful day my freshman year that I had somehow managed to acquire some of the dread LSD, I had read an article in Playboy about acid. Actually, it wasn't an article but a letter to the Playboy Adviser. Somebody was curious about tripping, and the answer was quite good. It said that before somebody chooses to trip, they should read as much as possible about tripping, and then make sure that wherever they were going to trip that the place be cool and without hassles. Also, that the people with whom one tripped be as cool as possible. I could dig all that. So I had gone to the library and dug up a couple of articles from the mid-1960s and read about tripping. I still viewed myself, on acid, as some sort of fragile mutant, but things would be cool as long as I didn't have to interact with a lot of assholes, or if I was around other people who were tripping.

I walked back to my room, and hassled with the door. I wanted to get the taste of the acid out of my mouth, so I grabbed a beer out of the 'fridge. As I did so, I saw the copy of The Electric Kool-Aid Acid Test sitting there beckoning me to pick it up. I shrugged and grabbed it. I stopped to take a piss then went back to Phil's room. He and Sid were sitting there, waiting for the effects of the acid to hit them, like passengers in an airport terminal waiting for the flight to take off. My basic metabolic rate has always been extremely fast, so I knew I would start getting off in about a half-hour. I felt those first rushes right on schedule.

The rushes were very physical, a ticklish sort of feeling that emanated from deep down inside me, working up through my collar bones and out. I chuckled. The Cosmic Laugh. I heard someone else chuckle and saw that Sid and Phil were also laughing. When our eyes met, all of us broke out laughing. I could feel the acid taste still in my mouth, so I drank another slug of beer. Phil put on one of the all-time great acid albums—Sergeant Pepper's. I smiled, and sank back into my seat. I looked at the armrest of the old, velour chair in which I was sitting. The thing seemed ancient, but it was extremely comfortable.

I picked up the book. The cover was a bright blue that suddenly seemed to glow. On the front was a brightly-colored drawing of a cube of sugar—of course! The infamous sugar cubes of the 1960s onto which had been applied the acid—with plain white wrapping paper coming off of it and, beneath that, psychedelic figures revealed as the heart of the sugar cube. I opened the book and immediately was sucked into it. The fucking book was all about acid and California in the 1960s. Ken Kesey. I'd heard of him. And I'd heard of the Merry Pranksters. As I read, I identified with so much in the book. Once in a while I would notice other sensations. I was sweating slightly. My skin seemed slightly moist, and the air that would occasionally move across it would feel cool and slightly wet with the sweat evaporating. The book was a couple of years old, and the pages were slightly rough with age. As I would turn the page, I would have to re-focus on the words. The letters themselves stood black against the off-white paper. Then I saw that the paper actually had a sort of pinkish and orange glow—very faint but still noticeable. I heard more chuckles and looked up. Sid and Phil were laughing about something else now, a joke I'd missed because I was reading. They both looked at me and Sid started to gesture to Phil, as if Sid was about to explain why they were laughing, but then they both started laughing again, and I nodded like yeah, I know, tripping. And I went back to the book.

The letters moved a little bit as I read. I was amazed that I could make sense of reading like this. I'd always had trouble reading when I was stoned on pot. I had assumed that the impediments to reading while tripping would be even more pronounced, but I was doing quite well. The only problem was that the letters were moving ever-so-slightly. My eyes would catch a phrase and nail it down physiologically, but then the letters would pull free and shunt slightly to the—right. My eyes would have to run back and catch them all over again. But that was a minor battle. And my eyes were doing okay. I was getting into the book. I read about the bus trip to the 1964 World's Fair, everybody doing acid. And the Merry Pranksters and the games they played. I'd felt like such an outsider at times here in the frat. And there one of the characters was, also feeling like an outsider. I could identify with that. But I really could identify with each of the characters at one point or another.

My eyes continued the battle, my brain happily accepting every bit of information. For example: each of us is never in the present moment; there is one thirtieth of a second between a sensation and our mind processing that information. Fuck an A! Then the Merry Pranksters partied with the Hell's Angels. And then Kesey did a bit with the American flag. Kesey said not to name things, because when you name something, you automatically know what it is not. And through it all was Dayglo paint. Everyplace. They painted their trees, their hands, their faces, the bus they had.

I heard chuckling again and looked up. Sid and Phil were sharing another cosmic exchange about something. I was being left out. Well—that was unavoidable. I was getting sucked into this book and reading it while they were getting into a trip together and sharing whatever thoughts that they had. I felt uncomfortable. I reached down and grabbed my beer. It felt a bit warmer to the touch, not as cold as it had been when I'd pulled it out of the 'fridge. I took a slug from it. The taste was weird, transformed by the acid into something else. The beer tasted as if the container, the bottle, was made of stone and I was drinking some elixir of ancient recipe. I drank again and felt the carbonation in my mouth. I put it down as Sid and Phil continued to laugh. I felt even more out of sorts. I looked at them as they shared whatever joke it was. I had been excluded. Well, what did they expect? I was reading. But I was still an outsider. I had moved into the frat earlier in the year from the dorms and I had missed out on my freshman year being in the house. Phil had been in the house only as long as I had been, but he was a freshman while I was a sophomore.

I needed to go back to my room. I stood, excused myself, then walked down the hallway. I passed the house president. What was cool was that normally I would have felt compelled to speak to him, even though I didn't like him. But I was tripping and so I was immune! Yes! He avoided me, as I walked past him! Marvelous!

I got to my door and turned the knob, and for once the fucking thing opened without a fight. I walked in and was enveloped by the silence. There was a slight hum, but that was about all. I looked at the white, plaster walls, ancient and with painted-over faults. But when I looked more closely, there were tiny patterns in there. I stepped closer to the wall and really looked. My eyes were a bit sore, but I could see patterns there, little paisley shapes. They weren't in my eyes—the paisley shapes were actually in the plaster. When I moved the center of my focus, the shapes stayed where they were. These were patterns that were within the plaster of my room. I'd always overlooked these patterns, but on the acid I could see.

The air felt cool now on my skin, but there was still a moist quality to the coolness, and I realized I was sweating slightly. I became aware of standing there in the silence of my room, still holding the book in one hand and the beer I'd been drinking for quite some time now—how long had it been? I didn't know. I looked down at the Ernest J. Borel watch I'd had since junior high. The watch face was curved as I looked at it, and the second hand moved along against the goldish cream color of the rest of the watch face. I tried to make sense of the time, but the effort was futile. What was time anyway? I chuckled to myself. I could make sense out of the words in the book, but I couldn't make any sense out of the simple position of clock hands on watch face. I usually tried to keep track of things when I was tripping, sort of life Dr. Jekyll watching the clock during his experiments with drugs. But that was a useless exercise at this point.

What if someone walked in? This would look weird, my just standing there. But so what? The silence became more pronounced, and I thought about putting on an album. I set the book down, then flopped on the floor in front of the stereo. I began flipping through the albums. One after another. Some of the music was definitely not for tripping. Some was just hard rock and roll, meant for listening to while high and/or drunk. My mind began to wander.

I looked up at the wall, and realized that it was bending. My vision took on the aspects of a fish-eye lens used for security on a door. The wall came out towards me and bent in the middle. As I moved the focus of my eyes this way and that, the bend in the wall moved with it. This was certainly a new way to operate my eyes.

Operate my eyes! What a gas! I started laughing, and then caught myself. What if someone heard me, just sitting in my room laughing maniacally? They would probably think I was crazy.

Suddenly, there was an announcement over the intercom that dinner was served. I looked at my watch and realized it was 5:30, but even having been informed by the announcement on the intercom what time it was, the information on the watch face meant nothing.

I shook my head and realized I had never put on an album. But at that point I surrendered. What was the point? The hassle of putting on an album was proving to be too much. So I leaned back on my mattress and felt something underneath me. Ah! The book. I had forgotten about it. I picked it up and it fell open to the page where I had left off reading. I thought this was some sort of omen, so I continued reading.

It felt as if I were a character in the book. I was one of the Merry Pranksters, tooling along in mid-1960s California, doing acid, being cool and accepted by Kesey and the others. Then I would read about the Sandy guy, how he sort of felt left out, and I would identify with that. The letters continued to move on me, their shifts becoming even more pronounced. Now when I looked up at the wall, the bend was even more pronounced, the tiny paisley shapes shifting even more, as were the letters on the pages. In a moment of insight, I realized that the shifts of the letters and the tiny figures resulted from my needing glasses. My vision was fucked. Goddamn! Major insight! Now I could actually feel the fatigue in my eyes. It was a physical sensation.

I lay there for a while, my eyes closed and resting. I was tingling—no, there was something more to it than tingling. I was zinging. No, zooming. No—more precise. I tried to find a word to describe how I felt. Then I realized that that was pointless. If I knew how I felt, why did I need to have a word or some words to describe that feeling? With my eyes closed, I could see patterns forming. Shapes appeared, geometric things, in vivid colors, spun and twisted and became replaced by others. The paisley thing was a constant. In the background. Always there. I opened my eyes and wondered how long I'd been sitting there, getting into the inner space. I raised my right arm in front of me, then turned it slightly so I could see my watch. Again, the positions of the hands meant absolutely nothing. I tried to concentrate, to make the watch make sense, but no use. I just chuckled.

Suddenly, I remembered a bit of folklore that had been passed around. It had to do with people who went off and tripped by themselves. There was a negative in there somewhere to it. I couldn't remember. Maybe if I looked at myself? Whoa, I thought, was that safe? I laughed at that question to myself. Another Cosmic Chuckle. Yeah, right. Was it "safe" to look into a mirror. Better be careful there, could be damaged by reflection of ego. And, after all, ego had fucked up a lot of things over the course of human history.

I had a mirror above and to the right of my makeshift desk. I stood up and moved toward it. I looked into the glass and saw myself looking back. I smiled. My image bowed into the mirror, just as the walls were doing. In psych the semester before, we'd read about physiology related to people's sensory systems, and how senses become distorted. The eyes, naturally enough, were part of that section of the course. I realized right then, standing before the mirror, that acid intensified colors. Like real, total enhancement. The eyes' receptors for color are the cones. The rods, the black-and-white receptors, provide night vision. The rods are at the edges of the eyes. The cones are located at the centers of the eyes, and that is why at night, in darkness, one's vision is better if one tries to focus on something on the periphery of vision. And now I realized that the cones were stimulated while I was tripping and that that was why everything seemed to bend outward, in the middle. It was the distortion effect of the stimulation of those receptor cells.

Wow! I leaned back from the mirror and looked at myself, exchanging with self a look of achievement and mutual conspiracy. A mystery solved! I was proud of my achievement, a melding of my higher education with daily experience. I wasn't just reading the things I was studying, but living them as well. I noticed that my skin had the same sort of colorful glow emanating from it as did everything. The skin on my face tingled. I saw beads of sweat—tiny, almost negligible—that had formed at my hairline. I was aware of them, their feeling of coolness. Coolness! I was cool! I chuckled at that. Then I began to wonder how long I had stared into the mirror like that. Was this a sign that I was crazy? I shrugged. I had no idea how long I'd been standing there like that. No use in looking at my watch, so I just chuckled again and sat down next to the stereo. So what if I was crazy? What did that mean? Besides, I was ready for music now.

I had read a book by Leary in which he set forth a list of his favorite tripping albums. "Their Satanic Majesties Request" by the Stones had been among his top three favorite. I pulled that out and put it on the turntable. I had always thought that the scratchiness of the needle on my albums would cause me, when I was tripping, to experience some sickening physical reaction, but it never did. In fact, that made the music that much more familiar to me. "Why do we sing this song together? Open our heads let the pictures come . . ."

I had given up on reading. I had gotten through two-thirds of the book. But now my eyes were tired—I was tired. Only not like regular fatigue. There was some sort of pressure that was pushing me down, my head down. Forcing me to close my eyes. I lay back on the mattress listening to the Stones. With my eyes shut I saw all sorts of images. As I watched these things spin and shoot past and transform into still other shapes and colors, I realized I had not yet peaked on the acid. I was still riding the stuff up. That scared me a bit, but I was without any ability to do anything about it. I was just an observer. Hey—that was a thought. Maybe if I just "observed" I'd be okay?

The weird instrumentation of the Stones album played through, and soon the album ended. I practically lunged at my album collection, and pulled out "Are You Experienced?", the first Jimi Hendrix album. That was something that surprised me, that Hendrix wasn't big in the frat. Anybody in the dorms who got high at all dug Hendrix. So what? I just kicked back and stared into space now.

The instruments in the song separated from the vocals, then from each other. The sound of the lead guitar emanated from a point in space, and not from either of the speakers. The sound was located about three feet in front of me and slightly above, right—there. The background noise separated from everything else and lay aside. When "I Don't Live Today" started, the chords of the lead guitar sounded weird, as though they were being played on a toy guitar of some sort.   I was riding the peak of the acid through my own personal space. Yeah, I was moving right along, and I had achieved something I had always wanted to do. I was now hallucinating. I was out of control of my perceptions. Too far out. I knew that I was okay and that the descent was about to begin. I had survived.

There was a knock at the door, and I said to come in. Jennings walked in, a look of uncertainty on his face. He said hi and sat down across from me. The stereo must not have been too loud. I had no gauge of anything at that point, but especially the proper volume for a stereo. But Jennings didn't have to yell to be heard. In fact, his voice was conversational.

"Heard you did acid," he said. I nodded. "Heard you did a lot." I nodded again, then looked back into space. "Getting any visuals?" he asked. I nodded yet again. "Like what?"

I pointed out into the air in front of me. "Right now I see a Mobius strip in various electric colors wrapping itself around a spheroid with angular edges, all of it about four feet tall and rotating in space right there."

Jennings turned away from me to where I had pointed. Then he looked back at me, said "okay," got up and walked out.

I sat there for a good long while, enjoying the ride. The album ended, and I sat there, wondering what I should do. Put on another album? Walk around the house?

I leaned over next to the albums to see what was there, what seemed like it would be good. I pulled out the Moody Blues. "Every Good Boy Deserves Favour." I replaced albums, carefully taking the Hendrix and placing it in its album cover. My hand trembled a bit as I did so. I stopped to look at my hand. It had a vibrance to it, a current running underneath the skin. The skin itself felt slightly moist and cooling. I willed my fingers to move—to clench, then unclench. I chuckled at the movements. I became aware of the fact that I had been staring at my hand for a good long while. I chuckled again, and then put the album on. I placed the stylus onto the surface of the album, then cranked the volume. A male chorus yelled "Desolation! . . . Creation!" Definitely a weird album. Quick transitions, through flute to a caravan sound, then organ, and finally tight guitar starting on "The Story in Your Eyes."

I understood something then. When I was a lot younger, the uninitiated described head-banger music—Black Sabbath, Alice Cooper, Uriah Heep—as being "acid rock." I understood now that there definitely was such a genre, but the music itself was much more subtle. True acid rock was music that had hard edges to it, but fed the experience of tripping. I smiled to myself—Ah! Realization! Learning!

But where did Self fit in to all of this. What was that thought? It sort of popped out of nowhere. I leaned back a little bit. What had I been doing in here? Again, I remembered something that was sort of taboo about tripping by oneself. Why that was, I didn't know. Could it be that people who did that were sort of warped? Or did the acid, when they were not in the company of other people, in turn warp them? Hmm. Was I subservient to the acid? I chuckled at that. That was absurd. Then I realized that there were points at which I did not have control over myself when I was tripping. I got up then and walked over to the mirror and looked at myself again. The person there, the face, was somehow—absurd. How could this all be taken so seriously? I chuckled at that, too, then thought better of standing in front of the mirror and moved back to the bed. What was I anyway? And why was I here? Why were any of us here?

I sat there getting into all of this, and listened to the entire side of the album. The visuals were far less intense. I still saw the subtle geometric shapes and patterns, a few paisley things here and there. Sound was still distorted, but not nearly so much as it had been. I was beginning to come down. When the album ended, I decided it would be a good idea to go upstairs to Criminal Phil's room and visit my fellow journeyers.

I stopped before going out the door, realizing I needed a prop. Some of the people in the house were not too cool right now about drugs. Not because they hadn't necessarily done them—but because by opposing certain things they could obtain a "bargaining chip" in the ongoing civil war. If I was walking around fucked up as I was right now, and they found out that I was doing acid, that could be marked down in a book somewhere and the information fed into—where? I didn't know, but I figured I would do something to camouflage my intoxication. I checked the half-full—I was still an optimist—can of beer that had been sitting next to me for a long time. The can was long-since warm. I walked over to my little refrigerator and pulled out another beer and popped the top. There. While some people might have found my tripping on acid to be objectionable, nobody could fault a frat boy for walking around with a beer in his hand. After all, that was what frat life was all about. I took a big breath, opened my door, ventured into the hallway and closed the door behind me.

I only had to walk 30 feet or so to the bottom of the stairway, then up the stairs, and around, then down a short hallway and I'd be at Criminal Phil's room.

While in my room I had felt that I was coming down and the sensations from the acid seemed to be far less pronounced. Now, out in the hallway, I wasn't so sure. The carpet was thick and soft as my legs and feet carried me along. I saw Rudolf—who was definitely not cool about drugs—coming down the hallway. He was carrying a beer, too, so I tried to emulate a drunken person and said something to the effect of "catch a buzz." I thought, "Fuck! I'm had!" I quickly reflected on my efforts at appearing drunk and thought I was far too brittle in the way I talked. I didn't have the sloppy, slurriness of speech and character necessary to carry it off. He would surely see through my act. But he was drunk, so any subtlies were lost on him and he said something back in like kind. Hey—I might get away with this, I thought.

I realized then that I hadn't taken a drink in a hell of a long time. As I walked up the stairs, I drank from the beer, spilling a bit as I tried to drink and walk and trip all at the same time. The beer had lost some of its stony flavor, but it went down really nice. I took another drink as I topped the stairs and went down the short hallway.

I could hear the muffled sounds of music coming from behind Criminal Phil's door. The Allman Brothers "Brothers and Sisters." Not real acid music, I thought. More like music for coming down from a trip. I knocked, and there was a hesitant, "Come on in." I opened the door and Criminal Phil and Sid were both looking at me, then they realized who I was and they both started laughing. I sort of shuffled in with what I thought internally to be a sort of self-mocking Cosmic type of laugh. Ego was anathema to me.

"Having fun?" I asked. For some reason this seemed funnier, still, and we all laughed again. I sat down on the edge of the bed and exhaled. The exhalation brought laughter, too.

"How was it?" Criminal Phil asked.

I shrugged. I'd shrugged a lot so far tonight. The shrug was turning into an important form of expression for me. "Saw a lot," I began. I started to say something about staring into the mirror at my face, and the problems that we all have contemplating ego, but I decided not to say anything at all. If I did say something, they might think that I was crazy. I sensed they were watching me and waiting for me to continue.

"You saw a lot—you mean visuals or what?" Criminal Phil asked.

I explained the things in the plaster and they both nodded. "We saw those, too," Sid said. "The wall sort of bulged out."

I told them why that happened, and that was a new thing for them to ponder. The mystery of the bending of light was explained through physiology. Then I added the part about the psychedelic Moebeus strip turning in space, and they both looked at me with eyes wide.

"Man, you were fucking hallucinating!" Sid exclaimed. I smiled. "Are you still that fucked up?"

"No, I'm still off some, but I started coming down a while ago."

The album came to an end at that point, and Criminal Phil took the Allman Brothers off and pulled out another album. I couldn't see what it was.

"Yeah," Sid explained. "We started coming down a while ago, too."

"Have you guys left the room?" I asked.

Sid and Criminal Phil exchanged glances, and Sid answered, "No. Maybe we ought to go down to my room and listen to my stereo for a while."

Criminal Phil nodded, pondering that suggestion. The expression on his face was one of deep thought—he was rubbing his chin and contemplating the situation very deeply, or so it seemed, and that sent us off into another spasm of laughter. That moving to another room involved such deep thought.

So we left. We passed a couple of people, and we probably looked a bit weird, walking along with these intense looks on our faces. I just wanted to get the fuck out of the hallway, so I held my beer tightly, proof of my "drunkenness." When we got into Sid's room and he closed the door behind us, we all let out heavy sighs of relief, then started laughing again as we realized what we'd just done.

"I don't think I can handle a trip like that again," I said, meaning the walk up and back to Third Old. But Sid and Criminal Ray looked at me sort of funny, as though I'd meant the trip on the acid. "I mean . . ." I started to say, but Sid quickly said, "I think that we need some music."

He flipped through albums and came up with "American Beauty," by the Grateful Dead. Awesome album, maybe their best. What was cool was that I'd just been reading about them a while before, about their early days as the Warlocks, and when they were playing at the acid tests with Kesey and the Merry Pranksters. I explained this to Sid and Criminal Ray. As always, any recitation of facts from counterculture's history was gratefully received. Then Sid reached back next to his stereo and pulled out a large envelope.

"I got this from a Deadhead fan club, or something," this last was added because in our state the concept of a fan club sounded rather silly. "They have a statement in here from the Dead, about what they're working on now. They're trying to develop home hologram machines. The machines will be the size of cigarette packs and will attach to your stereo." He leafed through some of the paperwork. "'Albums themselves will consist only of small pyramid shapes approximately one inch in height and will fit into the player. The images evoked by the songs being played will then be projected as three-dimensional forms in space.'"

66

"Sounds like they're on acid to me," Criminal Phil observed.

I sat back and thought about that, as Criminal Phil leafed through some of the paperwork Sid had handed to him. The three-dimensional forms being projected into space— I could understand that concept. I'd just done the same thing. That sounded kind of hip.

The music was pretty cool. The Dead had a way of continuing notes beyond the measure that was playing, carrying the song on further than it should have gone. They were supposed to be a heavily acid-influenced band, but the music we were listening to now didn't have the acid "sound" to it. Maybe their really early stuff had, but what we were hearing didn't have the sounds coming from different places like Hendrix.

I looked at my watch and realized it was finally making sense. I could understand the fact that it was now well past midnight—nearly one o'clock in the morning. The volume on the stereo wasn't all that radical, so we were cool as far as any noise was concerned. My eye sockets felt as if someone had lined them with sand. They hurt. I was sure that all that reading hadn't helped, in terms of fatigue. I looked over at Sid and Criminal Ray, and they were doing the same thing I was, just sitting and thinking. The chords of the music seemed cool and soothing. Maybe the Dead had written this music for people coming down off of acid. I mean—why not? Write different songs for different aspects of the LSD state.

The album ended, and as Sid took it off of the turntable, he told me to "do the honors" of picking out the next album. He had about 300 albums, some from Roach having left a few dozen when he'd moved out at the end of finals the previous semester. There were some really good choices, then there were albums that didn't seem to fit the mood right then. I found one I didn't recognize and pulled it out. The cover looked as if it had been bought the day before—very little wear.

"Who's Syd Barrett?" I asked Sid.

He looked up at me, then looked at the album. It took a few seconds for the question to register. "Oh—that's one of Roach's albums. Syd Barrett—he was one of the founders of Pink Floyd."

"You're kidding," I said and flipped the album over. It was a double album and involved Barrett's band—the Madcap Laughs. The album cover was weird. It depicted a long-haired white male looking very twisted and crouching on a hardwood floor, with a naked woman sort of draped across behind him.

Sid took the album from me and, as he screwed around with the turntable, handed the cover back and continued to talk.

"Roach never played this," Sid explained, then looked up at the two of us and chuckled. "He bought it because this was sort of a hip album to have—I mean, Barrett supposedly started Pink Floyd in an insane asylum."

I could see Roach buying an album to say that it was in his collection. I could also picture a rock-n-roll band getting together in an insane asylum. At least this night I could identify with it.

The music was the most fucking weird shit I'd ever heard. The guitar chords were bare, and the voice was strained and hoarse. Behind some of the songs was a weird sort of organ sound. The lyrics were, at the very least, bizarre. One song was "Effervescent Elephant"—definitely some acid influences there. Another song was just as bizarre, talking in garbled phrases, about the other person being "different from me," and the rocking backward and forward like the "red and yellow mane of a stallion horse."

The three of us were now laughing. We'd hear a new burst of chords/weird lyrics, and launch on a new set of laughs. There was mention of "poppy birds way" and a woman brandishing "her wand with a feathery tongue."

I picked up the album cover again and looked at the guy. Definitely wrapped a tad bit too tight, this Syd Barrett guy was. But some of the lyrics were really very good, and some made a weird sort of sense. And here he was, the founder of a rock-n-roll band that was pretty famous, at least for one album, and had a sort of cult following for their albums previous to that. And who was I?

As another song played, Sid said, "Wait a second—I know this poem."

As Sid went to his bookshelf and pulled out a couple of volumes, I followed the titles of the songs with my finger to try and figure out where the album was. The name of the song was "Golden Hair."

Sid slapped the book in his hand, having found the thing he'd been looking for. "This is a poem by James Joyce!"

"What?" I asked, and he handed me the book.

It was an anthology from one of his English courses. The book was opened to a poem titled "Chamber Music" by James Joyce. It was the song's lyrics.

Suddenly, this Syd guy was making a lot of sense out of things. He was transforming great writers' poems to quasi-rock-n-roll works. Neither Sid nor I chuckled nearly as much now as the songs came out. He flipped the album when it reached the end. Criminal Phil was still chuckling, and he'd look up to us for encouragement, but when he saw we were beginning to listen to the songs in earnest, he became a bit paranoid, as though he were being excluded from the "in" thing about the album.

I'd wondered about my sanity at one point during my trip. Now I was wondering about sanity in general. What was sanity? What was sane? Listening to Syd Barrett I felt a sort of kinship with him—a kinship with the insane. The album was part of a conspiracy that linked us. The words came out and entwined me into this conspiracy. And what about what I'd read earlier in the evening? All that stuff about the Merry Pranksters and the one guy—Sandy?—who was paranoid and who'd had to be hospitalized. What about him? I'd felt a sort of kinship there, too. Suddenly, I wanted to go back to my room. I wanted to be alone. I wanted to sleep. I told Sid and Criminal Phil I was done, that I was going to crash out. I walked back across the hall, not really caring if, in those few feet, I ran into anybody. I didn't really give a rat's ass. But nobody was up except for the pre-meds in the house, the people who were nocturnal. And none of them walked by at that point.

I got into my room and stripped and crawled into bed. The fabric of my jeans also bore the small whorls and paisleys of the acid, fading now and nearly done for the evening, but still there. The sheets felt weird against my skin. As usual on acid, I had a really rough time getting to sleep. The hisses of the evening seemed to be voices that said things that weren't distinct. Finally I forced myself to relax, and then I fell into a deep sleep and wondered if I would make an album one day, start a rock-n-roll band. Or if I would go insane.

Chapter 8 - More Winter Term Fun And Games

On Monday, everything started all over again.

I was studying in the mornings, then the rest of the day I'd read whatever I damn well pleased. I'd finished the Castaneda book. I picked up *The Autobiography of Malcolm X* one afternoon. I could barely put it down. It was a book that was popular among the hip professors on campus, one that a sociology or philosophy or political science or English prof could assign. So a lot of them did just that, to try and introduce their upper-middle-class, white students to concepts of recognizing the racial polarity in our culture on a basis other than that of ordering around servants. Prior to reading that book my understanding of Malcolm X was culled from the racist statements of Eva and Adolf, and various teachers I had in grade school and high school. Even the sound of the guy's name—Malcolm X—sounded threatening to them. Stir that into the talk of "Mao Maos" butchering poor, defenseless white people in Africa, and the riots that hit this country in the 1960s, and it all became a huge threat to them. I got into the descriptions of Malcolm Little's changes, transformations, and how he really bridged gaps, especially toward the end of his life.

Doc had me come to his debate class one morning to lecture. The class was made up of people who had never debated before but wanted the experience. I gave about a half-hour talk on organization in argument. Weird, coming from a person inclined, at the time, to nihilism. I'd acquired nihilistic tendencies over the last couple of years, but especially during the second semester of freshman year. I'd gained confidence in myself and my existence in college. One night, one of the guys in the dorm did Tarot card readings for anyone who was interested. He made a big deal out of it, but several of us thought the whole thing was pretty funny.

According to his cards, one guy was supposed to be an insurance executive and have three kids. Another guy would be an attorney. Shit like that. When he did mine, he sort of blanched. I asked him what was wrong. He told me he had never had a reading that was that bad. I asked him how it was bad. He told me I would die before I reached the age of 22. I thanked him for the reading. He told me he'd be glad to do another reading for me before I left school. I guess that was so I could get a more precise idea of how much time I had left on the planet. That sort of shit just made me not care a whole lot about the world. We all die some day. Anyways, the half-hour lecture I delivered was good. Doc thanked me, and I went on my way, my Winter Term obligations now complete.

I went over to Indy a couple of times with people. Once, Clancey and I went to the Lafayette Square Mall. He had to rent a tux for a wedding or buy a present for a wedding, or something. Whatever the reason, it was an opportunity to get out of Glendale for a while and see the flat, snow-laden countryside whiz by. Another time, Austin and I were really wasted and got into an argument over who was better at air hockey. There was no air hockey table on campus or in the town, so the next day we went over to an arcade on the west side of Indianapolis, near the Indianapolis Motor Speedway, and played a pretty ferocious best-of-seven series of air hockey.

Another day I accompanied Clancey to the A & P. He always kept a couple of cases of RC Cola in 16-ounce bottles in his room. For some weird reason, he also bought tins of kippers. While he was in the A & P, I ran into the Hook's Drugstore just next door to grab a couple of packs of cigarettes. The A & P was out of Vantage Menthol, my brand. I had cut down on my smoking, but I still had the Jones, the little nicotine monkey on my back. I went into the grocery and found Clancey walking down the aisle pushing a cart, headed for the check-out. He was going by a section that had albums. Like—I had never seen a grocery store selling albums before. But hey—I figured I'd flip through them. I found an album with a red fist on the front of it. It was about the strike at Harvard, and I grabbed that fucker and took it to the checkout. After we checked out, Clancey and I walked to his car, him wheeling the cases of RC in a cart.

"Hey look," he said, and pointed into the distance. A couple of miles away I could see a helicopter moving across the sky. The sound of the engine was barely discernible. "They're coming to get you," he said, laughing.

As he loaded the cases into his car, I watched the chopper. It sort of moved funny, then began to grow larger.

"I think you were right," I said with a grin. Then my grin wasn't so whimsical. The fucking thing was headed straight toward us. Clancey got everything into the trunk of his car and took the cart back to the area next to the entrance to the grocery. The chopper was now less than a mile away, dropping in altitude and still on a bee-line for us. We both just stood there staring as the thing flared over us and landed in the parking lot. It turned out to be a Hook's Drugs corporate helicopter taking their board chairman on a tour of outlying stores. The corporate logo was on the side of the aircraft. I was just glad I hadn't been tripping.

In the evenings I partied. Winter Term was, after all, still Winter Term. Beer and other concoctions of alcohol were plentiful. Then the pot started drying up. I ran out first. So did Sid. Then we started roaming the hallways, searching for people who might have a joint. That was about the time Paul Merriman came through.

Merriman was an alum. He had graduated before I had entered DeForrest. We had been introduced the previous spring, right after finals and shortly before I'd left for the summer. I'd spent those last couple of days on campus at the frat. I'd dragged my possessions over from the dorm and into a vacant room in Second Old. I had slept in a ratty sleeping bag I had had since my Cub Scout days and partied, savoring every moment before I would have to return to Kilkerry. Merriman was a raconteur of stories from the "old days" on campus.

He showed up one afternoon in his Porsche. That car was rather impressive, unless you knew very much about Porsches, which I didn't. The model he had was basically a VW with a light chassis on top that bore the word "Porsche." I had walked back from campus in mid-afternoon, and there the car was. I didn't know whose it was at that point. I only knew we had a Porsche with Kansas plates in the house parking lot.

Alums like Merriman—and older students, for that matter—provided a really important link for us. There was an oral history that was handed down. Well—there's that aspect to any culture. I thrived on that. It was very important to me. I first had been drawn into it at the start of my freshman year, listening to the stories of the sophomores and others. Then the stories that they knew from personal experience became blended with stories they had heard from others of the times before them—the burning down of the ROTC building in 1968 or 1969, for example, where the vice-president of the student body had torched himself by mistake, or the guy in the dorm who had chased out the campus cops with a samurai sword (and was expelled for a semester).

I had been perusing the albums that I had grabbed from the Cousin's forgotten collection in the Japanese House, along with some pamphlets and things. Among the pamphlets were paperback catalogues for poster stores and head shops in the Haight-Ashbury district of San Francisco. Mecca to me. The pages were in black and white but I could still see pretty hip and weird patterns to the pictures of Hendrix, Bob Dylan, or just weird designs that appeared to be pretty cool and acid-oriented. Each one of these artifacts— the albums, the catalogues—were little bits of treasure for me, things to which I could cling. Where the Cousin came up with them I never knew. I was certain that he never bought any of the items advertised. I mean, nothing like that ever popped up at the Japanese House or at the apartment he kept in the basement of the house next to the Shop that the Uncle had had divided into three apartments. Two upstairs and one down. Not a very nice place, but one to which the Cousin hoped he could lure dates. I mean, he wasn't like most other people in their late twenties. He was still living at home.

When I came up the stairs on the way to my room, Sid's door was open, and I could see him standing and talking to someone. As I rounded the corner, I recognized Merriman. I stuck my head in and said hi. He looked at me in this weird way he always had, with a sort of smirk on his face, chuckling at the World. I'd heard that he'd been a casualty of acid, taking too much one semester and having to quit school, then coming back and finishing his degree in five years, instead of four. Sid asked me if I wanted to join them, and I said sure

"Merriman pot" was legendary. I'd never had any before, but Sid and Roach had told me about it. If they thought it was awesome, then it had to be.

I sat down while Sid put on "Their Satanic Majesties Request," by the Rolling Stones. That album was sort of the Stones's answer to "Sergeant. Pepper's" and "Magical Mystery Tour." The front of the cover featured a picture of the Stones, with Brian Jones still alive. They were sitting, cross-legged, in front of a bunch of dolls and cushions and stuff. But the cover had a layer of plastic over it, and when you moved the cover back-and-forth, the picture changed slightly, so the Stones' arms moved. Pretty weird. Pretty acidic.

Merriman had a way of talking that seemed very patrician, very "old world." I mean, his accent was definitely not midwestern, most assuredly not southern, didn't betray his roots in South Dakota, but didn't really have the sharp edges of a New York accent. He drew out words as he pronounced them. The total effect was one of condescension. But he would throw in chuckles and little jokes so you didn't feel insulted.

"I remember my third Winter Term," he said as he rolled the joint. The pot was weird-looking—dark color, but I could see little streaks of bright green in it, and I could even smell it from a few feet away. "I was taking a course that was really a comparative religions sort of thing." He went on to describe the course by way of telling his story, the point of which was that everyone in the class was a moron, except for Merriman, and he partied that Winter Term more heavily than he had any other.

When he had finished rolling the doobage, it was a real pin joint. It was the usual length, but only the width of maybe two toothpicks put together. He said something about being careful of the pot, as if I didn't already know. He handed it to me and I fired it up.

Regular pot of the time, what we called "Mexican," had a nice flavor to it. In a bong it would expand a bit, and you would have to cough some, but not a lot. Really good pot would expand without having been condensed through the water of a bong, and you'd cough pretty hard for a minute or so. I took less than a normal-sized hit off of the joint. It started expanding immediately. This shit was nuclear. It pushed my lungs to the limits, and I started gasping for air between coughs. Something like 99 percent of the intoxicants in marijuana are absorbed by the lungs on contact. That's what I'd read somewhere. Well, it sounded good to me. That way I wasn't guilty about coughing. Sid was having a similar reaction as he passed the joint on to Merriman, who sort of chuckled as he took a hit. He did not cough. Altogether, Sid and I had three hits each off of the joint. A couple of minutes later, I was floating. The shit was really good. Really good.

That's when I realized Merriman was talking about his income and his job and art. I couldn't make sense of it at first, but then I realized he sold art. He mentioned a guy by the name of Brancussi, and prints that were down in the car.

"Can we see them?" Sid asked.

Merriman chuckled and said "sure," as though he had meant to do that all along. He asked us to help him bring the stuff up, so we trooped downstairs. I didn't bother putting on a coat, even though it was hellaciously cold outside. His car was only a few feet from the back door. The car's engine was in the rear, and the trunk was in front, so he popped the lid. As he did so, I stared around me, at the trees covered with light snow and ice, the snow on the ground, and the light bouncing off of everything in early evening. It all had a crystalline effect. Merriman handed Sid a big, black carrying case, about four feet by three feet, then startled me as he handed one to me also. Merriman himself brought two more out and we went back into the "physical plant."

Up in the room, Merriman set the cases against one wall and opened up the one I had carried. Inside were about 15 or 20 prints of various dimensions. Some were less than a foot square. Others reached nearly the edges of the case. And they were all of different styles and periods. As we made our way through the works in the cases, he showed us pen-and-ink drawings of cathedrals, with details so minute I needed a magnifying glass, and he carried one in a pocket of one case, in order to see the little stones that were drawn in under the windows. There were serigrams of large blocks of color and some portraits. I had never seen such high-quality work. Not "live." I'd never been to an art museum. Eva and Adolf viewed art, unless done by Norman Rockwell, as faggoty, silly crap, especially work like Picasso or Van Gogh, the style that wasn't simply a painting as replacement of a camera. Every semester someone came onto campus and sold prints—two bucks each, and a lot of neat stuff, abstracts, Picasso, Salvador Dali, M.C. Escher—in the Union Building. But those were just cheap prints. This was different. Everything was signed and numbered. It was really amazing. The prices were just as amazing. When Merriman showed us one nice print, he quoted a price of Thirty-Five Hundred bucks! That about blew me away. Then I became really paranoid. What if I knocked something over and spilled shit on that print? Then I began to wonder about it. Why would anyone want to pay that much for a print? Why not get a nice reproduction, frame it and hang it?

Merriman was rattling on about the value of the art. I was a bit confused, I guess, because I thought he was talking about the esthetic value of the art. But after a couple of minutes, I realized that he was talking about the economic value of the art. The phrasing was so familiar to Merriman, and certain hooks that he had in his shpiel were so trite, that I figured this must be the sales pitch he gave to people who were thinking about buying some of the stuff. He was talking about appreciation, not in the sense of enjoying the paintings, but in the sense of their increase in value, tripling and quadrupling over time.

"Art will never lose its value," he said. "Inflation might hit other investments and make them less than advantageous for the investor. But once these works have attained a specific dollar value, they can only go up."

"But they can't produce food," I said. "They can't be eaten."

He looked at me whimsically, as though I'd said something absurd. "I don't suppose they could. But the money you'd get for selling one would buy quite a few groceries. Or," and he said this with a wink to Sid, "a very fine dinner at a four-star restaurant."

"That's not what I mean," I said. "You were saying that these pieces would always be worth something and never lose their value."

"That's right." His manner was really condescending now.

"And that's for all of time—a hundred, two hundred years into the future?"

"Yes," he said, now seeming bored.

"But only if there's an economic system in place that would give these pieces value. I mean, if there's a nuclear war—and that's a very real possibility—then currency, art, stocks, bonds, gold—anything that isn't food or some other essential commodity for our existence—loses its value. You cannot eat a drawing."

"Your point?"

"That your general, conclusive statement, that art will never lose its value, is not true."

He shook his head as though pained with having to deal with me. I waited, expecting him to address my argument. Instead, he launched into a narrative about some obscure Belgian artist who specialized in lithographs during the 1920s.

I sat there for a while, then lost interest. I said good night, and walked back across the hall to my room. I fell onto the mattress and lay there staring at the ceiling.

Good pot can really knock a person out. But really, really good pot causes one to stay awake for a while, the mental wheels and gears turning. I lay there, pondering Society, wondering what it would be like if there were a nuke war in the morning. Could I survive in a state of chaos following the bombs? Could I provide my own means of making food? Did I have any skills in that regard? Fuck—did I even have the skills necessary to survive in this society? Did I have the skills to survive in a society as soft and kind to upper-middle-class white males as ours? I fell asleep confused, listening to the echoing sounds of three or four stereos playing different music throughout the house.

Chapter 9 - Getting Into The Rhythm And Feeling Good About Myself

There was one activity I was involved in that had the formal support of the university—debate. No matter how fucked up the rest of my life might be at any given time, I could always count on debate. I was damned good. I also enjoyed debate. I'd been debating since I was in high school. My freshman year, I'd originally signed up to be on the speech team. Our high school didn't really have a debate team. The speech "coach" was a woman who was near retirement age and into theatre, and wasn't on the same wave-length as me. I did well in extemporaneous speaking. Each competitor drew a topic based upon a recent article in *Newsweek, Time or U.S. News & World Report*, and then gave a four-to-six minute speech on that topic. One weekend, the coach had told us she needed people to go to a debate tournament. Schools that sponsored debate tournaments were always short of teams. They needed a lot of teams to provide competition. The coach of that tournament was a friend of hers, so as a favor each year she fielded a debate team for just that tournament. I "volunteered" and dragged a friend of mine into it. In the first round a team from a big high school in Indianapolis pummeled us, and I smelled my own blood flowing onto the floor. In the next round, we debated a team from Columbus, Indiana, and turned the tables. I got to smell their blood. I became committed to debate and pretty much bagged being on the speech team, although I made state finals in both speech and debate. Unfortunately, I lost a friend in my debate partner. We came to hate each other's guts, although we debated as partners for all of high school.

In three semesters of college, I'd gone through eight different partners at sixteen different tournaments. For the most part, after the first or second round of a tournament, whatever partner I had and I ceased speaking to one another, or if we did speak to one another, we did not speak to one another in civil tones. Debate was a vicious activity, and I regressed in the rounds. There was only one problem: I was getting burned-out on debate. There were a couple of reasons for that:spreading and squirrel cases. About those shortly.

I was studying for next semester's classes early in the day, then going to the library in the afternoon to work on debate. The infighting at the frat had seemed to hit a cool point. Had I realized the crap that joining the frat would involve, I probably would have not pledged. I mean, this house was supposed to be free of any such bullshit. There was a meeting of pledges one afternoon, and people discussed having our "walkout." That was one of the traditional rites of passage, an event in which, in the middle of the night while everyone else was asleep, the pledges would vandalize the house, then leave the frat and travel to the chapter on another campus. Once at that other chapter, everyone would party for a couple of days, creating mayhem and offending people whom they would probably never see again, before returning to campus. In the days leading up to a walkout, the upperclassmen would regale the pledges with stories of their class's walkout, the idea being that they were goading the pledges into being more outrageous than they had been. The idea was to really fuck things up for the people who were staying behind, all very rah-rah. I'd forgotten that our walkout was the coming weekend. I was glad I couldn't go—I had a tournament—because the pledge class had, for whatever reason, chosen the University of Tennessee as its walkout school. I didn't thrill at the thought of going to a place that had provided the concept for *Deliverance*. The meeting was held, and everyone tossed in ideas about how to leave the frat in a mess. I drifted out of the meeting and back up to my room to get high.

Stan Howard and I were scheduled to be partners at the Loyola tournament that coming weekend. Howard did not like me, and I did not like Howard. In fact, no one on the team liked Howard. He was an arrogant prick. That aspect alone was not damning. I mean, I was an arrogant prick. What was damning in my eyes was that he was not very good at debate. My usual partner, Randolph—not "Randy," but "Randolph"—Anderson had agreed to go to the tournament with Candace Shelstein. Candace was one of the de facto student leaders of the debate team. Hers was a leadership in the sense of organization. I was the other leader, due to my being the best debater on the squad. Candace and I had been partners at the I.S.U. tournament the year before. Indiana State University was in beautiful Terre Haute, Indiana. During the first round, she had tried to order me to argue several issues the ways she thought they should be debated. But this was the thing: she probably knew more about debate—techniques, philosophies of argument, minutiae of that form of expression—than anyone I'd ever known. But she had no concept of executing worth a shit And what she had wanted me to do in that round was tactically fucked. I'd told her that. I'd refused to be ordered around. As a consequence, she and I had only recently begun associating with one another. Her partner had graduated the previous semester, however, and she wanted to go to the Loyola tournament, and so it was that Randolph had agreed to debate with her, and I was going with Howard.

There was a sense of belonging in going to tournaments. A small group of us would travel a dozen or so weekends over the course of the year. At the end of the year, we always went on the "big trip"—Delta Sigma Rho-Tau Kappa Alpha Nationals in the spring. Or DSR-TKA as they were called. This year they were being held at the University of Kentucky in Lexington—not a long way away, as had been the site the year before, the University of Massachusetts at Amherst.

We usually attended tournaments around the midwest, but to me they still bore a sense of the exotic, if only because I got to travel outside Indiana. The campuses differed in some ways, but did seem to blend after a while. There was usually some goddamn tower or building or obelisk or emblem or structure or thing that stood at the center of campus as the phallic strength of the school. Class buildings and buildings for offices or labs stood close by. On the outskirts were dorms, and then, if allowed by the school in question, were the frats and sororities. They were located on "the Row" or "the Acres" or whatever name had been applied to their section of the campus. The campus architecture was of various styles, but the classroom interiors were of only two types: 1960s cement block or the cracked, painted plaster of the older buildings of the late nineteenth or early twentieth centuries.

Our coach, "Doc," was in his late 40s. Rather quiet, always polite, never angry in any way, he was the epitome of the "academic." I stopped by his office in the Performing Arts Center to touch base with him, and find out when we were leaving for the tournament on Friday. The rest of the week I interspersed working on debate and studying with doing bongs and quaffing ales. The graffiti on the walls of my room was multiplying, and had even spread to the ceiling. I had tried to do a day-glo Escher-esque thing on one wall. Somebody had written their philosophy: "There is no hope where there is no dope." I went to a kegger on Thursday morning. Later that day I got a call from Howard. He wanted me to journey the three or four blocks across campus to his frat to go over some things for the tournament. I told him we could do all that on the way to the tournament, that I already had an affirmative case. He started to lecture me so I hung up on him.

Friday morning I got up early and walked down the hall to the showers. I sensed that something was wrong. When I walked into the shower room, there was trash spread all over the fucking place, with motor oil poured on the tile floor of the showers themselves. Obscenities were written in what looked like soap or, worse for scraping off, paraffin. I realized then that my pledge class had taken its walkout. I stepped around things and was able to shower. Then I went back to my room and dressed. When I went down to the dining room I saw that the vandalism was worse. All the chairs were missing. I went into the kitchen and Clancey was there, talking with Edwards. They were both cussing about the pledges. I guess they'd forgotten about their tales of class walkouts. Right away I could sense that the walkout had had the effect opposite than that for which it was intended. Instead of being the sort of fraternal thing that pulled people together, it was pissing people off. I fixed a big bowl of cereal—part of the walkout pranksterism had been to call the breakfast cook and tell her to stay home—and stood there munching Cap'n Crunch as the two of them cussed about what the pledges had done. Somehow they connected the walkout with Carson and blamed him for the things the pledges had done. I quickly finished my cereal and got out of there. This would not be a nice day in the frat.

I got to my room and packed up the sample case I used to carry my files, then stuffed clothes into a gym bag that had seen far better days a couple of decades before. I went down the hallway to call Doc to let him know I was running a little late. Actually, I wanted the team to come by and pick me up. But when Doc answered the phone in his office, and I tried to talk, I realized that one of the pledges' little tricks was to remove the speaker chip from the phone. I ran up to Third Old and checked the phone there. They had "fixed" every telephone in the house—even the pay phone in the mail room. I walked across campus to the PAC. I was wearing tennies, even though there was snow on the ground, because the fucking hiking boots were not working out. When I got to the PAC, everybody was loading the car, a university-owned station wagon. One thing DeForrest never scrimped on was its vehicles. While other schools might have cheap vans and beat-up sedans bearing their official seals, we rode in big, gold-colored Dodge Monaco station wagons. They were big and beautiful and carried nine passengers, with a seat in the back popping out of the storage space and facing backwards. I always rode there so I could crack the rear window and blow smoke out as we flew down the interstates. I tossed my shit in and climbed into the back. Everybody was dressed for the tournament—ties, suits, all that happy horseshit. Of course, I had on jeans and a turtle neck. When I looked over at Howard, I about shit. He was wearing a plaid leisure suit. A plaid fucking leisure suit.

Randolph saw me staring at Howard and said, "Looks like a real tuna, huh?" Everyone heard Randolph's comment. That was when Howard's leisure suit came to be called his tuna suit. And yes—the reference was derisive. From the moment that pronouncement was made, he hated it.

As we settled in our places in the car, Howard badgered me about our case, our rounds, the evidence he'd found, blah blah blah. The topic was the same year, a by-product of Watergate—Resolved: That the power of the Presidency should be significantly curtailed. I knew that I'd done more research on it in the last week than Howard had all year, so I just handed him a copy of the affirmative case, and told him to review it and shut up.

We were all of two blocks into our journey when Howard yelled that he had to hit the bookstore. He always maintained that he couldn't—read that "wouldn't"—debate unless he had one of those four-colors-in-one pens for keeping his flowsheet of arguments. We did a group rolling of eyes as Doc turned the car back to campus and Howard ran into the store and bought one of the goddamn things. Finally we were on our way, taking the highway to the interstate, then going east on I-70.

There are several institutions of higher learning called "Loyola." One in Illinois sometimes spawns good basketball teams. Another is in Ohio and spawns some debate teams and quite a few derelicts. We often encountered teams from the latter Loyola. At tournaments we always partied with them. We always hosted an impromptu party DSR-TKA. Loyola was about a two-hour drive from DeForrest, one of the closer tournaments we attended during the year. It was in our "region" and it was a cheap stay.

We knew there were limitations imposed on the debate program by the budget. With only so much money to spend during the year, and one tournament—DSR-TKA— eating up a big chunk of that budget at the end of the year, our trips were limited to schools in the midwest. Wisconsin allowed anyone 18 or older to drink anything that they wanted. So did Michigan. Those were our favorite states for tournaments. Next came Illinois—19 for beer and wine; followed by Ohio—3.2 beer for people 18 and older. Bringing up the rear was Kentucky. The drinking age was 21, and had "dry" counties.

The landscape of central Indiana rolled by us, flat and barren and covered with snow. At least the day was sunny, but that meant I had to wear my shades. Every 15 or 20 miles, or so it seemed, we passed a Stuckey's offering its world famous pecan logs. We stopped at a Greasy Mac's just shy of the state line. As everyone ate, Howard asked me questions about the case. He wanted to make changes and I told him no. Any changes he made would be weak points that I would have to attempt to repair in my speeches. I blew him off, and then everyone finished eating, and we were off once again. We got off of the interstate at Richmond and embarked on the last leg of the trip.

Once we got to the campus, we had about 20 minutes before our first round. We congregated with the 70 or 80 other debaters and the 25 or so coaches in the lobby of the building where the tournament headquarters was located. Most of the debaters were wearing "business wear"—males in jackets or suits with ties, females in nice dresses or pants outfits. Some of the coaches were dressed up, most were not. Doc always wore a jacket and tie. He registered us, then came over to tell us who we were all debating, or "hitting," as was the parlance.

We had four rounds that afternoon and early evening. While Loyola students made their ways to classes, we wandered between buildings with the tournament schedule and our pairings on mimeographed sheets in hand. The next day we would have two rounds in the morning, and then the top eight teams would debate each other in single-elimination rounds with panels of three judges—comprised generally of coaches from other schools.

Debate, at that time, consisted of two, two-person teams. Each person had one ten-minute speech, known as a "constructive,"and one five-minute speech—the "rebuttal." There was no cross-examination, or questioning, of one side by the other, at most tournaments. I missed that aspect of high school debate. Anyways, the speeches alternated. The first constructive was that of the affirmative. So that speaker was called the first affirmative. Then came the first negative constructive, the second affirmative constructive and, finally, the second negative constructive. Rebuttals flipped with the first negative commencing things, followed by the first affirmative, the second negative and, finishing the round, the second affirmative rebuttal.

As I said before, I'd begun to experience burn-out on debate. It wasn't the traveling. I really liked that. And it wasn't the stress of debate itself. I'd always managed that pretty easily. No. The irony was that debate was becoming a mindless activity.

Most of the coaches and any of the debaters worth a shit would keep track of arguments in a round on what was called a "flow sheet." All that a flow sheet consisted of, usually, was four columns on one page, recording the arguments in each constructive, illustrating where clashes occurred, and four columns, generally on another page, tracking the arguments in rebuttal. Some people had really elaborate systems for flowing arguments. People would show up at tournament carrying artists' sketch pads so they'd have enough room to "flow." And the flow sheet generally provided the outline for the speaker of every speech after the first affirmative constructive. That speech was the only "canned," or pre-written, speech.

The problems in debate arose from the use of flow sheets as they developed in the mid-1960s. As judges would keep track of arguments, quantity began to supplant quality in arguments. A speaker who could put ten arguments into a ten-minute speech did better on points than did a speaker who put only eight arguments into that same time span. Debaters soon extrapolated from that rule. The more a debater could say in a speech, the more arguments that debater could put on a flow sheet. Debaters now spoke at rates that would put the guy in the old Federal Express commercials to shame. Speaking rates were hitting, according to one study, 250 words per minute. This approach was called a "spread." I had started debating in the spread style at the start of my junior year of high school. By my senior year, I was pretty fast. I had to be. My high school debate partner would read a canned negative constructive every round, regardless of the case we hit. In other words, he wasn't really arguing against what the other team said. He was just delivering a canned speech. He was happy because it meant that he didn't have to do any work. Unfortunately, it also meant that he put very little on the judge's flow sheet. That meant that I had to argue against everything that both the first and second affirmative said, plus make arguments against whatever they said that they were going to propose as an alternative to the status quo. In debate parlance, I had to argue both "case" and "plan." In a backwards sort of way, it worked as a strategy. There was so much the first affirmative rebuttalist had to respond to that we usually won. By the time I hit college, spread tactics were well-ingrained in me. To make matters worse, there was incentive to use bullshit arguments, called "squirrel arguments," in the debate. See—nearly any claim in an argument had to be supported by a quote from a journal or book or other publication, of opinion or statistics, whatever. If you didn't have a quote to counter an argument raised by the other team, you could be seriously hurt. So, like on the affirmative, if you could surprise the other team by interpreting the topic in some weird way—on this topic, for example, arguing that the power of the president of Guatemala should be significantly reduced—and the other team didn't have any evidence on Guatemala, then some judges would say that the other team was in quite a pickle. On the negative side, there were similar squirrels. The more obscure the argument and the sources for it, the happier some judges were.

Freshman year Randolph and I upset the University of Kentucky and made semi-finals at the tournament at the University of Saint Louis by basing our affirmative case on an article that Randolph had obtained from a back issue of his father's *American Legion Magazine*. The topic that year had been on energy, and our case relied upon some obscure process, no one had heard of, for generating energy. What no one realized was that the scientist who was quoted extensively in the article had been prosecuted at Nuremberg. But—back to squirrel arguments.

This soon resulted in an approach that meant that any argument, no matter how attenuated, if supported by a quote or a couple of quotes, was valid. For example— affirmative would argue that the powers of the president of the United States to appoint members of the Federal Trade Commission should be curtailed. Negative would argue that taking such powers from the president weakens the president—and they read a quote— then their next point would be that born-again Christians value a strong presidency— another quote—then they would say that if born-again Christians get pissed off, they will take over the country—quote again—and, if they do that, they will invade the Middle East because they will want the Holy Land—a quote about them wanting the Holy Land. If that happens, we'll have nuclear war because the Arabs would be pissed off and the Soviets would nuke us in coming to the aid of the Arabs—quote. Nuclear war would result from curtailing the power of the president in appointing members to the FTC.

We were affirmative against a spread team first round, then alternated after that. We hit a squirrel case in our last round—concerning the powers of the president of Senegal. I could tell that the judge in that round bought the arguments about Senegal. I thought we'd split, two wins and two losses. Howard thought we'd won all four. But then, he thought that he'd scored perfect rounds, too. I just wanted to have dinner and party.

I knew there was a chapter of my fraternity at Loyola. I'd heard that it was pretty wild. Our team had dinner downtown, at a stereotypical college campus bar/restaurant. There were pictures of Loyola sports heroes and former coaches—and a plaque declaring Loyola to be the "cradle of coaches." Pennants with the school name and seal hung every place. We had big burgers and fries. Then the team dropped me off at the frat. After Doc was done with his coaches' meeting, he'd come by to get me. I had my pledge pin affixed to the lapel of the old suit jacket I was wearing. I didn't know if the people in the house were going to be rah-rah jerks.

As I approached the fraternity in the January darkness, I could hear music and laughter from inside. Their "physical plant" was an old brick, multi-storied structure, kind of colonial in design, standard fare for a college fraternity house. I walked up to the front door then into the foyer. There were about 20 or 25 people standing around, or sitting on the steps of the big stairway directly in front of me, males and females lounging about holding translucent plastic cups of beer. Yes, I'd walked in on a kegger. A couple of the guys turned around and looked at me, and one looked at my lapel and crossed the foyer.

"You one of our pledges?" he asked, over the noise.

I said no, and explained where I was from and why I was there.

"No shit—you got lucky. We just ended rush. This is our party for our rookies."

I brightened at those prospects. The party we threw for our pledges at the end of rush was always a big one. I figured this party could be no worse. And from the looks of it, it was pretty big.

The guy stuck a cup of beer in my hand, then ushered me around, introducing me to various brothers. I killed one beer, then another. Things began to get fuzzy around the seventh or eighth beer. Someone handed me a joint. I remember I was jumping back and forth between a fire escape and a roof several times. Someone handed me what looked like a thimble and explained that it was 190-proof plum wine. The last thing I remember is making out on the floor of the kitchen with a girl who was introduced to me as "Space Chick."

The next thing I knew, I was waking up and it was morning. I was face-down on my bed in the motel, fully clothed. Randolph was in the shower and Howard was bitching at me to get up. My head hurt, I was dehydrated, my eyes were gritty, my mouth had the awful taste of hangover, and my body had been drained of every molecule of blood sugar. I managed to sit up. My clothes felt prickly from my having slept in them.

"I got dibs on the shower," I mumbled, and began pulling off my clothes.

"Like hell you do," Howard barked.

"Fuck you," I told him as the shower was shut off. Randolph exited the bathroom a few moments later, drying his hair. I lunged for the bathroom door, beat Howard to it, then locked myself inside. The shower felt good, and I made sure I used up every bit of the hot water our room had been allotted. Howard was cussing as he quickly took his—cold—shower, as I got dressed. I had to wear fucking slacks because my jeans were too gross. When Howard came out, he "ordered" me not to embarrass him that day. I told him to fuck himself, any success that we had at the tournament would be due to my abilities and not his. That was pretty much true. Besides, wearing that plaid leisure suit and butterfly bow-tie, the fucker looked like a polyester clown.

The two rounds that morning were power-matched—in other words, we debated teams with like records. I could tell we'd done all right the night before, because the teams we hit that morning were pretty good. We broke for lunch and went to a pizza place where I inhaled several pieces of deep-dish sausage and quaffed about a pitcher of ice water. I felt approximately human when we went back to the awards convocation. We were the only DeForrest team to make elims. We'd gone 2-2 the night before, but we picked up both rounds that morning. I even got a speaker award. We went to our elim round, and won on a 2-1. Then we dropped the semi-final round on a 3-0, so we placed third.

On the way back to DeForrest Howard thought he'd left his shoes back at the motel. He wanted us to turn around and drive back and get them. By this point, we were 50 miles along on our trip back, already on the interstate and sailing. We all blew him off. The car kept heading west.

"I can't believe I had to debate with this son of a bitch," I observed.

"I had to put up with your shit and be embarrassed," he shot back.

"I was embarrassed to have to hear you argue every round," I replied.

"At least I didn't pull the shit you pulled last night."

"So what? I got drunk at a frat party."

Everyone was quiet, then Doc said, "You remember what happened last night, don't you?"

I looked around at everyone, but nobody was saying anything. "Sure. Sure I do," I said, but the tone of my voice was not convincing.

"What happened last night?" Randolph asked, smirking.

"I went to the frat and partied. Doc picked me up on his way back from the coaches' meeting."

"You don't remember how you got back?" Dufo asked. He was another debater, a freshman Randolph had nicknamed after a character on a National Lampoon album.

Everyone waited. I looked around. They were all waiting for Doc to tell the story. "I went to pick you up at the fraternity like we'd agreed." Doc sort of drew out the story, very patiently, as he negotiated traffic. "I got there and had to find you. I kept asking about you, and everyone seemed to have met 'the guy from DeForrest.' I finally found you in the kitchen with some young lady you introduced as your future wife. You said you'd meet us at the tournament this morning." Doc stretched a little bit at this juncture of the story. "About two o'clock I was wakened by a call. A gentleman asked if I was the coach of DeForrest's debate team. I said I was. He asked if I could pick up one of my debaters. I said sure, that I'd be right there. He said, 'Don't you want to know where he is?' I said the name of the fraternity. Well—that wasn't where you were. I guess you'd decided to walk back to the motel from the fraternity, and you'd forgotten that it was five miles. About six blocks down the street from the fraternity, you must've seen this guy's light on. You banged on his door, explained to him who you were and that you needed him to call your coach. When I got there, you were sitting in the living room with a drink in your hand, and you appeared to be having a pleasant time."

Everybody got a good chuckle. Everybody but me, that is. I just shook my head and tried to nap. My system needed some rest.

Chapter 10 - A Marvelous Evening At The Cinema

One evening after supper and toward the end of Winter Term, I was sitting in Sid's room. We were listening to some of the cassettes he said he hadn't heard in a while. The sound was a bit muffled, as though a layer of fuzz had developed between the magnetic impulses on the tape and the tape heads. He had three Doors albums, and two albums by the Jefferson Airplane—"Volunteers" and "Worst of Jefferson Airplane." Altogether he had 18 or 20 tapes that had sat there gathering dust for a year or two. If Sid had a small unused collection, mine was rather sizeable by comparison. When Eva and Adolf had sprung for my stereo as a graduation present, it had been the Spring of 1973. At that time, and in that area of the universe, 8-track tapes were the thing. During that time I had found— and I know this sounds weird, but hey, it was real—a chain of dry cleaners in Indianapolis that sold bootleg 8-tracks for a buck each. Why a dry cleaners was doing this, I don't know. But back then we would have thought that having a McDonald's in a gas station was pretty weird. Over time I had purchased 40 or 50 8-track tapes. When the time had come for me to get a stereo, I had gotten the Hitachi as a discontinued model. It had a good tuner in it, a pair of miniature speakers and—ta da!—an 8-track player built-in.

The 8-tracks had been developed for automobiles. They were functional for riding around and getting high in a car. The play was continuous, so you had minimal hassle. The tapes themselves were light and easily transported, but the sound was inferior—sort of muffled—one was constantly cleaning the heads of the players. The tracks would change, sometimes in mid-song, with a reverberation then a huge ka-chunk! and then the song would fade back in. The things were not meant to play indoors, or at least they shouldn't have been. The systems were also prone to breakdown. Mine fried out at the end of freshman year, as I mentioned earlier. They weren't very convenient. Most decks did not have fast-forward or reverse, so one had to wait for the track to come around again to hear a specific song. I only knew one person who had an 8-track system that could record. Cassettes were preferable and, had I been able to travel back in time, I would have bought a system with a cassette deck in it. So my 8-tracks sat, unused, in a grocery bag in the closet of my room, just as Sid's cassettes had sat on the shelf in his room.

There was a knock at the door. We were out of pot, so neither of us was paranoid. Sid said to come in, and in walked Mooter. That was weird because not all of the circles of friends I had overlapped. Mooter had never partied with—or even met, for that matter— Sid. Mooter was known as the "God of Smoke." We had met during our first day of classes freshman year. We began conversing before the class started, then resumed the conversation afterwards and burned a joint. Since then we'd partied together a lot. Mooter partied as much as I did. In fact, his nickname—Mooter—was another word for a joint.

"Hey man," Mooter said, his eyes bloodshot and squinting, the ubiquitous smile crossing his face. "I knocked on your door and somebody said you were in here, but I didn't smell pot smoke." Mooter laughed at his own little joke.

"We're out," I explained.

"Have a seat," Sid said, after I introduced them.

"That's kind of why I came over here," Mooter said.

"You have pot?" I asked, sort of perking up.

Mooter shook his head. "No. But I've got some pretty good blotter acid."

"What kind?" Sid asked.

Mooter grinned even more as he reached into his shirt pocket. "It's Berkeley White, man."

With that he had my attention, as well as Sid's.

"You turned me on last fall to that Mr. Natural, so I figured I'd return the favor."

"How much?" I asked as I stared down at several small, white squares of paper.

"Four bucks a hit."

We did the math and bought three hits each. That about wiped me out. I had maybe two bucks left. Mooter left after that, on his way across campus to spread chemical cheer. I went across to my room and did two of the hits. I hid the other one in an envelope, and replaced the envelope in a box that held the other hundred or so envelopes. I walked back across the hallway and Sid was talking with Criminal Phil, and when I walked in I caught something about Criminal Phil paying Sid back.

"You done yours?" Sid asked. I said yeah. "How many'd you do?" I told him. "Shit," he said. "Your buddy came back after you left and said that half a hit would be plenty."

I just shrugged, like oh well, another one of these crazy LSD trips.

"You gonna do yours?" I asked both of them.

Sid said why not, and sat down. He tore a hit in two and put the rest in a tiny plastic baggie. Criminal Phil set about doing the same.

After they each did half a hit, as we were sitting there, Criminal Phil said, "The UB is showing *Easy Rider* tonight."

"Sounds cool to me," I said without even thinking about the hassles of being out in the general public on acid. I only considered whether I had the dollar admission and maybe 36 cents for a coke. I grabbed my coat. Then we all took off down to campus. The movie started at seven, and it was about a quarter 'til.

The air was really fresh and cold. The light played off the snow crystals and all was right with the World. As we broke across the lawn of Mason Hall, I gazed at that portion of the campus—at East College, a frat on the far side of the East College Lawn, the Academic Quad, the library—and it looked pristine and safe. Life would never intrude on anyone, as long as they stayed here. I was safe here. No one could touch me. I was light years away from Kilkerry.

When we got into the UB, I felt the first rushes from the acid. That was also the first point in time when I wondered if it was wise to go out like this. But I decided fuck it, that if things got too heavy, I could always walk back to the house. No one could arrest me for things that were going on in my head—like hallucinations. But then I'd have to cross Bloomington Street if I walked back, and I didn't know if I'd be able to gauge the speeds and distances of cross traffic and—well, I got a little paranoid.

We went down to the Hub and I got a large coke. They always seemed to max out on the syrup in their mix at the soft drink fountain, and to minimize on shpritz or whatever the technical name would be for the carbonation. I managed to execute the right moves for getting my coke, then paid the lady. Sid and Criminal Phil were already walking across the Hub, heading back upstairs to the ballroom, where the movies were always shown. They were giggling hilariously, and I had to catch up with them.

We got to the door and paid our dollar to a student who was getting work study money. Then we walked in and looked for seats. That was when I saw Austin and Michelle sitting in the second or third row of a nearly-deserted ballroom. I waved, and they chuckled and waved, and Sid and Criminal Phil followed me over. We took seats behind them, and they turned and chuckled again.

"What's up?" Austin asked, then he started laughing again.

"We're tripping," Michelle explained, suppressing a giggle.

"Berkeley White?" I asked, and they looked at me with an expression of surprise. "So are we."

All five of us laughed. Then the lights dimmed, and we prepared ourselves for some cinema.

The Union's flicks were pretty cool. They always opened up with a cartoon, then went into the main feature, just like movie houses used to do. That night was no exception. We had a Roadrunner cartoon. Wiley Coyote was buying various products from the Acme Corporation, all of which failed him miserably in his quest to bag the Roadrunner for dinner. The one that we saw that night was the one where Wiley Coyote buys rocket-propelled shoes. It was one of the good Roadrunners, too, before they had Wiley Coyote talk.

Pretty soon the movie came up. Peter Fonda and Dennis Hopper score a coke deal in a junk yard near an airport with some midget and a bald guy. Then they put the money from the deal into long plastic tubes that they feed into their motorcycles' gas tanks. The soundtrack was grainy. The ballroom's bare wooden floors, plaster walls and metal folding chairs offered bad acoustics, but that didn't matter. The songs were good and the storyline sucked us in.

After a couple of minutes, I stopped thinking about tripping. I just tripped. Mooter had been right—the acid was clean. I wasn't gritting my teeth at all. After the first rushes had subsided, I wasn't laughing maniacally. As I looked around in the dimness of the ballroom-turned-cinema, I saw that the couple of dozen or so people there appeared to be hippies. I guessed that was the type of audience this movie attracted. People wouldn't stand up and yell for the police if they discovered that someone among them was doing LSD. But how could they tell? They couldn't read my thoughts. What if I made weird noises to myself? How would I really know?

Jack Nicholson came into the movie, after Fonda and Hopper got busted in a small southern town while trying to ride their motorcycles through a parade. Nicholson was the small town's drunken lawyer, and he joined the trip to Mardi Gras. When he took his first drink of whiskey for the day, he flapped one arm and made a "yee-hoo, nik nik nik" sound, then said, "Here's to a new day." Pretty cool shit. Then he got killed while they were camping out, by some southern rednecks, and for a second I saw the axe blade split his face. The boys continued on their journey. They picked up a hippie who was hitch-hiking. He took them to a commune, where Fonda and Hopper met two women and had sex in a river pool. Fonda kind of got into the commune on some deep level which Hopper couldn't identify with. Then the boys had to be on their way. They got to New Orleans and did acid in a graveyard with two more women. Then they left New Orleans. As they sat by a campfire, Hopper says something about how they have it made. Fonda says, "No, we blew it," and I knew he was referring to their having left the commune. The next day they get up and are riding down the highway and—sorry to spoil the movie if you haven't seen it—they get blown away by a couple of rednecks with shotguns in a pickup truck. That's where Cheech & Chong came up with "East Rider rifle racks."

The lights in the ballroom came on and we walked out. The image of the guy wearing buckskins and hitchhiking across the west was indelible on my mind. We pulled on our coats and walked out into the cold air. The street lights seemed so distinct in their "spheres."

"Good flick," Criminal Phil commented, the first words spoken by any of us since the end of the movie.

"I really got into the commune," I said. "I don't necessarily agree with that one"— it appeared to have a vegetarian bent, and I couldn't imagine living without steaks or chicken—"but I can see the concept."

"Did you see Fonda glimpsing his death when he was tripping?" Sid asked.

I realized I had! It was just a couple of frames, a split-second, and I was about to reply when a voice behind us said, "You guys just see that movie?" There was a straight-looking guy, hair barely touching his ears, walking our way. Sid said we had. The guy said, "That's nothing. Go see *Billy Jack*." Like "show me gore" or "show me brains exploding."

I looked at the guy. He was very smug. He was an asshole. "Is that all that you got from that film? Violence? I mean, except for a half-dozen frames where Nicholson gets killed, and the bit at the very end of the flick there's what"—I looked at my companions— "A minute? Less? That's all that you got from that flick?"

Suddenly the guy was defensive. He snorted, kinda like Eva. "There aren't hippies walking around doing LSD anymore!"

We broke up in hysterical laughter right as we got to his living unit, and he scurried up the path. The guy was talking to "hippies doing LSD," and didn't even realize it.

We crossed Bloomington Street—always a challenge to the impaired, and, for that matter, the unimpaired. A student was hit at that crossing every other year. There was very little traffic for us, though. As we reached the curb, I realized I felt impervious to the cold. In fact, breathing felt great on my lungs. I had not smoked a cigarette all day, and that was the first moment I had even given cigarettes a thought. I looked up at the trees. I saw them as great, inverted lungs, their snow-laden branches representing the clean cilia of the lungs of a non-smoking, acid-eating hippie. I decided then that I would quit smoking. Then we were crunching across the gravel and snow of the parking lot behind the fraternity—and by "fraternity," I mean the physical plant.

I was still caught up in the movie, especially the whole freedom/hitch-hiking thing. I walked into the Informal and some guys were watching a movie. Maybe if I had just sat down then and watched that movie, things would have turned out differently later, but I was into the movie that I'd just seen. So I walked on through the Informal, oblivious to anyone or anything, and out the French doors and onto the porch, where I stood and stared out at the street, ignoring the winter. I heard the door open and close behind me. Sid was standing there, grinning, wondering what the hell I was doing.

"The movie," I said. "Where they moved on after the commune."

"Yeah, that's what Fonda's character meant when he said that they'd blown it."

I shook my head. "I don't think the commune they had is what I would be happy doing, but the whole idea of taking off . . ." In Kilkerry the World seemed unreal—New York City existed only in the movies or on TV. Europe was an abstract concept to which no one from Kilkerry ever traveled. Major cities and subways appeared on the news and the news never happened. Major league baseball and professional football occurred with actors. Pro basketball games were on another planet—nobody actually grew to be seven feet tall. Great paintings never really existed. They were just prototypes for two-dollar prints sold at campus art shows. The movie had somehow made the World seem real. I don't know why it had that effect on me. Watching the movie now, I think it's rather shmaltzy. But that night it seemed to open my eyes. Maybe it was the fact that the two main characters rode their motorcycles across such distances, from California, across deserts, to New Orleans and the Deep South. Maybe my mind was just coincidentally spinning that way that night and the movie came along at the right moment and I mistook correlation for causation. Whatever the reason, it had seemed to make plausible the existence of people and things outside this little slice of whatever you'd want to call it in Indiana.

I looked down at my feet. I said to Sid, "Look—the porch leads to the sidewalk. The sidewalk leads to the street. The street goes down a block and hits the state highway. Turn left and go nine miles and you're at the interstate. And from there, you can go to the World."

"I see what you mean," he replied, and we stood there staring out at our means of egress to the World.

Then Ridgeway stuck his head out and said Sid had a phone call, so we went back inside. I went up to my room and fried out the rest of the night listening to my acid albums and contemplating the concept of "World." Eventually my body remembered how to sleep, and I dozed off, thinking about the possibilities my life held.

Chapter 11 - Saint Louis

Our next tournament was at the University of Saint Louis. Randolph and I, the year before, had pulled a couple of upsets, making semi-finals in the varsity division against Kentucky before losing on a 2-1 ballot. I wanted to try to repeat our success the year before. Randolph had some function at his fraternity for which his presence was semi-required. The only other person who wanted to go was Howard. Even Doc wasn't going. He had some prior commitment, and so Doc had a former debater, who actually lived in Glendale, go with us.

Robert Donato was in his mid-thirties and lived with his mother. From time to time he would travel with the team and help Doc out by judging some rounds. If a school that came to a tournament had more than two teams per judge, then that school had to hire judges at the tournament site. Robert traveled with us on occasion. It was cheaper for the school to pay for his meals and a few bucks a round that he judged than to pay for a hired judge at the tournament site. As Randolph had once said, Robert's relationship with his mother and an interest in a rather odd form of fourteenth century Catholicism seemed to be

Robert's only pursuits in life. His appearance seemed consistent with his life. He wore wire-rim glasses, but not out of any sense of style. They were functional, not hip. He also wore madras shirts and chinos of styles that had been in fashion among college students about ten years before. The effect was of a bookish, aging fan of the Beach Boys. He wasn't employed, as far as any of us could tell. But he was intelligent. He had a doctorate in divinity from an Ivy League school.

As usual we left on a Friday morning, in a whale of a university station wagon. The usual flat, snow-laden landscape flew by us. The ride on I-70 from Glendale to Saint Louis is not very memorable. It's boring, in fact. For that matter, most of interstate Indiana is dull. As we approached Saint Louis from the East, the urban congestion became more noticeable, traffic heavier. Then the Arch appeared. It didn't take us long to find the campus and the tournament headquarters. We went straight to our rounds. We had four, then we were off for the evening. Howard was more frustrating than he had been at Loyola. But I was in a real groove. By the time that we broke for supper, Howard was fuming over the fact that I wouldn't listen to what he wanted to do, and I was annoyed by his whining.

We found a neat place for dinner, a kosher pizza place in a section of Saint Louis called Clayton. The place was packed, and everything about the place was old, from the waiters to the furnishings. As we ate, Howard was trying to tell us about a private survey he had more or less undertaken, comparing different types of prophylactics that he'd tried with his girlfriend back home. I tried my best to ignore him. There was something perverse about how he was discussing it, as though he was talking about the new oil he was trying in his car. Everything was so mechanical. Rubbers seemed to distance or separate one from the act of sex. At least it seemed so to me, although I had no personal knowledge of the matter. All that latex separating the two people involved in the act. This was, after all, the 1970s. Most college women were on the Pill. There was no AIDS. There were only distant rumors of herpes in any of its forms. Condoms were for the prevention of pregnancy—and for guys to carry around in their wallets as signs of the "fact" that they were sexually active. I think Robert was oblivious, munching on pizza and looking at the photographs of celebrities who'd visited the restaurant. Then Robert started talking as though someone had hit a button on his neck and told us about when he'd lived on the east coast, and how he hung out for a while in the Village. "I even saw Dick Cavett try to do stand-up comedy one night," he said.

"What?" I asked. "Cavett doing stand-up?" The summer following my graduation from high school, when I'd had mono so bad, I'd lain on the couch in the living room after everyone else had gone to bed and watched Dick Cavett's talk show on ABC. I was a fan.

"He was awful. Everybody could tell what he was trying to be funny about, but it just didn't work. He bombed. Everyone was politely silent and he got off the stage."

I tried to picture that. It was pretty cool, having a link like that. Knowing someone who had been there to the Village and seen a show like that. It was also pretty cool that Robert had effectively silenced Howard.

On our way back to the Holiday Inn, the motel where most of the teams at the tournament were staying, we stopped at a liquor store so I could get some beer. I wasn't carded. When we got back to the motel, there was a party going on next door to the room Howard and I were sharing. As we walked past, I saw through the narrow window next to the door that some debaters from Indianapolis State were in there. I put the beers in our room, grabbed a couple and walked next door. One of Indy State's debaters let me in. Because of the proximity of our schools, we knew their team pretty well, and soon we were drinking beers and chatting about the tournament.

I began talking with one woman from their team. I'd debated against her a couple of times. We'd always won, but she was pretty good in rounds, given her level of intelligence. She was a very serious person, one of those people who mistakes seriousness with intellect and tries to approach everything on a serious level. If someone tells a joke, for example, instead of laughing at the punch line, the person asks what is funny about it, and tries to diagram the joke. I wasn't in the mood for that. Not that I ever was. I was into a whimsical mood, instead of my usually irreverent attitude. I was tired and blowing off some steam.

"What is it you want to do with your life, though?" she asked.

I felt just like having some fun. So I quoted Firesign Theatre, from "Don't Crush That Dwarf, Hand Me the Pliers." "Gee whiz," I said. "I want to climb a tree, cut off the soles of my shoes, and learn to play the flute."

For the next half-hour I sat there trying to explain things to her. At first I tried to tell her I was only kidding. But she wouldn't let go like that. She started seeing something deeper, sort of Freudian in a way, that maybe I really did want to climb that tree. And why did I want to cut off the soles of my shoes? She never questioned the part about the flute. I guess the flute was an instrument that was, in her way of thinking, sufficiently intellectual to pass muster. I realized there was less effort in just going along with it and playing the game than there was in actually saying what I felt. So I told her the key was cutting off the soles of my shoes. By doing so, on the surface, I was complying with convention—it would look as if I was actually wearing shoes. But beneath the veneer of shoe, down at the "sole"—play on words, right?—I was barefoot.

I finished my beers and got the fuck back to the room. Howard was already asleep, and I was glad. I didn't think I could have handled one more of his lectures on rubbers.

The next morning first round we hit the team from Indy State with the woman on it from the night before. I did really well in the round and we won. Our last round was against a team from Illinois College. The team was comprised of a guy and a girl. The female was immensely cute, and was wearing a boa. I could dig that. We broke for lunch, and I bade Howard and Donato adieu. I had been invited to party with the people from Illinois. We went to their van and they pulled out a quart bottle of vodka. I pulled out a couple of joints that I had stashed in my sock. The more vodka we drank, the cuter she appeared to be. We were out there for a long time. We all ducked down the two or three times security police had driven by. The afternoon was sunny and chilly, but then the sky began to turn a dark shade of gray. The more we partied, the more I flirted with the girl with the boa. I got her address and told her that I would write. I stuffed the slip of paper with her address into one of my pockets.

After an hour or so, we saw debaters heading back inside the building where the awards convocation was being held. We were thoroughly smashed. We were loud and boisterous as we staggered into the auditorium to the glares of some of the people. As it turned out each one of the kids from Illinois got speaker awards, as did I. In fact, I was second-highest in points for the tournament. I vaguely recall the bummed-out expressions of most of the people in the auditorium as we, the very drunk people, kept going up and taking hardware from the tournament director. My trophy was pretty good-sized. Like all the rest of the trophies given at the tournament, it was a miniature of the Saint Louis Arch. The kids from Illinois made elimination rounds, though, while Howard and I didn't. So I bade them farewell and good luck—luck that they would need in the elim rounds, as drunk as they were—and staggered alongside Donato and Howard to the university station wagon. By now the sky was really fucked. Snow started to fall. Donato didn't want to drive, and I was so screwed up I couldn't drive, so that left Howard. As we left Saint Louis, I fell asleep with visions of the girl and her feather boa, dancing in my brain.

When I woke up, it was dark outside. I looked over the front seat and into a blizzard.

I heard Donato, somewhat pissed, say to Howard, "Either leave them off or leave them on." I sat up and looked over Howard's shoulder. The speedometer indicated that we were traveling at 30 mph. Donato noticed I was sitting up. "We're almost to Indiana," he said, and added it was ten o'clock. I'd been asleep for about seven hours. All I could see outside was the snow slanting in at us from ahead and everything else fading into blackness.

It was then that I noticed that Howard was reaching down and fucking with his shoes. He was wearing platform shoes with three inch heels. They'd only been out of style for about two years. But Howard continued to wear the fucking things, especially when he was wearing his tuna suit. Apparently he did not like to wear those shoes when he was driving—they put his foot into an unnatural angle—so he was pulling them off. What became apparent to me was that, after he had them off for a while, his feet would get cold, and so he would put them back on. Doing so would not have been a problem, but we were driving in a blizzard on an interstate in the dead of night. Anybody else who was stupid enough to have attempted the task would still have had the sense to do so with one hand while keeping their eyes on the road. Howard, however, had to use both hands, attempt to steer the car with his shoulder, and look down to take off or put on his shoes. Every time he did so, he lost a bit of control and the car fishtailed. Howard was oblivious to the situation on the road. He was more concerned with the comfort of his feet. I could see why Donato was disgruntled.

We drove that way for a good 30 or 40 miles, the snow-laden landscape passing by, our whale of a university-owned station wagon carrying us closer to DeForrest and home. Then Howard complained about his feet, and he started fucking with them again. The car fishtailed.

"Christ, Howard," I muttered. It wasn't enough that he get the shoes back on—he had to tie them, too.

"Either keep them off or leave them on!" Donato was disgusted and the closest to blowing up that I had ever seen him. "Watch it here—it looks slick . . . and careful! I think that semi behind us is gaining!"

Altogether the process of the shoes took Howard about five minutes to complete. And every time we nearly wiped out. We continued to travel that way—shoes on, shoes off; near-spin, quick recovery—until we were about five miles from the Glendale exit. I mean, we were almost home. So what does Howard do? He starts the whole process again. The car began to fishtail, then it spun. The car skirted across what there was of the left lane and down into the median. Howard looked up, with both hands on his shoe laces, and froze. Donato grabbed for the wheel and tried to steer the thing in a kind of half-assed manner. I sat there in the back seat, clutching my trophy. I glanced behind us, expecting to see the word MACK above a huge grill and bumper bearing down on us. But there was only blackness. No one was close to us. The car came abruptly to rest, and we sat there for a few moments, listening to the engine hum.

"We're about 15 miles outside of town," I said, pulling on the coat I had only too-recently been using as a blanket. "Not too bad of a walk in this snow."

"I'm not walking anywhere in these platforms," Howard spat out, as though we had other options.

"Well fuck you then, you shouldn't have wrecked the car."

Donato was miffed but tried to hold things together. "All we can do is get out of here and get help."

There was a tap at the window, and all three of us turned. Donato rolled down his window, and we saw a man in his forties standing there.

"Saw your car wipe out. Need any help?"

"Are you going near Glendale?" Donato asked.

"That's where we live," the man replied then, seeing Howard and me, asked, "Are you with the school?" We said yes, and the man said, "Come on, let's get your stuff into our car."

I grabbed my night bag and the sample case I used to carry all my debate shit. Howard, of course, had five or six satchels, suitcases, a suit bag, a brief case—just a whole bunch of crap. Donato and I let the fucker hassle with all of it. We were not in a mood to act as porters. I laughed as I watched Howard struggling, in his platforms with three-inch heels, up the incline of the median on the thick snow, carrying his bags. It took him three trips to get everything, and if he'd fallen and busted his ass, I would have absolutely howled with laughter.

The man was with his wife, and it turned out that they were both alums. Donato and I chatted with them as the guy navigated their sedan through the blizzard and into town. Howard sat, silent and sullen, staring out into the night, pissed off at us, I guess, for having not helped him with his bags. Mine was the first stop along the way. I got out and thanked the couple, then walked carefully on the snow into the frat.

It was a Saturday night and there were people up and partying. I got to my room and hassled for what seemed like an hour with the lock. I finally got it open and tossed my shit into my room, took off my coat and tossed it on the floor. I walked across the hallway to Sid's room, still carrying my trophy.

Sid was there and so was Roach, whom I hadn't seen since finals the previous semester. They were getting high, and Sid offered me a bong, which I gladly accepted. Sid filled me in on the last two days and the shit I'd missed. Apparently the situation in the frat was one of turmoil. Some new crisis had erupted. Somebody had insulted the house president's girlfriend, and so the president had taken a swing at somebody else: a situation about which I didn't want to hear. I shrugged, said goodnight, and stumbled back to my room. I thought about the girl with the boa. She was really cute—a little bit of a sexy overbite, shoulder-length brown hair, a nice figure—and we had a lot in common—dipsomania, debate, and whatever the topics were that we had discussed as we were getting fucked up. I couldn't remember what those topics were just then in my room. I reached for my pants that I'd discarded on the floor next to my mattress. I fished around in the pockets for the piece of paper with her address—and what was her name? I checked each pocket, but could find no slip of paper. Oh well, I thought as I lay back, I'd find it tomorrow.

Then, with visions of the Illinois girl naked in my playful sleepy mind, I fell asleep.

Chapter 12 - The Semester Begun

Winter Term had ended. I had partied the whole time and then wakened one morning having to attend classes. However, I was ready. As the first week of the semester turned into the second, the calendar I had drawn on the wall above my makeshift plywood-brick-and-beer-box desk took on a mark for each class I made. I hadn't missed one yet. I was even taking good notes. But that good old high school back in Kilkerry hadn't exactly put me through intellectual boot camp in preparation for college. There had been no "orientation" for college. Of course, since only 25% of the members of my graduating class went on to post-secondary education of any sort, the parents and taxpayers did not place the same kind of stress on college; not like the parents and taxpayers in, say, Lake Forest might have done. I guess I had thought that in college you just went to class and listened, absorbed data in a form of osmosis, then took a test on the reading matter. Doing a Vulcan mind-meld on the textbook could be a plus.

My favorite class was political and social philosophy. There were only eight people in the class, so it was taught in a seminar format, with a lot of discussion/arguing. Nearly everyone, including the prof, good old Gleason, smoked. Everyone but me was either a junior or a senior, so I felt pretty cool to be mixing it up with upperclassmen. The only drawback was that we were starting the semester with Hobbes, and, as I said earlier, he was a rather bleak fellow writing bleakly during bleak times. But if I had to re-read something four times to navigate the archaic language, then hey—that's what I was there for.

Con law was weird, if only because we were discussing specific cases of the U.S. Supreme Court and, on top of it, using the Socratic method that was employed in law school. Add to that the odd mix of students, most of whom were poly sci jocks, some of whom were among the most conservative people on campus and a couple of people who were among the most radical—and it made for some weirdness. The textbook was a big, thick expensive son of a bitch—like forty bucks, kind of unheard-of in those days. I mean, university bookstores have always raped students, but on this text book the act took on the proportions of a capital offense. So, since we were studying U.S. Supreme Court cases anyways, and since the library had all of the U.S. Supreme Court's cases in U.S. Reports, I dispensed with buying the textbook and saved the money for other things. After all, I was going to make every class that semester, so I would keep good notes of each student's presentation of his or her case.

Speech Pathology was innocuous: very clinical, easy to digest. There was nothing much there that I would ever use.

Ed Psych was strange. I was taking it so I could have, nicely lined-up when I graduated, all of the requirements for obtaining a teaching license. Yeah, right. Like a school district would hire me. The prof was one of the older, revered profs at the school. By the second class session I hated the son of a bitch. He talked to us as though we were all fourteen years old. The first day he told us we would have three hourly exams and a final and, as in all of the classes in the psych department, those exams would be multiple choice. And what did the first chapter of the ed psych text say about multiple choice exams? That they are the worst type of exam to give. That should have told me something about the course and the prof. But I'd read ahead and I felt pretty good about knowing the material.

I wanted a three-point for the semester. After my first couple of days of classes, I was confident I could achieve that. My GPA coming out of first semester was a 2.1. I had to pull a 3.5 to get my GPA up to a 2.5, which was what I needed to keep my scholarship. After having reviewed all of the factors, I felt confident that I could hit that. And if I kept my scholarship, I had to have met whatever standards had been set in my trust back at the bank in Kilkerry.

The door of my room was still fucked up. The house manager had quit after the conflagration, so there was no one I could go to to get the lockset replaced. I took things in stride and hassled with it every time I locked it. We didn't have any thefts in the house, so

I left my door unlocked whenever I was actually in the fraternity—and by "fraternity," I again mean the physical plant.

Oh, and the fraternity bullshit. What a fucking time suck. I couldn't simply walk away from it. After all, I didn't have wealthy parents like a lot of people at DeForrest. Hell, I didn't even have parents, just stingy old Eva and Adolf. Moving out of the physical plant, as several people had done, was not an option for me. So I continued to live there, with emotional turmoil surrounding every day's existence in the place.

At the start of the third week of the semester, I enjoyed a fine Monday of getting buzzed. It was the start of a tradition. Classes were over for the day. My one o'clock class was con law, and at 1:50, I picked up my books from the standard, college classroom chair with the one arm that was wide enough for a notebook, and started back to the physical plant. As I headed up Anderson Street, I saw Ridgeway ahead of me. His clothes looked ratty and beat-up, as if they were purchased from Goodwill. His father, being a stockbroker in NYC, made sure that his son's clothes were actually new and expensive. It's just that in putting them on, Ridgeway transformed them. He always wore corduroy pants, plaid flannel shirts and Chucks for tennis shoes. He was a real basketball freak. He was on his way back to the physical plant as well, and so I caught up with him. He was just coming out of a history class. That was his major. He had a weird memory for arcane details.

"Done for the day?" I asked. It was a silly question because I knew he had no more classes.

"Got studying to do," he replied.

"I was thinking about maybe getting a 12-pack."

Ridgeway gave me a wry look, as though I had uttered a heresy. "Nobody gets fucked up on Mondays. That's the one day during the week that everybody studies."

If he hadn't said that—or maybe if he hadn't said what he said with the same inflection as he used that day—whatever the case, I started a new tradition for myself. There was no rule that applied so steadfastly to everyone. I viewed myself as being an exception to just about everything. If there was a rule that people did not party on Mondays, then goddamn it, that rule would not apply to me.

When we got back to the physical plant, Tom Buchanan made a run to the liquor store. I rode along. On the way, we passed Marya's house. At the liquor store, I sat outside, as Buchanan went in and bought a 12-pack of Stroh's cans for me. On the way back, I had him drop me off at Marya's.

Marya was an old lady I had never met—nor seen, for that matter. She owned a big, old house off-campus, and students rented rooms from her. There were two common bathrooms and a big common kitchen, then like five or six rooms let out to students. She didn't live in the place herself. I never knew anyone who rented from her who wasn't a hippy. The house sort of attracted that element. It was three stories, with a tower on one corner that sort of rose into a top floor that was meant as an attic, but another room had been shoe-horned into it for a student to rent. The exterior was turn-of-the-century, with a bunch of gingerbread touches, like intricate wooden latticework on the front porch, all sorts of neat stuff like that. Inside, the walls had been papered with weird, paisley designs, and the trim was painted all sorts of weird colors, with a predominance of plum and raspberry and pink. Some colors were even day-glo. I'd been there a couple of times for parties, and I knew Barry Lane had moved in there right before break. I'd seen him a couple of days before, and we'd chatted. He'd mentioned that he'd moved into Marya's. That was a surprise—that he hadn't been living there all along. It wasn't that he'd invited me to stop by or anything. And it wasn't as if we were close friends at all. I'd been at maybe a half-dozen parties, mainly at Austin and Michelle's, where Barry had been. He was an interesting person. He'd actually hitch hiked, and he would tell stories of his trips thumbing. I don't mean hitch hiking a couple of miles, or maybe down to Bloomington. I mean long trips. He'd been all the way out to Arizona once. Austin once said that Barry had thumbed up and down the east coast There was a mystique to hitch hiking: a freedom, a severing of ties. I enjoyed listening to the stories. I figured I'd stop by and see Barry. At worst, he'd either ask me to leave or, if he wasn't at home, it was only a block-and-a-half back to the physical plant and I could party back in my room.

Buchanan let me out in back of Marya's and I trudged in, carrying my 12-pack. A tall, slender guy was standing in the kitchen, and I recognized him from campus working as a janitor. He fit into Marya's, with hair that was just brushing his shoulders. It was weird to see him here because DeForrest students did not mix with townies, much less townies who worked on the janitorial staff of the school. He was talking with a girl I recognized from one of my classes previous semester.

They both looked up as I walked in. He asked me what I wanted, not in any sort confrontational way, just asking me my business. When I said I was looking for Barry, the guy jerked his thumb towards a stairway and said, "Upstairs, second door on the left." I thanked him and walked on through as he and the girl continued their conversation. I wondered if one day I would look as natural talking to an attractive woman.

As I walked up the stairs, I could hear muffled music, some sort of heavy metal, coming from above me. As I approached Barry's door, I could tell the music was coming from there. I heard someone cough above the music, and I could smell the "sweet, sickening smell of burnt rope," the drug posters' description of the odor of pot. I knocked. The music was turned down. The door opened a crack and Barry peered out.

"Yeah?" he asked.

"Figured I'd stop by and see what you're up to," I said, feeling weird standing there in the hallway.

Barry seemed to ponder this for a moment, then opened the door. As I walked in I saw another guy who had lived in the dorms sitting on a couch against the wall. I introduced myself and we shook hands but he didn't say anything. I realized that I didn't really know Barry that well, or this friend of his at all.

"What's up?" I asked. Obviously I knew the answer to that. They'd just burned one. Their paranoia would have been understandable. A person that one of them sort of knew and the other one knew not at all pops out of nowhere to walk in with the scent of drugs hanging in the air.

My views on the subject of drugs had evolved from early youth and "Dragnet," Joe Friday standing there delivering a staccato lecture on !!!!!!!!!DRUGS!!!!!!!!! "Pot, weed, sticks, cannabis, Mary Jane, reefer. Different names for one thing. Dope. It gets you high. You want more. But one day that isn't enough. So you go on to some speed. Then maybe some downers," etc.—you get the picture. A lecture on marijuana delivered by an anally-retentive asshole who later died of cirrhosis due to downing a quart of vodka a day and chain smoking non-filter cigarettes. Horrors were committed against children by people smoking pot. I remember one episode where a couple was getting high and they forget that their baby was in the bathtub and Joe Friday goes in to find the kid drowned. Or another episode where a kid whose face was painted half blue and half yellow sat down to a healthy bowl of variously-colored pills to see how many he could eat. Then somewhere in there in my childhood the Beatles started acting weird. I'd believed in the Beatles in some ways. My world was turned upside-down when Sergeant Pepper came out. They grew their hair long and started hanging out with the Maharishi. I didn't know what to think. My freshman year of high school I did a paper and a presentation for civics class about drugs. I read up on the subject, and a couple of my classmates thought that I was talking from personal knowledge and experience. But it would be several years before I would be an active participant in the War on Drugs, a volunteer in the guerilla war that was being waged.

Drugs had been an important part of my transformation from a high school geek dressed in Sears mix-and-match double-knit polyesters, the transformation to whatever it was that I found myself to be now. Don't let anyone tell you differently. Drugs do constitute a cool thing to do—especially if your life is major-league fucked up before that. You get a really good idea that the people who are supposed to be "together" are themselves major-league fucked up and that there is some kind of truth beyond everything. I might not have had a whole bunch of answers to things, but I was far better off than I had been back there in high school. The irony was that, in high school before my transformation, I'd been so goddamn certain of things. Then, when I'd first gotten into this lifestyle, first started the experimentation, I'd felt odd. I was trying to adapt. One dickhead in my high school class called me a "plastic hippie." I felt that "label" was hypocritical and unfounded. But then I saw people who were like that. One guy from the frat, Stent, was overseas that semester. He was quick to tell you what a druggie he'd been in high school. I'd met him the previous year when I'd been over to the physical plant for a couple of parties. But the only time that I'd ever seen him smoke a joint, he ended up lying on the floor in the Third New hallway crying to his date—who was really bummed out—about having rockets on his shoes. And I smoked that pot. Like I fucking wish it had had that effect on me.

When Barry sat down on the couch, I sat down on the floor, on the far side of the coffee table. I set down the 12-pack and asked if either of them wanted a beer. Barry declined but his friend didn't, and that really seemed to ease things a bit. Why, I don't know. I mean I'm sure that if a narc knew that offering a beer would gain a bust, then that narc would walk around with a cooler full of beer all the time. The stereo was on but not very loud. I looked at the album cover leaning against the stereo. It was "Mystery to Me," by Fleetwood Mac, a cultish kind of band at the time. Their albums had not hit "mainstream" and to listen to them or to have their albums was a bit arcane.

"We were just going to smoke another joint," Barry's friend said. I said that that was cool and slugged down some more of my beer. I'd run out of pot, and everybody else in the physical plant was getting low, too. Barry pulled out a number and lit it up, then passed it to me. His friend asked me where I lived on campus and I told him. He nodded, like what did it matter.

"So when are you leaving?" Barry asked his friend.

The friend shrugged. "I figured Friday morning. Get some good traffic then, headed south."

Barry shook his head. "I don't know. The South's always bothered me. And with your hair as long as it is . . ." He let this last part sort of hang out in the air, then took the joint and inhaled.

"Where you going?" I asked.

"Down to Florida. I got a cousin down there right now, and I can kick out of a week of classes without any problem. I have a bunch of psych classes." That meant that there was no attendance taken and nearly everything on the finals would be from the book. "He's at Mexico Beach. It's in the panhandle. Not very commercial. The sand on the beaches is white, like snow, and as fine as talc."

One song on the album ended, and another one started up. It was just a drum beat in a weird rhythm with four notes and a rest, repeating several times. It was one of those weird things, where a song grabs your attention. Then guitars came in. The lyrics were weird. And I realized that the song was talking about Castaneda. Barry and his friend kept on talking while I zoned out. Towards the end of the song, the lyrics were really cool, and spoke of a place down in Mexico where a man can fly without an airplane over mountains, and that what matters most is the perceptions that one has when hypotized.

The pot was pretty good. I'd copped a quick buzz. When the song was over, I reached over for the album cover. On the cover was a color drawing of a baboon tasting something that was on its finger.

I was drawn back to the conversation. Barry was saying something about the Kentucky and the Tennessee cops not being that bad, but that the Alabama cops were real motherfuckers.

"Just fill up on gas before the Alabama state line," I volunteered, "and make sure that you drive the speed limit."

"I'm not driving," the guy said. "I don't have a car. I figured I'd thumb."

That hit me: standing next to a highway, with all of one's possessions in a backpack or some sort of duffel bag, heading to who the fuck knows where. The whole concept of it was so alien to anything I'd done or experienced up to that point in my life. Of course, the prospect of just taking off had pushed me to go away to college in the first place. I remembered riding in the car with Eva and Adolf one time, and for some reason the AM radio station in Kilkerry was playing "She's Leaving Home," from Sergeant Pepper's, and I was afraid they'd listen to the lyrics and realize what I was thinking. Thumbing had that same secretive I'm-sneaking-the-fuck-out-of-here-to-another-World kind of feel to it.

Barry went on talking about the cops. He said the Arizona cops were real bastards. One time when he was out West, an Arizona state trooper had pulled up to where he was standing at an on-ramp for an interstate. "It was rush hour in the early evening on a Friday. I was hoping to make really good time. Sometimes it's tough getting a ride at night. I thought maybe I'd get a ride from somebody splitting town for the weekend to go to California. The cop pulled up. Looked at my hair. Started asking questions. I had my ID out. Handed it to him. He started asking me about drugs. I just stood there, shaking my head. I never carry when I'm thumbing. Finally he gets out of the squad car. Makes me dump the contents of my pack out on the shoulder of the on-ramp. People are driving past staring. He's poking through my possessions. Just to hassle me. He detained me for something like an hour there. Radioed my name and date of birth in to the dispatcher. Had them checking on me while he poked through everything. By the time he was done and pulled away, rush hour was over, and I stood there waiting for something like three hours before I got a ride."

I hadn't thought about that aspect of it, being hassled by the cops. Barry's friend went on talking about getting rides at truck stops, and how long he thought the trip would take, then he bummed another beer off of me. Barry put on a different album, and I soaked up all they were saying about hitch-hiking. The guy from downstairs in the kitchen came in then and sat down. He pulled out another joint, and then he and Barry started talking about some guy named Mel as we passed it around.

"Yeah," the guy said. "He's coming through next week."

"Shit," Barry said. "I haven't seen him in like a year."

"Cut his hair off and everything. Got a job at some computerized steel mill."

"He always was a capitalist."

"Last guy I knew who paid his tuition to this place by dealing pot."

They went on like that for a while. The joint was roached. Another album was put on. I sat back and listened. The guy was an alum and yet he was a janitor at the place. He was obviously intelligent. Why would he still be here? I listened as they talked about life in the dorms of only about two years before, the year before I'd gotten there. The guy seemed to know everything about everyone. He even mentioned the names of a couple of guys who had lived in my frat.

Another album side was almost played through, and I figured it was time to leave. I thanked everyone, grabbed the bag that held my 12-pack, and walked carefully across the floor so as to not make the needle jump on the album.

The air was crisp, and the day was still overcast as it had been when I arrived. I knew my eyes had to be redder than shit. But the walk was a quick one, and soon I was in the physical plant, crossing the foyer and bounding up the stairs to my room. I really had to hassle with the door. I pulled one out of the 12-pack and put the rest of the beers in my fridge. By now it was 4:00. I heard Sid's stereo going. I walked across the hall and banged on his door. He and Criminal Phil were listening to "Meddle" by Pink Floyd. There's another group that was of cult status at the time. Again very obscure, very arcane. They'd had a major hit with "Dark Side of the Moon," released the spring when I graduated from high school. But the older albums were really cool. They'd originally been called The Pink Floyd Sound.

"You got any pot?" Criminal Phil asked. I just shook my head. He looked closely at my eyes and said, "Like hell you don't. You're fucking stoned."

"Just because I'm high doesn't mean I have any pot."

I told them where I'd been. About how much we'd smoked. I sat down. I knew that everyone was getting low on pot. I was out. And hell, if Sid was out then I knew that everybody had to be out. The album ended. Then I heard my name paged on the intercom. I got up and walked down the hallway to the little phone booth. It was the pledge trainer for the chapter at Loyola of Ohio. He said that their freshmen were going on their walkout and he wanted to know if it would be okay if they came to our house. I told him he'd have to ask the house president, that I couldn't say. I took down his number, scribbled a note to the chapter president, and left it on the dude's door. Then I staggered back to Sid's room.

We sat there, wasted, listening to tunes as the sky went from gray to a gathering of darkness for dusk. When it was almost time for supper, we headed downstairs and waited in the stairwell with everyone else. As usual, the housebitch was escorted past us and into the diningroom as the waiters announced the evening feeding. The paranoia that seeps into one's being when high can sometimes be significant. At this time I did not want to have to sit at the housebitch's table. In fact, I successfully navigated to the table farthest from her. As somebody said the prayer, I and several other of the frat's atheists stood impatiently, heads not bowed, waiting to dive into the food. And I certainly did that with gusto. We had roast beef, and it wasn't too bad. Add to that the starch of dinner rolls and the omnipresent mashed potatoes and I was able to fill my gullet for the evening.

The house president was sitting at the housebitch's table, as he always seemed to do at meals these days, and tapped his glass to get everyone's attention. We all stopped in mid-mastication to listen.

"I got a call from the chapter at Loyola of Ohio, and they're taking their walkout here this weekend." There were a few groans, a couple of laughs. "They're getting here Friday night. I figured that we'd just give them the Old Cold sleeping dorm to camp out in." He paused and looked down at the table. "Then next week we have a traveling secretary from International coming to see how we're doing." More groans. Somebody said, "Moronic jack-off." The house president looked around, an angry look on his face, to see who'd said it. I didn't know if the person had meant the traveling secretary or the house president was a jack-off. "Listen you guys, I'm serious about this. Having good relations with other chapters is the kind of stuff that International likes to see. We can score some brownie points doing this right." Still angry, our esteemed president sat down.

"They're taking their walkout here," Symington said. "Great—that means they're going to fuck this house up like our rookies do when they do a walkout."

A couple of people finished dinner and just stood up and walked out of the dining room without requesting permission to leave from the housebitch. A couple more did the same. So I joined in and headed upstairs. I saw Snyder heading up the stairwell to Second New, and I followed him to his room. He turned around, saw me, and mimicked smoking a joint. Ah! He had marijuana. So I went back to my room and grabbed a couple of beers.

TV had "Retrospective," the best of the Buffalo Springfield. He put that on and I grabbed the album cover as he rolled a doob. I didn't realize until right then who all was in the Buffalo Springfield—Neil Young, Stephen Stills, Richie Furay, Jim Messina. A couple of other guys not well known. Wow. What a cool group! There was another knock at the door and Sid and Criminal Phil came in. They must have detected marijuana-related activity. So it was a party. We got high listening to old tunes. At one point TV made a batch of popcorn in his ancient popcorn maker. The thing looked like it was made in the 1920s and constituted five or six fire hazards, but at least it was functional.

We sat there getting high. Eventually my eyelids grew heavy, and I almost crawled back to my room. As I crashed, I smiled to myself. Yes—I had gotten wasted on a Monday. Others had, too. This would be a nice little tradition.

I fell asleep thinking about a girl I knew in high school. The dreams were lucid and pornographic.

Chapter 13 - The Firing Of Farina And Frat Wars Continued

I was in the Hub when I first heard about it. The Daily DeForrest even came out with a "special edition" to cover it, an event that would turn out to be another one of those "epochal" events in my life. I was in the Hub with Austin and Michelle, and TV and TV's girlfriend, drinking a coke between classes when Sammy Taylor, the reporter from the paper, came in, all breathless and wide-eyed. He came straight up to our table and addressed everything to Austin and Michelle, whom he knew from Farina's classes. The rest of us were just sort of an audience.

"Farina got dinged," Sammy said. "The faculty appeal committee affirmed the decision of the department. Farina's gone at the end of this semester."

"Who was on the committee?" Michelle asked.

"Don't know," Sammy replied. "The membership is secret and their meetings were secret. Even Farina doesn't know who was on it."

"We have him next hour," Michelle observed.

I was pissed. I had hoped to take one of his courses. We sat there for a while, venting our anger. Technically it wasn't a "firing"—Farina had been denied tenure. But the university's rules were such that a faculty member had seven years in which to make tenure, or that person had to leave. This was Farina's seventh year. All around us in the

Hub people were talking of nothing else. Copies of the special edition were being passed around.

I got up and headed back to the fraternity—and by "fraternity," I still mean the physical plant. I walked up the middle of Anderson Street, wondering what we could do. Some sort of action was called for, but I wasn't sure what. As I crossed the gravel parking lot behind the frat, I decided that whatever was to be done, I wanted to be involved in it, and that the time to get it going was now. I struggled with the lock on my door. I tossed my books onto the mattress and then went down the hallway to the phone. I started calling people, friends and acquaintances culled through getting high. I had friends in every living unit except Omega Dickhead, and I knew quite a few people who were OIT. I got hold of twenty or thirty people. One problem we had was finding a place to meet. Trying to use a room in one of the university buildings was out. The university would allow only organizations officially "recognized" to use a room in that way. We didn't have an organization and, besides, we didn't want to tip off the administration that anything was going on, although they probably had a pretty good idea that something was going to happen. There wasn't a good place to meet in any of the dorms, OIT people lived in small apartments, and people in Greek houses didn't think that their brothers or sisters would tolerate hosting protest meetings. Apparently there was an image problem with that. But I figured our house was cool.

The first meeting was held that evening after dinner, after the dining room was cleared and cleaned. What started out informally stayed that way. I tried not to play chairperson, but I talked a lot, as did everyone. Austin and Michelle were there. So were Jillian and Cindy and their friend Patricia. TV and a couple of other guys from the house were there. We discussed alternatives, all pretty vague at that point. None of us had ever organized student protests. But each of us had read of such things, myself avidly. We'd been raised on healthy servings of student protest on the evening news throughout grade school, then junior high, and finally high school. Our clothing, our hair, our beliefs and our music had all been shaped by protests.

There is no specific point in time at which those events had begun for me. I know that it was after the Cousin worked in Goldwater's campaign for president in 1964, and after he'd bought the "Don't Blame Me. I Voted for Barry" license plate that had gathered dust over the years, never making it to the bumper of a vehicle.

The first protests were dismissed by Eva and Adolf and their contemporaries as being the work of crackpots and communists. Eva and Adolf, after all, had never questioned any role that the United States had taken in any war or military action. They didn't believe such protests could be homegrown. Eva had even abandoned the Democratic Party for good in 1952 when Truman sacked MacArthur.

Nationwide the protests heated up as I entered seventh grade. Discussions at school were not very sharp, not compared to what such discussions would later become. Most of my classmates were descended from long lines of hilljacks. In Kentucky, it was said, they taught the "three Rs"—readin,' 'ritin' and Route 31, the highway northbound out of Kentucky that carried people to the factory jobs in the factory towns of mid-north Indiana. Route 31 ran right through Kilkerry, and the car factories there drew many of the hilljacks. The men were lantern-jawed, long-armed and sharp-elbowed. The women were of a stocky build similar to that of good defensive backs. Our area's high school football teams had outstanding secondaries. The people never questioned the propriety of U.S. involvement in Vietnam. In fact, they favored it. Ironically it was from out of their class of people that many of the white people who served in Vietnam were drafted, although many of them outright volunteered. There were several satin jackets in our high school, worn by girls, that bore military insignia on pockets and backs—huge embroidered dragons with the names of Southeast Asia military bases. The girls were 15, 16, 17. The jackets were from their boyfriends or husbands, not their brothers.

Once the demonstrations really picked up in the late 1960s, I watched the national news every night for the latest riots, demonstrations, bombings, and especially college students shutting down their schools. In the back of my mind was the notion that one day, when I reached college, I would have the opportunity to be a part of demonstrations that shut down whatever school I attended. The firing of Farina posed just such an opportunity.

We knocked around ideas of what we could do, especially staging a strike. We set another meeting. No one was named as chairperson or head dude or anything; but of anyone there, I agreed to do the most—calling more people, making fliers to announce the next meeting the following Monday, and offering the dining room of the physical plant as a meeting place.

Once the meeting was over, Austin, Michelle, TV and I went upstairs to my room to get high. Austin still had a little bit left. We sat in my room and listened to the Harvard Strike album, a collection of tapes of live broadcasts from the student radio station. At one point the dean announces that Harvard Yard was to be vacated or else people would be arrested. People around or near the microphone are talking, shocked at the prospect of arrest. The four of us sat in my room, digging the whole thing. We were looking forward to confrontation on this level. Maybe I would see my childhood dream come true, and I would lead demonstrations that would shut down my college—too cool.

Against this backdrop I was still doing well in classes, and the bullshit of the frat wars had not lessened. In fact, the wars had heated up.

It didn't help that one of the seniors had called the housemother an illiterate slut. There were insults hurled back and forth between people. A couple of guys exchanged punches. And then the Loyola pledge class was on its way to the frat for their walkout.

They were supposed to arrive in the early evening hours of a Friday. At about 6:30 the house got the first phone call from a very drunk guy who wanted to know how to find Glendale. The guy that answered the call discovered that the guy was the pledge trainer for the Loyola rookies. Our guy asked where they were.

"Indianapolis."

"Then find I-70 and take it west."

"We've tried."

"But you were on I-70 to get to Indy."

"Yeah, but we got off of it."

"Do you know where you are in Indy?"

"A phone booth."

"Where's the phone booth?"

"Somewhere in Indianapolis."

So it went for about ten minutes. Finally, our guy determined that the Loyola people were somewhere on Indy's north side. Our guy told the Loyola fellow to take I-465 west, then south, and catch I-70 at about nine o'clock on the beltway around Indy. Fine.

About an hour later, the same guy called. Standifer answered this one.

"Where are you?"

"Same phone booth," the guy slurred, and then started laughing maniacally.

"Cars break down?"

"No. Ain't in no fucking car. We're in a fucking truck. And we been around this city twice and there ain't no fucking I-70 west."

It took a while for Standifer to calm the son of a bitch down. The Loyola guys had made two laps around Indianapolis on the Interstate. A lap around the city on I-465 is about 40 miles. Finally, someone else from the group, not that much more sober but more adept at understanding directions, wrested the phone from the pledge trainer. About an hour later, a big rental truck with a huge box for cargo came screaming into the gravel parking lot. When it came to a stop, the doors and the overhead door on the cargo section in back exploded open and, amidst empty beer cans clattering onto gravel, out rolled about a dozen drunken frat boys. They began whooping in joy over having reached their destination.

We had a keg going already downstairs in the basement party room. About 40 or 50 people were down there drinking and dancing. More were upstairs in rooms, getting high and listening to music. The Loyola guys staggered in, oblivious to the welcomes and greetings of our people. A few of them stayed downstairs for more beers and music and dancing. Most were so plastered they just went upstairs to the Old cold dorm, which had been set aside for them, and crashed in the bunks. All of them, though, were in ugly moods from being cramped all that time in the truck and they somehow—vaguely—blamed the guys in our house, either for bad directions or the way in which the interstate had been built around Indianapolis or for the location of DeForrest.

Their Pledge Trainer—PT—and another upperclassman with him apparently were people with whom I'd partied at their place. I didn't have a clear recollection of partying with them, but they certainly remembered me and hollered when they saw me, slapping my back and shaking my hand. I apologized for not being able to get them high as I was out of pot. Greg, the guy who wasn't the PT, said that was no problem and patted his shirt pocket with a grin.

I fought with the lock on my door, but this time, finally, it won. I could not get the thing open. The two Loyola guys were willing to break down the door for their ol' buddy from DeForrest. I declined the offer, and told them to follow me. We climbed through the window on the stairwell, walked across the roof, and climbed into my room through the window I had left ajar. They were laughing, but I was pissed. Greg pulled out a briar pipe and loaded it with what he said was "bomb herb." We smoked that and I put on "The Worst of Jefferson Airplane." They were staring at the graffiti-strewn walls and ceiling. My room's decor seemed to verify, to them, that I was insane. We got seriously fucked up. I followed JA with "Who's Next," and we smoked some more.

When my body shuts down and demands sleep, that shutdown is absolute and swift. I have about 15 minutes before unconsciousness. That kicked in at about the start of the third bowl. I told my guests that I had to pass out and escorted them to the window. They departed, chuckling over the means of egress. I crashed out for one more Friday night in college, on my mattress on the floor, empty or nearly-empty or nearly-full beer cans surrounding me.

By crashing early, I arose at 6:30. I'd forgotten about the door and tried to go out that way, but the fucker wouldn't give. I traversed the gravel-covered roof in my ratty-ass bathrobe. Nobody else was up as I walked downstairs to the kitchen. I loaded up on Cap 'N Crunch, my favorite cereal since I'd been a delegate from my high school, between junior and senior years, at the American Legion's Hoosier Boys' State. I read *The Indianapolis Star* to grab the right wing's views on the events of the day, chain-smoked Vantage Menthols and drank a cup of tea. I showered and dressed, then did my housework for the week. Once more I had the pleasure of cleaning the can—the john, the head, the restroom—on Second Old. The person we called the Mystery Zooker had struck again—i.e., someone had vomited all over one of the stalls and had been too drunk and/or inconsiderate to clean up after himself. I put on rubber gloves and cleaned. Benson, the house manager, checked me off. I was through with any housework for the day. Even if someone used a fire extinguisher on the bathroom—and that had been known to happen, although it carried a very heavy fine—I was done.

I went downstairs to the Informal and switched on the cartoons. I grabbed a Pepsi and replaced some more of the fluids and blood sugar I'd lost the night before. This was a dead Saturday. Except for the Loyola guys being at the house, nothing was going on. The Loyola guys didn't start rolling out until at least ten o'clock, hungover as shit. They all looked terrible, too. That basic death-warmed-over look from sleeping in someplace other than one's own bed: Bloodshot eyes, wrinkled, reddened faces, and your basic hair fuck—hair oily and in a crazy mess sticking out at weird angles.

By the time the first of them were getting up, the kitchen was closed, so a bunch of them got directions, piled in their truck, and headed to the Burger Chef on the edge of town. Glendale had an ordinance that prohibited drive-in restaurants within the town limits. McDonald's was fighting the ordinance. They wanted to put one of their golden arched cathedrals in yet another small town. Ronald McDonald *uber alles*. So far a group of DeForrest profs had been successful in blocking those efforts. The profs efforts were doomed. First, they had only one small-town lawyer walking from his office to the courthouse to file the occasional motion and attend a hearing now and then. McDonald's had high-powered firms from Chicago and Indianapolis at their beck and call. On the right signal, they could bury the courthouse in paperwork. Greasy Mac's attorneys were arguing that McDonald's is not a drive-in restaurant. Go figure. The other strike that was against the profs was the townies, who wanted McDonald's in their hometown. Burger Chef didn't have the greatest fast food in the world, so when the Loyola guys got back to the house, they were bitching about it. They were implying that maybe our chapter hadn't acted in the best way as hosts.

Eventually, one of the Loyola guys mentioned the word "beer," and they all realized that they were missing an important element of their walkout weekend. The PT was 21 and asked me for directions to a place that sold kegs. There was only one place in beautiful Glendale that sold kegs, and they only sold two brands—Stroh's if you got there early, Pabst Blue Ribbon if you got there late.

The Loyola guys dispatched a couple of their number to obtain a keg. The rest of them kicked back and watched "Johnny Quest," but that particular cartoon was too much of a strain on their intellects. They switched over to Moe, Larry and Curly. It wasn't long before their guys returned. The run on kegs had been hot and heavy already that weekend and, consequently, they returned with a pony keg of PBR. They were vocally indignant. They were even more offended by the fact that they had to send one of their number on a return trip to the supplier to rent a tap. For whatever reason, our house tap could not be found at that moment. I think our guys were not into the role of host house to these particular members of our national fraternity. Those negative feelings were understandable. There was some sort of ritual in which the Loyola people sought our participation. Something about singing songs of the national fraternity. That died a quick death with us. There was a pile of copies of a songbook titled "Songs My Brothers Taught Me" gathering mildew in a corner of the library in the basement. The closest any of those copies had ever gotten to being employed in the production of music, since I'd been around, was to prop up the corner of the table on which TV had stationed his stereo, to level it. And the Loyola guys kept asking about "choppers." I thought they meant motorcycles at first, but then I realized that they were talking about people—members of another fraternity. They made the people sound sinister, as though choppers were their worst enemies. The Loyola guys tapped their beer, and set the keg out on the front porch in the cold air of an Indiana February afternoon, right there for passing traffic and all the World to see. I didn't see anything wrong with the Loyola guys setting their keg out onto the front porch. Sure—alcohol was illegal on campus, but the policy was a tad bit hypocritical. I had never heard of any fraternity being "written up" by the University for an alcohol violation; just the dorms.

I went out and drew a beer for myself from the keg, at Loyola's invitation. They still viewed me as a "good guy." I went up the first flight of stairs and was halfway out the window to cross the roof to my room when Benson saw me, and came storming up.

"The Loyola guys have a keg," he fumed.

"Yeah, I know," I said, lifting my plastic cup. "I already got one. Thanks."

"That's against the rules."

"What?" I didn't think that I'd heard him correctly.

"Alcohol's against the rules below second floor. They will have to move that keg."

"We had quite a few kegs last night in the basement," I pointed out.

"That's different. That was in the party room. This is on the front porch."

"Why are you ragging at me?" I asked. "Go down and tell them yourself."

"They're your friends."

"They're not my friends. They're our brothers." I felt artificial and rah-rah. I hated that. The weird thing was, here our house was doing something of which, we presumed, the national fraternity would approve—hosting another chapter's walkout. But all of it was going badly. I looked at Benson and said, "You go down there and tell them what you've just told me. In the meantime, you're house manager. Can you fix my door so I don't have to keep entering my room through the window?"

He muttered something and something and gosh-darn. I mean, Benson not only believed there was a supreme deity, and not only believed that it was the Judeo-Christian deity, he also went to church every Sunday. So I had just heard him use the most extreme profanity he ever used. I turned and walked across the gravel on the roof, then climbed in through my window, being careful not to spill any beer. I put on Neil Young and sat down on my mattress. Then the window opened and the Loyola PT and his buddy came in.

"What's the hassle with your brothers?" the PT asked. I grated at the word "brothers," almost pointing out that I was an only child and an orphan. "We buy a keg and a bunch of people go ape-shit."

"They're saying that you gotta have it on a different floor or something."

"Okay. But they don't have to be dickheads about it. I felt like we were being busted by the cops."

"Yeah," the PT's buddy added. "This Benson guy acts like a real shithead."

Well, I couldn't disagree with him. All that I would have been able to say was that he was a dickhead in general, and not specific to this situation. I didn't say that, though, because I could sense that the whole weekend was devolving. Our guys were getting pissed off at them and they were getting pissed off at our guys and I didn't want to get caught in the middle. It wasn't like I was planning on transferring to their school and they were going to be close friends or anything. They got up and went out. I waited until I was almost out of beer, then I got up, pulled a screwdriver out of my makeshift beer-box desk drawer, and popped the hinges off my door. I set the door inside my little closet. I now had no privacy, but at least I didn't have to crawl across the roof to get into my room.

I went downstairs in search of the keg. It had been moved from the front porch to the stairwell landing between first floor and the basement. The tile floor was beginning to get wet. I went up to the Informal, where a couple of guys were watching a college basketball game. Ridgeway was sitting there, sipping a draft beer. I asked him where the Loyola guys had gone.

"They got pissed off. Went to the bars or down to campus or something." Ridgeway shrugged and stood. "At least they left their beer. Not bad guys on that account." He walked out of the room and into the stairwell. I heard him cuss when he hit the landing and slid on the puddle of beer.

The afternoon went further downhill. I went up to TV's room and got hammered. Then we had lunch in the dining room. Everybody was talking about what assholes the guys from Loyola were. At least the housebitch did not come down. One of the waiters fixed a tray for her and left the dining room to take it to her apartment. The friction between the factions in the house had increased. The house president sat at the housebitch's table— her seat was ceremoniously left empty—with his buddies, Benson among them. They talked amongst themselves in hushed tones. Something was going on.

I went back upstairs to my room with a pitcher of beer. The pony keg only held seven-and-a-half gallons, and I wanted to be sure to get as much as I could.

During the afternoon, the Loyola guys returned. They had met some girls down on campus. The girls, as it turned out, were on campus for a high school visitation weekend. There were probably a hundred or so high school students here for that activity. They stayed in the frats and sororities. That was one way the Greek living units rushed high school seniors. This was the first anybody in our house knew of a high school rush weekend. Apparently the university had chosen to exclude us from this activity. Anyways, the Loyola guys took the keg to the sleeping dorm, and set up a boom box they'd brought with them, and began dancing and partying. None of our people really cared, by this point, what the Loyola guys were doing, as long as they didn't bother us. One of the girls they'd brought back obviously had few cares or concerns, either. She had sex with four of them in succession, then walked around the sleeping dorm naked, trying to goad some of them on for more. At least that's what Ridgeway claimed, because he'd walked in right in the middle of things to bum some more beer. The Loyola guys were too preoccupied to notice Ridgeway filling up a pitcher from their keg. I believed Ridgeway, too. He rarely embellished facts. Besides, the next day, when several of us went upstairs to clean up after Loyola's mess, we found several discarded rubbers.

We had a party ourselves that night. Somebody ran over to Plainfield, a small town just west of Indy and the next closest place to buy kegs, and picked up a full keg of Budweiser. That was something of a delicacy in Glendale. It even required a special kind of tap. The stereo got cranked and people got a bit rowdy. Miraculously, by the time I headed upstairs to crash, the Loyola guys and our guys had not mixed.

The next morning I got up, showered, and went downstairs. The Sunday morning breakfast cook made my eggs nice and goopy, just the way I like them. I ate everything pretty quickly because I was starved, then I walked up to the Informal. Standifer was watching television. He looked up when he heard me walk in.

"They got them out of jail," he said.

I stopped and stared at him. "Who got whom out of jail?"

"The guys from Loyola."

"What were they doing in jail?"

"Public intox, disorderly conduct, disturbing the peace . . ."

"When did that happen?"

"When they went over to beat up the Lambda Chis."

"Why'd they do that?"

Standifer laughed when he saw the confused expression on my face. "They were talking about it all weekend. Going over and beating up the choppers. The Lambda Chis are their big enemies at Loyola, apparently. The Loyola guys came downstairs to our party about midnight. They wanted to know what we do about choppers here. Porter was the first one to figure out what they meant. He said we beat 'em up all the time and that the Loyola guys were wimpy shits if they didn't go over there right then and take care of business with those choppers."

"Oh no," I said. "Was anybody hurt?"

"Not any Lambda Chis. As soon as the Loyola guys left, Porter called the Lambda Chi house and warned them. The Lambda Chis ambushed the Loyola guys and beat the crap out of them."

"How'd the cops get involved?"

"Neighbors, I guess, called GPD. The Lambda Chis were smart enough to get the hell back inside their house. The Loyola guys were too drunk to realize what was going on. The chief of police called here this morning and said that they'd released the Loyola guys on condition that they leave town immediately and never come back."

"Lucky them," I said.

"No," Standifer said. "Lucky us."

And that was the story of the weekend that the Loyola chapter's freshmen took their walkout at our chapter. Ironically, the national wrote this down as a mark against us. The national was pissed because we refused to sing fraternity songs or stand up for our brothers from Loyola. Nothing was said about their dalliance with the high school girl or their arrest en masse while trying to commit battery. Oh—and we racked up points with the university, too. Even though no officials from the university had stopped at the house or anything, we got written up for a violation of university policy against alcohol—and not for the keg in the basement that we had, but for the pony keg that the Loyola guys had had on the front porch of the fraternity. The university placed us on "social probation" for the rest of the semester. What that meant, no one really knew. It certainly didn't interfere with our partying at all. But anyways, somebody had turned us in. We all figured that it was the housebitch. And, as it turned out later, those suspicions were correct.

Chapter 14 - Consisting Of Pure Intellect

I hadn't heard about it until two days before the event was to take place. How I missed it, I'll never know. But David Bowie was coming to Indianapolis.

Bowie at that time wasn't a superstar—well, maybe in parts of the Civilized World, but not in most of Indiana. He was a cult star, a lot like Fleetwood Mac, or pre-Dark Side of the Moon Pink Floyd, when they were doing things like "Pipers at the Gates of Dawn." Why Bowie would want to come to Indianapolis had me stumped. The reason certainly wasn't the size of the venue Indy had to offer. He was going to play downtown in the convention center's "big room." The big room held about six thousand people. The reason couldn't be that Indianapolis was some sort of oasis of hip culture in the middle of the prairies. The booking of Indianapolis must have been a last-minute development because we didn't hear about the gig until two days before it was to take place. The ads on WNAP talked about "having appeared in New York, Boston, Chicago, and Los Angeles, David Bowie will be live!" Then the announcer said "Indianapolis." Without the number "500" tacked on to the end of the name of the town, it just didn't sound World-class.

Bowie's popularity was weird. As soon as news of the concert hit, Austin and Michelle and Jillian and a bunch of others immediately made plans. I had some money, and I said sure, even though the price of tickets was outrageous. We had never heard of anyone before charging Eight-and-a-Half bucks for a concert ticket. However popular Bowie was in the dorms and among the people OIT, nobody in the frat seemed to take any notice. Maybe it was the style of the rock-n-roll that the guy did, the "glam" bit. Or maybe it was because of his androgynous image, wearing dresses and talking about bisexuality. I don't know. But I paid for my ticket and arranged to ride with Michelle and Austin in Austin's ancient Chevy Impala station wagon.

The day of the concert I ran into Mooter on campus. "Hey, man, gonna go to the concert?" he asked. It was nine o'clock in the morning and his eyes were already red and formed into slits from being stoned and smiling. I told him I was, and he smiled and shoved an envelope into my hand. "Check it out, later," he said.

I shrugged, shoved the envelope into my pocket, and headed back through the chill to the fraternity—and by "fraternity," I mean the physical plant, of course. I was pretty sure that whatever he had handed me was illegal. We're talking about Mooter, after all. I got into my room and opened the envelope. There it was—a small brownish bit of plasticene substance. It was windowpane, but not like I had done before. This was the infamous brown windowpane. I examined it carefully. It was slightly more than half of a four-way, I figured about two-and-a-half hits. I thought about matters for a moment, then figured I would do it for the concert.

After dinner, I got dressed and then took the acid as I was about to head out the door. I grabbed some necessities and started down the street to Austin's and Michelle's. The air was crisp and felt good. When I got to their little bungalow, there was a crowd in the living room. Austin's station wagon was a nine-passenger vehicle, and there were nine people going to the concert. So, as we all piled into the big thing, and I was wedged in between two people in the middle seat, I started getting off on the acid. I don't mean that I was kind of getting off on it, easing into the trip or anything. I was exploding. We started down the street, and I was just staring straight ahead, trying to focus.

Everybody was chattering away about the concert, and as soon as we were outside the city limits, somebody broke out a joint. It was passed to me, but I declined, explaining that I was tripping. There were a few chuckles, but that was about it. When smoke happened to hit me as the first joint was passed around and another fired up, I felt a twinge at the gritty smokiness of it.

Austin picked up speed gradually, the weight of the vehicle with its cargo of nine people being so great, and we hit 55. Then the back of the vehicle started this rhythmic swaying. I didn't want to say anything about it. Maybe there wasn't really a swaying motion. Maybe it was just me and the effects of the acid. I must have chuckled or something because a couple of people glanced at me with concern. Jillian asked me if I was okay, and I said yes. I didn't want to say anything about the swaying motion. If it was real, I didn't want to alarm them about the peril, and if it wasn't, I didn't want to alarm them about how fucked up I was.

And how fucked up was I, and not in any existentialist sort of way, I wondered.

I hadn't noticed the passing scenery, but I looked out to the left now, and saw that the bare branches of the trees were very delicately detailed into fine webs of limbs going down to branches going down then to the tiniest of twigs on the ends and then into space, seemed to blend into the atmosphere. Hmm. Concept there. Where did the tree end and the air begin?

Then we turned onto U.S. 40, the familiar "back" road to Indy. I must have chuckled again, because I got a few more Looks of Concern from others in the car. I smiled. It was a rigid smile, one meant to show that I was obeying societal convention. I was being polite.

But inside my head what was I doing?

I realized then just how badly I was losing it. I had to keep control! I tried to focus again on the passing scenery, fading as it was into darkness. The windows of the car were smudged here and there, where nicotine had coated them and somebody had pressed a finger up to the glass. I was paying more attention to the smudges, now, than I was the scenery outside. But maybe that wasn't scenery passing by outside? I thought. Maybe the windows were really all TV screens, and we were watching a program that showed sequentially, on different screens, starting with the big screen at the front, the windshield, splitting to go down the two sides of our little theatre, then ending in back with the glass over the tailgate. Now there was a concept!

I must have laughed again. Again more Looks of Concern. Someone asked again if I was okay, and I tried to say, "Most assuredly! Not a problem in the World!" But I couldn't talk very well, so I just nodded my head and chuckled a "yes, yes" like some sort of village madman.

I really realized then that I had to get control of myself. After all, what would my friends here do if I FREAKED OUT!? We were miles from home. They had shelled out all this money for tickets to the concert. I couldn't very easily ask them to turn around. But then again, I couldn't talk very easily. Once we were at the convention center, what then? Would I FREAK OUT in the midst of thousands of people? I could see it now, the police and ambulance attendants all surrounding me. The whispers about "drugs." Then I'd be shipped to some ER, then the mental ward of a large, urban hospital. Eva and Adolf would be called, and they would sit there, triumphant looks on their faces.

Man, what was this shit? I was getting into warped thoughts. I glanced around the car, but everyone seemed to be looking elsewhere. Maybe that was good.

I had to get control of my mind and the course of my thoughts! Or else I would go—what? Crazy? Is that the word I was looking for? I had to get control of myself, or I would go crazy. Yes, I would do that. Get control.

I thought about the concept of "control." What does it consist of? Nixonesque images arose in my mind of control freaks—people who were too rigid. Rigidity was not a good thing. I remembered the first time I had flown in a jet. I was with Adolf and the Cousin. I was about nine years old. The plane had hit some turbulence. I freaked when I saw the wing flapping out there. I thought it was a signal that the wings were weak or about to snap off and that we would go plummeting to our deaths. Then Adolf had explained to me, in an exasperated tone, that the wings were flexible, and that if they were too rigid, they couldn't take the stress that turbulence caused. Now here I was in a car, or a room with TV screens showing continuous images of passing, darkening countryside, and I was trying to adapt to my environment through rigidity, and that wasn't good.

I looked up again, and thought that a couple of people glanced away from me as I looked up, so as not to make eye contact.

"How are we doing back there?" Austin asked. Again I chuckled something. I don't know what it sounded like, but I thought that it was a reasonable facsimile for "okay."

I tried to get back into a "proper" state of mind, but I had a lot of trouble with that. What was proper and why was I thinking these things? Then I got pulled into a whirlpool, a fatal "circle of logic." I thought that, in order to maintain sanity, I had to maintain "control." I would feel as though I was rocking and repeating "control" as though it were a mantra. Then I would transform, in my state of mind, from that mantra and a semblance of control, into a wandering, and my mind would sort of drift, and I would think about things like reaching across and opening a door to see if we were really in a stationary room with continuous TV screens or if we were actually moving and — I would think, "I'm going insane!"

And then the whole circle would start again.

The deserted motels passed by, cars on cement blocks rotting next to cars only slightly better off in front of the doorways, the grass very bare. I continued in the circles, alternating between rocking with my mantra of control and sitting starkly and straightly up at the realization that I might be crazy. I was glad the acid had been free. I would hate to think I'd actually paid for the experience I was going through.

We then entered the outlying reaches of Indianapolis, then passed within a half-mile or so of the airport—Weir Cook Airport, I remembered. Traffic was heavier as we neared the downtown area. I blanked out into my mantra, then someone was shaking me, saying that we were "here."

I concentrated as I got out of the car. I slid across the middle seat there in the back and swung my legs out and stood. We were in the middle of a huge gravel parking lot. I thought it was unseemly to have an unpaved parking lot at the center of what promoted itself as being an urban area. There were huge parking lights spaced around the parking areas, giving off a pinkish chemical glow. People were moving toward the huge box-like structure of the convention center. The closer we got, the more everyone seemed funneled into the area ahead of us, doorways we would have to enter with the rest of the multitude. The sounds were weird, too, combining into a sort of communal hissing of feet and coat fabrics and talk and passing vehicles.

I noticed that, still, from time to time, others in our group were casting sideways glances at me. The person would not want to make eye contact with me. But I would catch their glance in my peripheral—or, as most Hoosiers say it, "periphial" vision. Then the glance would slide away, and the person would exchange a look with another person in our group, as if in a sort of agreement of "we're okay so far."

Austin was ahead of me, and he kept glancing back and smiling, and I could almost see the reflection of the lights from the parking lot on his teeth. I tried to smile back, but even now I'm not sure how successful I was in projecting a humanesque expression. Then we were passing under an awning or some sort of structure that shielded the 30 or 40 feet of cement in front of the front doors. The doors spread across the front of the building; nine or ten pairs of chromium/plexiglass things, very space-age looking. Beyond the doors, I saw ceilings 40 or 50 feet high it seemed, with chandeliers extending down. Then, as we shuffled along, I concentrated again. I had to get through this crowd thing in order to get into the concert. I shuffled along, only a foot or two at a time. We were that tightly packed, and nothing was moving very quickly for some reason. The closer that we got to the door, the more slowly we were moving. I twisted my hands into my jacket pockets, my right hand holding my ticket. Weird—I hadn't taken any special precautions to safeguard it, and here I had it at the right time!

Then I redirected my attention to the door. FUCK! The crowd was forming into six lines going through specific doorways. As each person reached a doorway and that person handed her or his ticket to an usher, two deputy sheriffs—brown uniforms crisply starched and menacing—examined the person. If that person looked "suspicious,"the deputies patted down that person. Once searched, the customer was free to go on through for the evening's merriment of anarchistic rock and roll.

Fortunately, I was so fucked up I didn't have the capacity to reflect on "peril." I was more in tune to the reflections of the individual lights of the chandeliers off the huge plate glass panes surrounding the entry area. I just shuffled along with the crowd. Then I was right behind Austin. He handed over his ticket, received the ticket stub back, then was patted down and passed on through. Then it was my turn.

As I stepped forward, I concentrated on each required movement. I pulled my right hand out of my jacket pocket and handed over the ticket. The usher didn't look up at me. She took the ticket, tore it in half, and handed the stub back. I took it, then shoved my hand into my pocket and moved on. I didn't make eye contact with the deputies. Ahead of me, Austin was looking back at me, a smile still on his face. Things seemed to slow down then. I heard someone to my right, then to my left, say, "His pockets. Yeah, check his pockets." As I took another step forward, someone grabbed my right arm and spun me around. I was looking straight into the face of a deputy. Both my hands were now out of my jacket pockets. I thrust my hands forward and said, "All I have is my ticket stub!" I stood there, a look of vindication—I was sure at that moment, although I'm not so sure now—crossing my face.

Then a weird thing happened. As the cops stood there, slowly attempting to decide what to do about this strange-looking, obviously drug-crazed hippie, I felt people behind me pushing me. They started propelling me down the hallway, through the rest of the crowd as others seemed to fold in behind to block the cops. I didn't recognized any of them. They just had surmised what was taking place and took charge of my rescue. We passed through huge doors and were now in the "big" room, where I rejoined my friends. They were standing in a small group in the aisleway behind the huge bleachers that had been set up for the concert.

Austin was staring at me, his mouth agape. "What the fuck happened?"

I smiled, and my brain kicked in, trying to help me formulate the words that constituted speech. I'm sure that I tried to stammer something about cops and the crowd pushing me away. Then Farris said, sort of smiling, "At least you weren't carrying any pot."

"Yes, I was," I replied, and started to reach down into my pants where I'd hidden it.

Austin grabbed my arms. "Don't do that here!" I looked up and everyone else looked alarmed.

Then somebody said, "Let's just find our seats," and the group headed around the end of the bleachers, a couple of them looking at ticket numbers and trying to figure out coordinates of section, aisle, row and seat. Since we had bought all our tickets together, all our seats were together. I just followed along, counting on the rest of our group to guide us. I was too busy watching people. The people were weird.

Well, people at rock concerts in the 1970s were weird in general. Bowie's fans, though, were thoroughly bizarre. I saw several people dressed exactly as Bowie was on the cover of "The Rise and Fall of Ziggy Stardust and the Spiders from Mars." There were a couple of people who had gone to the concert in the make-up and orange hair of Bowie on the cover of "Alladin Sane." There were a couple of people made up as he was on the cover of "The Man Who Sold the World." There was even one guy who had tried to put together something similar to Bowie's appearance on the cover of "Diamond Dogs," although minus the paws. Others had glittered themselves out or died their hair bright colors or worn outrageous make-up. I saw one guy who had made a sort of glitter business suit complete with a tie that had, spelled out in glitter running down, "1984."

We found our seats. They were floor seats, smack in the middle of everyone. We moved sideways past legs and knees and feet and sat down in the metal folding chairs. I finally took my coat off and sat on it so I wouldn't lose it. That would be just my luck here, to lose my only jacket. The others in my party conversed with one another, and I tried to listen so that maybe I could participate, but my mind was absorbing the weirdness. A lot of the people were smoking cigarettes, so the huge room had a layer of smoke hanging above it like smog over a large city. It made the room seem bigger.

I glanced at my watch a couple of times to see if time made any sense, but the hands were still meaningless. I wondered if anyone else was getting antsy for the thing to start. Then I heard murmurs of impatience around me, little bits and pieces of "what's taking so long" and "I wish they'd get fucking started." Then an old woman with no teeth sitting two rows and directly behind us yelled out in this bullfrog voice, "All right, goddamn it! Let's boogie!" And a bunch of people started clapping and I started laughing because she was right, yeah, goddamn it, let's boogie! Then as if on cue the lights went down and people started cheering.

At this juncture of a rock concert in the 1970s, people usually fired up joints and bowls and what-have-you, little fires springing up all over the venue, from matches or lighters. Tonight was no exception, but as that happened, a huge group of uniformed cops came into the room and started grabbing people near the aisles or on the edge of the floor seating. As the chords of a song strummed, people were being grabbed and dragged out of the place. Then the band really fired up and Bowie came out, everybody cheering. I wondered if anyone was watching what I was watching as the busts continued.

I turned my attention back to the stage. Bowie walked to the center, close to the front edge, and started into "1984." He was dressed in some kind of suit with shoulder pads built into the jacket. The way he stood there, with his legs apart and this real gritty determination, I got the feeling that he was the quintessential rock star. As he went through his song list, I sat there mesmerized. I wasn't all that familiar with his albums. I had listened to them but I didn't own any. One song became another and I just absorbed the sensations. I recognized "Suffragette City" from Ziggy Stardust, and I really got into that.

Everyone I was with was getting impatient with trying to see over everyone. Austin grabbed my arm and pointed to an empty section in the bleachers. Looking there I could see that the place wasn't sold out. Fucking weird. David Bowie plays Indianapolis in a venue that holds only six thousand people, and still doesn't sell the place out. I got up and grabbed my coat and followed, past the sea of legs and knees and feet, through the aisle and up the bleachers. Once we got up there and sat down, I was a hell of a lot more comfortable.

We had sat there for several minutes when people two rows in front of us lit a pipe and—Boom!—they were busted. Cops came out of nowhere and nailed them. One guy was slammed into the floor, his arms pulled way out behind him. I thought something had to have popped in his shoulder the way the cop had him. I started to lean forward to say something, but then Austin on one side and somebody else on the other side put me in like arm locks or something, and Austin said into my ear, "You'll just get busted, too." I leaned back, and by that time the cops were dragging the poor son-of-a-bitch away.

Then the concert was over. Just like that.

"What the fuck!?" Austin said. "He played less than an hour and a half."

Everyone in the "big room" seemed disgruntled. About half of the people stood and raised matches or lighters, the universal signal for an encore. None came. People started stomping their feet and clapping, but then the house lights came on fully, and an announcer said, "Mr. Bowie has left the building."

We shuffled down the bleachers and out with the crowds. I carried my jacket with the lining out so that a cop would not so easily recognize me as a person who had escaped their clutches. I realized I was in a lot better shape than I had been going in. Things in my head were calmed down.

We got to the car and joined the jam of traffic leaving the parking lot. Because we were near the back on the bleachers and most of the people had seemed to be crunched together in the floor seating, we seemed to be among the first getting out of there. I thought it was weirdly appropos that we drove by Central State Hospital, Indiana's primary insane asylum. The ancient steel fence surrounding the place flashed by and looked menacing. Soon we were cruising through the night, across the flatlands of Indiana on old U.S. 40, heading back to Glendale.

My brain had calmed down. I was no longer caught in the circles of logic. The music from the concert was rattling around too much. It's not that the acid had completely worn off. I was still tripping, but the peak was past. Now I was copping a good mellow acid buzz. Everybody in the car was quiet. Austin turned on the radio to WNAP. One of the deejays had been at the concert and was talking about what a gip it was for eight-fifty.

In order to get to his and Michelle's house, Austin had to drive by the good old fraternity —and by "fraternity," I mean the physical plant. So he stopped at the end of the sidewalk and let me out. I said goodnight and headed on up the walk, my hands crunched in my pockets. The lights from the windows cast weird glows of colors as I looked up at the building. I shrugged and went in through the front door, then bounded up the stairs. It was a Tuesday night, so the place was as quiet as it ever got. I reached my room and tossed off my jacket, then walked across the hallway to Sid's room. He and Criminal Phil were about to smoke a bowl.

"How was the concert?" Criminal Phil asked.

"Okay I guess. I don't know." I tried to explain to them about the ride over and the hassles with the cops and how short the concert had been and how everybody was getting busted. They looked at me incredulously. Then Criminal Phil said, "Yeah. Right. Sure."

They offered me a bowl, but I declined. I went back to my room and turned on "Harvest" by Neil Young, the first of a long series of mellow, coming-off-of-acid albums to which I would end up listening that night. I sat there with the lights out and listened to the music and, in between albums, I listened to the building hum. Finally I was able to go to sleep.

Chapter 15 - Evenings Crossing Water On Inflatable Shoes

That winter was cold. People went to keggers or, more often, partied in small groups in their own or friends' rooms on campus. That meant that people got into stereos and TVs.

Television was just emerging from its adolescence. I was raised on it. I loved TV. I watched it a great deal even before college. There was no cable in the Kilkerry area yet. I hadn't really heard of cable until my freshman year, when the dorm TV was able to receive WGN from Chicago. Eva and Adolf were still dependent on the TV antenna. When I was very young, their antenna was a simple thing four or five feet high attached to the peak of the roof. That antenna gave us reception for three stations—one for each of the network affiliates in Indianapolis—and, if the weather was clear or the atmospheric conditions were favorable in some other way, we could get Channel 4, the independent station out of Bloomington. When I was a kid Channel 4 was my favorite channel, because it carried Tarzan movies, Bomba the Jungle Boy, Clutch Cargo, "Superman" with George Reeves, all the stuff I really loved. Later, when I was in high school, they carried "W.C. Fields Theatre." Saturday nights meant Sammy Terry and his "Nightmare Theatre." Half the time I had to watch Channel 4 with a blanket set up as a tent enfolding the screen on one of the sets in the TV Lounge. That cut down surrounding light. Then I would watch "Tarzan and the Leopard Women" through a heavy snow effect on the tube. In 1966, Adolf, to his credit, tried to catapult us into a new era of TV reception. He actually paid somebody to come out and build a television tower. It was about 30 feet high, and the antenna itself would rotate, controlled by commands from a little box on top of the set in the living room. That gave us better reception of Channel 4—yay!—and got us snowy reception of a couple of UHF stations in Fort Wayne. The Fort Wayne stations constituted the real reason for Adolf's purchase of the system. He wanted to watch Kilkerry's team play in the Fort Wayne Semistate of the Indiana High School basketball tournament. The antenna worked okay for the Semistate—Kilkerry lost in an afternoon game and did not advance. The whole set-up functioned for a few weeks after that. During that period I remember staying home sick from school one day. That was rare for me, to miss school, but I was really sick. Anyways, I was playing around with the antenna and the channels on UHF. A primitive form of surfing, minus the remote. I was able to pick up the weirdest thing. It was a surveillance/security camera on a branch bank in Jeffersonville, Indiana. Jeffersonville is on the Ohio River, directly across from Louisville. I though that was pretty cool and watched it for a while as people walked in and out of the place. The fact that I did that tells you how fucking boring it was to live in the environs of Kilkerry. Not long after that the rotational control for the antenna malfunctioned. The basketball tournament, as well as Adolf's needs for the equipment, were over, and so, since repairs cost money, the system was never repaired.

Like I was saying, I rarely missed days in elementary, junior high and high school. It's not simply that I hated being at that house. It was also, to a degree, the fact that I would be cooped up in the same place all day with Eva. Not a pleasant prospect. Eva blocked out the day from 10:30 a.m. to 4:00 p.m. soap opera by soap opera. I have always hated soap operas. The only one I ever cared for was "Mary Hartman, Mary Hartman," and that was a spoof. I have always found those fucking shows to be extremely depressing and pointless. I remember what they were like when I was really young, around 1962, before the shows had realistic sets. They didn't have reproductions of living rooms or bedrooms or offices or kitchens or hospitals. As simple as such things are to make, I think the programs had to have been on tight budgets. The sets had black flats for everything. A living room would have black walls with a picture or a window frame hung here and there. For a new scene all that the techies on the set had to do was remove the picture, move the window frame to one side and replace the couch with a desk and there—ta da!—was an office. The characters and the story lines seemed to join with the blackness of the sets, of the void that was behind everything. Nor did it do any good to try and read. The television set was on and loud so that once Eva was through with her hours-long recitation of the rosary, she could hear the TV while she gossiped for two or three hours with Delores Pottman about the latest sexual peccadillos in the neighborhood. Once in a while, if I was lucky, I'd sneak over and switch the channel to reruns of the "Andy Griffith Show," but that was rare. Consequently, I stayed home only when I was extremely ill which, in my younger days, seemed to happen frequently.

In college, I'd grown accustomed to cable. There were far more choices in television programming—old movies, old reruns, the works. Staying home from classes did not mean that I was forced to watch the soaps. Eva wasn't there. I could smoke some hooter, drink some beers, catch a buzz and have some fun. In the evenings, if there was a particularly big television event—a presidential press conference, a major sporting event, the world television premiere of a James Bond flick—we all gathered in the Informal and enjoyed a communal thing.

If television was important, our stereos were absolutely critical. Music was one of the most important aspects of my cultural existence. I'd wanted to be in a band nearly all of my life. I had been in The Renegades in the sixth grade, and for a very brief time during the summer before my sophomore year of high school, I took part in an abortive effort to start another one. Somewhere in there, though, I'd given up on the idea. The lead guitarist of The Renegades had moved to another school district and the rest of us sort of floated away from the concept. On top of that, I think the people who ran the factories in Kilkerry paid off the music teachers in our school, trying to get the teachers to discourage as many people as possible from pursuing music as a field of interest. The factories didn't want their workers to be anything but culturally challenged. The factories did not want workers who think. I think the people who ran the factories also probably put something in the water. The people of Kilkerry could not have been that stupid and malicious naturally. Well, maybe, given the gene pools of Kentucky and Tennessee, one could explain the situation. Anyways, the main music teacher in our school was always hoarse from screaming in class. She would scream over the piano, scream in the absence of any competing sound, scream sometimes it seemed just for the sake of screaming. We were required to take music through and including freshman year. Once I had in my requirements, I never looked back.

Between my freshman year in high school and my senior year, I was very limited in music. Once I started getting high, though, music took on an entirely different—meaning? Texture? Feel? All of these and more.

I had not anticipated a new influence emanating from my stereo. By "new influence" I mean something that was coming out of the stereo that wasn't music or stand-up comedy. We were getting high in TV's room one evening, and he happened to mention the "Firesign Theatre." I thought he was referring to a campus group. TV said that no, he was referring to a group that did albums of some sort. I shrugged, thinking that this would be another set of albums of radio shows from the 1930s and 1940s. TV chuckled and put on "I Think We're All Bozos on This Bus." My life was changed forever in one more way. The album was about people going through an amusement park—they weren't called "theme" parks yet—consisting of holograms operated by computer. The name of the place was The Future Fair. Comedy was infused with drug-induced humor. I was hooked. It was wild because every time I played one of their albums, I gained a new insight or two into what they were doing. I was tripping the night I realized they had a character on one album place a telephone call to a character on another album. And I was really fucked up the night I realized that their album "Don't Crush That Dwarf, Hand Me the Pliers" was about that person's past, and that that album ended where "Bozos," the album featuring The Future Fair, would then begin. I had to have these albums. When I had spare money I bought "Bozos" and "Dwarf." There were three or four other albums of theirs that I wanted, and I resolved to get them. The upshot was that listening to Firesign quickly spread throughout the hippies on campus as more of us listened to Firesign. Randolph really got hooked. Soon our language changed to adopt Firesignisms. Cool.

Chapter 16 - Listening To Stereo And Traveling Through Time

Another one of those epochal moments occurred when I first heard music while high. My musical tastes had centered on Simon and Garfunkel, and Chicago, and maybe the Guess Who, and a lot of folk singers. And Tom Lehrer. I always had enjoyed listening to tunes and singing along with them. I'd even been lead singer of a band in sixth grade. We called ourselves the Renegades, as I said. I think we played like maybe four gigs. Our playlist included instrumentals like "Pipeline" and "Wipeout," the song with a constant drum roll. Really a bitch of a song for a drummer. We also included many of the tunes we felt—in our eleven-year-old minds—were classics. "Farmer John," "Gloria," "Louie, Louie," "Sweet Pea," and even one we wrote ourselves. I wrote the lyrics and the lead guitarist did the tune. We called it "Gertrude." Lennon and McCartney we were not.

The problem we had was locating a drummer. The lead guitarist and I both played snare drum in our elementary school "band," but the qualifications for playing drums in a rock and roll band were different. The main qualification was owning a drum "kit"—a full set of drums. We had a constant turnover in the position. We thought we finally had a guy. Both of his hands had been broken somehow, and he was three or four years older than we were. But he owned a drum kit and could make it to the gigs, even though he had obvious problems with "Wipeout," what with his hands being broken and all. The Renegades played their fourth—and final—gig at the party of a girl who was a classmate of ours. There was a cemetery nearby the party site and our drummer took a fairly long break with one of the girls at the party and the chaperones found out about it and we were all thrown together with the drummer as being bad influences, and so came the demise of the Renegades.

As the years passed and I took on the polyester threads of a dweeb, my musical tastes became more dry and mundane. Then my senior year of high school I got high. Man, did that ever do a number on music.

I would go out driving around on the old back country roads of our part of the county, getting high and listening to tunes on my 8-track. Once I got back to the Farm, I would spray the eyes with Visine to get the red out before walking through the living room past Eva and Adolf, go up to the room I shared with the Cousin, and put on the headphones of the AM/FM/shortwave radio I had. I would tune in WLS or WCFL in Chicago, both of which came in more clearly than the Indianapolis stations, and tune out the world.

Once I got to college, I was exposed to a lot of different rock and roll. One guy down the hall from me in the dorm was the son of a sergeant in the Army, who had been stationed in Germany. The guy had a couple of hundred cassettes of different weird European and Japanese bands we had never heard of. Guys from other parts of the country, too, had tapes or albums of regional bands the rest of us had never heard of. Then there was the larger body of music I'd not been exposed to, "mainstream" rock bands that everybody else knew about but I'd not yet discovered.

I would listen to the stereo with other people, but then I also would get really fucked up and sit in my room alone, as I'd done at the Farm there right before coming to college. A lot of times I would listen to the music and the words and sit there a bit transfixed. I would try to pick apart lyrics—understanding some rock and roll lyrics as they are sung is always a challenge. There were some songs, of course, that were easy to comprehend. But going back to the days when I sang "Louie, Louie" and "Wooly Bully," I knew the task was not always easy. Today I still will hear a song on the radio and realize, for the first time, what a specific line was. It was always a help to have liner notes or some fold-out that had the lyrics printed out. A few times I read in reviews of albums that did this that the artists were trying to be taken as "serious." I didn't think that was necessarily the case. I just thought the artists were trying to be helpful. Anyways, I would think about what was said in the songs. As I did so, my love for headbanger music diminished. Uriah Heep's songs about wizards and such were no longer "deep" in any way, although the tones of the chords sounded rather good when one was high.

Then came times when I wouldn't listen to the songs for what they said, but to imagine myself being a rock star, singing the parts of the song in question; or playing whatever instrument was to be played—guitar, of course, was a frequent choice, but piano, even sitar or xylophone—don't forget "Under My Thumb" by the Rolling Stones—could be played in "air" simulation. They could definitely be played in one's mind. And so I would sit there, imagining myself in some venue playing whatever hit was in question.

But something was missing. I would sit there imagining singing these songs, but they were—covers. In other words, in these mind gigs, I would be playing songs originally done by other bands, just like any other Holiday Inn lounge act roaming the midwest. Somehow such gritty realities weren't very appealing to me sitting there, so I would try and come up with some way of accommodating these problems into the way I would drift off listening to tunes.

Eventually, I came up with the concept of being able to travel back in time, to a point before the song or body of songs in question had been written. Somehow I would acquire the ability to play the musical instruments necessary—but that question became easy after a while. The guitar was the essential instrument. The piano was nearly as important but hell, as much as I'd read Lennon and McCartney talk about learning the various aspects of the guitar, neither of them had commented on learning how to play the piano. Learning to play the organ was an adjunct to the piano. I developed rules as to how I could acquire the songs in question. I couldn't just "rip off" songs from people whom I respected, and I didn't really like songs by Pat Boone or the Carpenters or Jay and the Americans, so the question of taking those songs by traveling back in time was moot. I had a rule. I could not purloin more than two songs from any one group by traveling back in time. That pretty much knocked out taking songs from "one-hit wonder" groups, because that would be denying them any claim to whatever fame they'd achieved. So like I could go back and arrive in 1966, during my sixth grade year. I would teach the others in the Renegades the words and chords of, say, "Sympathy for the Devil" and "Brown Sugar." Yeah. Play those at that "fall festival" in the elementary school. Sure. Or play "Stairway to Heaven" and "Whole Lotta Love" my junior year of high school. Well, you get the picture.

There were a couple of other rules, the main one was that I could not purloin any music by the Beatles. Period. They were unassailable. The other was that I would never flag in my use of drugs as I performed these songs.

Chapter 17 - The Semester Chugs On

Things quieted after the Loyola fiasco. Something was going on—the house president was talking with the house corporation and the national fraternity. Everybody knew that. It was just that nobody knew exactly what was being said. Sure, bitching about things in the house was understandable. The question was—had any "plans" been developed concerning the rest of the house membership? Other houses on campus had gone through "splits" before. The Delt house seemed to purge itself of half of its membership every year. That would be a hassle if it happened in our case. People would have to scramble around to find an alternative place to live. I didn't want to do that. I liked the frat. I just didn't like the bullshit.

My classes were going well. I had a borderline A/B in speech pathology, a borderline B/C in ed psych—quite an achievement, considering it had the weird multiple-choice exams, tests that were more exercises in testing theory than gauges of substantive knowledge of the course material. The prof didn't impress me as being a deep thinker. I had a solid B in con law. And I had an A in political and social philosophy. I still had to work hard, but the goals of a 3.5 for the semester, and making dean's list, were still quite feasible. Even if I missed the 3.5, but came close to it, I had an excellent argument to the financial aid office that the first semester that year had been an aberration, and that I deserved to keep my scholarship for one more year. I was sure that if the university was on my side, then the bank, and its interpretation of the terms of my parents' trust, would be as well.

The Farina matter was in its formative stages. We had another meeting set for a Thursday, again in the dining room of our frat. The talk was of a strike. We were trying to get more people involved. The irony was that the student election campaigns—for student body president and academic council chairperson—were going on right then, and none of the candidates was addressing the issues of academic freedom or the denial of tenure to Farina. They were focused on grasping the brass ring of elected student office so they could pad their applications to law school. So the one formal structure into which the students had the most effective input—student government—was one place that was void of any discussion about the most burning issue at the university.

One afternoon, I got back from classes and, walking across the parking lot, I saw Roach's car parked next to the fraternity—and by "fraternity," I mean the physical plant.

During the 1970s, everyone knew at least one person whose nickname was "Roach." It was nearly a statutory requirement for college students. The Roach that I knew was one of the first people I'd met when I had visited DeForrest that fateful weekend second semester of my senior year in high school. I had arrived at DeForrest on a Friday afternoon for an admissions conference. The campus was crowded. I had trouble finding a parking place. I checked in with the proper registration people and attended the welcoming ceremony. Each high school senior was assigned to a Greek living unit of the appropriate gender. We could see up close what the university experience was all about. For me it was two fun-filled days of partying before I returned to Kilkerry. That weekend sold me on DeForrest, especially at one point, when I looked across the Dells at one of the old brick dorms, and the place looked so Eastern, as if it were cut from the pages of a Fitzgerald novel. I drew, as my house assignment, the frat in which I would later live. Roach was a freshman at that time, and he was one of the guys I partied with.

Ah! But the previous semester of my sophomore year he had flunked out. Maybe it was because he and Sid had been roommates. Or that his room had been next to the one in Third Old that Criminal Phil and I had split. Third Old only had four rooms, and ours were at the end of a dismal little hall with no means of egress. It had been almost like an opium den from Sherlock Holmes. It was great. But it wasn't great for GPAs—either Roach's or mine. After finals, Roach knew the bad news and packed up all of his possessions into his Monte Carlo and headed back home. His plans were to transfer to I.U. in Bloomington. Then he could either graduate from down there, or work his grades back up to the point where he could transfer back to DeForrest.

When I got up to my room, I heard the music from across the hall and knew Sid and Roach were partying. I dumped my shit into my room and knocked on Sid's door.

When the door opened, a cloud of smoke enveloped me. It was the sweet smell of hemp, so rare the last few days. Roach was ready to do a bong and waved to me. Sid chuckled. I sat down and waited my turn.

A rift had developed between Roach and me the previous semester. Maybe it was the daily exposure we had to each other. I don't know. But it seemed to be gone now, and when he handed me the house bong, I took it. The smoke expanded in my lungs, there was a tickling sensation at the back of my throat, and I coughed as I handed it back.

"When'd you get in?" I asked after I recovered.

"I've been on campus since this morning. Got into the house about a half-hour ago."

"You didn't waste any time," I commented, nodding at the bong, and Roach smiled. "You into I.U. yet?" The question caused Roach to frown a bit.

"Fuck no. And I'm not gonna. Went down there a couple of weeks ago to talk about transferring in. They were only gonna let me keep about a third of my credits. I woulda been starting as a second-semester freshman. The woman in the admissions office was lecturing me about what a fine fucking school I.U. was. Like I'd been going to some ditch-water place. Fuck them." By now he had another bong loaded and handed it to Sid. "I talked to the dean here." By "dean" he could have meant any one of half-a-dozen people, but I let that slide. "He said if I sit out this semester, I can come back in the fall. I'll be on academic probation, but if I get my GPA up to a two-point, I'm okay."

"You gonna live in the house?"

"Fuck no," he said. By now the bong was back to him and he took a hit, balancing the bong on one knee while he held the flame from the butane lighter to the pot in the bowl.

There was another knock at the door, and this time Criminal Phil came in. He had a 12-pack and passed beers around, saying hello to Roach. Roach handed the bong to him and he gratefully accepted it. Then another knock and in walked Tom Feldman. Not a minute later Ridgeway knocked on the door, as did TV shortly after that. The scent of cannabis was wafting through the fraternity and drawing people to Sid's room. We ran out of chairs, so people started sitting on the floor. We ran out of beer, so somebody made a run to the liquor store.

Roach told us about life back in his hometown. He was working for his uncle's construction company, making good money, and spending most of it on partying. He was the only child of an affluent family, so he had no concerns about tuition money for his return to DFU. Sid changed albums to "Stop All That Jazz" by Leon Russell. The tones were very clear and mellow on Russell's keyboards. I was extremely stoned and watched the clock on top of one of the speakers. It was a digital from that crack in time between the dominance of round faced clocks and the lighted electronic display things that came to dominate the telling of time. It consisted simply of tiny cards mounted on wheels. As each minute passed, the card would flip over to the next minute, from :07 to :08 and so one.

Every hour the number for that portion of time would click over. Very primitive. I began to wonder about peoples' concepts of time. Until now, time had always been told in a circular form. The clock face was round and whole. It bore the one-ness of a circle. Everything was part of a cycle. Twenty-four hours and the next day would begin at the same starting point. The Earth rotated at the same speed as the clock! Everything was in synch! Then digital clocks came in. Everything was linear. There was never closure. People had no holistic . . .

Ridgeway was shoving my knee. "You got a phone call," he said above the blare of the stereo, and I nodded quickly that I understood and walked out into the hallway to get the call. When I got to the phone booth, my name was announced over the intercom again, and I looked back toward Sid's room. The smoke hung outside his room, heavy and fragrant. I chuckled and turned to the phone.

It was Austin. He was calling to update me. Apparently some of Farina's students, people who had him as an adviser and/or been in a lot of classes, had heard about the meeting we'd had and the one that was coming up. They were going to be there. I told him that was good, but his tone was rather strange.

"Jimmy Natas is in the group, used to be president at one of the men's dorms."

"Yeah," I said. I remembered him, a real face man. His was the kind of visage that sells cigarettes and all sorts of things. That was about all I knew of him.

"I just thought I'd let you know," Austin said, as though warning me. But I was too stoned to really care and just blew it off. He asked me what we were doing and, when I told him, he said that he and Michelle would be right over. It was almost as if the smoke was now wafting out of Sid's room, out into the open air and down to campus, drawing people to party.

I went back to Sid's room and wedged my way into a spot on the floor. I asked Roach if I could bum a joint from him, and he said sure, pinching off a good amount of hooter and placing it in my palm. Everybody watched him as he did that, and I have no doubt that in the next little while he was hit with many more requests. I thanked him, grabbed the 12-pack I'd gotten, and walked back across the hallway to my room. I nearly bumped into the house president as he walked past. I said hello and he grunted. I was surprised he didn't walk into Sid's room and party. He and Roach had always gotten along. Roach had even voted for the guy the previous semester. But the house president just walked on down the hallway, to the stairs and down. I shrugged and walked through the open doorway to my room. I put on an album and waited for Austin and Michelle to arrive. I was not long in waiting.

There was a knock at my doorway, and Austin stuck his head in, a grin spread across his face. He stuck out a bottle of Yago Sangria, a favorite wine of his and Michelle's at the time, and came in, Michelle close behind. I grabbed a couple of glasses and he poured.

"We smelled pot coming up the stairs," he said maniacally. "Where is it?" I pulled out my frisbee, the seeds and stems already sorted out. I grabbed the little bowl I had and loaded it, then handed it to Michelle. "I was serious about Natas," Austin said. "He's really a control freak."

I was nonplused. "Yeah?"

"I mean—watch him."

"Okay," I said, still unclear about what he meant. Natas hadn't been to the meeting, hadn't done anything, really, about the Farina issue or affair or whatever. And he'd been in

Farina's classes and had plenty of opportunity to do things. Hell, he was a senior. For that matter, very few students had done anything at all in the year that the events had transpired.

Austin now took the bowl as Michelle flipped through the albums. When the last song playing was through she handed the strike album to me and asked if we could listen to that. I said sure.

Listening to the album was weirdly in synch with what we were experiencing. A strong baritone voice-over talked about the 1960s and the unrest and upheavals that had occurred at Berkeley and Columbia. "But not Harvard," he said. Then came the heart of the album, recordings from broadcasts of the Harvard student radio station. Austin and Michelle and I sat there, our puffings adding to the haze of smoke that was escaping from my room and out into the hallway. There were four sides to the album, and we listened to all four. The thought of shutting down the school seemed real. We could actually do it. Maybe we could even keep Farina's job for him. When the album was over, we sat and shot the shit for a while as I looked for another album. "Have you ever read *The Strawberry Statement*?" Austin asked. I shook my head. The album covers sort of blended together and I had a rough time focusing. "It's about the 1968 strike at Columbia."

"The Cousin visited there," I said.

"Where?" Austin asked.

"Columbia. He went out there on a student bus trip like in '67 or something. He wrote to them for a bulletin. Thought about going to grad school there. Like—fat chance."

"You oughtta read it. It's pretty good."

I asked Austin if he had a copy, but, as was true with any reading materials of the counterculture that passed among us, he had had a copy, loaned it to someone, and then it had disappeared.

Michelle had been sitting there for a while, staring at the walls and ceilings. A lot had been added since their last visit. People had been expressing themselves to the max in dayglo colors—and I still had paint left.

The afternoon ended with the call to supper. Michelle and Austin got up and said good bye. I went downstairs with them and turned into the dining room as the last of the members of the fraternity were taking their seats. As I sat down, the president of the house tapped his glass with a spoon. Everyone quieted down to listen to what he had to say. Probably for the last time.

"Somebody's been smoking pot in the house this afternoon," he said, and about got drowned out by laughter and ridicule. He tried to add something about the image of the frat down on campus, and stuff like that, but nobody could take him seriously. If someone had made a similar pronouncement the previous semester, he would have been as vocal in ridiculing that person. We just started passing the potatoes and roast beef or whatever it was we were being served, and mowed down, oblivious to what he was saying.

After dinner I went back up to the Informal and watched the news. The stock market had closed eight points up that day due to some unfounded rumor. Ridgeway, whose father was a broker in New York, said, "The market closed up—my old man's getting drunk tonight."

The rest of the news was about the impending fall of Vietnam and the recent fall of Cambodia. Cambodia had been really weird. The government had been so corrupt that generals and colonels overreported the numbers of military personnel in their units so they could collect the pay, from the American government, to the ghost "troops." That would not have mattered, were it not for the fact that in planning the ensuing military operations, the American generals based their actions on troop strengths that were eight to ten times more than actually existed. This sore point of managerial accounting was lost on the American military supervisors until the Khmer Rouge had nearly finished their eviction of the American-backed regime and begun their genocide of millions.

Among the magazines and newspapers that lay strewn on the huge, square coffee table was the latest edition of the national fraternity's magazine. I flipped it open for yuks. There were the usual ads for various items featuring the fraternity crest and name and symbols. There was a letter from the national president, although the national always referred to itself as "international" thanks to two chapters on campuses in Canada. There were sections describing the fundraising at the various chapters, and the latest events occurring there. Our chapter did not have a mention under anything. I smiled when I realized that. Then I saw the guest column. Some old fart of an alum from another school wrote about "true individualism." I thought that was interesting in the context of a communal effort such as the national. A couple of sentences into the article, I saw where the guy was going. He decried the "fake individualism" of people "doing their own thing" and "putting self ahead of everything else." What he called for was a return to "true individualism," a system of beliefs where the individual knuckled under and toiled for the group cause. In other words, his "true individual" wasn't an "individual" at all, but just somebody following the herd in knee-jerk style. It had been that way all through grade school and junior high and high school, too. The stories that were taught would extol virtues of standing up to the crowd and obeying an inner voice that said that something was wrong. Like Rosa Parks refusing to sit at the back of the bus—although we were never taught that lesson in my school, since that involved "coloreds." No matter how virtuous the hero or how compelling the story, when it came to actually acting, the people who taught these things hit the brakes and said no. The thing to do is go along. This guy was even bastardizing that sentiment and calling herd mentality "true individualism." And this guy was a college graduate?

I got up as Ridgeway was telling about his latest conversation with his brother— his real, biological brother. He was at school at Washington and Lee, and he and the guys in his house had gotten drunk and thrown a piano out of the third floor window of their fraternity. That sounded pretty funny. And hey—we had a piano in the Formal Living Room of our frat.

Chapter 18 - What A Wonderful Night For A Party

In the days before lawsuits had rendered dangerous the concept of a fraternity holding parties in where alcohol was consumed, the frats on campus had keggers and parties involving mixed drinks on a pretty frequent basis. The tableau of each frat's parties was different. At one house, known for being a "jock" house, the reports from campus were that the guys would be on one side of the room and the women would congregate on the other side and interaction was rather weird. No latent homosexuality there. No sirree. At most of the houses, people got pretty trashed in a basement party room while the cranked stereo belted out party tunes from a tape usually put together that afternoon. Everyone would risk fractured limbs dancing while the spilled beer spread. The place would usually be packed from about ten until one or two in the morning.

My freshman year, our house had been known for "feel good" parties where everybody danced and had a good time. They were the types of parties that parents could have attended and the reputation of the house would have been none the worse for wear.

The parties drew women from about every sorority and the Freshman Quad. But 17 seniors had graduated the previous spring and the main contingent of "feel good" partiers were in that number. They had been replaced by us—people who had a little bit different idea of what constituted a good time. There were still hold-overs from the days of yore. The "feel good" period had, after all, been only the year before. But one year had made a serious difference in the attitude towards parties. There was more of an edge to the parties. Things were a tad bit more dangerous. The feeling was that, at any given time, anything could happen. Also, there was a pretty good-sized contingent of people in the house who would pay their respects at the party downstairs, then grab a pitcher of whatever was being served and repair upstairs to their or another person's room and party to the stereo and many bowls of pot. Perhaps this lent a bit of an antisocial element to the party as well. There was just a good number of people in the house who didn't like the false airs of the usual frat party—putting in face time, talking trivial shit. People would rather have been upstairs consuming dangerous drugs, listening to music and maybe getting laid by their date. As a consequence, the number of women attending our parties had declined somewhat. The women from the "best" sororities very rarely came over. They were usually at the parties at Omega Dickhead or one of the other "better" frats, lined up on one side of the room and the guys from that frat lined up on the other.

Things were still tense in our house. Some people did not speak to others. The housebitch had ceased coming down to meals on the same day that several of us had decided to start a food fight and nail her dyed hair and wrinkled face with mashed potatoes and whatever else was lying about handy. Somehow word must have gotten to her, because she hated to skip meals. From that point on, though, we never saw her in the dining room again. House work on Saturdays was done willingly by only a few. I was among them because I didn't want any hassles from anyone. I usually cleaned the bathroom in Second Old, and I didn't mind doing that. Maybe it was because of the grossness of the toilet back "home" at the Farm. The fact that I did that work held me in good stead with the "powers that be." Overall, though, the atmosphere in the house was something like that of a war zone where a battle is about to be fought. The birds and animals have all flown, scurried or slithered away to abandon the countryside to the combatants.

In this atmosphere, some genius decided that we should have a hairy buffalo.

Some parties featured keg beer: sloppy but fun and predictable. Other parties featured mixed drinks—Saturday mornings before football games in the fall, Bloody Marys or Screwdrivers would be served. Hairy buffaloes, however, meant a crazy time. A tad bit twisted, a tad bit bent.

The concept was simple. The social chairman would buy a cheap, new trash can and place a plastic liner in it. Into that would be dumped a bunch of ice and a shit-load of cheap mix—fruit punch or red Bev-Aid, the cheap substitute for red Kool-Aid that was always available in the dining room. Then each member of the house would dump a pint of booze into the mix. The pint could be anything. Vodka and gin were favorites, if only because they were usually the cheapest concoctions available. But anything would do, as long as it wasn't beer or wine. So the mix would have scotch, bourbon, sloe gin, schnapps, tequila—you get the picture.

I generally liked parties that started earlier in the evening. When they started late, I was usually leaning toward bed time. On this evening I had consumed a couple of hits of speed. I was ready to party into the wee hours of the morning. I was wound up enough and was looking forward to a good time.

The party started at about 8:30—pretty early. Guys from the house arrived in the party room downstairs with dates or by themselves. I'd bought a pint of really rot-gut vodka, a brand that was very popular that evening because it had been on sale at Eastside. Once there was enough alcohol in the can, we started consuming the stuff. I sat off to one side sipping it, talking to a couple of women who had arrived from Candace's sorority. They had been in one of my classes the previous semester, and we talked about various bullshit.

I went upstairs a couple of times to get high. Sid had about half-a-dozen people in his room, everyone doing hits on the house bong. They were working through an evening of Traffic. There's a clear line of demarcation in the history of Traffic. Before Dave Mason and after Dave Mason. This was all post-Mason: "Shootout at the Fantasy Factory," "John Barleycorn Must Die," "The Low Spark of High-heeled Boys." Walking down the hallways of the Second floor, both Old and New, one was hit by a dozen different stereos playing in that many rooms, and under the light of the fluorescents, there was a haze that seemed to hover a foot or so from the ceiling.

When I went back down, at about 11:30, the party was getting a little bit weird and twisted. Rudolf was knocking down drinks at a fairly brisk clip and talking fairly loudly about the "other" faction, whose members were largely absent from the Bacchanalian celebration. "Altamira," a song by the Edgar Winter Group from their album "They Only Come Out at Night"—the most famous song from which is the immortal and instrumental "Frankenstein"—was sort of a house song. It was to this song that several people from the house usually would go out into the middle of the room and dance what was called the Dirty D. That night, however, nobody got out into the middle of the dance floor as they usually did. People just stood around. A few moments after the song ended, Jones came down the stairway, but he wasn't walking. He was riding a bicycle. He almost ran over two people sitting on the stairway. Everyone got a hearty laugh out of harmless fraternity highjinks.

It was along about that time that the drugs began twisting me around. I decided to go upstairs and paint my face in day-glo colors a la "The Electric Kool-Aid Acid Test." It seemed a good idea at the time. The paint job took a good 20 minutes. By the end of it, I looked into the mirror in my room and admired the weird face looking back at me. I had covered every square inch of exposed skin above my jaw line and in front of my sideburns. There were blue stripes across my forehead and yellow wings traversing my nose. My jaw was painted in orange in a pattern that was mechanical. I thought it looked fine and fit into the weirdness of the evening. However, when I walked down to the party, people either ignored me or looked at me as though I were crazy. Jones, he of the recent bicycle-down-the-stairs fame, came up to me and advised me to go upstairs and wash it off, that it looked rather strange. I was tempted to tell him to fuck off, that a person who rode a bicycle down a stairway wasn't exactly in a position to criticize anyone else for being weird. After all, what I was doing at least had roots in a recent literary work. But I didn't say anything at all, except okay. I hadn't realized that the fucking paint, when left on for a while, would start burning like a son of a bitch. So I went upstairs and washed my face with soap and water. Standing in a room later that had a black light, my skin shone in spots fluorescent.

It was toward one o'clock that the incident occurred. Streaking had been "in" the previous year. Jones thought it would be funny to streak the party. He had done it once or twice before at parties. The previous year it had been the thing to do once in a while. Nobody ever complained. Jones came running down the stairway, naked except for a ski mask, took a lap around the room and everyone had a good laugh. Ha ha. Then he pulled off the ski mask, and that was a bit of a humorous touch. Ha ha ha. More laughs, not as heavy but still there. He stood near the trash can, having stopped to speak to Buchanan. That would have been that. In five seconds he probably would have gone back upstairs to his room and gotten dressed and the whole thing would have been over. The party would have continued to wind down, and that would have ended another Saturday night of fraternity frivolity. Unfortunately, Carson chose that moment to walk up to Jones and tell him that he should go upstairs—Now, goddamn it—and put on some clothes, as the whole bit that Jones had done had embarrassed Carson's date. And that bit about embarrassment might have been true, as Jones and I were probably two of the few males on campus whom Carson's date had not seen naked. Be that as it may, Jones did not react well to Carson's order—and that's what it was, an order. Jones told Carson to fuck himself. Buchanan stood there for a moment, and then blurted out that he thought that being naked was a wonderful thing, and he dropped his pants, peeled off his shirt, and stood there just as naked as Jones. Rudolf picked up what was happening, and so did Edwards, and they stripped.

Now it wasn't so funny. This wasn't about streaking or pulling a harmless college prank. There was something angry and confrontational about it, and people don't respond very comfortably to several drunken, angry, confrontational guys just kind of standing around naked at a party. I left to go upstairs while there was this lull in activity. The speed was wearing off and, besides, this was not too cool of a scene. I followed several other people up the stairway and I went back up to Second Old.

The party in Sid's room had lost its momentum. I explained to the people in there what had happened downstairs, and a couple of people got up, thinking that maybe there was going to be a fight and, if so, Jones would need some help. So we trooped downstairs, where the party had taken the weird twist. Rudolf was sitting on the stairway, naked. Two women were trying to talk him into grabbing his clothes and getting dressed. He said "No" every few seconds. I needed a drink so I walked on past and down. Jones and Edwards and Buchanan, still naked, were milling about talking to people. The rest of the people in the room were reacting uncomfortable. The party was thinning out, fast. I glanced over and Ridgeway was standing behind the little bar that we had, his pants down around his ankles, sort of adding his partial statement to what was appearing to be a protest. It had all gotten too weird for me, so I went back upstairs to my room and crashed.

The next morning the Sunday crowd for World War II Theatre in the Informal was more sparse than usual. The word that was going around was that there was going to be a visit from National. I just blew that off. Who cared a fuck? This was our house, we lived here. I watched flicks all afternoon and took it easy.

The next day, Monday, was the day the rest of the living units on campus held their "meetings." In the frats and sororities that meant attendance was mandatory. If you weren't there you were fined or suffered some other form of retribution. In our house you lost a rung on the seniority ladder for room preferences. Rudolf, Jones and Buchanan took an absence each so that they could go to every sorority and women's dorm and apologize for their behavior of Saturday night. I thought that was a bunch of horse shit. Hell, in all the time that I'd lived there I'd never seen members from a couple of the sororities that they visited enter our fine fraternity—and by "fraternity," I mean the physical plant. But the three of them apparently thought it was necessary, that somehow it would work to their advantage to "'fess up" and admit their wrongdoing. What a bunch of crap, as it turned out. We were in a war.

Chapter 19 - A Visit From National - Ha! Ha! Ha!

The people from the fraternity's national—they called it "International," as I've already said, because of two chapters in Canada—had only to drive the 40 miles from their headquarters in Indianapolis to visit the DeForrest chapter. I soon picked up on the idea that visits from national meant a high degree of trepidation in the house. Our chapter wasn't very popular with the people from national. After all, they wanted a "show place" close to Indy to which they could point with pride. Their vision of the proper house was one in which short-haired, clean-shaven, proper Conservatives in neatly-pressed suits lock-stepped to whatever national dictated, and for whom alums from the 1930s, 1940s and 1950s—times of real liberalism in the country, sure—could freely and happily donate $. Unspoken was the notion that the members of the fraternity would intermarry and interbreed with girls from the proper sororities, thus ensuring propagation of the American upper-middle-white-class.

The president and his buddies had taken personally the nakedness at the Hairy Buffalo party. The defiance that was expressed there was a protest against the president and his cabal, the housebitch.

The guy from national came in about mid-week. He was a former small college All-American football player, tall and wide and muscular—the stereotypical jock. That did not settle well with me. I've always hated jocks. Most of them, at least. The high school I'd graduated from placed jocks—not on a pedestal; something higher. As though jockdom was the focus of all existence. At DeForrest I knew jocks who were human. Others weren't. Wilson in our house wasn't a bad guy, not a bad person to party with. I'd gotten high with a few people—more than a few, actually—who were on the football or baseball teams. But this guy from the national fraternity was a cartoon. His name was even suspect—Greg Best. I mean, come on. The names of the traveling secretaries had to be like strippers' names. Candy Cane. Lotta Love. Except the traveling secretaries' names would have to fit into some archetype of "excellence." So this guy picked "Greg Best." There was probably a "John Pride" and a "Steven Sureness." And he was so Aryan-featured. I knew that whatever his real last name was it didn't end in "berg" or "stein." His appearance was highly reminiscent of the Nazi tank commander played by Robert Shaw in *Battle of the Bulge*. This guy was the offspring of some mad Nazi breeding experiment. He was sitting in the Formal Living Room with several moving boxes resting on the thick nap of the carpet beside him. He was talking with Benson. They were chuckling and having a high old time.

As far as I knew I still got along with everyone in the house, even the president and his buddies. Benson and I got along fine because I always did my housework and didn't bitch about it. I didn't know what was going on with the moving boxes, so I walked into the Formal, straight out of class, books under my arm.

"What's up?" I asked, innocently enough.

Benson introduced me to Greg Best as though they were old buddies. Of course, I was more athletic than Benson. Shit, Helen Keller was more athletic than Benson. Benson obviously felt cool now. Greg Best stuck out his hand and about crushed mine, I guess for effect. He was looking at me strangely, as though he was confused. I looked like one of the "enemy"—long hair, jeans, aviator shades, yup, just like the DEA "most wanted" poster child for drugs. But then Benson and I seemed as though we got along, and apparently Greg Best had been filled in on the fact that Benson wasn't getting along with the people who were the "enemy." I just smiled as my hand was crushed—never a good idea to piss off a guy with that much testosterone—and pulled it back.

"What's with the packing boxes?" I asked.

Benson was really beside himself with joy, he wanted so much to tell somebody. "Rudolf, Buchanan, Jones, Whale Man and East are all being booted from the house."

This was sudden. Rudolf, Jones and Buchanan. Their little peccadillo had happened Saturday. Still, there hadn't been any house meeting about it or anything. On top of that, then, Whale Man and East? Whale Man was TV's extremely obese roommate. East was a tad bit psycho, but I couldn't figure out why them and then—oh yes. The housebitch. Whale Man had always referred to her as "that illiterate slut." And East had shot a bottle rocket at her once causing her to split her gold lame pants in the parking lot. Ah! Things were becoming clearer.

"Just like that?" I asked.

The guy from the national fraternity was the Voice of Authority. "Just like that," he said. "That's why we have the packing boxes. We want to help them any way we can."

"Some help," I said. I was thinking about the economics. The national fraternity got your hundred dollars when you pledged. They got another hundred and fifty when you activated. I was sure that this fucker wasn't going to be handing out refunds along with the packing boxes. Then they booted people out over personal vendettas. What horse shit. And this was supposed to be an institution of higher learning?

"If people choose to oppose this, are they out, too?" I asked.

"You bet," Greg Best said with an All-American smile of white, capped teeth, the corners of his mouth now hardening. "We've heard that there's been meetings here of student protesters, too, and that stops today as well." I guess he'd just remembered my name and fit me into the grand jigsaw puzzle of things.

"In that case," I said, grabbing a box. "I'll need one of these, too." I turned on my heel and went upstairs to my room. I tossed everything down and stood there staring at the floor for a minute. They were going to try to turn this place into another Omega Dickhead house. We would all salute the fraternity flag like members of the Waffen SS, maybe even learn secret German or KKK phrases. They'd want us to dress in sheets and kick small children. I was lost in thought for a few moments. I realized I'd have to move, once again. No way was I going back to the dorms. How about if I claimed to be a Tantric Buddhist so that I could go OIT? How would I survive? I'd never learned how to cook. There was a knock at the door and Jerry Halpert came in.

I don't think Halpert had ever been in my room before. Hell, I'd never seen him in Second Old before. When he wasn't studying, he was working out or riding a bike. He didn't smoke pot, didn't drink. But he wasn't an asshole about any of it. We weren't pals or anything, but we got along okay. He started to say something, but then he saw the moving box.

"You heard already?" he asked.

"Yeah, I just talked to the Nazi in the Formal. When did they make the decision to kick people out?"

"Edwards is talking to Carson right now, trying to find out."

"Oh—that must be a fun conversation to hear. Where are you gonna move once it's over?"

"If I have to—not the dorms. I know you lived there, but I just think it would suck too much. OIT, I guess. Or transfer. But you know, this thing isn't over yet. We can still beat them."

"Yeah, sure. Like, let's see who all we have on our side." I held up one hand and started turning down fingers. "Obviously the national fraternity is against us. Then there's the university—can't forget our social probation. The house corporation and the alumni. Then there is our own president. And, finally, as if we didn't have enough against us already, there's the housebitch." I was left standing there with my fist. "Did I bother to mention that we don't have anybody on our side."

He shrugged and started to leave when Buchanan poked his head in. "Meeting tonight," he said. "Lemon session." This last was said with a certain sense of gravity, as though a meeting named after a fruit was one of the great important things of our lives.

"Is it only for members of the house," I asked, "or are you guys gonna be there, too?"

Buchanan gave me a look of disgust, and started to say something, but before the words could leave his mouth, Criminal Phil brushed past him and came into the room.

"What the fuck is going on?" he demanded.

"You heard?" Halpert asked.

"Yeah. Who the fuck is making decisions around here?"

"Apparently Jimmy is," Halpert replied.

"I say we kill the creepy little fucker," Criminal Phil said. With Criminal Phil one could not always tell if what he said was in whimsy or serious.

Again the pace of events was so fast nobody had time to react. We heard a door slam down the hallway. The slam was really fucking loud, and it came from the direction of Carson's room. We heard footsteps and then Edwards was standing in my doorway, his face bright red, out of breath.

"Fucking Carson," he panted. "Motherfucker met with national over in Indy yesterday, they brought in a couple of alums, and then they got the dean on the phone. Carson got to pick and choose who got the boot."

"Shit," we all muttered fraternally; well, communally at least.

Although I had planned on studying, I did not. The rest of the afternoon passed in similar fashion. Somebody would burst into my room, joining the small group that was there, as one or two others drifted out. There were certain faces—those from Jimmy's cabal—that were not appearing in my room or Second Old. The only sightings were on the main floor and the hallway leading to the housebitch's apartment.

At dinner Greg Best sat at the housebitch's table. It was the first meal in a couple of weeks that she had taken in the dining room. She had this vile smile on her face, a sneer that contained hate and avarice and malice and pettiness—and, behind it all, the arrogance of a coward's victory.

The house chaplain, one of the housebitch's "boys," actually asked for everyone to bow their heads for prayer. The president of the house and his buddies barely fit at the housemother's table. They'd had to slide in an extra seat to wedge in Greg Best. They stood dutifully as the house chaplain began with "Dear God." The rest of the people in the room hesitated, but then Rudolf sat down, and then Jones and East and Whale Man, and then the rest of us. We started passing around the food, as the prayer droned on requesting guidance and what have you "through these times of trouble." Excuse the fuck out of me. They had the national fraternity, house corp, the alums, the university and the officers on their side. Now they were invoking the intervention of an almighty deity. Get real! A couple of people from our side laughed, and then the prayer ended and the meal dragged on slowly. A bunch of us finished as quickly as we could manage, all at about the same time, and we stood and left the dining room together, a breach of courtesy that I saw Greg Best note in a little blue book he pulled from his shirt pocket.

The meeting was held in the Formal Living Room. People flopped down on couches and the floor and the wide window sills. Greg Best and the house president were the last to enter the room and they walked in together. Jimmy actually seemed to smirk, until he got a good look at the faces looking back at him.

"Gentlemen," Greg Best began. I noticed then that, somehow, in Indiana in late March, this guy had a good tan. Maybe he had acquired it while visiting the chapter houses in Florida. Then something else struck me. From the guy's swagger, and the way he used the word "gentlemen," he reminded me of any of the coaches I'd heard in junior high and high school. I'd quit track my sophomore, junior and senior years. If I had wanted to have someone from that aspect of the world exercise any authority over me, I would have stayed in sports. There were people who did that at my high school—guys who had little or no athletic ability but still hung on in sports, like track and cross-country and football, where nobody was cut. But the whole point was, I hadn't wanted that. I'd quit. And I certainly didn't appreciate having that same mentality assert itself through some moron like this asshole, here at college, where I had thought I would be safe from such idiocy. Besides— wasn't this guy supposed to be addressing us as "brothers"?

"Gentlemen, you all know why I'm here. The International Fraternity"—and the way he said it you knew that not only were both words capitalized in his mind, but they were probably gilded as well—"is concerned over this chapter." He put his hands behind his back, and acquired this pained look, as if he were suppressing a fart. I got this image then of all of the national fraternity's traveling secretaries attending some motivational seminar where they were taught to speak in this manner. It reminded me of my junior year of high school, when our cheerleaders returned from cheerleader camp. Apparently they had been taught to maintain this facial expression as they did their cheers. The expression consisted of eyes wide, lips pursed and extended, as though someone had just goosed them. This guy's expression was just as contrived. I figured that the big thing in his seminar, though, was learning how to walk without one's knuckles dragging the ground.

"The International has watched this house for several years now. This used to be the best house on campus. Now," he waved a hand. "Mere participation in intramurals." Oops, there was a real serious one. "Low GPA." Maybe it would be higher if we didn't have stupid fucking meetings like this. "Nobody active in campus concerns. Except that protest meetings have been held under this roof lately." Well, we all knew at whom that one was pointed. He looked up. I think he meant to look each of us square in the eye, some man-to-man sort of thing, but the effect was more that of a politician in a 30-second TV ad. "I understand that some of you refer to this fraternity"—here I assumed he would have had trumpets sound had he had the option available—"the 'Omicron Hilton.' I certainly do not find this amusing. I assure you that the International does not either." He sat down on the back of the couch. We were about to get the heart-to-heart. "When you joined this fraternity, you joined it for a reason. You joined it to be a part of one of the oldest fraternities in the World. Those are not just Greek letters on the door outside there—they mean something." He then said a couple of Greek words, then interpreted. "That stands for 'liberty and knowledge.' But," he interjected, shaking his head, "I guess a lot of you might not know that. I understand there was no pledge training this year." He shook his head again, as if he'd found out that it was true, that we had not learned the pledgeship crap and that we were mass murderers and that we tortured animals and children. Those were the depths to which this chapter had sunk. "Gentlemen, there are going to be some changes here.

International wants those changes. The university wants those changes. The house corporation wants those changes." He shook his head, then began again. "As you know . . ." He stopped when he saw the hand raised. It was Dennis Rickard's. Dennis was my pledge father. Greg Best looked a bit confused, thrown off by the fact that anyone would interrupt him. "Yeah?"

"I thought we were here for a lemon session. That's what this was billed as, and all we're getting is a lecture. Do we get to talk at all, to complain about things?"

At Dennis's use of the word "complain" Greg Best's squinty little sun-wrinkled eyes lit up. He even might have mistakenly thought that Rickard was one of the buddies of the president of the house. "Yeah, sure," he said. "This is a lemon session. Sorry I started off like that. Go ahead."

Rickard had a way of talking in a reasoned sort of beat, his chin tilted slightly upward. "What you're saying about the national fraternity. I didn't join this place because of a set of Greek letters or what the chapters might be like at the University of Oklahoma. I met guys here that I liked, that I thought I could get along with better than the other houses on campus. It seemed like there wasn't any bullshit here. I came here for an education. This place didn't have hazing, hell week, tests over memorized shit in a fraternity manual or any secret handshakes. It didn't matter to me what national fraternity the house was affiliated with. I liked the people."

A few people said "Yeah," a few more of us applauded. The look on Greg Best's face darkened. "I guess, then, that you're happy with the way things are around here."

"Actually, I'm not," Rickard continued. "The guys who supposedly were our officers kick out our friends without any notice or hearing, you come in here preaching this rah-rah bullshit, and I have an organic chemistry exam tomorrow morning at 10 and I should be studying for it instead of listening to you."

There were more sounds of approval, and then Edwards spoke up, wanting, again, to know how the Five, as they were now being called, had been chosen and the procedure by which they were booted from the house, whether there could be an appeal, etc. It was then that I looked around and realized they weren't here, that they had been excluded from the meeting. Then I glanced out the side window and saw that it was open, and that, about three feet away, one of the windows to the housebitch's apartment was open. The bitch was getting to listen to the meeting, and the Five, who were members of the fucking house, didn't have that privilege, which should have been one of their rights as members.

Greg Best was trying to explain the expulsion procedure, but every time he added a new facet, Edwards asked him another question, thankfully without any malapropisms.

"The officers made the decision . . ." Best began.

"I'm an officer, and I wasn't included."

"House corp and the International were the two final . . ."

"Fine, but how did they pick out these individuals? Did they draw names out of a hat?"

"It was more complex than that. Certain considerations were given to maturity and leadership abilities, to grades and campus reputations . . ."

"What bullshit!" Rickard said, and, shaking his head, as most of us were laughing and applauding his outburst, he walked out of the room. Greg Best pulled the notebook out of his pocket and, after consulting Carson, wrote down Rickard's name.

"Jimmy really named the people to kick out, didn't he?" Edwards asked.

"No," Greg Best said, and the laughter grew louder. A few more people stood up to leave, and I joined them. The meeting was over as far as everyone, except the president and his buddies, were concerned.

As we walked out of the Formal, Greg Best started talking in a sort of high-pitched staccato, trying to machine gun us with words at our backs. "I'm going back to International tonight! I'll tell them what the situation is here. It's bad, that's for sure. Not the worst I've seen, though. Not the worst I've seen by a long shot! You guys think that you're bad! Ha ha! Next week the house corp wants to come in here and interrogate—er, uh—interview you all—one at a time. They want to make a decision: to close this place up and start from scratch, or to try and salvage something out of here. You people think that you're necessary. You're not. International has plenty of money. We don't need your house bills. We've done this many times before, and we'll do it again!"

Chapter 20 - Das Kapital

We held a couple of more meetings on the Farina matter. Even though the "structure" of what we were doing was very loose, we were getting a lot of things done. One group of people had started sending letters to alumni, trying to get some support from that sector. That was a nice idea, but the only alumni they knew were recent graduates. Those recent graduates, in turn, did not contribute large sums of money to the university. Only the older alumni did that. Those were the people the university would listen to, and that was where we needed the leverage. Unfortunately, most of the older alumni did not really care about the issue of academic freedom. They were more concerned with how pretty the campus looked on alumni weekends, or how well the football team was doing. Another group was making picket signs. We had decided to picket the Union Building on Mom's Day and we figured the same picket signs could be used for the strike. Yes, the strike. That was bubbling to the surface.

Robert Wolff came on the scene at about this time. Robert had graduated the year before and had been a student of Farina's. He was tall and skinny. His hair wasn't long, by our standards, but it wasn't short, either, just curly and unkempt. He always wore denim pants and denim jacket, and I never saw him when he wasn't smiling. He was radical as hell. He was the first anarchist I had met. He had caused a bit of a hubbub the year before by suggesting that the International Students Association re-name its newsletter "Rising Fist." The suggestion came surprisingly close to succeeding. It failed only when those who were debating the matter realized that Robert was not eligible to take part in their affairs. At the time we were organizing, he was working with a couple of unions in the midwest. He became involved in the Farina matter and attended our meetings when he was in town. He was also an old enemy of Jimmy Natas's.

Since Natas had become involved in our activities, he had seemed to stay on the fringes of things. He rarely spoke in meetings, but at the most recent such gathering, he had installed himself at the table at the front of the room. I was too busy to notice that at first. By the time I did, it was too late. He had papers spread out and was talking to a couple of the women who were among his "groupies."

By this time, I was spending a lot of time on the Farina thing. I had started missing classes. It bothered me, especially after I had compiled such a good record for the semester to date. But I had been doing so much—meeting with other students, reading up on DeForrest history in the university's archives, finding out that DeForrest had done this same thing with other professors in the past. As I read through the past three years' issues of the student newspaper, I realized that over the past several consecutive years the university had dismissed outright or denied tenure to its only Jewish professors. The quota seemed to be one per year. The university was down to two, and Farina was one of those two. I raised this issue at a meeting. I thought the university's anti-semitism was important to address. Others agreed but Natas and a couple of his cronies went nearly ballisitic, saying that any such actions by the university were misconceived by us as being discriminatory, that they were sure that the matters were merely coincidental, that voicing any concerns over side issues would obscure the real thing on which we should focus. Natas said, "We need to protect his job and get him tenure or else we've done nothing." Natas projected a good profile, almost posed, when he said that.

Even with all of the effort I had put into the thing, I had yet to meet Farina. I knew what he looked like from the student newspaper. I resolved that problem one day. I had a "nine-0" and a "ten-0" in DeForrest parlance—a nine o'clock and a ten o'clock class. I knew Farina had an eleven-0, so I figured that after my ten-0 I would walk over and wait for his class to let out.

My nine-0 was speech pathology. For the first hourly exam I had made flash cards of all of the relevant terms and gotten an A. We'd had the second hourly, and although I wasn't nearly as prepared—what with the rebellion and strife in the frat and all of the planning and activities related to Farina, and then my quota of partying, I hadn't the time to prepare as well—I'd still scored a B. So I was borderline A/B, and figured I'd better not miss any more classes. If I didn't and I got an A on the last hourly and an A on the final, the prof would see no problem in giving me an A. I about fell asleep in the class that morning, as I did any morning in speech path. I was not fired up about the subject. I went to my ten-0 after that, ed psych.

I really hated the prof. We had seat assignments, and I'd made the mistake the first day of sitting near the front, so my recent absences were pretty blatant. Fortunately, I was current on the reading. When the prof tried to nail me with questions twice that morning, I answered them correctly. It was obvious that he was pissed off about that, but hey, what could I do? We'd had one hourly already in there. I'd gotten a high B, a miracle for me to do so well on psych multiple-choice exams. We had one more hourly and the final after that, and I figured that, if I held in there okay, I'd have a B.

I loitered after that. When the bell in the tower rang, and students began pouring out of the classrooms in Asbury, I walked to Farina's class. Farina was at the front of the lecture hall standing next to the podium. He was short, wore a goatee, had radical hair fuck, as if he really didn't give a shit, and was garbed in the classic left-wing professor uniform of the day—jeans, flannel shirt, corduroy jacket. I waited at the back of the room until the last student who had wanted to speak with him had finished, then I walked to the front of the room to introduce myself. Farina looked at me warily, as if he wondered if I was a process server or something. When I stuck out my hand and we shook I told him who I was and that I had wanted to meet him.

He said, "You're the cocky little shit that's been working on the protests and things." He laughed as he picked up his books.

We walked over to the Faculty Annex, where he had an office that had been made out of a broom closet or something smaller. The room had enough space for a tiny desk, two chairs and a ton of books, stacked floor-to-ceiling. We sat talking for about an hour, about the school, about everything that had happened to him. When I told him what I'd noticed about the anti-semitism, he laughed. "Once they get rid of us, they'll start on the

Catholics!" As I left, he asked me if I was going to be at the bars that night. Hell, I didn't look my age of 19, much less 21. Being a college town and all, the bars—especially the ones that catered to DeForrest students—carded heavily. But I wanted to appear cool, so I said sure. He said he'd buy me a beer.

We'd talked through lunch, but I didn't care. I figured I could hold out the few hours until supper, then gorge myself on mashed potatoes and dinner rolls. I headed back toward the fraternity—and by "fraternity," I mean the physical plant—and as I started up Anderson Street, I ran into Mooter.

"Hey, man," he said. His eyes were squinted and, when I looked more closely, I saw that they were a deep and bright red. Had the British at the Battle of New Orleans had an army of Mooters attacking Andrew Jackson's forces, the British would have won. Jackson had ordered his men not to fire 'til "you see the whites of their eyes." Mooter had absolutely no white in his eyes—that day or most any other day. But his grin was certainly wide. He walked up to me in conspiratorial fashion. "I just got some hash, man."

"Cool," I said and figured he was about to invite me to smoke some with him.

But he shook his head. "Good stuff, man. And I can get you an ounce real cheap."

Hash was sold in increments of grams. A gram went for anywhere from three to seven bucks, depending upon the quality. Only someone who was going to deal would buy an ounce, and I had never dealt anything. It's not that I had any sort of moral problem with it. After all, in the grand scheme of supply and demand, it was necessary that someone be there to provide the supply. My reasons were more practical. I was not a business person. I viewed myself as holding a combination of several beliefs or philosophies, none of which embraced capitalism. Then Mooter told me the ridiculously low price and I compared that number with the number of grams and the price per gram and I figured I could sell enough in our frat alone to get seven or eight grams for myself free.

I told Mooter I would be at his house later that afternoon, after my two-0, which was philosophy. I walked back to the house wondering where I would come up with the money. When I got back, I checked my mail, and there was an envelope from the bank back home. I opened it up and immediately saw the check. For some reason—weird, apocalyptic, whatever— the bank had sent my house check directly to me, and it was made out to me. In other words, I was being paid the money that was supposed to go to the frat for my room and board. The figure on that check was about fifty bucks more than what I needed to buy the hash. I figured I could buy the hash, sell it off, recoup my money, and have free hash for myself in the process. Immediately, I went in search of someone who had a credible bank account so we could go to their bank and cash the check, since I had no account in Glendale or anyplace else on the planet, and the sum on the check was far greater than the limits imposed by the DeForrest book store.

Jerry Leone was a very quiet sort, very non-drug and non-alcohol oriented, but he wasn't a pain in the ass about it. He was scrupulously trying to stay out of the fray in the frat. He wanted nothing to do with any of it. He also had a lot of money and bank accounts in Glendale that were larger than the check that I was trying to cash. On top of that he had a car—a classic, as a matter of fact. It was a 1954 Porsche Spyder, just like the one James Dean was killed in, he always used to brag. It had an aluminum shell for a body and looked pretty mean—and low enough to slide under a compact car and kill the passengers it was carrying. Riding with him in it was always something akin to riding shotgun in a grand prix race. I caught him at about 12:45. Since there were no one o'clock classes that day, and since he wasn't really doing anything, he agreed to drive me to his bank and sign off on my check. Everything was processed fine and dandy and I had a shitload of cash.

Later, I was antsy sitting through political and social philosophy class. We were discussing Rousseau. In high school, I had written a paper on Rousseau, and I found him to be an interesting, hedonistic, hypocritical kind of guy. In philosophy we were studying his first and second discourses. I thought the whole notion behind his first discourse was pretty cool.

He wrote the first discourse after he saw an ad for an essay contest. The topic was whether the restoration of the arts and sciences has contributed to the purification of manners. While nearly everyone else was answering that question "yes," and then explaining why they took that position, Rousseau said "no," and blasted contemporary society. By the second discourse he was writing about a "noble savage," a person whom he acknowledged as being fictional, but who was primordial, who was unblemished by any of the vulgarities or artifices of modern society. Rousseau really wailed on the theatre. He also decried the way artists of his day had to prostitute themselves by painting the sides of carriages for money. I flashed on the fact that the artists of my day were doing the same by painting murals and what-have-you on the sides of vans. When I thought about it, I realized that none of the people whom I had ever met who painted the sides of vans seemed particularly disgruntled or viewed themselves as "prostitutes." I imagined that the artists and artisans of Rousseau's day probably were glad to be making a living doing something they enjoyed.

None too soon class ended, and I shot out of the room and went across campus to Mooter's. Mooter's frat was nearly in the middle of campus. As far as campus culture went, it was fairly middle-of-the-road. It had its share of freaks and hippies along with the academic types and jocks, and the basic anonymous college student.

I knew Mooter was moving from his old room to a new room in the basement. I had been to maybe one party in their party room in the basement, and the stairway down was around behind something or other, so when I walked into the foyer and saw a guy whom I knew from my psych class the previous semester, I asked for directions. He told me where the stairwell was, and then said, "When you get to the bottom, turn left." But when I got downstairs and turned left, I entered a small room and figured the guy must not have caught my question correctly. The room was very small—three feet deep by about 12 or 13 feet long—and the "wall" that faced me as I stood there in the doorway was comprised entirely of dark, wooden cabinets about four feet tall and a foot-and-a-half wide, arranged in two rows, one atop the other. It looked like a coat/locker room from a movie about an English boarding school. I stepped back and tried to see if maybe there was another room in the basement that could be Mooter's. But all that I found were the party room, a laundry room, and the boiler room.

I stepped back into the room of cabinets, and that's when I caught a muffled sound of talking, then an album beginning to play. The sounds seemed to come from behind the cabinet doors. I opened one of the lower doors, through which the sounds seemed to be the loudest, and was surprised to find a small hallway, almost a tunnel, the height and width of the cabinet door, about five feet in length and running straight away from me and into what looked like another room.

"Mooter?" I called, loudly enough to be heard over the music.

Mooter's face popped down into the space at the end of the tunnel. He was grinning and holding a bong.

"Hey, man! Come on back!" he said.

As I walked, scrunched over in the small space, I flashed on what Lewis Carroll and Alice's journeys from the real world. When I popped out at the other end, I was in a room that was larger than the usual frat room, but pretty conventional in most ways—

waterbed, small TV on a table, books on a couple of shelves, stereo, albums. Mooter had even purloined a coffee maker somewhere along the way. And, because it was Mooter's room, the Head was there.

The Head was a styrofoam millinery display stand in the shape of a human head, but very basic. It didn't have a nose, eyes, ears or mouth. In a drug-induced fit one day (or night. I wasn't there, so I don't know), Mooter had painted it with various designs in different colors of dayglo paint. He had also come up with a neon feather and headband a la 1920s flapper. The effect was weird, but–hey, that was Mooter.

"Do you like the cabinets, man?" he asked. "The house was gonna throw them out. They were against this wall, and this was like a storage room. And when I heard that and I got to thinking, and we were doing room prefs anyway, I thought—Man! How cool!"

A couple of Mooter's frat brothers were ensconced there, one on a beanbag chair, the other cross-legged on the floor. The scent of smoke hit me, and Mooter must have seen my head cock slightly to one side, because, still grinning, he said, "Hash!"

Hashish—the refined product of marijuana—was not rare, but it wasn't on campus every day. It was a pleasant, occasional treat. The flavor and scent of the smoke were different from pot, slightly perfumey. The buzz was the same, but because it was concentrated, one needed far less to hit that buzz. As Mooter filled a little pipe and handed it to me, he repeated what he'd said earlier about an ounce. He said it would be $110. I did the math. Five bucks a gram time 27 grams. I'd have four grams for myself. Not too shabby. So I said sure. The hash was "blonde"—in other words, it was a light color, combining a light green and a gold. I could still make out, on some of the larger chunks, the press of the seal that had been placed on each huge wheel of hash, when it had been made, sort of like Edam cheese. The stuff was pretty decent, too, as I caught a good buzz. I handed over the money, and he handed over to me more hash than I had ever held before in my life. It was already divided into grams, so I was spared that labor. All I had to do was sell it. When I left, I shoved it into my pockets and began the trek back to the fraternity— and by "fraternity," I mean the physical plant.

The day was sunny and in the 50s. When I got back to the house I went straight to my room. The door still didn't lock, and that bothered me. Anybody could come in and rip me off. But the house was pretty secure and, besides, I could hide the hash in my closet so it would take a while for somebody to rip it off. I did just that, then walked across the hall and knocked on the door to Sid's room.

I sold two grams each to Sid and Criminal Phil. That showed that I could dispose of the stuff. Maybe I'd be able to get it all taken care of in the next couple of days. Then I could pay my house bill and all would be right with the world. I figured I would get right onto that task after supper, and that maybe I could unload the lion's share of the stuff that evening. Then I'd go to the bars and meet Farina and everyone.

At dinner the house president and his buddies sat at the housebitch's table. He stood after the meal was nearly all consumed. He hit his glass with his spoon to get everyone's attention.

"Tomorrow," he said. "House corp will be here. They will interview each member for ten minutes. The list of times and people will be posted in the stairwell here. The interviews will start at 1:00. If you miss it for some reason, you are automatically expelled from the house." At that several people went "oooh" in mockery of him. He sat down and there was a pained silence, then people just got up and went to the Informal or their rooms. By this time the president and his buddies didn't mix with the rest of us.

I wasn't able to call people and unload the hash that evening. Instead, my room became a meeting place once more for people who wanted to bitch about the turmoil in the house. At 9:30, I gave up, turned off the lights in my room, closed the door, and headed to the bars. I would take care of business the following evening.

This was the first time I'd hit the bars, although I knew quite well where they were located. There was a mystique to "the bars." I'd heard, since my first day on campus freshman year, upperclassmen tell stories of long discussions and fights and women and professors and, of course, intoxication. I thought that now, maybe, I would be a part of this milieu. I'd go down there and caught up in the whole thing. I might even meet the right woman and, finally, after all these years, get laid. Glendale had only a half-dozen bars. Students couldn't go to one of them— the Double D, a redneck place on the square. Its patrons looked as if they'd been relocated from Kilkerry, very hilljackish. Of the other bars, only two were really DeForrest hangouts. Stan's was not one of them. It was just off campus and I'd heard that while students were not barred there, we weren't made to feel at home, either. The Railroad Crossing was up on the north side of Kilkerry, and it was pretty nondescript. It did featured country western music, however, so students automatically avoided the place. On the other end of town, there were three bars. The walk was all of about six or seven blocks from my frat. That part of Glendale did not feature prime real estate. The closer one got to the bars, the worse the houses, then houses and duplexes, got. In the last block or so before the bars, doubles butted up against one another, white paint cracked and peeling and covered with layers of dirt. Paint was long since gone from the flooring on porches, the boards gray and weathered and warped. To furnish their front porches, the residents used old, stuffed couches and arm chairs from their living rooms, tufts of cotton stuffing escaping from seat cushions or arms. "Yards" were expanses of bare dirt with children's broken toys strewn about. The sidewalks were narrow and, at several places, cracked and buckling. This was not an area upon which the town fathers intended to bestow expenditures of community monies for improvements.

In contrast, as one neared the bars, one saw the variety of Glendale student cars. Sure, there were a few old beaters—early 1960s cars with oxidized paint that looked as if they'd seen better days. But then one saw the other cars, the expensive toys that Daddy wanted Baby or Junior to have as the "right" set of wheels at college. There were Corvettes, Mercedes Benzes, an Alfa Romeo, a couple of new 260Zs, a couple of Porsches, and a real rare one, a Jensen Interceptor, a couple of motorcycles, one an especially expensive, new BMW—and the Glendale residents in their quasi-slum housing could watch these cars move past their hovels on a nightly basis as the students came and went. No, the townies weren't bitter at the students. No way.

Of the three bars, only two catered to students. The 714 had been frequented by DeForrest students the previous year. But then a change of management, infusion of CW music, and a crackdown on IDs had led the students to avoid the place and go elsewhere. "Elsewhere" was Sullivan's and Neal's. I tried Sullivan's first, if only because I stood less of a chance of being carded. Charlie Sullivan was one of the few black people in Glendale. He was big—6'2" or 6'3" and about 200 pounds. It was said that he had fought in Golden Gloves and then had gone pro for a couple of fights. He was one of the most genuinely nice people around the DeForrest community. Amongst his more noble traits was a great disdain for certain types of rules, particularly those that concerned age requirements for the consumption of alcohol. In fact, his place had a very strict policy toward underage drinking: If you were underage, they would serve you a drink. If you wanted a lot of drinks and you had the money, they would serve those to you as well. Of course, if agents from the ABC—Alcoholic Beverage Commission—were in town on a periodic crackdown of underage drinking, Charlie and one of his bouncers would stand outside and card everyone. This cut the number of customers on such an evening by about seventy-five percent, but it was necessary to do so for Charlie to keep his license. But crackdowns only occurred three or four times a year. His place was down one side street turning off a second, and then a third from the state highway. It was a wooden-frame structure in the middle of the block. A few concrete steps climbed to a narrow doorway with a peaked roof. The plate-glass window read "Charlie Sullivan's Bar-B-Q," but from the inside the window was covered, so no one passing by could see in. Of course I knew where it was, having ridden past it as a passenger in several cars. But I had never been inside.

As I climbed the steps, I heard the loud, muffled music of a bar with a good-sized crowd behind a closed door. When I opened the door, the music and the smoke and the noise blasted out at me, along with the humidity of a lot of bodies and drinks. A short, skinny fellow was standing inside the door, looking official. I realized that he was the guy "working the door" for the bar that night, and that meant, inherently that the place was carding, or checking for IDs. My spirits sank for a moment.

"You 21?" he asked. I stammered that I was. "Okay," he said, and stepped aside to let me in.

I thanked my luck and the skinny fellow and walked on past.

The place was crowded with DeForrest students. I'd heard that the black people in town who frequented bars went to Sullivan's, but there were very few black people in Glendale and besides, the students obviously had control on this evening. Everyone was a professor or a student. The students were upperclassmen. I saw no other sophomores. To my left was an old bowling machine. It was about ten feet long and a couple of feet wide. It had a wooden alley, just like a real bowling alley, of polished, laminated wooden slats. The bowling balls were black and the size of softballs. I watched as an Omega Dickhead grabbed a ball. He gripped the whole thing, as it didn't have holes. He rolled it down the alley. The "pins" hung down from mechanisms built into the ceiling of the machine, and were struck or tripped by the ball hitting trip-wires that stuck out of the surface of the lane. The pins would flip up, and the machine would keep score to the accompaniment of bells and buzzers and multi-colored lights.

The players barely had room to bowl because of the juke box. It displayed a panorama of 45s. The music wasn't CW. It was Aretha Franklin and Marvin Gaye, plus a couple by the Commodores. The juke box had seen better times, but belted out tunes. Opposite the game and the juke box, half-a-dozen booths lined one wall. There was some seating on a ledge next to the plate-glass window, and opposite the door, at the other end of the narrow room, was the bar. It had seating for only four or five people, booze bottles rising in tiers behind it. In the middle of the place, the main features after the alcohol, were two pool tables.

There wasn't much room to move around. People were pressed against the walls, the bowling machine, and the ends of the pool tables, parting now and then to let someone shooting a game to take their turn. Hooded lights hung down giving the green felt surfaces a warm glow. The color was soft. But however soothing and welcoming the tables appeared, as bar owners the world over know, where there are pool tables, there are fights. There's something about holding a polished stick of wood that sets some people off. Just then, I heard someone yell at someone, and I looked up to see, about ten feet away from me, one pool player crack his cue stick over the back of the other player, who lunged. Like a flash a huge black gentleman— assumed correctly that it was Charlie—swept across the room, grabbed the two miscreants, moved them through the crowd by the necks, and tossed them out. With males around the age of 20 present, and hormones and alcohol pumping away at high-speed, fights occurred with regularity. I was very careful and polite in making my way toward the bar. The irony was that although this was the only bar owned or frequented by black people in Glendale, the frat most closely identified with it, Omega Dickhead, was generally regarded as being the most bigoted.

I laid down my thirty-five cents and got a mug of beer. I sipped carefully and looked around for Farina. I did not see him. But then I felt someone tug at my elbow, and I was face to face with Professor Gleason, my favorite prof. I said hello and he grinned.

"I wasn't aware that we had any twenty-one-year-old sophomores at Glendale, although the stories of such creatures are legion." He grinned, in reference to tales of people growing into old age as undergrads, unable to leave the partying and freedom, I guessed. Or unable to push their GPAs above the 2.0 required to graduate.

"I was going to tell the guy at the door that I wasn't twenty-one, if only he'd asked." I smiled.

He looked around the cramped room. "This place was operating as a bar when I was a student here." He had a lit Camel in one hand and a mug of beer in the other. The Camel was nearly out and, as he talked, he pulled out a new one, lit it with what was left of the old one, and went on smoking and talking.

"When did you graduate from here?" I asked.

"1964."

"They didn't allow drinking at all here then, either on campus or off," I observed. "That was around the time of the Black Friars scandal, and when female students were required to wear skirts whenever they were outside their respective living units."

Gleason looked at me, a tad bit surprised. "How do you know about that?" I told him about my research in the DeForrest archives—not the why of the research, just what I'd found. "It's nice to see that someone is interested in the history of this old school, although I guess that it can be pretty boring."

"Not as boring as some of the shit I've had to study."

"You don't like my course I take it," he said, suddenly with a note of seriousness.

"No, no," I said quickly. "That's not true at all." I went on to tell him how much I'd learned, how much I had enjoyed Rousseau in particular.

"Yeah, that much came through in your comments in class," he said, then waved to a waitress and ordered a pitcher. I offered to chip in on it, but he waved me off. "My contribution to the undergraduate cause," he said. "I was a student once, remember."

We went on discussing the class, and I explained the problems I had in following Hobbes, in particular, although Locke wasn't any walk in the park. "I had to read Locke in poly sci one. What a bite in the ass. I think I missed that more than any other class first semester freshman year."

"You shouldn't skip class for any reason," Gleason said, knowing full well that I hadn't missed his class even once.

"You mean you never missed a class, skipped on purpose?"

He grinned. "Fall. 1962. World Series. The games were all during the day—it was before they had all this night shit for the networks—and I didn't want to miss even one game. So yeah—a bunch of us got some beer." He laughed. "They didn't have pull tabs on the cans back then. A lot of guys always tried to wear church keys on dog tag chains."

"Church keys?"

"Yeah. You know. Bottle openers, can openers, one of each on each end. Well, anyway, about ten or a dozen of us piled into a couple of cars—and they were even more illegal on campus then than they are now—and we went out to the country." He stopped and his brows furrowed as he tried to remember. He gestured into the air. "There's a bridge. It's about three miles—you turn off Indianapolis Road, then you go north a couple of miles."

"On Round Barn Road?"

"Yeah," he said, looking up, finally remembering. "We called it that, too." The lit end of his Camel was nearly down to his yellowed fingers. He pulled out a new one and lit it with the old, then stamped the old one out on the floor, where it joined several dozen other butts. "So we drove out there. The banks next to the creek out there are steep, but we climbed down them and walked out onto a couple of sandbars. Well, they were half sand and half mud and rock. A couple of the guys had transistor radios, and we set them up and listened to the game." He smiled. "The New York Yankees and the San Francisco Giants. The whole thing."

"Wasn't it on TV?"

"Well, I guess so. But we really didn't want to watch the game. We wanted to listen to it. Sitting there on one of the last warm sunny days of fall. Baseball. Beer. My best friends. Out there next to a creek in the woods." He sighed and shook his head. "Coming back to the dorm, we had to be really careful. Remember—alcohol was illegal on campus. You could get expelled."

"So DeForrest was just as hypocritical back then as it is now?"

He smiled and looked at me as if I was being silly. "There was some hypocrisy, yes. But there is at nearly any college or university."

That hit me the wrong way, I guess. And he asked me if I had a problem with that. "Yeah. This is supposed to be an institution of higher learning. I would think that a university is the one place that tries to free itself of hypocrisy." I then used that specific topic as a springboard into my description of what could best be called a "world view." I had never put it into words before that night. It was rough and there were holes and splotches in it. But it was formative. It was something that instinctually, as I said it, I knew was something upon which I could build. It was my view of how the world is, how it was going to something else, what it was going to be, what it could and should be and why. It was a romantic concept that bordered on fascism: the people of the world, the masses, did not know what was good for them but I—a college sophomore—did know what was good for them and I would tell them how to live. This was offset, though, by a belief in civil rights and liberties such that I could only tell them how to live. They could ignore my words, like as not. The content of my world view reflected the one-and-a-half semesters of course work behind me. There were elements of Mazlow, Piaget, Freud and Jung, Plato, Thucydides, Rousseau and Locke. I stumbled across writings related to anarchism and the writings of Michhail Bakunin, the Russian anarchist whose words began an embryonic tug at my mind. Always there were the authors of various literary works—Shakespeare, Moliere, Albee, Williams, Faulkner and Fitzgerald. Fitzgerald was there from my teenage years, forming my ideals and giving shape and rationalization to my penchant for the consumption of alcohol. Vonnegut was in there, too, providing a leavening measure of common-sense. I stirred in a broad reading of radical movements, and historical descriptions of events that had been benchmarks of radical history, both abroad but, more particularly, in this country. My reading and research in this vein was still in its early stages. I knew just enough to get myself in trouble. I'd picked up Revolution for the Hell of It by Abbie Hoffman. A shorter work, "Fuck the System," was appended to it. I also had recorded an album that Warren had. It was Abbie Hoffman's "Wake Up America!" comprised largely of speeches that he had given around the time of the trial of the Chicago Seven (Eight). I'd picked up a copy of Jerry Rubin's Do It!, but Hoffman was much more introspective. Through all of this, I held to the idea of a coming revolution. It would not be bloody, but it would turn all of our social order on its head. Marijuana would be legal—and that was not merely a "given" in my world view, but a necessary event from which all else flowed. There would be worldwide peace. Richard Nixon would be in prison for life. Property would be equally distributed around the world. Gleason had given me the springboard I needed. He had allowed the steel ball to roll in front of the plunger, and I had pulled the plunger back and let fly, bouncing off the blinking bumpers of conversation, verbalizing some things for the first time. I KNEW that there would be a Revolution. Not just a Revolution, but THE Revolution.

Suddenly, Gleason demanded, "What is your premise?"

I stopped. "What?"

"What is your premise? What is the basic principle upon which you base that whole thing you just went through?"

I sat there for a few seconds, confused. Then I remembered I had to be someplace else. I looked at my watch then, remembering I had to meet Farina. I didn't really want to break off the conversation with Gleason, though, because I was enjoying it, and I didn't want to be rude.

"You meeting somebody?" Gleason asked, startling me.

"Yeah. I was supposed to meet them at one of the bars and they aren't here."

"Try Neal's. They're probably down there."

I told Gleason we had to do this again, and soon, and that I would ponder what he'd said about premises.

"Yeah," he said, "otherwise you get a little too cosmic."

I killed the beer and then made my way through the crowd and to the door. Clancey had arrived at some point, and he was playing the bowling machine with one of the Omega Dickheads. I glanced at the scores and saw that he had a decent lead. I didn't bother him, though, and slid out without his seeing me.

I enjoyed the clean feel of the night air. The air in the bar had been close and heavy with cigarette smoke and humid with the evaporating beer and moist exhalations of drunken students. I trudged along towards Neal's, only a half-block away. Neal's was back towards the state highway, occupying one end of a three-store-front building painted a shitty greenish-gold. The other two-thirds of the building were vacant. Although it had no "second story" as such, the front of the building had a brick facade that rose to a height of about two stories. There, on the roof, two stories above the cracked sidewalk, was an old metal and neon sign that read, simply, "Neal's Tavern." It had probably been a century since Neal had owned the place or since a Neal had worked there, but each of the succession of owners had not seen fit to change the name, whether out of respect or out of lethargy— they didn't want to climb up to the roof and change one of the few neon signs in all of Glendale.

A couple of weeks before, The Daily DeForrest had run a story about the "new owner" of the place. He was a retired member of the Merchant Marine and he and his wife had looked for a place to buy and run so that they could augment their Social Security and his pension. As I approached the front door, my hopes rose as I saw that there was no one carding. Once inside, I quickly ordered my beer, and it was served to me. I took a sip—I was in! According to student folklore concerning Indiana law, I could not now be refused a drink on account of age or lack of ID. I looked around, my first time in the place. The ceiling was low and made of fiberboard. It was painted a lime green, but when I looked at it more carefully, I saw that there was a layer of grease and gunk on it, no doubt from the grill in the back. I could smell the grill even all the way at the front of the oblong, narrow room. The bar ran along one wall to the right, and there were a dozen or so people pulled up to it on stools, or standing there talking to people who'd gotten stools. The rest of the seating in the place consisted of small, square cabaret tables that, I could see, people pushed together to accommodate the numbers of larger parties. The tables were covered by cheap, red-and-white checkered tablecloths, probably bought in gross. The tables had matching chairs, too: cheap, vinyl-covered plywood, with a thin layer of cotton batting to make the chairs "soft." The frames were made of cheap, chrome-plated steel tubing. The walls were covered with the same fiberboard and paint and grease as the ceiling, except for behind the bar, where tiers of bottles of various booze rose. I could see right away that there wasn't much to do in Neal's except get drunk, talk, and play the juke box. There were no pool tables or pinball machines.

By my second sip I spotted Farina with a group of ten or a dozen other people on the far side of the juke box, tables pulled together and people talking. At least two other profs were with the group, Dr. Ahmed of the sociology department and Fred White of econ. They were amongst that group of profs who were hip and always trying to talk with students, and get to know their students better. I'd heard that in some seminars, there were profs who would hold the last class of the semester in Neal's. I'd also heard that students would get together, be partying, and decide to call up a prof or a couple of profs to invite them down to the bars. That was an advantage of going to college in a small school. The profs were readily accessible.

I made my way over. I felt like an outsider. When I got to the group, Farina looked up and saw me. I saw then that the guy he'd been talking to, whose back was to me, was Robert Wolff. Wolff turned, the omnipresent grin on his face.

"I see we have the new radical leader with us tonight," Wolff said merrily and tapped his mug against mine as a sort of cheers, I suppose.

"Hey—the kid's okay," Farina said with a grin.

"I've told him to be careful of Natas," Wolff said to Farina. "He needs to watch his back."

"Oh, you guys still have a hard-on for each other because of freshman year," Farina said, a bit impatiently, downplaying Wolff's statement.

They continued to talk, and I tried to interact, but it was obvious that I was just a bystander. After a few minutes, I looked around the bar. I drained my mug and walked over for another one. That was when I ran into Jillian and Cindy. They were with people who looked like townies. Jillian waved at me, so I walked over.

"We're drinking tequila!" Jillian gushed exuberantly. I said that that sounded like fun. Cindy then introduced me to the people they were partying with. I didn't catch any names, but there were five people, three men and two women, all of whom appeared to be in their early twenties. One of the guys was black and his eyes were weird—squinty with one eye veering off to the side. The five weren't DeForrest students. Two of the guys were from Terre Haute, and the other three were from Glendale.

Jillian handed me a shot of tequila. Things started getting splotchy after that. I remember starting to tell her about coming up with my world view. It was a new discovery for me, about which I felt great, and why shouldn't I share it with people? My narrative was interrupted by shots of tequila, and I remember having my beer refilled a couple of times. Then we were moving—leaving Neal's and heading down the street to Sullivan's. Gleason was gone by then—it was getting quite late. At one point I remember trying to explain my theory of worldwide revolution to the black guys. I mean—if a black person couldn't understand the need for righting the social disorder, who could? I remember that at one point he asked me if I had anything to smoke and I said sure, but back at the frat. It was not long after that—and more beers and more tequila, of course—that I remember the fuzzy visuals of walking up the center stairs at the fraternity with the black guy and one of the white guys. One of them asked me why my door looked so funny and I explained that the lock wouldn't work. I remember pulling out the hash and loading a bowl. I also remember going to the restroom down the hall. There are bits and pieces that play back in my mind: explaining to them the concept of worldwide revolution, as they stared at the walls and ceiling of my dayglo room, their eyes rolling back in their heads. There was a point at which I excused myself to go to the restroom again. I remember coming back to the room and my guests rather hurriedly explaining that they had to leave.

The next morning I awoke with a tequila hangover. My eyes burned. My mouth tasted like shit from all of the cigarettes I'd smoked. When I sat up on my mattress, my head was spinning and I thought I would faint. I gave myself a couple of minutes to try and adjust. The clock said almost ten. I made it to the showers, and that helped, as did the lunch a short while later. Then Sid came by the room and told me he wanted to buy a couple more grams of the hash. I told him no problem and went to my dresser. The hash was not there. Over the next hour, tequila hangover and all, I combed every inch of that room. Only later did it dawn on me that my guests of the previous evening had absconded with it.

I tried to get hold of Jillian and Cindy by phone, but they would not answer their page. After dinner I walked over to their dorm and had the switchboard page them again. Jillian finally came down. When she saw me she said hey, and asked me how I was doing. We went to one of the couches in the public area on the main floor and I told her about what was missing. She was appalled, said that she didn't know those guys, that she'd only met them drinking in the bar the night before, and then she asked about the lock on my door, and I said, that it still didn't work. "Maybe someone in your frat took it," she suggested. She also suggested that I hit the bars more often and keep an eye out for them—as if yeah, I'd confront them physically and beat their asses or something. No, I didn't think so. I thought about the possibility that someone in the frat had taken it, as I left and headed back to the house. No—it couldn't be anyone in the frat. If someone in the house had taken it, at some point they'd be getting high on it and they would be caught.

I didn't know what I would do about making house payment. The money I'd sunk into the hash was not easily replaced. I sat in my room the rest of the evening. The tequila hangover and depression enveloped me. I felt like such an ass. Sure—I was really going to spark worldwide revolution. My guests of the previous evening were probably still chuckling over the dumbass DeForrest student that they'd ripped off. They were probably telling the tale to their friends even then. Eventually I fell asleep.

Chapter 21 - A Visit From Hitch-Hiking Friends

One of our assigned readings in political and social philosophy fairly blew me away. The only other philosophical piece that had had such an impact on me before was Thoreau's "Civil Disobedience."

When I'd read the syllabus, I had noted that we had to read "The Crito" by Plato. I thought that this would be one of those assignments I'd grit my teeth through, find some Cliff's notes, and go on with life, hoping there would be minimal impact from that assignment on the final. But once I got into it, I found that it was really cool. "The Crito" is one of the dialogues. In it, Socrates, who has been sentenced to death, is about to drink hemlock so that the sentence can be carried out. A friend attempts to stop him. Socrates says that he cannot. He explains that he had been raised, educated and protected by the State. At the age of majority, one makes the decision to agree to live within the State and accept, or to go away into the wilderness and live on one's own. By remaining in the State after that point, one has agreed to abide by its laws and judgments.

That placed the entire concept of the social contract into perspective. I had the right to accept that contract, and thus live within the State, or to reject it. Cool.

Once we got into the discussion, something hit me. Everybody else was talking about acceptance of the contract, but something was missing.

"This isn't really a contract situation," I pointed out.

One of the seniors in the class grimaced and said, in a desultory tone, "What do you mean by that?"

"If I make a contract to buy a car, I not only have the option of buying that car, I also have the option of buying any of the other cars on the market. I have that freedom of choice."

"There are over a hundred governments on this planet," the senior replied, before anyone else could say anything.

"It's not realistic to say that we are free to be able to choose whatever country we want to live in. People in other countries sure don't have that choice about the United States. We deport thousands of people every year who are in this country illegally. I'm sure that at the age of majority, most if not all of them would have opted to live here. And I certainly can't opt to become a citizen of Saudi Arabia. They wouldn't let me in to their country just like that. 'Hi! I'm 18. I read a lot about your country and it's for me!'"

Gleason smiled. "You have a good point. The concept of a 'contract' might not be very accurate."

"It's an adhesion contract," somebody else said, and Gleason's smile became a grin. I was listening intently. "If you're buying a car, you also have the choice not only of being able to buy any car on the market, but also the choice not to buy a car at all. You don't have that choice in a social contract setting. In other words, they're pointing a gun at your head and saying 'choose.'"

Gleason said, "That's right. In the time that this essay was written, people could reject the State and go off to live in the wilderness. We don't have that option anymore."

"All of those hundred-plus countries," I said, "have already carved up the territory for themselves. Even the high seas are subject to 'international law.'"

This all sunk in and I contemplated the legitimacy of my rejecting the State. I stumbled back to the house after class, lost in the thought of there being a legitimate, articulated basis for rejecting sovereign authority over me.

It was in the midst of all of this—the frat wars, the Farina mess, my own turmoil— that Bramberg came into town. I knew Brammie from freshman year. Not that he'd ever enrolled at DeForrest. He'd been enrolled at Ball State for two quarters before flunking out. But Simos, Brammie's best friend from high school, lived just down the hall from me in the dorm. They were Air Force brats. Their high school was about 20 miles north of mine. Our high schools were even in the same athletic conference, so we knew a lot of the same people and same places. Simos was a partier, so of course we became good friends freshman year. When Brammie started visiting from Ball State I got to know him pretty well, too.

At the beginning of my sophomore year, I'd heard that Brammie had taken off from school and gone back to rural Kilkerry. Davros, a buddy from the dorm who'd also pledged a fraternity at the same time as I had, had received a letter from Simos that bore that news. Simos had flunked out of DeForrest after two semesters and headed to some goddamn place in Maine, where his father had been transferred. All I knew was that the new base was somewhere in the far northern part of Maine. Simos had gotten a job there at the base exchange and was making a living—partying, living in a cheap apartment, the whole bit. I was surprised that he'd write anyone a letter. Freshman year I saw him with beers in hand, and quite a few joints in hand, but I'd never seen him with a pen in hand.

Davros called me on that Friday afternoon. It was bizarre weather for March in Indiana—but then all the weather in Indiana in March and April is bizarre. We'd gone from 20 degrees one day to 80 degrees the next. It was sort of like hitting one of those warm valleys that exist among the huge expanses of ice and snow in Antarctica. The sky was clear and the sun was shining. It seemed as though everyone in our house who owned a car was outside washing and waxing it. There were people in the front yard throwing frisbee and people in the back playing hoops. All the windows in the house were thrown open, and a cool breeze carrying promises of spring blew out the stale air that had been coagulating over the winter. When I heard my name paged over the PA, I went to the phone booth and punched the button that was blinking. I yelled "Got it!" and said hello. I recognized Davros's voice immediately.

"You'll never guess who's here," he said.

I thought for a second or two, then said, "Simos?"

"No, but close. Brammie's here!"

I had never thought of Brammie visiting our campus without Simos being there, too. I mean, Simos was the connection, and with him gone I never would have thought that Brammie would stop by. I told Davros I'd be right there to his frat. He and two other guys from our dorm had pledged to the same frat when I had pledged my house the previous spring. Their house was right down on campus, catty-corner from campus security. That was sort of a weird place to locate a frat with the reputation of being a party house. It was only three or four blocks away from my frat, so I immediately set out down the street. I knew where Davros's room was from Winter Term, so I went straight there and heard Brammie's voice as I came down the hall. When I stood in Davros's doorway, Brammie looked up and grinned.

"We goin' to the country or what?" he asked.

I looked down at the floor. There was a huge, old-fashioned metal tub filled with ice and probably four cases of beer. "Sounds like a plan to me," I said, smiling. I also noticed a couple of big packs with sleeping bags attached to them that were over in a corner.

Brammie introduced me to a friend of his who was standing there. They called the guy Hendo. "We started out going to see Simos," Brammie began.

"In Maine?" I asked.

"Yeah. Way fucking north in Maine. Loring Air Force Base."

"It's right near Caribou," Hendo added.

"Sure sounds north," I said. One of Davros's frat brothers handed me a joint.

Brammie said, "It's all pine forests, fucking gorgeous. There's a bluff overlooking this little valley. Two rivers come together there to form a third. We'd go up there to sit, get high, and watch the sun set."

"How'd you get up there, drive?" I asked.

"Shit no," Hendo said, laughing a bit.

"We thumbed," Brammie said. "Took off in September. Went up there." In between hits off of first one, then the next joint, Brammie started telling us about hitch-hiking. How they'd gotten side-tracked in Pennsylvania, and again in New Hampshire. What motherfuckers the cops in Ohio and New York were.

"But they ain't nothing compared to the cops in Texas," Hendo interjected with a tight voice, as he held back a cough after he'd taken a hit.

Brammie said. "Wasn't much work in Maine. So we went down to Texas."

"There's whole bunches of work there," Hendo added. "But for shit pay."

"Yeah," Brammie agreed, chuckling. He described how they'd gotten a ride with a semi driver and into Amarillo. How the driver them gave them a lead on a job, and they found a cheap apartment to sub-let from a guy who was a DJ who was moving to West Virginia. "The place is really shitty. I mean, we were living there in November and it was still hot and dry and miserable. The people were all shit-kicker rednecks. To top it off, we didn't have a car so we had to walk everywhere." Brammie crushed the empty beer can he was holding.

"At least we had air-conditioning," Hendo added.

"Yeah," Brammie agreed. "But we woulda died down there without it." He paused to accept the beer that Davros handed to him, tossing the empty into a corner, near a waste basket. "Anyway, we got fed up with it. Walking to work one morning, we saw this dead armadillo lying next to the road, been hit by a car. I told Hendo that was what the whole place reminded me of—Amarillo, dead armadillo. It was pay day so we just took our checks and cashed them, got drunk a couple of days and split."

"Went to New Orleans," Hendo said, chuckling.

"Now there's a wild place," Brammie said. "Took off from there a couple of days ago. Figured we'd stop by here and see you guys. We're on our way back to Maine to visit Simos again. He's getting married."

"Simos? Married?" Davros asked.

Hendo said yeah and started talking about how Simos had met this girl who lived just down the street from his folks at the air force base. I started asking Brammie about hitch-hiking—didn't they have problems getting rides with two of them instead of just one, what they did to avoid cops, a bunch of questions about logistical aspects of thumbing. Davros had arranged to borrow a beat-up, massive, 10-year-old Chevy from one of his fraternity brothers. We lugged out the tub of beer and put it into the trunk, then piled into the car and took off. Once we were heading out of town, I knew that Seven Arches was our destination. There were dual railroad tracks running side-by-side from Indianapolis to Saint Louis, and those tracks passed right through Glendale, down next to the student bars, and on out through the country. A few miles outside of town, where the tracks crossed Walnut Creek in a gorge, a bridge rose about 25 or 30 feet into the air, carrying the tracks. The structure was so long it was made up of seven arches of reinforced concrete. Inside the bridge itself, within and between the arches, ran tunnels for maintenance crews. We parked the boat of a car and climbed up the hillside and into the bridge. When we were half-way through the length of the bridge, the concrete began to tremble, faintly at first, then very noticeably. We all started laughing. When the train hit the bridge the noise was deafening.

The train seemed to be a hundred cars long, and it had to be hauling a bunch of coal cars to Terre Haute.

I looked over at Brammie and Hendo. The stories of thumbing held such a sense of freedom. A part of me wanted to try it. But I didn't know how I'd go about it. There seemed to be too much to it, too much to know. There was a confidence that it required, a confidence I lacked. I knew that if I tried it, I'd fuck it up somehow. Then again there was always the possibility of being picked up by a weirdo and murdered.

Finally the last car passed and the noise subsided. We crawled out of the structure and down the slope next to it. Somebody grabbed the tub of beer and brought it down beside the creek. We took off our shoes and waded in the water, still cold as hell from the winter. We stayed there a while, just throwing rocks and shooting the shit and drinking, all of us buzzed to beat the band. Then we headed back towards the car. I grabbed the tub, figuring it was my turn to tote it. It had water in it and not much beer, by that point. I wasn't thinking about effective strategies for carrying tubs of beer up hillsides. When I was nearly at the top of the mud path up to the road, I lost my footing and started to fall. The path was so steep that my fall was nearly straight down. Davros had brought a Polaroid camera and at the exact moment I lost my footing, he snapped a picture: Me, from the middle of my chest up, a surprised look on my face, and a column of water rising three or four feet into the air from the tub. I was helped up the hillside, and we all laughed at the picture as we headed back into town.

The guys dropped me off at the house and I said goodbye to Brammie and Hendo. They were going to split the next morning to head up to Maine.

I had just enough time to change out of my wet and muddy clothes. I headed down to the dining room, but Clancey signaled to me as I entered. He reminded me that I hadn't paid housebill yet, so I couldn't eat.

I went back up to my room, hungry as hell, and put on the Doobie Brothers' "The Captain and Me." That had sort of been an anthem album the year before, when I'd lived in the dorm. I sat there listening to it for a while before, stomach growling, I dozed off.

Chapter 22 - The Semester Rolls On

My attendance dropped. I was accurately noting my record of attendance on the calendar I had drawn on my wall. There were more and more oblong empty marks to denote classes I'd missed. I was making about half of my classes. Compared to semesters past, that was actually good attendance for me. However, compared to the first weeks of the semester and, my own expectations, it sucked. I was also hungry much of the time. In order to make up the money I'd lost in the hash deal, I waived off the meals portion of my house bill. That meant I had to scrounge as best I could for food. I'd bought some cheap vitamins, thinking I could supplant the nutrition I was losing. The worst time was when the meal was announced over the intercom. I would sit there in my room by myself, listening to my stomach growl, and try to concentrate on other things. After the first couple of times that this occurred, I just made sure to absent myself from the fraternity—and by "fraternity," I mean the physical plant—when mealtime approached. I would go down to the library to study or, as was more often the case, I would go off to some far corner of campus and get high by myself. The other bad part was the stomach cramps and diarrhea I soon experienced as a result of eating only vitamins. Goodbye nutrition! One positive thing was that my door had been fixed finally and I could lock the fucking thing.

Gleason's class was pretty cool, and my attendance there hadn't faltered much. We got into arguments with him and with each other as the classroom filled with smoke from everyone's cigarettes. I think a couple of the people in class, a couple of the real ass-kissers, had even taken up smoking just so they could meet with his approval: anything to get a good accume and into the med or law schools of choice. Hey—even increase the risk cancer if it meant a good GPA. Gleason went to Sullivan's all the time, I now discovered, so I was going down there and continuing the arguments we'd had in class. I knew that if I had 35 cents—the price of a mug of the cheapest draft beer—I could bum refills from people who'd bought pitchers. The arguments at Sullivan's were excellent. I was learning to improve the form and structure of argument

I was also taking acid about once a week, maybe twice. I was getting into the feedback in my head, listening to tunes differently, and pondering existence. I was seeing everything as being developed from ego, and I wanted to laugh—at myself and at everything flying around me. The thing about it, though, was that the effects of acid didn't merely last for the duration of the trip. They reached into daily existence. The acid reshaped the lenses on my eyes, helped them to physically alter the way light entered my soul. I began to doubt so much. I was observing more, too. Life was much more subtle than people realized.

We were just hitting mid-terms and so everything was a bit hectic. I was really humming in speech pathology. I had a high B, with two more hourlies and the final to go. I figured that I was okay in Gleason's class. I thought I would need to work on ed psych. I was getting tired of the prof's stories about teaching coaches during the summer. I was getting the distinct impression that my strategy of having a public school teaching license I could fall back on was not going to pan out. I couldn't stand the bullshit at the college level—I would never be able to acclimate myself to the worse bullshit at the secondary level again, having escaped it once.

In con law, Cindy and I had joined forces to challenge the established "right wing" of campus. Of course, in 1975 on most college campuses a right-winger was someone who apologized for Vietnam and, as a purist, felt that the country would have turned out better had Goldwater won the 1964 election. There were several of these people in con law. On one day there was a big confrontation when the focus of the day's discussion was the concept of stare decisis, the principle in law that case precedent controls. The conservatives in the class were staunch defenders of that particular principle, since it was fairly accepted dogma that the right wing would never take the White House again, and so the Supreme Court would be purged eventually of its Nixon appointees. Consequently, old case law protected the vestiges of conservatism, and judicial activism would mean that the forces of truth, justice and freedom would be advanced. Of course, at that time, as I've said before, Ronald Reagan was a senile joke, none of us taking him seriously for the 1976 elections.

The class began, as usual, with one student going to the podium and reciting the facts and holding of the case that had been assigned to her. Dr. Fredrick began the discussion after that. He was seated to the side of the room, away from the windows, in one of the ancient student chairs that festooned the rooms of Asbury Hall. Except for the obscenities and crude representations of various anatomical structures that were carved into the wooden desk tops, the chairs looked as if they were the original furnishings of one of the school's buildings in 1835. Fredrick was extremely intelligent but very soft-spoken. The Court case in question was a pretty difficult one. The majority of the Court had wanted to go one way, one could tell from the opinion, but had been held in check by prior decisions. I thought that this was bad. Hell, the Court in question was the Warren Court, and the changes that the justices wanted to make in the law in the particular case being discussed were changes that expanded free expression, one of those cases where Black and Douglas refused to participate in oral argument because they believed that the First Amendment was absolute. For whatever reason, that particular day I was pissed about the forces of Evil. Blood was pumping pretty rapidly in my body as I tapped a foot and listened to Dr. Fredrick describe the Court's dilemma. Others in the class must have felt similarly charged.

The class had quite a few poly sci jocks—people who were majoring in political science and, so, had a lot of classes with each other. For the most part they were juniors and seniors. My being quite vocal was not smiled upon by my "elders" in the class.

After Fredrick had finished describing the situation that the Court had faced, one of the seniors in the class raised his hand and, after Fredrick nodded his head towards the guy, the guy spoke.

"The Court had to do what it did. They had to follow precedent," he said. His name was Bob. He was from a house known for its jocks. Only at DeForrest would that identification have clicked in everyone's mind at the same moment—the specific fraternity followed by stereotype. In this guy's case, however, the stereotype was valid. He started on the football team's offensive line. In a Division I school, he would have been eaten up, but in Division III, a short white boy like him could exist. His hair was anachronistically short, and his beard was neat and trimmed. "If the Court ignored precedent," he continued, "the stability of the system would vanish."

Fredrick next called on one of Bob's buddies, Eric. Eric had begun the semester sitting in the front row of the class. After Fredrick had described the format of the class, and had begun sitting a different place every day among the members of the class, Eric was thrown into a state of confusion. He could not predict, from class to class, where the prof would sit. This was critical to Eric's strategy for getting into the law school of his choice. He was one of the students who had raised ass-kissing to the level of high art. In any class, he always sought the seat closest to the prof. He would heap praise upon the prof and smile like Eddie Haskell. By Dr. Fredrick moving about to different parts of the room from class to class, Eric had been placed in a position in which he would have to think—where do I sit today? That was the depth of his intellect. "The Founding Fathers," Eric now intoned—probably the voice that he envisioned one day as being useful in a campaign for state representative—"foresaw just such a check. They built it into the structure of the Court to ensure stability."

Cindy spoke before I could. She was even more unpopular among the members of this class than I was. Maybe she had already pissed in everyone's men's rooms. I don't know. But the big factor was that not only was she a hippie and a female, but she wasn't an attractive female. The opinions of attractive females, after all, could be tolerated. In the eyes of DeForrest male fraternity society, assessing, as those eyes were, future upper-middle-class breeding stock, an attractive hippie female could be tolerated when she expressed herself because such a woman's opinions could be characterized as being "cute." Once married and yoked with the burden of motherhood and raising upper-middle-class children, she simply would be told to shut up. Of course later, after class, the "boys" would share their jokes and each would speculate aloud as to the size of breast or skill of mouth. But an unattractive woman who was vocal and opinionated and Irish and way to hell to the left of center and who lived in the goddamn dorm for chrissakes—such a woman should not have been allowed to enter the hallowed halls of DeForrest. Margaret Mead probably had chafed at these aspects of DeForrest's "culture" in the short period before she had transferred out in the twenties. She had allotted a page-and-a-half in her autobiography to the two years that she had spent at DeForrest. On this day, Cindy started out cussing, and that threw them—the right-wingers—even more. "Bullshit," she said emphatically, not bothering to raise her hand or wait for Dr. Fredrick to call her. "Judicial review wasn't anticipated. Nobody planned for it when they drafted the Constitution. It just happened. That's what *Marberry v. Madison* was all about."

"They did, too," Eric countered.

I wanted to say "Did not" but Cindy was getting into it. "Who the fuck is 'they'?"

"The Founding Fathers," Eric replied arrogantly. He was on safer ground now, and addressed Cindy as though she were an idiot. Maybe she had pissed in the men's room on his specific floor of his specific frat when he had been the one taking a crap.

"Name me one," Cindy challenged. "Show me anywhere during the Constitutional Convention or in *The Federalist Papers* that one person said, 'And hey—look. The Supreme Court can look at the actions of either or both of the other branches and declare those actions to be null and void.'"

A female voice now arose. Lindie was a member of the sorority on campus that was considered to be the place for a female student to go if she wanted to have a high GPA and still be considered "cute." Lindie might have had a decent GPA, but if so she didn't acquire it through intellectual prowess so much as shopping for classes to pad the grade point. Con law was a good class, but it was not the bitch that some of the other poly sci classes were. To paraphrase Steve McMichael of the Chicago Bears, she "wasn't gonna win no Nobel Peace Prize for intelligence." She wore all the right clothes and she was very attractive in that anorexic way that most models have. Oh yeah—she modeled during the summer and other breaks from school. "I'm certain that Thomas Jefferson considered the matter when he wrote the Constitution," she shot off and, having done so, struck a profile that she probably thought would emphasize a critical point.

I really didn't like Lindie, and I couldn't pass this one up. "Jefferson didn't 'write' the Constitution. He wasn't even at the Constitutional Convention. He was in Paris at the time."

"But I remember," she said disdainfully, cringing at the very notion of having to converse with hippie scum, "in one of *The Federalist Papers* that he wrote. He specifically mentioned starry whatever." She might have been big on the date scene, and she might have been in demand as a model, but she had the brains of a turnip.

Cindy jumped in. "You mean stare decisis, honey. And Jefferson didn't write any of *The Federalist Papers*. Madison, Hamilton and Jay did."

Dr. Fredrick interjected a comment to get things back on course. He explained, for about the eighth time in the course, what the justices had considered in the case at hand—why each justice had gone one way or another. "In the end," he said, "the deciding vote went the way it did because that justice either did not want to destroy 80 years of case precedent or, like in *Brown*, precisely because they felt that they had to."

I raised my hand and Fredrick nodded in my direction. "But that's exactly the point—why make an exception because of the nature of the issue?"

"Because," Eric said, sensing an opening to portray himself as having some higher moral standards than the Seven Deadly Sins, the pursuit of which actually set the direction for his moral compass, "the Black case, or whatever, involved discrimination."

"So what?" I replied. "Presumably each case that's before the Supreme Court is important. I don't think the Supreme Court is determining cases involving the throwing of spit wads in school." A couple of people laughed. "Why say that on some issues precedent must be followed while on others it can be ignored or dispensed with? And I don't see why the 'Founding Fathers' and their views are necessarily all that important. Those fuckers are long since dead, and most of them were slave owners in an agrarian culture that was ruled by a white, male elite where only landowners could vote. Why should we be controlled by them from the grave?"

The argument was cut short by the ringing of the bell in East College. Cindy and I, each as hypered as the other, walked across East College lawn to the Hub where she inhaled a cheeseburger, I sipped an ice water, and we re-capped the argument. I got bored after while—and hungry thanks to sitting there and watching her eat.

Of course with mid-terms came the demand for speed. I was out of money, thanks to the hash deal and the gentlemen from Terre Haute. But that didn't mean I was out of the picture on obtaining drugs. A couple of guys asked me about speed, so I called Bloomington and my old acquaintance Dial-a-Drug.

I knew Dial-a-Drug from partying down at IU with people from Kilkerry. I was never really clear where he was from, as in what part of the state or the country. I made his acquaintance the semester before at a party down there, and he'd said that if I ever needed anything to give him a call—that he delivered. I thought he had meant that figuratively, and that we would still have to drive the 50 miles or so to Bloomington to pick up whatever it was we were buying. But no—he meant he would deliver. Just like a pizza place. During finals the previous semester I'd obtained some speed for nearly everyone, and some mesc. So it was that I pulled out the beer-box drawer of my makeshift desk and rummaged through the crap in there, looking for the scrap of paper I had written his telephone number on. I found it, then hustled up some change from a couple of interested people. It was long distance. The phone rang several times but was finally answered. I recognized his voice and told him who was calling, keeping my identity very cryptic, in case the phone was bugged. Of course, if the phone was bugged, the cops would know who I was just from the toll records. Nonetheless, I said I was the guy "from Glendale." He chuckled and asked me how I was doing.

"We're approaching mid-terms up here."

"So are we," he replied. "And I imagine you could use some help."

"You got that right."

He rattled off his inventory and prices. I was familiar with the types of speed he was listing, but he was adding embellishments to help me understand quality. "Got some basic white cross, a nickel a hit, get you off but not too wired. Got some black beauties, a quarter a hit, big and black and will really wind you out. Got some speckled birds, also a quarter, more for fun than for work. And the real gems—pharmaceutical quality time-release capsules. Fifty cents per, developed by some high-level research teams somewhere. They are good."

I did some quick calculations in my head. I rattled off numbers of the specific kinds of speed, and asked him how soon he could be there.

"Two hours," he replied. "Need anything else?"

"Like what?"

"I got some basic Mexican for $185 a pound. It won't kill you or anything, but you'll cop a good buzz. But I do have some blond Columbian that'll really blow you away."

"I don't think so," I said.

"Don't even want to try it?"

I told him no, and that I'd see him in a while, and hung up.

Only two other people in the house knew anything about speed coming in, but mid-terms were fast approaching, and people were getting desperate, and pretty soon my name was being paged every three or four minutes over the house PA as someone else was calling me to find out about the speed, that's how fast the news hit campus. Some of the people who called, I didn't even know—and I really loved that. We were only bringing it in for people in the house, though, so I told anyone who called that I didn't know what they were talking about.

I knew I was not a capitalist. No—that's the wrong way of stating it. I was not a capitalist by belief. I felt that that system was corrupt. It used people. Only a few benefited from it. Since it was based upon growth, that inherently meant that once growth was exhausted, oligopolies, then outright monopolies, would be the natural outcomes of the system. I was also under no illusions by this point that I was a business person. I could not function as a capitalist. I was not ruthless enough. When I had pot for sale, for example, I would always indulge the "customer" by smoking more than I should have from my portion—the profits. However, the prospects of obtaining a good bit of speed held out hope for me that I could (1) at least have a cash flow from which I could exact money for a few meals and some trips to the bars and (2) perhaps even recoup the heavy loss I had suffered in the hashish fiasco. Suddenly, I was not as depressed as I had been only a short while before.

Sid joined me in my room as I waited for Dial-a-Drug to arrive. Sid was looking foward to perhaps buying some pot and bringing an end to the lock that the Arkansas pot had had upon everyone. Even though I'd told Dial-a-Drug that we didn't need pot—my instinct for self survival had caused me to say that, to try and avoid losing more money— I knew he would bring some along, in the hope of making perhaps one sale.

A little over an hour after we'd talked on the phone there was a knock on my door and Dial-a-Drug entered. Of course, the first thing he did was to stare at the Day-glo walls and ceiling. "Man, you got a weird room," he said as he pulled off his backpack.

I introduced him to Sid, and then I got up and locked the door. Dial-a-Drug withdrew the contents of his backpack—speed and pot—as he talked. He was chuckling about the deluge of speed that had hit Bloomington. I told him about the acid we'd had come through, but he sort of blew that off. Then I remembered a story I'd heard from Warren. Dial-a-Drug was one of the most profit-oriented people I've ever met. He was not from the love-everyone-in-the-world school. He handled pot, hash, and speed. He never touched acid, and professed to have never taken it. When I brought up acid, he switched from his usual happy-go-lucky mannerisms to a bit more tight-lipped and quiet. The story went that the only time that Dial-a-Drug had done acid, he had reverted to a fetal position and murmured things about "god." He was a member of a fraternity at the time, and the people there thought that this was weird. For someone with as many hard edges as Dial-a-Drug had, I'm sure such behavior on his part was unacceptable. Drugs were for deadening things or speeding things up, but not for exploring deeply into the brain.

The hits of speed were already counted out and split up among different plastic baggies. I picked them up and sort of hefted them, one at a time, in my hands. Everything looked right. I took the money that had been given me and passed it to Dial-a-Drug.

"You sure you don't need any pot?" he asked.

"What do you have?" Sid asked.

Dial-a-Drug grinned. "I have some decent Mexican for $185 a pound, $20 a bag. Here, check it out," he said, and tossed onto the mattress next to me a large plastic bag that held a quarter pound. I picked it up, opened the zip lock, and smelled it. It seemed pretty good. "I'll even front it to you," he said to me, and that settled it. I shouldn't have done that, but, against my better judgment, I agreed. "But I have some Columbian that will blow you away." With that he whipped out a pin joint—a joint rolled as small as those tiny straws that they use for carry-out cups of coffee. He handed it to Sid, who immediately lit it and inhaled. "Be careful of that," Dial-a-Drug warned. "You only need two hits."

Dial-a-Drug handed me a bag of the stuff at the same time as Sid passed me the joint. I took a short hit and almost coughed from the density of the smoke. I tried to pass it to Dial-a-Drug but he shook his head, so I passed it back to Sid and exhaled. Then I looked at the bag that Dial-a-Drug had handed me of the "good" stuff. It was an ounce, but it felt different from any other pot I'd ever had. When I looked at it, I was struck by the color. At first glance, it was predominantly a blondish gold with streaks of bright green running through it. When I looked even more closely, I saw that there were flecks of a dark red color in the flower tops. I opened the bag and inhaled. The fragrance was almost overpowering—a smell of the primordial Earth, deep and rich. I traded with Sid, the bag for the joint, and I saw his eyebrows arch as he examined the pot.

"How much?" I asked.

"Thirty-five an ounce," Dial-a-Drug replied.

I think my jaw dropped at hearing the price. We were used to paying fifteen, maybe twenty a bag for Mexican. The year before some excellent Jamaican had gone around campus, among a select few, for about twenty-five a bag. And, the previous spring, a little bit of Colombian and a very little bit of Acapulco Gold had popped up here and there around campus at thirty a bag. But thirty-five was unheard-of.

"Just wait," Dial-a-Drug said, smiling.

He turned around and started flipping through my albums. I thought he was going to pull one out to play, and I contemplated that. What music would sound good at this point? I tried to visualize one of the albums. The albums in my collection were nearly all old and battered, the covers torn here and there, the spines worn to the point that whatever writing that had once been there was gone. But they were like old friends of mine. I could play an album and the sounds would visit me, dropping by to pay their respects and impart some pleasure. It was when I was on this line of thought that I realized that I was lying back on the floor, staring at the ceiling and trying to match the cracks in the plaster running here and there and through Day-glo paint with any road maps of the United States that I had ever seen, or perhaps places to which I'd been and—I realized then just how fucking high I was. I looked over at Sid and saw how bloodshot
his eyes were, and I knew my eyes had to be the same way.

Sid reached into a pocket of his jeans and fished out several bills totaling 35 bucks and handed the money to Dial-a-Drug. Dial-a-Drug tossed Sid the bag of pot.

"How much of this can you get?" Sid asked.

"I don't know. Maybe a couple of pounds."

"Uh-huh," Sid grunted and leaned back, lost in a foggy thought. "I'll get back in touch," he said, then added, with a grin, "Man, I'm fucked up."

The drought was over for some people. I passed out as people left to go downstairs to dinner.

Chapter 23 - Planning A Strike

Some of the guys in the house weren't too keen about playing host to a meeting that ran so heavily against the administration. We were in the throes of civil war within the frat and good relations with the university's administration would be something nice to have.

Of course, the administration would not have been on "our" side, demonstrations or no demonstrations. The administration had cast its lot with the old alums and national frat. Besides the guys in the house who gave a shit about the issue were on our side. So the meeting was set and I spent most of that day running around campus, making sure people knew the time and place of things.

A little before 7:00 I went downstairs to the dining room to make sure all was ready. Buchanan was sitting at one of the long tables—studying! I hadn't seen him studying in the entire time I had been at school. When I walked into the dining room and he looked up, I could tell there was going to be a hassle.

"What?" he asked.

Yeah, like he didn't know. "We're having a meeting in a little bit here. We need the dining room."

"I'm studying."

"Well, go ahead. It's just that the dining room is going to be full in a bit and it won't be real quiet."

"I'm going to complain about this."

"You already are complaining."

"No, I mean I'm going to lodge a complaint."

"With whom? Carson? Hey—and there are other places in the house to study, like down in the library."

He slammed his book shut—probably the first time that semester the book had been open— and stormed out. Oh well.

The dining room was big. The house had a capacity of 68, so the dining room had been designed to accommodate at least that many at the long, narrow tables. The room was a little larger, still, to allow for the occasional visitor. I'd hauled in extra chairs, and with the warm air of the spring evening, we'd opened the double doors out onto the patio. People began arriving. By the time we got started, the room was packed. I had my notes and things at the table at the front of the room. Natas had ensconced himself at the table as well, having claimed the space at the last meeting. The room was standing room only. People even sat cross-legged on the floor.

Absent were the leading members of student government. The SBP—Student Body President—was a face man like Natas. He'd never made any statements or taken any side in this matter. He'd been elected, then gotten laid a bunch of times, and had his picture in the yearbook. His resume was safe. The members of Academic Council—the group that should have been most concerned with the issue of academic freedom—were not there either. To read in The Daily DeForrest about the meetings of the various organs of the campus student government, one never would have known that there was any type of controversy brewing on campus. But student government for these people was a vehicle for getting into law school, and a resume padded with references to Student Senate or Academic Council or—plum of all plums—Student Body President—was good. In that way, the darlings could hedge their bets against a bad GPA and/or lame LSAT score.

I had talked with several people to finalize an agenda. Natas was talking with several of his people as the meeting began. I had seen them with him a couple of times on campus. They were like his groupies. Jeanna and Chrissy or something and another woman. Right before the meeting I tried to talk with Natas, but he was aloof. I had no idea what his problem was.

I asked someone to act as secretary and someone volunteered. I went on to say what all had been done so far. Then I got into the main point. "Over the last year, we know what the university has been doing. On the one hand, DeForrest has said that it is committed to academic freedom. And yet, on the other hand, the university has been determined to rid itself of Dr. Farina for no apparent reason. Finally, a couple of weeks ago, the university let us know that when it comes to choosing between academic freedom and the consolidation of university power, academic freedom can go to hell!" I said that last bit with a little oomph, and some body English. There was applause. I felt really good. I glanced down at my notes and tried to focus. Every TV news bit from the 1960's was coming to mind now, and I was getting into a rhythm. "There's going to be a rally next Friday. We're going to hold it on the back steps of the Union Building." I added a couple more things, and then others spoke.

There was a consensus that the situation was bad, and that something dramatic had to be done to shake up the university. There were several proposals. I suggested a strike. That was the next-to-the-most radical position offered. It was a very popular choice. The most anemic was a letter-writing campaign. One of Natas's groupies was ardent in suggesting that. She got heckled. Another of Natas's groupies suggested we lobby. I asked her whom should we lobby, and who would be the lobbyists. Those questions shot that line of thought. Other suggestions were tangential, like how to do picket signs, etc.

Natas startled me by speaking. I was reminded of Robert Redford toward the end of The Candidate, when his character has sold out. Natas suggested that we strike for one day. That would send a message to the university. We could call it a moratorium, he said, a term that he knew harkened to the antiwar days.

I objected to a one-day strike. "The only message that will send," I said, "is that DeForrest students are willing to bag classes on a spring day for something other than a country run." There was applause at my cynicism. But Natas was confronting a major dilemma for most of the people there: moral beliefs v. GPAs. What would happen to people's grades in the event of a strike? What would happen to their apps for a Top Five law school, or the med school of their dreams, or that position for which so many of them would vie in the Corporate Management Scheme Of Paradise?

As this debate took place, two chemistry majors sitting close to the table signaled me. I leaned over to one of them and he said, matter-of-factly, "We can blow off the back half of the administration building."

I looked at the guy, and when I saw that his expression was serious, I waved him off. That was too crazy, too weird. Besides, the people who played those characters in the movies always ended up being bad guys.

Meanwhile, the debate had turned a couple of directions and arrived, finally, where Natas wanted it. There was going to be a one-day moratorium on attendance of classes. On top of that, Natas picked a Friday for the moratorium to occur. With very few exceptions, DeForrest didn't have Friday classes. Shit. And I could just see it. The weather would be nice, people would be playing frisbee, and it would have all the appearances of Spring Break at Daytona Beach without the beach. There was a vote then—not on whether to have a moratorium, no, that matter was decided without a vote by Natas. No, one of Natas's groupies suggested that after the rally at the UB, we march "someplace." Someone suggested that we march on the house of the university's president. That carried resoundingly. Only problem—the president of the university was never home. He was always fundraising all over the fucking country. With any luck we'd confront the maid. But I could see that, at this point, naysaying would not be greeted well. One of Natas's groupies raised her hand and asked who would speak at the rally. I said we should try to get one of Farina's colleagues in the faculty to speak. That seemed pretty logical. There was general agreement on that.

She continued, "That's all well and good, but I mean, who is going to speak on behalf of the students?" There were a couple of people in the crowd who said my name, a couple of whom were rather loud. Somebody said, "Vote on it!" And a lot of hands went up, a lot more than half, and I said, "I guess that carries!" Everybody except Natas and his groupies laughed at that.

I figured the meeting was over, but Natas spoke up.

"It would seem that we need structure to what we're doing. We lack structure."

"Okay," I said. "What do you have in mind?"

"I think we need to name ourselves, so that we can identify what this organization represents."

There seemed to be agreement with that. But I shook my head. I thought about Kesey and what he said about naming things. "Once we name ourselves, we tell the university what we are not."

"I thought Students for Academic Freedom sounded pretty good," Natas said, ignoring me. "That's what we are."

There seemed to be support for that, but I continued to argue against it. "That's precisely my point. Right now we constitute an amorphous force of discontent. The university can't be sure that we're limited to the issue of Farina and academic freedom. I mean, there are a lot of other things on this campus that need change. If we don't adopt a name for an organization, then the university can't be sure what we'll be pissed about next week or next month."

"No other issues are as important as academic freedom in a university," Natas intoned.

"Sure there are. OIT policy. Unequal treatment of women. The fact that we can't have a car on campus without some Mickey Mouse excuse. The fact that university security can walk right into a dorm room at any time without cause—it's in everyone's housing contract. Christ—the food in the dorms."

When Natas said the dorm student government groups can deal with the problems there, four or five people said "Bullshit."

By now, I noticed, Natas's groupies had fanned out, taking up positions that made it seem as if he had support throughout the room, just like fake bidders at a rigged auction. They took up the argument for naming the thing Students for Academic Freedom, as though without the name, plans for the "moratorium" would not go forward. Some of the people there were convinced. Others simply wanted to go home—we'd accomplished the important things. One of Natas's groupies made the motion—actually, she said "I motion that . . ."—and another one seconded it and it quickly passed. Then that same groupie said, "I think we need to appoint committees."

"That's a good idea," Natas said. "We need committees. One for publicity, one for planning, one for letter writing, one for affirmative action."

"What's affirmative action?" I asked. But my question went unanswered because another of Natas's groupies reminded him about lobbying, that we'd need a committee for that, too.

Jeanna quickly volunteered to head the letter writing committee. And what could I say? How could anybody object to people volunteering to take on work. Despite my misgivings, Natas had his committees. Curiously enough, he and his groupies were all installed as chairpersons of those committees. Natas, Cindy, Austin and I were on some sort of central committee. The meeting finally adjourned. I glanced over at Natas, where he was talking with his groupies, all newly-appointed committee chairpersons. There was a hand placed on my shoulder, and I turned. The two chem majors were standing there.

"I tell you," one said in an insistent whisper. "We can take out the back half of the ads building. It's really simple."

"I don't believe you guys," I said. "This thing's non-violent. Hell, we aren't competent enough for anything else."

"You don't understand," the other chem major said. "All we take is a simple benzene ring . . ." Some crap like that for a minute or two, then his buddy interrupted him. They started arguing about the chemical sequences involved in making explosives. That was their real interest: How to create bombs for maximum effect. Defense contractors should have known about these guys and recruited them. They would have been real catches. "Don't pay us any overtime—we love staying here designing bombs." I told them to forget any such plans. I reminded them of the story we'd all heard about the DFU students in 1969 who'd tried to burn down the ROTC building. Those students had only succeeded in causing major burns to themselves and then getting arrested and expelled.

"We ain't blowing anything up," I said. "Got it?" Reluctantly they agreed and left.

I turned around and the only persons left were Natas and his band. They were discussing something, in hushed tones, and I took a few steps towards them. One nudged another and then all discussion stopped.

"I think we should meet tomorrow," I said.

"I don't think that we can," Natas said, turning to the others for prompt approval.

"Well, we should at least get together before the rally on Friday," I said a bit impatiently.

"Okay," Natas said. "In the Fishbowl at the UB. Fifteen minutes before."

"I'll arrange for a faculty speaker," I said, and Natas said that was fine.

I walked back up to my room as they filed out. The situation was very strange. I wanted to call Austin and Cindy and talk about it, but I figured it could wait until the next day. I also wanted to talk with Robert Wolff.

Chapter 24 - Drug Bust Worries

Then the rumor went around that there was going to be a drug bust. Not just a drug bust, but some kind of campus-wide thing that would hit nearly every house, all the dorms, and a bunch of people OIT.

There was a hierarchy of vulnerability as far as the police state and DeForrest were concerned. The most vulnerable people were those who lived OIT, those "asocial nonpersons" who had decided that communal living was not for them; the people who had decided that privacy, and freedom from the fun and games of Greek life in particular, were more appropriate concepts in the face of being released into adult life. Presumably, given DeForrest's policies, such maturity was not viewed positively by the DeForrest administration. So if the cops busted someone OIT, it was as if that person was a renegade to begin with and so deserved his or her fate.

The residents of the men's dorms were were even more vulnerable, because of a clause in the housing contract that allowed those acting on behalf of the university to enter any room at any time without warning. A lot of people in the dorms got high. On weekend nights, even when parents were visiting, it was almost possible, on a couple of the floors in particular, to get high by walking down the hallways. But about every two years there was a token—no pun intended—bust in the men's dorms. My freshman year the dorms got skipped. The previous fall, one of the guys in a dorm had left a small amount of pot in a baggie in one of his jackets and had sent the jacket to the cleaners. Anyplace else, the people either would have thrown the pot away, or kept it for their own use. Not in Glendale. The guy who ran the cleaners was among the great many adult males in the community who was duly sworn as a part-time deputy—he directed traffic at the area high schools' football games and longed for the opportunity to be a real cop and swagger around wearing all that patent leather—and when he found that bag, it was five-alarm city. The cops called the university, got permission to enter the room of the student in question, and were accompanied by the head of security as they stormed in and busted the guy, with three of his friends, as a joint was being burned.

Of course a big gulf existed between the policy of toleration toward the men's dorms and the university's policy towards the women's dorms. Whereas the university more or less ignored the rabble in the men's dorms, it took on the protection of women paternalistically. Women could party only outside their living units or under the greatest precautions within.

And that brings us to the frats. People in a frat had to be blatant in order to bring down the wrath of the police. It was believed that the frats were protected by their alumni. Actually, they weren't. Not in the sense that the people in the house could call up their alums and say, "Hey—call the president of the university and tell him to call of the heat." However, the university perceived the alums from the frats as being those alums most generous in donating to the ever-ongoing fund drives. And in that sense, the university didn't want to screw up fund raising by having the alums read about rampant drugs on campus. Those 90-year-old alums from the class of ought-six wouldn't want to read in the Star or hear from other alums that busts had taken place on campus, much less in their old house. The frats were also protected by the fact that they were privately owned. The cops needed warrants to go in. So it was a hassle for the cops to bust frats. But busts had happened. One frat had been busted twice, its members nailed because they were using rooms to grow plants. The busts were never official and never appeared in the town's or the university's newspapers. The university did not want its students busted for drugs. Not that the university was motivated out of any concern for the health and well-being of its students. Stories about drugs busts would fuck up fund raising. And the university could make its desires be carried out without any publicity. The university was, after all, the largest employer in about eight counties of that area, including the county in which Glendale was located. The university had more than a little clout. If the university didn't want its students to be busted, then by god they wouldn't be busted.

Paranoia had run high on campus since a bust at the dorm the previous fall. Students were sure that something was "coming down" at "any time," a view that waxed various days of each month since the previous fall. Each rumor that made the rounds carried with it a few details sufficient to lend it an air of legitimacy. Now we were through mid-terms, ready to go on break, and, after that, end the semester. The times would have seemed hardly propitious for a bust, but then the world has a strange logic to it.

I was at the house, sipping a beer and watching TV in the Informal. I was paged—I was getting a lot of phone calls, what with the Farina situation and also with DSR-TKA nationals looming. I went over to the phone booth just off the foyer, thanked whoever had paged me and took the call.

The person on the other end of the line said my name, and it took me a second, but then I recognized Mooter's voice. I started to say something but he cut me off. "Shut the fuck up, man!" His voice was urgent. "Don't say my name. Drop what you're doing and get the fuck over here. I'm not kidding." Then he hung up.

I stood there for a couple of seconds. Then I shrugged and went upstairs. Whatever was up, Mooter had good reason to ask me to come over to his house. Probably a party or something. I grabbed a light jacket and stuffed a beer into each pocket, then finished the one that I was drinking and headed out. The trees were still bare, although a few had budded. The air was cool. As I walked along, I could feel my hair brushing down the sides of my face. I felt like a real hippie. I chuckled and as soon as I was on Anderson Street, I popped open one of the beers and took a big swig.

It was the middle of the afternoon of a weekday, so very few people were out roaming about. Most were inside studying. That was a perfect time for Mooter to throw one of his parties. The walk over to his house was only about four blocks—long by DFU standards, a short hop anyplace else. Once I got there, I bounded up the stairs and knocked on his door. I thought it odd that there was no music playing. Mooter was always playing music, especially if he was throwing a party. When Mooter opened the door, he grabbed me by the arm and pulled me inside. There was a girl sitting on his couch. Mooter always had women around. This girl was a townie. I recognized her from someplace, a party or something. I smiled and said hello, although Mooter was acting weird.

Mooter threw a lot of parties and was a really weird guy, but he had this mellow aspect to his craziness—very laid-back but always thinking. His room was definitely weird, as I said before, rather trippy. When I turned to Mooter, I realized he was uptight. I'd never seen him agitated before.

"This is Tina," he told me. "She works downtown."

"Yeah, we've met," I said, giving Mooter a look of uncertainty but trying to smile at the same time. I offered my hand and she took it, a bit nervously I thought. Then I thought that probably most hilljack guys didn't offer their hands to shake upon meeting women. Maybe they touched the bill of a cap and said, "Ma'am" or sacrificed a toothpick to a match's flame or something. I don't know.

"Tina works at Glendale Police Department—in the records section."

I about shit when Mooter said that. What in the fuck was he doing with a girl who worked for the cops? Maybe she was a cop! Maybe they gave her a badge and an ID number and the whole bit, and she was deputized and duly authorized and could haul our young white asses to jail right now. Then I thought—I don't have anything on me. But what about at the house? In my room? They could take me into custody, then hold me while they got warrants . . .

"Tell him what you told me," Mooter said to Tina.

"They've been investigating the drug traffic on campus, and a bust is going down. I saw the warrants. There are seventy of them. I saw Mooter's and a couple of others." She reached into her purse and took out a piece of notebook paper and unfolded it. She handed it to Mooter, and I stepped over to look at it with him.

"You didn't tell me you wrote down the names," Mooter said.

"You didn't ask me," Tina replied.

I saw my name and Sid's and TV's. I also saw a bunch of other names I knew.

"When's it happen?" I asked.

"Tomorrow night," Mooter answered. "They got university, county, city and state in on this."

"Fuckin' A," I said. "I'd better be moving. Thanks, Mooter. And hey—thanks, Tina."

I got out of there and headed straight for Michelle and Austin's. When I banged on the door, Austin opened it, grinning when he saw who it was. The grin disappeared as I explained what I'd learned.

I got back to the fraternity—and by "fraternity," I mean the physical plant—quickly, and told TV and Sid. We put our heads together. We figured that if any drugs were found in the "public" areas of the house—any places outside our individual rooms—then the police couldn't bust any individuals. So each of us wiped fingerprints off our baggies, wrapped what we had into paper bags, then shoved those paper bags into the candy machine that stood, unused, in the main stairwell. Once I had those items secured, I grabbed one of the house sweepers and went back to my room. I carefully swept my carpet, going over the whole room twice. I handed off the sweeper to Sid so he could do the same, and then I got down on my hands and knees and, starting in one corner, began working a very patient grid, looking for any flakes of pot or any seeds the sweeper had missed. I was surprised by how much I had at the end of that closer examination. I had enough for a bowl. So I took that, placed it in an ancient aluminum film cannister and, minus fingerprints, stashed that as well. I went back to my room and started on the closet. I pulled every single item out and swept the floor with a whisk broom. I meticulously examined every corner as well as every inch next to the base boards. Finally, I examined my desk. The surface appeared to be clean. Then I took out the "drawer" and emptied it entirely, replacing each object carefully and only after close inspection. By the time I was done, three hours had passed, but my room was definitely clean. I promptly opened a beer and got very drunk.

The next day was weird. There were eight million rumors circulating. The telephone was constantly ringing as some new rumor was issued. I had even bagged classes for fear of walking down to campus and getting picked up by the cops. Late in the afternoon, Sid broke out a joint of the blonde Columbian he had stored in the candy machine and he, TV and I went up to the fire escape to smoke it. The smoke felt good and tasted good and the buzz really helped after such a fucked couple of days.

I'd never been in a situation such as this before, waiting for the cops. I went back over my room several times, just to make sure I hadn't missed a seed or a tiny flake of pot. I was paranoid. I also felt a weird satisfaction over having made a list of some sort of Enemies of the State. That had a certain appeal to me. I wanted a copy of that search warrant. Then I realized—"Copy," hell, I'd get served with the original! Never having been through the process, I could only make guesses about it. But I figured that, if they gave me an actual piece of paper, I would have it framed, maybe get a picture of me with the officer who served it on me. No—the cops wouldn't cooperate like that. After all, apparently this was supposed to be a "big" bust for them, and they soon would realize that it had been blown, and when they realized that they would be pissed. And then they would probably see the huge Day-glo badge I had painted on the wall, the middle of which read, "Fuck the Pigs." That would not endear me to the law enforcement officers who would soon be our visitors. Hey—maybe they'd take pictures of my room for use in their little anti-drug presentations to high schools! That would be cool.

Early in the evening, after dinner, we gathered in Sid's room. He had a damn good view of the front lawn and Seminary Street. I didn't even have a beer in hand. I figured if they were going to bust people, they would bust people for anything, including underage drinking. Everybody in the house knew what was happening. Everybody in the house who smoked, even though only three of us had made the "list," was paranoid. After all, names could have been added after Tina had nailed the list, or she might not have seen the entire list of names.

At about 6:30 I was paged once again. I got up, disgruntled, and walked down the hall. I pressed the blinking button and said hello. After the caller had finished giving me his message, I thanked him and ran down the hallway back to Sid's room. TV and Sid both nearly jumped when I ran into the room.

"That was Tony, the guy that drives for the pizza place."

"Yeah?" Sid asked.

"He just drove by the police station downtown. Seventeen cop cars. All parked down there. County, city, state, university. Plus some vehicles that look like they're government issue but aren't marked." Sid whistled, and TV rolled his eyes. "They oughtta be here any minute."

Simple math on the cops' cars went something like this. The town of Glendale only had two cop cars—G-1 and G-2. The county sheriff had four. The university had three. That meant that the State of Indiana and, I imagined from the unmarked cars, the DEA had contributed to the "operation" about to take place.

We opened the windows. The air was cool, but if sirens were wailing en masse we wanted to be able to hear them. We were freezing our asses off. Ten minutes became twenty, and we were about to close the windows, bust or no. Then two cop cars—G-2 and one of the unmarked cars—stopped at the end of the walk out on Seminary Street, lights rotating and blinking. The vehicles didn't seem like machines. They were almost animate, like carnivores in search of prey, looking at their quarry holed away safely in its lair, out of reach. The cops sat there for a couple of minutes. They had to have known which rooms belonged to whom. Sid's lights were on, so they could see us clearly, staring out at them. I thought that maybe some cursing was going on. Then, just as quickly and quietly as they'd pulled up, the two cars pulled away.

There were no busts that night. Cop cars pulled up in front of the houses and apartments of the people who were on the list that Tina had, but no warrants were served. No cops even left the warmth of their cars. I never got to frame my piece of paper. Tina kept her job and nobody was the wiser. In the weeks that followed, the cops didn't even seem particularly pissed off about anything.

Then I got to thinking—maybe the university was behind the whole thing. "Let's scare the shit out of the little bastards and maybe this drug thing will die down." They didn't want to bust anyone. That was bad for the University's image as a safe place for upper-middle-class white people to send their sons and daughters. No—they could make the list available to that little girl that works in the department sorting records—she's friends with a couple of them. She can even copy it down if she wants to. And the students will get scared as all fucking hell and clean up their acts.

Yeah. Right.

Five minutes after the cops had pulled away the smoke in the hall was so thick you'd have sworn there was a fire going. Actually, there were a bunch of fires going, very little ones that would spark, and light a bowl or a joint. The university's plan was cause for amusement, but not for a change of lifestyles.

Chapter 25 - The Inquisition

At lunch one day, Carson announced to us that "we" had received notice, on that day, a Tuesday, that on Wednesday and Thursday evenings of that week the house corporation—or "house corp" as it was short-handed, the group of three or four old alums who acted as a sort of board of directors—would come to the fraternity—and by "fraternity," I mean the physical plant—to "interview" each member of the house, individually.

Somebody asked, "What do you mean by 'interview'?"

Carson said, "They want to know about the situation here."

Somebody else said, "That didn't answer the question."

Carson hemmed and hawed and said he didn't have any more announcements and then he got his ass out of there, his food only half-eaten.

As was becoming typical, we all wasted time that afternoon and early evening—after a supper at which neither Carson, the housebitch nor any of his or her cronies showed their faces—talking about what had been announced. Nobody knew what to expect. I figured several alums would come in and ask us about our majors, what we expected from the frat, about our goals in life, that sort of thing. There were other people, though, who thought the prospects were much more sinister. Whale Man was among that number. "Anything Carson's got his fingers into is gonna end up hitting one of us." By "us" I assumed that he meant one of "The Five." But I figured he was probably being paranoid.

I was fast running out of pot, and I had received the last of the checks I would get from the bank for "books." From these last bits of money, I purchased alcohol. I proceeded to blow off studying and get drunk. That was always a nice prospect. Candace and her friend Brenda, on whom I had always had a crush, were supposed to be over later. Candace wanted to see what I had done in preparing for DSR-TKA. I had done a lot, really, but mostly was from books and journals I had. The research I had done in the library was minimal.

I had to take a piss, and as I walked down the hallway to the head, I was witness to Edwards confronting Carson in the hallway outside Carson's room.

"Did you have anything to do with setting this inquisition up?" Edwards demanded.

Touche! I thought. "Inquisition." Right on! Edwards was being as paranoid as Whale Man.

"I resent the implication that this is any sort of inquisition," Carson replied.

"Come on!" Edwards snorted. "We're going to be called in individually to justify ourselves to people who haven't been here in 20 years or more and who haven't given any money in over a decade." Carson started to walk around Edwards, but Edwards blocked his way. "Are you going to answer my question!?"

"I don't have to answer your question," Carson snorted.

That was not a smart approach for Carson to take as (a) an elected house officer (b) with the title of "president" of anything (c) on a college campus (d) the year after Nixon's resignation was prompted by Watergate. If the house president had had any political smarts at all, he'd have realized that he had reached a point with which other autocrats in history—Czar Nicholas II and his wife Alexandra, Louis XVI and Marie Antoinette, Charles I—had become familiar. This was the point at which he should have cut his losses and run. But Carson had the illusion of being in control.

I went in and took a piss and, when I came out of the can, Carson was just disappearng down the stairway. I shrugged and headed back to my room, but I was intercepted by Edwards.

"You got a minute?" he asked.

I have always thought that is a weird question. Like I can possibly possess time. Or, if I can, is it infinite? Or is there only a finite amount of time that each of us has and if we give away one minute it impacts on the last few moments of our lives? How can I possibly know how many minutes I possess? I didn't think Edwards wanted to discuss anything on that level. If he had, he would use a plethora of malapropisms and word fragments. I said sure and led him back to my room where I picked up a beer. He looked around the room. The graffiti was in a constant state of flux, ever-growing, ever-glowing. Edwards had added his autograph up toward the ceiling on one wall, shortly after the room had been christened. This was his first visit since then and I could tell that he was impressed—or weirded-out, I'm not really sure which.

"You're house parliamentarian," he said. I nodded. When I had joined the frat, since I was the only person with any knowledge of parliamentary procedure—from student congress competitions in high school and in college—I had been made parliamentarian. It had been an appointed position, not an elected one. I was always involved in high school student government. But I had assiduously avoided any job in the frat involving authority or responsibility. It's one thing to piss people off on campus. It's another thing altogether to piss people off in the building where you have to live. I hadn't had any choice in being named parliamentarian. Since no one else in the house knew anything about parliamentary procedure and I had admitted that I did, the mantle of that office was thrust upon me. I did not see how that particular position could result in having to do anything of any consequence. Or anything, period. Until now, in fact, I had never been called upon to perform any duties. "Can we hold a chapter meeting without the approval of the president?"

That question didn't involve parliamentary procedure as such. I said I'd have to see the by-laws of the chapter but that, generally, yes, a membership can usually call a meeting if that membership can assemble a quorum, with or without the approval of the head officer. It's sort of what prevents despotism.

Edwards said he'd be right back with the by-laws, so I sat down and sipped my beer, trying to figure out what album to put on next. When he came back he had Buchanan and Jones with him. I took the dog-eared pages of the by-laws Edwards held, and flipped through it.

"We can have a meeting with a quorum," I said. "And a quorum is two-thirds of the membership of pledges and actives living in the house."

"How about removing the president from office?" Edwards asked.

That was certainly a weird twist on things. I looked through the by-laws again. "It says here that you can do so on a general motion. But there has to be a one-week waiting period for a general motion to be voted on. That's weird."

"Fuck!" Buchanan exclaimed. "That means that Carson'll still be in office when house corp gets here."

They went on chatting for a few minutes. I kept on drinking my beer. I even popped open another one after I'd killed the one before it. I flipped through the pages, and then an idea dawned on me.

"You don't want Carson in office when the house corp gets here tomorrow, right?" I asked.

Jones said that was right. "What do you have in mind?"

"How about this—we suspend the rules. We can do that under Robert's Rules of Order. Then we vote Carson out. Kyle here, as Vice-President, assumes the office of President. By the time that house corp gets here, it's done."

"Can Carson challenge that?" Buchanan asked.

I shrugged. "Yeah. But so what? If a majority of the membership of the house is on record as saying that he is not wanted as president any longer, who fucking cares? He'll have no authority."

"Can we make it retroactive?" Edwards asked.

"Huh?" I asked.

"Can we make it retroactive to when he called the house corp and national and invited them here?"

"I don't see why we can't. We're a self-governing body. If we're going to suspend some rules, we can suspend them all. The Constitution of the United States prohibits ex post facto laws, but that's for the country, not for this frat. There's no provision that I see in the by-laws prohibiting us from making measures retroactive."

"Then I'm calling a meeting," Edwards said, and the three of them left my room. The next thing I heard was Edwards on the intercom saying that there was an emergency chapter meeting in 15 minutes.

I actually owned a copy of Robert's Rules of Order. It had a chart that gave a nifty little short-hand of motions and how many votes were needed. I grabbed it and the sheets of the by-laws and went downstairs to the dining room. Edwards motioned to me to come up to the front table. Oh great, I thought. I get to sit at the front table of a meeting again. I was getting a bit tired of this. I mean, I didn't mind it when we were having meetings about the Farina thing, but a meeting of the frat was different.

It didn't take long for everybody who was in the house to come downstairs to the dining room. Even members of the "other" faction, all except Carson that is, were taking seats. Everybody was wondering what the hell was going on. Edwards called the meeting to order and had Jones, who as house treasurer was the next ranking officer, call roll. They had a quorum and Edwards started by saying that things were really fucked up, especially considering the fact that national and house corp were trying to boot people and interrogate people, etc., and that a lot of people wanted to get them the fuck out of our lives. "But we can't,"Edwards said. "Because the constituential components of this fraternal entreaty are resolutioned to stand on their own to . . ." And he went on for a minute or two. We all cringed. If he would have avoided trying to string out long words the meanings of which he did not know—or long verbal "things" that sounded impressive to the uninformed or illiterate but that were, in fact, not words at all—he wouldn't have sounded like such a hilljack, even with the accent. But that was Edwards. I had seen several copies of The Reader's Digest in his room and figured he did the vocabulary building section in it every month.

Carson's buddy Benson raised his hand and Edwards recognized him. "Why wasn't Carson told of this meeting?"

"He would've been if he was in the house," Edwards replied. "But this is an emergency meeting. The majority here want to do things differently than the president of the house is doing."

"You can't have a meeting without the president," Belzer, one of Carson's other buddies, said, somewhat tersely.

Edwards gestured my way and said, "Our parliamentarian says differently."

I nodded and said, "As long as there's a quorum, we can hold a meeting."

Edwards said, "The first item of business is to suspend the rules."

Jones said "So move." Buchanan added, "Second." Edwards said "All in favor?" and there was a hearty chorus of "Aye." Not that most of the people knew what was going on. I mean, all of this had come up in the last few minutes, and so not everyone had been told what was happening, but a lot did and the rest more or less sensed it. As long as it was perceived as a backlash against Carson, it would carry.

Then Buchanan said, "Move to remove Carson from office."

And as he said that, who walks in but Carson himself. Rather dramatic moment, that. Everyone turned and watched as he entered the room and strode to the table at which Edwards was sitting. "Care to tell me what the fuck is going on here?" he asked.

Edwards shrugged. "Emergency meeting of the membership."

"I didn't call a meeting. I'm the only one who can call a meeting."

"No you're not," Rickard said. It took a lot to get Rickard pissed off, but once he was, he was pretty vehement about whatever it was that was causing him to be pissed off.

I think Carson was beginning to get the drift that his popularity was definitely not on the rise at this moment, and so he said, "Well, I chair any meeting that's held," and he walked around the end of the table and took a seat next to Edwards. Edwards looked at me and I shrugged. Carson was right about that. Carson took the gavel away from Edwards and said, "What's the business on the floor?"

I said, "We just voted to suspend the rules."

Carson had this quizzical look on his face, trying to sense the way in which the meeting was going. That's when Buchanan said, "I just moved to have you removed from office."

"Well, that item's off the table," Carson said, as if that made it so.

If there was any doubt about how that vote would go, it ended in that moment. Carson was acting like Nixon, the worst thing anybody could do on a college campus in 1975. Jones was sitting there, and I saw that he was thumbing through my copy of Robert's Rules. He pointed to something and showed it to me and I nodded. Jones stammered a bit as he read the text for the motion and said, "I move to appeal the decision of the chair."

I turned to Carson before he could say anything and said, "You have to recognize that motion."

"No I don't," Carson replied.

"Yeah you do. It's one of the few motions that's an absolute right of the body to present on the floor. You have to entertain it."

Before Carson could say anything else, there was a second, then Edwards said, "All in favor, raise your hand." With only a few exceptions everyone raised their hand.

"I believe," Edwards said now, "that means that we are now discussing the motion to remove you from office."

Carson just looked up at everyone and said, "Meeting adjourned!" banged the gavel and stormed out of the dining room. There was a lull of several seconds as the door swung shut—it would have been slammed by Carson but for the fact that it had one of those pneumatic arms attached to it at the top. Then Benson and Belzer and a couple of other of Carson's buddies got up and followed their leader out of the room.

Edwards called for the vote, which was unanimous now that Carson and his buddies had left. Carson was removed from office retroactively to the previous week. As we all filed out of the dining room and into the Informal, we heard a slamming of a door. Carson had left via the heavy, oaken front door, going off to who knew where. "He's probably going to a phone to call national and house corp," Whale Man observed.

The next day was clear, sunny, and slightly cool, absolutely perfect for an inquisition. Those of the fraternity's membership who preferred to focus on classes instead of the fraternity's civil war went to lectures as usual. I came back to the house in mid-afternoon. I wanted to bag the interview for which I was scheduled at 7:15—they were running people in every 15 minutes. The house corp was ensconced in the library, a 20 x 20 room located down a side hall in the basement. There was a sparse collection of books on the shelves— an ancient set of Encyclopedia Britannica that still identified Iran as "Persia" and Thailand as "Siam," and a healthy number of books that had been ripped off from the university's library. It was quiet in there with heavy nap for the carpet, but damn few people ever used it for studying.

At this point, I wasn't sure of what to do. I liked living in the fraternity. The food was far better than the crap that was served in the dorms, and only a very few seniors had singles in the dorms, and meant that there was a lot more privacy than in the dorms. Also, there was far less likelihood of being busted than if I lived in the dorms, or if I lived OIT, for that matter. Now that the regimes in the house were changing, and the civil war was over, life would be different. Edwards had stood up at lunch that day and encouraged everyone to stay. "We all have to stick together," he'd said, then added superfluous analysis consisting of five or six sentences built around polysyllabic combinations of verbal fragments that were meant to be words, and maybe to Edwards sounded like words, but that weren't words at all. The contexts in which he used the words that did exist and were of four syllables or greater were at odds with any definition that could be found for the particular word in question. But hey, he had to justify his subscription to *Reader's Digest*.

The house corp had arrived. I saw them get out of their respective vehicles—no big luxury sedans here, nope. Just a couple of Fords, a Chevy and a 1972 Olds. The youngest one of the bunch looked to be in his late-50s with a Marine Corps haircut. He had the mean look of an ex-drill instructor. The other two seemed kindly enough, but those looks were more affectations of advanced age than the result of any feelings of kindness towards us, the present occupants of their fraternity. They promptly posted, on the dining room door, "instructions" for the interviews. We were supposed to go in, answer all questions "truthfully," then, afterwards, not reveal to anyone else what had transpired during our "individual session." Right.

The first people who went in were our now-former president and his cronies. I saw Carson come up the stairs and emerge into the foyer after his "session" and he wore a smug look of triumph. Edwards was the first to go in after that, then Jones. A couple of people who came upstairs during those "sessions" said that they could hear the screaming all the way upstairs in the Informal.

When Whale Man came upstairs, he said that the guy who looked like the ex-Marine was mean, asking pointed questions about Whale Man's lifestyle and personal habits. He was the angry, confrontational, accusatory Grand Inquisitor, carrying the banner of the national fraternity, the past generations of "brothers" into battle, and maybe even the Pope's own soldiers, the Dominicans. The other two just seemed to sit back and look dismayed. They asked a couple of general questions about the house, and Whale Man's classes, but that was about it.

We sat there waiting for the "next" name to be called. The process moved fairly punctually. First came the newly-installed officers. Then they moved through the Five. Then 'twas I.

I shook my head as I stood up and walked downstairs. A couple of people wished me luck as I exited Second Old.

Maybe it was how I was dressed. Everyone, even Whale Man, to this point, had worn a tie. Most of the others had worn jackets to go along with that look. I figured that, since my presence was "required," that they would have to take me as I was. I wore my usual turtleneck and jeans, with my Chucks and no socks. I had already assumed that my shoulder-length hair would not find favor with them. I really didn't care. My attitude was pretty much like that of the majority of the house. I just wanted to be finished with this fiasco.

I wish I could say that I told them to fuck themselves, turned around and walked out. That is what I should have done. That is what each one of us should have done. Why I didn't, I don't know. Maybe I didn't because I was 19 and they were each old enough to have been my father. I'd learned early on, from Eva and Adolf, to fear the iron boot of pseudoparental authority. Maybe it was because going down there for 15 minutes was the quickest and easiest way to do be done with it. Maybe it was because I was curious. I was not into having a fight.

The library door was heavy. I pushed it open and walked into the room. The two old farts smiled as I walked in, but there was some sort of hesitation in their looks. Crew-cut was seated to the left and slightly behind the only empty chair in the room. His eyes bore malice. Something was familiar about that set-up. One of the old fuckers nodded to the chair and I went to it and sat down. I said "hello" and waited for one of them to say something. When they didn't I figured I'd at least tell them who I was, beyond name, rank and serial number. I told them my major and that I was the leading member of the debate team and served as the house's student senator. I figured they would ask me a few questions about the split in the house and what I thought should be done, maybe ask some questions about the Naked Party or the Loyola walkout or something. Ask me about my goals in life and that sort of bullshit. I had learned a long time ago that when one is nervous, one should limit hand gestures so that the audience doesn't see the hands shake. And even though my voice was a little bit high and wound-up, it didn't sound as though I was scared.

One of the old fuckers tilted his glasses and looked down at a printed sheet. "It doesn't say here what your grade-point is," he said, then looked up at me expectantly.

I stared back at him, and there was silence. Then Crew Cut barked, "What is your grade-point!?" I had to swivel my head to look at him, slightly behind me and to my left.

"My grade-point is none of your business," I replied.

"It is our business," the other old fucker said.

"I don't see how," I replied. I found this whole line of questioning to be offensive. And, while I hadn't expected to be greeted as the Messiah, I didn't view myself as being one of the Five or one of the new officers, people who had had a long and colorful history of dissent in the house. It was, however, beginning to dawn on me where I ranked amongst the perceived misanthropes in the house. Hey—I'd made the Top Ten.

"Anything that anybody does when they're a member of this house reflects on this house," Crew Cut snorted. "If something reflects badly on this house, it's our business."

"Fine," I said, thinking I'd be cute. "I have a 3.8."

"You're lying," one of the old fuckers said with a hint of disappointment in his voice. He was looking down at a different sheet of paper and nodding to it, holding it out for the others to see that he'd found it.

"Do you people have a file on me!?" I demanded, outraged. I was reminded of the scene in Casablanca where Major Strausser is introduced to Humphrey Bogart and recites from a "dossier" on Bogart.

Crew Cut spoke again and I had to swivel 180 degrees back around to make eye contact. "You come in here lying about your grade point average. What else are you going to lie about?"

I was about to respond, but I hesitated. I was confused, twisting this way and that. Then I realized what they were doing. It was an effective interrogation technique utilized by generations of junior high school assistant principals and deans of boys and their ilk. Seat the questionee in the middle and spread the chairs of the questioners around in a semicircle or more. Get several people firing questions at once and the person being interrogated would be spinning his head around so much that he would become physically confused, almost dizzy. I'd heard one sadistic bastard bragging about it to a teacher once, and I had always remembered that. I stood up and moved my chair back against the wall so that I was facing them comfortably.

"You put that chair back!" Crew-cut barked.

I ignored him and sat down.

"We would prefer that you replace the chair to its original position," one of the old fuckers said.

"No," I replied.

I realized then that I was again face-to-face with the Enemy. Maybe, as they looked down the list of people to drill, they marked me down as drug user/hippie scum. Every bad guy from 1960s and 1970s TV, or their church youth group movies, came back to haunt them when they saw me. Maybe I reminded them of their own children. Maybe those kids hadn't spoken to these fuckers or their wives in a couple of years and they wanted to take that out on me.

"May I see that file?" I asked, but Crew Cut cut me off.

"You may not! I want to know just what the fuck it is you do in this house with your spare time—which seems to be most of your time, in light of your grades."

The old fucker who was holding the file looked uncomfortable with Crew Cut's use of the word "fuck." "What our brother means is that we aren't at liberty to disclose the contents of this file to you. International provided it to us and its contents are strictly confidential."

"Wait a minute," I said. "You people have a file on me and I can't see it? Besides— my grade-point average is confidential information that only the university is supposed to have."

The old fucker ignored my question and consulted the file. He wore a quizzical expression. "It says here that last December, after finals, you consumed alcohol on the first floor, in a public area of the house and burned one of your textbooks." He looked at me as though I were insane.

"Who gave this information to you? Do you have spies constantly working for you?"

"Answer his question!" Crew Cut ordered and seemed to move forward in his chair.

"It's not exactly right. I was drinking egg nog. The housebitch"—they cringed at that—"made it and spiked it herself, liberally. Everybody else in the house was downstairs— in a public area—drinking egg nog, too. Finals had ended. And I didn't just 'burn' the textbook. I fed it a page at a time into the fireplace." I thought that what I had just said was sufficient explanation. They hadn't taken broadcast comm with me. If they had, and they had been there then, they would probably have been sitting beside me burning their textbooks, too. Maybe not—these people were dicks.

The other old fucker just shook his head. Crew Cut seemed to be chomping at the bit. He really wanted to get into this thing. Hitler would have been proud to have some asshole like this in the SS.

"You're also the house parliamentarian, aren't you?" Crew Cut asked.

"Yep."

"There's something we're curious about." He reached back and opened up a legal pad. He consulted a page, and asked, "How is it that the house could make a vote retroactive?"

Wow. Here was a question the answer to which was no sweat. "Easy. We just did." There was a pause. No one said anything. Crew Cut sure looked confused.

Crew Cut said, "The U.S. Constitution says you can't do that."

I smiled. What a guy to give me the chance for a good one-liner. "But as you gentlemen are demonstrating, the United States Constitution doesn't apply here." Lob—smash. "Besides, it's like the infield fly rule. It's there because it's there. Organizations enact retroactive measures every day. The body of this frat is autonomous. Last night we voted to suspend the rules and remove the officers. We could do that."

"What a lot of horseshit," Crew Cut snorted. "And I'm an attorney. You're wrong."

I stared at him. I couldn't believe that this moron had made it into law school, had actually graduated and passed the bar. On top of it, his reply consisted of a fallacy:"I am an attorney, therefore I am right." Then the wheels of my brain started kicking in. The house corp and the national must have been really screwed when the officers were voted out. I mean, the house corp had lost a lot of leverage. Edwards had been right in that move. If the old officers were still in, the house corp would have probably just thrown out everybody but a handful. Now, in the last 24 hours, their plans had been fucked. Even if I was wrong about the retroactive bullshit—who cared? The move had bought us time and threw these fuckers off.

"Oh, let's cut the shit," Crew Cut said to his two buddies. His voice startled me. "What about drugs in the house?" He walked over to the old fucker who had my file and picked up the paperwork, flipping through pages trying to find something.

I realized that this was Jack Webb! I was looking right at Joe Friday! I expected the fucker at any moment to start mouthing all of the cliches of that period: "Pot . . . Weed . . . Reefer . . . Mary Jane . . . It all has the sweet, sickening smell of burnt rope . . . Go ahead, kid, the first one's free . . . Then a once-in-a-while thing becomes an every-day-thing, and the joints just don't do the trick anymore . . . So you find yourself in an alley with a needle in your arm . . ." Not just the hairdo. I mean, I realized that Crew Cut even looked like Joe Friday, complete with cheap, speckled sports jacket.

I realized when I spoke that I stammered, but yeah—I was nervous. I wanted the fuck out of there. "I . . . I wouldn't know about drugs in the house. I don't do them. To the best of my knowledge, nobody does them." Yeah, right. Instead, I should have told them to shove it up their asses. That people on this campus either smoked or were tolerant of people who did. This was the mid-fucking-seventies!

Crew Cut didn't buy it. He stopped shuffling through the papers and looked up at me. "Don't give me that crock of shit. You're known in the house as somebody who throws pot parties all the time." That term—"pot parties"—really threw me. I hadn't heard that expression since I'd seen re-runs of "Dragnet-1966." Maybe that was where all of this guy's knowledge of drugs came from. His terms all seemed so antiquated. I half-way expected him to ask me if I knew any "Negro jazz musicians." "You have pot parties in your room. You've used"—time for the heavy minor chords of organ music here, folks—"LSD."

I told him—again in a stammering, unbelievable voice—that I didn't know what he was talking about and that I'd like to see that file to see who my accusers were. One of the old fuckers said, "It's time," meaning the 15 minutes was up. The other old fucker told Crew Cut to cool it, that they'd discuss matters later.

But Crew Cut was livid. "We're talking about drugs here," he said. Man, he wanted to say, "We are right at the heart of evil in the United States, the thing that's fucked up the country." But the fucker couldn't verbalize that. Instead, he looked at his two cohorts and practically begged. "But I got kids."

The old fucker that seemed "in control" of things said they'd discuss it later, but that they had other people to interview. The old fucker thanked me, and said I could go. He reminded me of some kind of old Nazi from the death camps. He might have agreed with what Crew Cut said, but he had other fish to fry.

I got up and walked out. As I got up to Second Old, another name was announced. I went to my room and a couple of guys stuck their heads in to see what had happened during my interview. I was ashamed. I told them the basics, that the fuckers had files on us, etc. But I was ashamed because I'd been face-to-face with what I considered to be evil, and I had been the one who blinked.

I cranked some tunes, got drunk, and sought to pass out as quickly possible.

Chapter 26 - The Rally

After we had decided on a schedule, word had spread around campus fairly quickly. We'd even had time to run an ad—gratis—announcing the rally, to be held on a Wednesday night, and what was now being called The Moratorium the following Friday afternoon. Natas had placed the ad, and so, of course, it said "Students for Academic Freedom announces . . ." The rally was to be held on the back steps of the Union Building, where there was a huge, wide patio with steps that formed a perfect platform from which to speak. None of the other committee chairpeople who made up the "Committee of Committees" had any real notion of the purpose of the rally. I thought of it as being sort of a pep rally for the demonstration. I was going to speak as were Professors Ahmed and White. Then we were going to march from the UB to the home of the university president.

I met Cindy and Austin in the Hub the day before the rally. It was one of those weird days when Michelle wasn't with Austin. "She's finalizing quitting the sorority," Austin explained. Cindy sprang for a coke for me, and we started discussing what needed to be done for the rally.

"By the way," Cindy said to me. "One of my suite mates hangs around with that one chick who's friends of Jimmy's. I heard that Natas is really pissed at you."

"At me? What the fuck for? I barely know the guy."

"You were one of the ones who tried to abolish the hall government over in the dorms when you lived there. He was president of that whole thing. That didn't help matters much. But then you got the ball rolling on all this with Farina. Jimmy was the guy who circulated all those petitions last year for Farina."

"Shit, I didn't know that."

"Yeah," Austin continued. "He's had Farina for four or five courses. And here you come in and take away the glory of leading the protests. Natas doesn't like that."

I shrugged. There wasn't much to say.

"Oh, fuck hurt feelings," Cindy said. "We have to focus on the next couple of days. The rally then the strike. After that, we have to make plans. And hey," she said, turning to me, "don't worry about Natas, he's going to have to grow up."

I nodded and finished my coke. After that I walked to class, sat there for 50 minutes barely listening to the lecture. But hey—I made class. That counted for something. I just doodled in my notebook.

The day for the rally seemed to arrive rather quickly. Professors White and Ahmed were good friends of Farina's as well as being allies of his in the war against the university. White was a history prof in his mid-30s with just a hint of silver in his shaggy black hair and somewhat-trimmed beard. Ahmed was Syrian by birth. His bushy black hair had receded and he wore a goatee. His accent was noticeable but not overbearing and, whenever anything sparked his interest he had an intensity of expression that was riveting. He was a member of the faculty in the sociology department, the sister department of Farina's anthro. Both of these professors were among students' favorites, for their accessibility, openness and lack of pretense. There was very little bullshit about them. They wore jeans nearly every place they went. Added to these facets were their high levels of competence and knowledge in their fields. In short, they were credits to DFU's faculty.

The morning of the rally, Austin, Michelle and I sat at a table in the Hub comparing notes about the rally and the march late that afternoon.

"I think marching to the president's house is a good idea," Austin said.

"Why?" Michelle asked. "I don't see the point. It's redundant."

"It's a statement," Austin said. "We're saying to him: 'You can't shut us out. We can come to your front door.'"

"And he can say," Michelle replied, "'I am closing my doors and pulling my blinds and watching TV.'"

I shrugged. "It doesn't really matter. Everyone voted on it. So we're going to do it. We just need to work out the logistics."

"How far is it?" Michelle asked, as the three of us looked at the multi-colored map of the campus I'd grabbed a few minutes before from the office of admissions.

"It's about five blocks," I answered. "We'll march straight up Anderson Street, right up to his front door. Of course, we have to cross Bloomington Street."

"How many people are we expecting to march?" Michelle asked.

"A few hundred," Austin replied.

"And we're going to be marching the wrong way up the middle of Anderson Street, and then shutting down the busiest street in town as we cross it?" Michelle asked again.

"Shit," I said. Austin and I could both see what she meant.

"I don't want to go to the police," Austin muttered.

"Neither do I," I said, "but I don't think we have a choice. We might have to get a parade permit." I thought back to those free speech cases in con law where the "authorities" sought to place limits on free expression by enforcing trash ordinances or other laws. I was paranoid about Glendale's Finest using any means at their disposal to stop our march. And they would do so with the university's blessing.

Michelle and Austin had class, but Austin bagged it. Michelle would take notes for him anyway. So we walked with her to the academic quad, then went downtown to Glendale's miniature police station. GPD was located on the second floor of an old, beaten-up building just off downtown. The first floor was occupied by the Glendale Fire Department. Of course, the fire station was numbered—Number One. There was no "Number Two." I guess they were optimistic about growth. As we approached the building, we saw that G-1 and G-2 were parked beside the station. Either the War on Crime had reached a lull in their little hamlet, or the officers were taking a needed respite before heading back into the fray. Although I'd been rambunctious on campus over the past couple of years, I'd managed to stay out of the way of the local powers of law enforcement. As far as they knew, I was just another long-haired student walking down the street. The bust scare had given me an inkling that they might know me by reputation, but nobody had said that the files had included pictures, so I assumed that I enjoyed a bit of anonymity by way of appearance. Austin felt the same way, that they might know him by reputation, but that they had no face to match.

We entered the building and climbed long, narrow stairs, the walls of which were painted Institutional Lime Green. At the top, we turned a corner. The dispatcher was behind a counter, a radio emitting white noise as she read a paperback. An officer stood off to the side, pouring a cup of coffee. When he saw us, he called us by our names, said hello and asked us what he could do for us.

We both about shit, then looked at each other and shook off the shock of recognition. Oh fucking well.

"We're having a rally this evening . . ." I began, then went on to explain what was happening. The cop nodded and said that he'd have to get the chief for this. He used the station's ancient intercom system—he yelled for the chief, who appeared a few moments later. We declined the offer of coffee and went on to explain the purpose of our visit.

I'd seen the chief around Glendale before. He had an Elvisesque look: sideburns, pompadour hairstyle slicked back with grease into a ducktail. Very stylish—in the 1950s or Appalachia and hilljack America. "Where you gonna march?" he asked. He needed a toothpick hanging out of one corner of his mouth for full effect.

We told him where we were "gonna march," and I added that we'd be glad to fill out any necessary forms, then braced myself for the ream of forms that I was sure he would place on the counter.

"Oh hell," he said, "you don't need no permit. Just let us know the time you'll be crossing Bloomington Street. You know how the traffic is down there, living in your frat." It seemed even the chief knew who I was. "We'll just send a unit down there and shut down traffic as you go through."

The way he said "shut down" made it sound as if that was something that he enjoyed about his job, being able to exercise power and inconvenience a lot of people all at once. After all, his wasn't an elected job. He didn't have to worry about the wrath of voters.

We estimated the time we'd be marching through, allowing for three speeches and people walking the two blocks or so before they would have to cross the street. Then we headed back to campus. We had anticipated major hassles. We had also thought that we enjoyed a certain degree of anonymity. We were wrong on both counts. I was surprised that they didn't have our photographs posted on one of the walls there. Well, come to think of it, we'd only seen a couple of walls and those were in the public areas of the station. Who knew what they had hanging in other rooms and offices?

I had two classes that day. In one, my speech pathology prof acknowledged the reality that a moratorium of classes was going to take place, and so she canceled class. That move was rather redundant, since the class was on Friday and she had announced, at the beginning of the semester, as most DFU profs did, that there would be no Friday classes. The other class that I had that day was Gleason's. His seminar met only once a week. The moratorium would not affect that class.

We were sitting at the huge table when Gleason came in, hunched over, as usual, a Camel straight lit and in his hand. He walked around to an empty chair and set his armload of books and notes on the table. He took off his jacket and sat down, as though he were really caught up in something. Before he said anything, I raised my hand, and he said yes as he nodded in my direction.

The question I asked sounded as if it came from a college freshman or sophomore. Very naive, really. But the question was honest. I respected Gleason more than any prof

I'd had at DFU, and I wanted to hear what he had to say on the subject. Looking back, I'm surprised we hadn't discussed the subject of Farina during our many conversations about Life and the Universe and Truth and Baseball when we were in the bar. I said, "Professor Gleason, how can we discuss any matters in a university if we don't have academic freedom?"

At first he looked thoughtful, as though I'd asked a superb question. Then I saw a change —first in his eyes. They became colder and closed a little. His face began to turn color, from a rather jaundiced, life-spent-under-fluorescent-lights look to a blotchy pattern with a foundation of bright red.

"That's a rhetorical question!" He nearly yelled. "There is no place for a question like that in this class! I cannot believe the students here right now . . ." and on he went. He ripped into everything that had been done for Farina and everyone who had done it, including me. I hadn't realized, until his diatribe, the organizing that we had done was known widely by people in the faculty. Then Gleason went from the general to the specific—me. He called me naive— three times—adolescent—four times—unrealistic—twice—and grossly uninformed—eight times. At first I was too surprised to react. I mean, this guy was my favorite professor. We drank beers together and argued into the night. How could he see the university's actions as being anything but wrong? And on top of that, even if he disagreed with me, how could he be so personal in his attacks? As the shock wore off, the anger inside me rose. He was proving that we had no academic freedom. Oh sure, talk about Rousseau, and say things in different variations that people had said about him during discussions for the last couple of hundred years. Or talk about Hobbes and how valiant he was in the face of the despots of the day—big whoopee. But if we couldn't discuss whether we had the freedom to discuss whether we had the freedom to discuss anything that we wanted to discuss, then we had no freedom at all. I wanted to explode at what Gleason was doing right now, and call him names. But then my anger receded, and I seemed to float above the room, looking down on it and him and everyone in the class. The man looked ridiculous, his eyes slightly bulged, his face even a darker red, his arms flailing about. I'd respected the man so much, and all that he was succeeding in doing was looking like an idiot.

Once Gleason had exhausted himself, he sat down and picked up his notes in a jerking motion. He attempted to elicit responses from people about Rousseau. I wasn't the only person who was affected by what had happened. Well, one guy, a pre-med, naturally enough, saw an opportunity to kiss ass and started trying to involve himself in a dialogue with Gleason, but the guy hadn't read Rousseau. After a couple of comments, Gleason asked the guy, "Where do you get Cliff's Notes on this campus?" The guy said that he'd had to go to Bloomington, and then Gleason dismissed class, and we weren't even half-way through our allotted time.

I had several places to visit, at the last minute, on campus. There were "marshals" whom Natas had designated for the rally and the Moratorium. These students would wear white armbands, formed from strips of bedsheets, on one sleeve, and would act as "guides," Natas had informed me. I asked him what the fuck did people need guides for. In the first ten minutes on campus freshman year, a DFU student knew the campus layout. This was not a major metropolitan area in which a sprawling campus was located. But Jimmy was insistent. If we had been armed, I would have thought that the "marshals" were his answer to Brownshirts.

The rally was on my mind. I didn't have money to eat, as usual, thanks to the failed hash deal. So I sat in my room and went over the few notes I'd made for the speech. I was nervous. I mean, here I was, 19 years old, giving a speech to a rather large number of my fellow students, for a cause in which I believed. And it was aimed at a strike—well, okay, a "moratorium"—that would shut down—in part and only for a business day, true—the school in which I was enrolled. This was what I'd looked forward to since junior high.

The air was chilly, but I was warm. I had on the cheap, blue hiking boots that pinched my feet, but looked proper for attire in a student demonstration. I had on jeans, a sweater and the vented jacket of my one and only suit. I walked to the UB and around the back of the building to the patio where everything was to take place. Professors White and Ahmed were inside the building, staying warm and chatting. I could also see Natas and his buddies, the bulk of the membership of the "Committee of Committees," sitting in a corner of the main room on the first floor of the UB, all huddled in conversation that looked intense.

Candace and Brenda approached me from around the huge shrubs in front of the UB.

"Nervous?" Candace asked.

"What do you think?" I asked, smiling, the paper shaking slightly in my hand. I knew from all of my years of experience in competitive speech and debate to abandon the paper before my speech. There was no podium, and I didn't want my shaking hands to belie to the crowd how nervous I was. They wished me luck, and I sat down on the low stone wall that ran across the front of the UB. I pulled out a cigarette and lit up. I realized I'd smoked more today than I had other days of late. The slight breeze carried the smoke up and then dissipated it, through the branches of the tree above me. Maybe the tree would get a nicotine buzz. I glanced towards the windows of the UB. There were people in bunches of two and three and an occasional lone straggler heading out toward the back of the building, where the rally was to be held. I tossed my cigarette and walked inside, then across the lobby to the doors and out.

Professors White and Ahmed were leaning against the brick wall of the UB, talking with each other, one occasionally nodding or waving to a student in the crowd. I saw no other faculty members. There were several hundred students there, all gathered on the lawn, a few steps below where we were standing. Natas was off to the side and signaled to White, who jerked away from the wall, nodded and walked to the edge of the top step.

Everyone quieted as Professor White began to speak. He was very popular with the students: well-liked as a person and well-respected as a teacher and human being. He described the situation: the importance of tenure and academic freedom; what it meant for the American Association of University Professors to threaten DFU with censure. White was relatively young for the DFU faculty, but was used to speaking to groups of students, although maybe not groups of such size as the one to which he now spoke. DFU classes were usually in the size of 15-20 students. Only in the freshman intro classes and some of the psych lectures did the size go beyond 30. Nonetheless, his voice was measured and his manner calm. He concluded by stressing the importance of academic freedom to everyone at DFU, and to any other college or university. When he finished, he received warm applause from the students, many of whom had taken one or more of his courses.

Professor Ahmed followed. While White was very laid-back in his approach, Ahmed had a spirited way of talking. This isn't ethnocentric bias, either—"Oh, those Arabs can be so emotional"—but you had to know him. You had to see him speak. He was just as calm and deliberate in his speaking manner as had been White, but there was a tension and an energy underneath that manner. That spirit seemed to surface now. He related how the students in Paris in 1968 and gone to the barricades to defend their rights, and had nearly brought down the government of France in the process.

As he spoke, I noticed a tall guy walking around the edge of the crowd at the back. He was an Omega Dickhead with a reputation for starting fights, both down at the bars and elsewhere. He was wearing an absurd-looking derby and was saying caustic things. Several people shot him sideways glances. One woman pulled away from him. He was mostly ignored, but I hoped there wouldn't be violence instigated by him.

Ahmed said it was important to continue the fight against DFU on this matter, because this was a fight for freedom at every other college and university in the World. That gave me pause. I felt a comraderie with other radicals elsewhere. Then he added that this was a microcosm of the fight for rights everywhere. When he finished he received even more applause than White had. As he came back to where White and I stood, he shook first White's hand, then mine. I told them both that they'd made great speeches. They wished me luck.

I walked over to the spot where each of them had spoken. My notes were in my top pocket, but I didn't need them. I doubt that I could have read them anyway, even if I had had them out. Things were a bit of a blur right now, but I could make out pockets of energy in the crowd. Places where there was a murmur or a buzz of support for what was happening. "They've decided to deny tenure to a professor," I began. "A little short guy." People laughed, glad to have a bit of humor interjected. "But they picked the wrong guy. Because he's a fighter. And because he was voted Professor of the Year—by us." That got applause. I'd gotten the crowd onto my side. I was reading things pretty well. I could sense the crowd's reactions, as if the crowd was a continuous field of energy I could hear, more than see, and there reactions were like aural infrared light patterns—swells of energy registered, and then there were places where the energy was downturned. There was a block of freshman women who didn't seem to be as upbeat. I tried to address comments to them, while speaking to the whole crowd. The response was great. I had adrenaline flowing and I was into a really great buzz. In my speech I explained, in short-hand, the history of what had brought us all here, punctuating my narrative with cynical comments about DFU, and about specific people in the administration. I referred a couple of times to things that Professors White and Ahmed had said, and this lent some continuity to the evening's speeches. My energy level was picking up now, as was the rhythm of my speech. I was getting applause here and there, and I started winding into the conclusion of my speech. Maybe I could get laid some day, I thought.

"A lot of you have been wondering what you can do about this. What you can do to stop the university from the action that it's taken. Some of you have been to the meetings we've had." I stopped and pointed to some of the people at the front of the crowd. "You, Steve. And Rudy. And Lisa. You've been to those meetings." I looked back up at the rest of the crowd. "But for some of you, this rally is the first that you've been involved. That's a start, and it's an important start. You can build on that. In a few minutes, we're going to march down to the house—of the president of the university!" There were cheers at this line. People were getting a little revved up, and I guess I was caught up in that. When everyone had quieted, I continued. "But that's not all. You can really do your part on Friday. Because that's when we're going to have a strike!" People cheered at this line, too. I wanted to avoid addressing the obvious—that hardly anybody had classes on Fridays anyways, and those profs who did schedule classes on Fridays were generally recognized as being sadists.

Natas had moved off about ten feet to my left and a little behind me. He hissed at me: "Moratorium! It's the Moratorium!" And I mean, the way he was saying it, you knew that in his mind he saw the capital "m" on the word. His brainchild. Properly moderate. Not anything so radical as a "strike." I ignored him.

'We're gonna shut this sucker down. Friday afternoon we'll have music and speakers out on East College lawn. Do your part—be there! Aloha! Now let's march down to the house of the president and show that son of a bitch we're serious!"

I went down the steps and started around to the front of the UB. Professor Ahmed was clapping me on the shoulder and Professor White was laughing. Some of the students were yelling, things like "Way to go" and "Fuck DeForrest!" It was weird that we would all be paying so much money to an institution that, at the moment, we despised. Natas caught up with me. He tugged on my sleeve and when I turned and looked at him, I saw an expression on his face that appeared—well, miffed. He said something about "wrong attitude" and "objectionable language." I pulled away from him. I was too into the moment to really waste the time listening to him.

We started down Anderson Street, a one-way thoroughfare against whose traffic we were marching. The president's home was all the way at the end, and a block to the left. I was at the front of the column and, after we'd gone a block or so, I turned around and looked at the line of students, stretching back all the way through the arch at East College. The street was filled, and a couple of cars were blocked.

Every 40 or 50 yards there was one of Natas's "marshals," one more student wearing a white armband. They did nothing that I ever saw, just stood and watched as the rest of the students marched by. They were certainly of no help at Bloomington Street. The GPD was a bunch of real pros when it came to traffic directing. Glendale might not have gotten any murders or robberies in its recent history, but it had its fair share of high school football and basketball games, at the ends of which there was always the mass rush from the parking lot. By comparison, our march was pretty tame. All that the cops had to do was stop through traffic on Bloomington Street. That took one cop, but he had a buddy, I guess in case they had to radio for back-up in the event of a riot.

We got to the end of Anderson Street and turned left. We walked up the driveway of the president's house, politely and respectfully staying off the well-tended lawn. The mansion was a huge, old wooden-frame, white structure, a sort of East Coast design. It was in beautiful shape. The mass of people had stopped. Everyone waited as I walked up to the door and knocked, but nobody answered. I waited for a minute or so, then I knocked again. Finally the door opened and a woman wearing a maid's uniform—I couldn't believe that people actually made employees wear such demeaning things—peeked out and asked what I wanted. When I told her we wanted to see the president, she explained that he and his wife were out of town on a fundraising trip. I thanked her and then turned to the crowd.

I told them he wasn't home. Then someone up front suggested that we walk over to Farina's house, only a block or so away. It seemed like a good idea. I mean, I wasn't in favor of marching to the president's house in the first place, but so many people had marched all the way across campus to get here, I thought that it would be a shame to piss away the effort and just go home. After all, Natas wasn't jumping up there with any bright ideas. He was standing off to the side, talking with two or three of his little groupies. So I asked if everyone thought we should head over to Farina's, and there were shouts of approval. So the entire mass of people pivoted and headed in the direction of Farina's house.

When we got there, I walked up onto the porch and knocked on the front door. By this time, even though the air was a bit chilly, I was wet with nervous sweat. Mrs. Farina answered the door and, not surprisingly, was a bit startled to see several hundred students standing there, filling her lawn and spilling out onto the street in front of her house. She explained that her husband was in Indianapolis, meeting with his lawyers. Then she walked out to the railing of the porch and, in a loud voice, repeated what she'd just said, and added that she and her husband appreciated the students' support. Then she waved and went back into the house.

I turned around and looked at the crowd of students waiting for me to say something. But we'd done about all that we could, so I said, "Thanks for coming out tonight. Remember—the strike is on Friday! Meet on East College lawn and give the university a show of force! Venceremos!" I clenched my fist in a power sign and hopped off of the porch. The frat was only a couple of blocks away, so I went in that direction, being joined by Austin and Michelle and Cindy. When we got back to the frat, we got really wasted.

The next morning, as I woke up, I pulled the on-off knob on my Hitachi amp/tuner/tape deck to WNAP. It was early enough that I thought that I could catch "The Organic News," a sort of hippie national radio wire service. It was a syndicated feed of some sort, interspersed with local news, to which I always listened when I was coming down from tripping or pulling an all-nighter.

There was an item on the national feed about a study in which violent incidents involving cops were reduced in communities when the cops didn't wear uniforms and tried to relate to those communities. Then there was something about the Supreme Court. Then the local news and—ta da!—our march of the previous evening. We'd made the radio! I sat up in bed. As the announcer started, I wondered who in the fuck phoned in the story.

"It seems that DeForrest University students rallied on their campus last night for a protest. They marched on the home of the university's president, but he wasn't home. Then the students marched on the home of a professor—but he wasn't home either. Then all of the students went home. Gee, you'd think that if those rich preppies had kept trying, they would have found someone to protest to. Well, okay. The weather today . . ."

I cringed as I lay back down on the mattress. What fucking ridicule! I wondered who in the fuck could have phoned in a story like that? Sure, members of the administration. Right. Like they're going to know to call WNAP. No, it had to be someone from among the students. But even the right-wing dickheads, few as they were on college campuses of the mid-1970s, were on our side in this one. I tried to figure out the answer as I walked down the hall to take a shower and start the day.

Chapter 27 - The Coup And The Moratorium

I soon realized that I'd been cut out of any planning for what was by now referred to everyone as the Moratorium. I'd had no concrete ideas of what would happen during the event. I envisioned some people speaking, a little bit of music being played, and the public venting of anger by students. Natas seemed to have taken charge of it, with his committee of groupies. He had made no effort to include me in the planning of anything. And, while I had tried to keep lines of communication open, I had gotten the distinct feeling that by giving him information and receiving nothing from him in return I was somehow strengthening whatever position he held while weakening my own.

On the morning of the day between the rally and the Moratorium, several of us got together at Michelle's and Austin's to make picket signs. We had opted for yellow posterboard and black tempera paint—a play off of our school colors of Old Gold and black. Someone bought wooden staves and tack nails at a local lumberyard. Somebody bought a jug of Sangria, and we passed that around as we got artistic painting slogans on the posterboard. We started out with pretty basic expressions: "Academic Freedom Now" and "Don't Deny Farina Tenure." Then we started getting creative. I liked Austin's: "Academic Freedom? Academic Slavery!" I thought it caught the spirit. The poster I would carry said "DeForrest" in bold black letters, with a day-glo "Censured" printed across that. We painted and sipped wine from various glasses that Austin had acquired over time from miscellaneous gas station and jelly company promotions. Each glass was a different shape and size, and some were festooned with cartoon characters or petroleum corporation logos.

When we were nearly finished, the phone rang and Michelle answered. She spoke for only a few moments and then hung up. "That was Natas," she said.

"I can't stand that asshole," Jillian observed.

"Christ," Cindy said. "Remember when he was running the men's dorms? He and his little friends tried to combine the dorm governing bodies so he could be president of all the dorms. Who knows what for."

"Probably the power," Jillian said.

"The title sounds like 'Czar of all the Russias,'" I said.

Cindy shot Jillian an odd look, like Jillian was full of shit. "What 'power'?" Cindy said.

"What did he want?" Austin asked.

"He said that the Committee of Committees is meeting at about 4 in the Hub."

"The 'Committee of Committees'?" I asked.

Austin said, "Beats me. It's the first that I've heard them actually call it that. But if Michelle and I are on it, you must be, too."

"We'd better be," I said, and started the next poster.

Cindy leaned back in a chair. That particular chair was comfortable, but only if you got situated correctly. It was ancient, and its cushions were bound in vinyl. If you sat for any appreciable length of time, the vinyl would stick to the exposed areas of your skin. So Michelle or Austin—or hell, some previous tenant—had tossed a heavy bedspread over it. And that was fine. But it gradually would creep off the chair, and whoever was sitting on it would have a tendency to slide over the vinyl.

"I'd be careful," Cindy said to me.

"How's that?" I asked, daubing the final strokes of paint onto yet another placard.

"I heard that Natas was pissed off. He was overseas last semester. Lost a lot of his contacts, wasn't set up for anything. He'd had his eye on the Farina situation since a year ago last fall. He assumed he'd run the whole show this year. You started things up and took control out of his hands. He's pissed. He wanted to give that speech the other night. Fuck, he wants to give all the speeches."

I looked at Cindy. I felt a bit uneasy. "Let's just make sure that all of us are at the Hub at 4 today," I said. Austin and Michelle agreed. Cindy nodded.

We finished the last of the posters and stacked them next to the front door. The air smelled faintly of tempera paint, and the wine tasted very good. Austin pulled out a pipe and we drank and smoked, but I was careful about how much I consumed from that point. Michlle put Todd Rundgren's "Something/Anything" album on the stereo. Jillian had never heard the album, and that day it became one of her all-time favorites.

172

Eventually I ran back to the frat. I showered and brushed my teeth well. I didn't want anyone fainting from wine breath. Then I nuked my eyes with Visene. About five minutes later I checked in the mirror and my eyes weren't red at all. I headed down to campus after that, and just made it to the Hub as the East College bell tolled the hour. I saw Austin in a corner, sitting in one of the high-backed booths. I didn't have money for a coke or anything, so I plopped down opposite him.

"Where are Michelle and Cindy and Jillian?" I asked.

"Michelle had to study. Cindy and Jillian both said that they'd be here, but you know how they are."

"I've been working on my speech," I said. It was generally assumed that I would give a speech the next day. I figured that the Committee of Committees was meeting to hammer out the last-minute details for the next day's events. I quoted Jefferson and Thoreau. The speech wasn't even that inflammatory. It was just a good, solid jab at what the university had done. I explained all this to Austin. I asked Austin where everybody was, and just then, the door of the Hub opened, and Natas walked in with his entourage. His various groupies, whom he had appointed to "head" the various "committees," surrounded him. I had the feeling that they had formed some sort of miniature army, and that all that they needed at this point, for effect, was to goose-step and wear uniforms. Then I saw that they were wearing their white marshals' armbands.

One of them saw us and nudged Natas, who turned and started in our direction. They were all very polite to Austin, but none of them made eye contact with me. Nonetheless, I figured I'd get the ball rolling, and on a non-confrontational basis, too. "The picket signs are done," I said. "Finished this afternoon." They still weren't looking at me. "Anyways— we have about 35 or 40 signs altogether."

"That's good," Natas replied, his voice having a weird, mocking tone.

I started to feel paranoid. There seemed to be so many of them, and only two of us. I wondered where Cindy was. As if reading my mind, Jeanna, the Natas groupie who seemed to have the hots for him the most, said, "Where's the other one?"

"What do you mean, 'other one'?" Austin asked.

"You know," she said. "Cindy What's-her-face. The fat one."

A couple of the other Natas groupies laughed, and Natas said, "Oh, you know. She's probably off getting high someplace."

They all had a good, harsh little chuckle about that, until Austin said to Natas, "I never saw you turn down a joint that was offered to you."

There was a pause of embarrassment, and I spoke up. I figured we'd better get things back to business. "Everything's set, then. Fliers are already run off. Cindy did that yesterday afternoon. We have music all set. Willie Jeffries will be out there bright and early."

"Yeah," Austin started to say. "I saw him last . . ."

"Excuse me," Natas said, his expression pained. "We need to discuss something."

"Okay," I said.

Natas had one of the fliers for the day in his hands, and he wasn't looking at it so much as he was wringing it. "Just what time had you anticipated speaking?"

"About one," I said. "It was really just an introduction for Farina and his lawyer."

"Well," Natas said, drawing out the word. "The Committee of Committees met last night . . ."

"What the fuck is that!?" Austin demanded.

Anna, one of Natas's groupies whom I had not heard speak before, except when I think she had been throwing in comments from the crowd in the meeting at the frat, now chimed in. "The Committee of Committees is comprised of the committee chairs. Each has a vote. We met last night and elected Jimmy as president of Students for Academic Freedom."

"What!?" I said, sitting upright in a flash. "You didn't have the authority to . . ."

Jeanna cut in quickly and brutally, standing up at the table and nearly screaming. "We had to have some sort of leadership. The Committee of Committees made sense. And it was democratic. We elected Jimmy." She sat down and added, "We've decided to run this like a political campaign."

"That's all well and good," I said, now leaning back in my seat. "But let's get back to this 'democratic' thing a bit . . ."

"We felt," Natas said, ignoring my effort to speak, "that the proper way to approach this situation would be like an election. Trying to convince people."

I drew in a deep breath, ready to counter Jeanna's volume with my own if necessary. "Fine. I was working in local politics when I was 12 years old. Blocking neighborhoods and going door-to-door for liberal Democratic Party candidates in the heart of Klan country. How many campaigns have you people worked in?"

Natas stammered, looking to his groupies for help, but they probably only knew the lines they had rehearsed. This ad-lib shit was beyond their understanding or abilities. Maybe they thought that I'd just shut up, roll over and die. "I've . . . I've never worked in one."

"And I imagine that none of the rest of you has either," I said.

Jeanna sensed things were not going their way and she quickly spoke up. "That's not important," she said. And I have to hand it to her, she was not going to let her and the others' ignorance stand in the way of achieving what they had come here to accomplish. "We want to know what kind of reputation you have."

Natas broke in. "She means that we want to run this like a political campaign. We don't want SAF to be criticized for having people in it who might engage in . . ." He was trying to come up with an appropriate word or expression. " . . . antisocial activities."

"I still don't understand . . ."

Jeanna said sharply, "Are you involved in drugs?"

I looked around at them. Their hair was long or shaggy or in some other "style"— unkempt and growing—indicative of the "drug subculture." They wore jeans and flannel shirts. They tried so hard to appear to be "hip." And then they were reeling off these questions.

"'Involved in drugs'? Sure I'm 'involved in drugs.' Most of this campus is 'involved in drugs.' Most of the charitable contributions to this school come from one of the world's largest pharmaceutical companies. A majority of the students on this campus smoke pot. A good number do speed during mid-terms and finals. When acid hits this campus, people are falling in the street, laughing. I've seen some of you people at parties doing drugs"— I hadn't, really, but their startled looks told me that my bluff was right—"so don't give me that shit."

Natas was consistent and persistent. He ignored anything else I said and extracted only what he wanted from my comments. "See—that's my point. You're into drugs. We want to run this as a political campaign. If the university wants to discredit us, they point out that one of the leaders of SAF is into drugs."

I laughed. "You really want to run this as a political campaign."

"That's right."

"And yet I'm the only person here with experience in working in a political campaign."

"We voted last night," Natas said.

"Who's 'we'?" I asked.

"The Committee of Committees," Natas replied. "We voted you out of any position of leadership in SAF."

My mouth probably dropped open. I felt blood draining from my extremities and a ringing pronounce itself in my ears. "Wait a second. I started this organization."

Natas blew that off. "Furthermore, you will not be giving a speech tomorrow. The Committee of Committees voted on that, too."

"Let me guess," I said. "You will be giving the speech."

"He's the president of SAF," one of the groupies said, and I don't really know which one. They were all begining to look the same to me—longish hair, well-scrubbed and hypocritical little shits.

I stood up. "Well, since it's cut and dried, I don't see the point in my staying. Cute little power play, Jimmy. Man, people were right. They warned me about you. Shit. And using drugs as the pretext for shoving me aside. Slick. I mean, you all get high, every one of you." When I said that, the two or three who were still maintaining eye contact looked away or down at the table. "And you know that the university would never criticize any of its students for involvement in drugs. If it did that, it would be blowing its PR gig." I picked up the notebook I'd brought with all the little writings I'd scribbled out. For organization of the next day's activities. For a speech that I would never give. "Christ. Your idea of a political campaign is to simply boil everything down to inoffensive image. Make sure that everything is bland and neat. Well—fuck you all." With that, I turned and walked out.

I walked back to the fraternity—and by "fraternity," I mean the physical plant. I don't remember the walk. If I saw anyone I knew, I don't remember. I was just staring at the ground a few feet ahead of me, moving one leg then the other. I talked Jennings out of a quart bottle of very cheap vodka, then went back to my room. I slammed the door, opened the bottle, took a big swig, then put on "Houses of the Holy" by Led Zeppelin. When I awoke the next morning, I was still in my clothes, sprawled out on my mattress. At least the day was sunny, although it was pretty cool out. I showered and dressed warmly. I had on jeans, of course, and a sweater, with a denim jacket over that. I pulled out from a paper bag in my closet a bagel I'd gotten from somewhere. Of course I didn't have a toaster, so I had to eat it cold. My stomach growled. I walked into Second New to be by the water fountain. I washed the starch down after every bite. I walked over to Austin's and Michelle's. I was surprised that I wasn't more hungover. But then I'd been drinking vodka. I reflected on the events of the previous evening. I wondered why Austin hadn't said anything. He'd simply sat there. And when I'd left, he'd remained. And yet the attacks that Natas and his groupies had brought applied to Austin's lifestyle no less than they applied to mine.

When I walked into their living room, I saw that all but three picket signs were gone.

"They came over last night and got them," Austin explained. "I knew that you wanted this 'censured' sign, so I kept it back, along with two for us."

Michelle was standing in the kitchen doorway, munching on a donut. "You want anything to eat?" she asked.

I was always hungry, even today. "Sure," I said. I walked past her into the kitchen, and grabbed a couple of donuts out of the box that was sitting there. "It's pretty chilly out there," I said between mouthfuls.

Austin walked into the kitchen. The long sleeves of a thermal underwear shirt poked out from the sleeves of his flannel shirt. "I'm ready for the cold," he said and grabbed a donut.

"Why were you quiet last night?" I asked him.

Austin had been smiling, but now the smile started to fade. "Nothing much I could say. It all seemed so cut and dried."

"You could have walked out, too."

Austin shrugged and simply stood there, eating and staring at the table.

"I'm surprised you're still going to go over there," Michelle said.

"Well, I started the whole goddamn thing," I said. "I'd might as well see it through to its end."

"Its 'end'?" Austin asked.

"Yeah," I replied. "You don't think Natas and his little friends will do anything after today, do you? The only thing that he cares about is getting onto TV, having his few minutes in the limelight. That happens today."

"I don't know about that," Austin said. "He seems to have a lot of energy and . . ." Austin's voice faded.

I said, "But you don't trust the son of a bitch."

"No," Michelle answered. "We don't trust him."

I grabbed a couple more donuts, and so did Austin. By the time that we left, carrying our picket signs with us, the box was empty and lying in the trash. The ads building was only a block or so away. As we walked, I looked at my watch. It was 10:50. As if to confirm that fact, the bell in East College began ringing to signal the end of ten o'clock classes. But there were only a few students moving about. When we got to the ads building, no one was picketing there. I glanced across the lawn of East College and saw several of Natas's "marshals" putting the finishing touches on a temporary stage. Willie Jeffries was standing to one side, waiting with a couple of his buddies to move equipment onto the stage. Jeffries had lived in the dorm at the same time as I had the year before. He was one of the few musicians on campus who wasn't a music major and whose musical tastes weren't limited to classical music of the eighteenth and nineteenth Centuries. I'd been to parties where he'd whipped out a guitar, much to everyone's appreciation. The music majors couldn't do the same thing with a cello or oboe. When I had been "in" on the thing that was not yet "SAF" it had been agreed that he would play.

"What do we do now?" Austin asked.

"Why not picket here?" Michelle asked. "I mean, we're supposed to be meeting here at 11."

"Did that get changed?" I asked. "I mean—you're still in the organization, aren't you?"

Austin shrugged. "They were going to meet last night to go over what they called 'last minute details.'"

"In other words, they did change plans." I just shook my head. I wasn't angry. Hell, I was beyond feeling angry. I was more dead inside than anything else.

"Let's picket the ads building," Michelle said, repeating her idea of a few moments before.

"Why not?" I asked.

Austin's face broke into a grin. "Sure—why not?"

So there the three of us were, walking back and forth, picketing the administration building of DeForrest University. It was called Studebaker Hall. I have no idea why, except that maybe the Studebakers donated money. I am not aware that any Studebakers ever attended DFU. Perhaps some of the students owned and drove Studebakers at one time or another. Certainly some of the students' parents probably owned stock in Studebaker. One or two of the ancient secretaries that had staffed the university for decades walked by us on their ways back from breaks or errands, and one or another of them would shake her head in distress over our presence there.

At one point, as Austin passed me, he said, "They wouldn't try to arrest us, would they?"

I smiled and said over my shoulder, "They're not that stupid."

Michelle said, "They've done things more stupid than that."

We must have been picketing for half an hour or so when we saw Natas and a couple of his ever-present groupies walk out of the UB and start across East College lawn. They all wore denims and bright, white armbands firmly in place on their left arms. The Daily DeForrest had quoted Natas as saying that there would be no violence as a result of the activities of SAF—as if the possibility was very real. Other than the argument between the two chem majors about the logistics of building demolition, I knew of no discussion of violence, and even that discussion I took as being half-assed at best. The student body of our white, upper-middle-class enclave was not willing to sacrifice (please imagine a symphonic coda here) med school or, for those with lower grade points and slightly higher ethical values, law school, over the tenure of a prof whose classes most of them had not taken. Beyond that, any exuberance or creativity of expression had been squelched by Natas and his groupies.

As they walked across the lawn, one of Natas's groupies caught sight of us and nudged Natas. When Natas saw us, he turned sharply towards us. "Hey guys," he greeted us, half politely, half with an expression like he was wondering what the fuck we were doing. "What is this?"

I looked at the son of a bitch, and all that I could do was smile. "Figured we'd get an early start."

"Pickets aren't supposed to start until 2," he said, and held up and pointed at his wrist watch. I'm surprised that he didn't provide us with an interpretation of the reading of the big hand and the little hand. He pointed at the Union Building. "And when we picket, it's going to be over there at the UB, not here." He turned back towards us. "So put them away." He turned to go back to East College, his groupies in tow.

"Fuck you again, Jimmy," I said, smiling. My tone was still very pleasant, albeit laced with a few obscenities. "You can't boss me around."

"He can tell you what to do," Jeanna said for him. "He's president of SAF."

"By coup, maybe," Austin said. He seemed to be a lot more vocal in his oppostion to Natas today.

One of the other groupies started trying to explain, like in a civics lesson, very serious as if we didn't understand the mechanics of what had happened, and that somehow the mechanics of the whole thing legitimized it. She sounded kind of funny, rattling off phrases, like 'Committee of Committees,' as though they bore some religious significance. It made me wonder how their meetings were held, now that the prying eyes of the uninitiated were excluded. Maybe the meetings were in darkened rooms with a predetermined number of candles lit, and an incense censure burning in a corner, perfumed smoke billowing from it. As she spoke the words, her eyes were lit with the fervor of any other type of fanatic.

Finally, Michelle got disgusted with the whole thing and said, "You can't order us around, and I don't want to listen to this crap anymore." She began picketing again, walking the same path that we had been following before. Austin and I followed her lead.

Natas started walking alongside us, talking, his voice rising in volume. "Come on, you guys! You look ridiculous here!" He looked at his watch. "It was bad enough the other night when we marched all over the place and nobody was home. I want this to be different!"

I stopped and looked at him. "The march was your idea, asshole."

"Look," Natas said, ignoring my last comment. "Did you hear the radio the other morning? The DJ was making fun of us . . ."

Jeanna snorted in disgust, "I couldn't believe he'd never even heard of DFU. I had to explain . . ."

"You called him!" Austin said, dumbfounded.

Natas shot on, covering up the mistake of his cohort. "I don't want the same thing to happen today. I don't want the TV cameras showing just three people picketing the ads building." Then, in the midst of his tirade, Natas finally hit the truth. I don't think that the moment constituted an epiphany for him, or any great Zen moment of insight. I think he blundered into stating the truth by losing control and allowing his anger to take hold. "This is my day, goddamn it! I'm going to be on TV! And I want it to go right!"

He was nearly shouting by now, and little white pools of spittle had formed in the corners of his mouth. He was actually foaming at the mouth a bit! I'd never seen the son of a bitch lose that superficial, calm, valiumesque demeanor. And all because I threatened his—image on TV?

The whole thing was making sense. This wasn't about academic freedom or the tenure of a popular professor. This was about ego and Natas's urges. Maybe mine, too. Sure, why not. And he had won at this round. The rally the other night was only for the campus paper and maybe radio. But Natas had the part about TV figured out. That was his baby. The coup of the day before had all been carefully planned, exactingly timed, and flawlessly executed. The steps had begun with the committees being set up, and Jimmy's groupies being appointed. All of this had been done so Jimmy could admire his own face on TV. I wondered if he'd be screwing one of his groupies later on as he watched the footage on the 6 o'clock news. Maybe switch off and screw another one during the 11 o'clock news. Or just get right down to it and jack off. And I was about to say something along those lines, maybe toss in the fact that we were protected by the United States Constitution here, the First Amendment to be precise—that we were protected even from him. But then I glanced over his shoulder, and I said, "TV news crews are here, it looks like." Everyone turned to look in that direction and saw the vans pulling up to the UB half a block away. The vans bore the logos of the television stations from Indy and Terre Haute, as well as the logos of the networks for which those stations were local affiliates. Reporters and camera people got out of the vehicles, one or two of them stretching and yawning. A couple of them looked around and saw us, then a camera person nudged a woman who looked like a reporter. Then a guy started retrieving equipment from the back of one of the vans.

Just then Jillian, Cindy and their friend Patricia came out of nowhere, each of them carrying a picket sign. Cindy, angry and Irish and I would guess somewhat high, bore down on Natas.

"What's this shit I hear about you taking things over!?" she demanded.

Jeanna made the mistake of trying to speak up for Natas. "You weren't even there! What right have you to say anything?"

Cindy turned on Jeanna. Only a woman can use the "c" word and get away with it. "Shut up you little cunt! If I'd have been told about the meeting I would have been there!"

"Yeah," Austin said. "Why wasn't Cindy called?"

"I didn't think . . ." Jeanna stammered, still shocked from having been called a name she had only seen in a Harold Robbins novel. "I mean, I tried, but she wasn't in."

"Bullshit!" Cindy replied. "I live in the suite next to yours. You knew I was there. Fucking asshole."

I saw Natas turn and look up the street. TV people with their gear were trying to decide which direction to go. Jeffries had hooked up his equipment, and begun to run sound checks. That seemed to have drawn a couple dozen students. But the media people were pointing our way, and a crew started towards us.

"All you did," Cindy said, turning on Natas, "was take this thing over for your own sake. You've been a two-dimensional little shit ever since I've known you."

Natas quickly put up his hands, a grin breaking across his face. "Do you want the media to see us arguing?" Then he leaned over towards Cindy, but also so the rest of us could hear him, and the mask slipped again for a few moments. "I'm not going to step aside. If I have to, I'll argue with you, or even Mr. Debater here, on TV. I don't care. If you want to make asses of yourselves on TV, go ahead. But this is my gig. I'm doing it. And if you value anything at all about 'academic freedom' or Farina's tenure, you'll let me go ahead. Besides, he already has a settlement with the university and another job lined up in Boston." Man, Jimmy was good at being a weasel. By the time we realized what he'd said and done, he was making a bee-line for the TV crews.

I guess I'd about had it by then. The air was a bit cool, but I was goddamn cold all of a sudden. I was numb, too. I was shot the fuck through. I mean, I didn't want to, but I believed what Natas had just said, especially about a settlement. I think we all felt the same way, because we just stood there staring after the little group as it joined the media. This whole thing had become so tainted.

Jillian's friend Albert walked up just then. He was the only one among us without a picket sign. He was Jillian's "special friend" although we didn't know it at the time, and we wouldn't figure out until later what that meant. He had only started hanging out with her recently.

Then the quiet was broken when Jillian said, "Fuck it. I'm still picketing. At least we can embarrass the shit out of the university."

She and Albert started their march then, picketing on the same path Austin and Michelle and I had followed. I don't think we'd worn any sort of marks into the pavement or anything. It just seemed the natural spacing of an "orbit" there in front of the ads building. We watched as Natas's little group headed toward the vans, Natas conspicuously in the lead. He stopped when he encountered the first camera crew, already on its way towards us. Lights came on, one microphone then another stretched out. Natas seemed to be making a statement from a folded piece of paper, then answering questions, then finally turning and pointing in the direction of the stage in front of East College. A couple of hundred students, about the max that would be there at any one point, had gathered, and Jeffries, playing his guitar and singing in his odd, back-of-the-throat voice, started the entertainment for the day.

And we continued to picket. We got 20 or 25 people with us by the middle of the afternoon. Two of the film crews even came over and shot footage of us. About that time

Farina took the stage for a quick pep talk, accompanied by his attorney, who also spoke, basically saying that they couldn't say anything. Neither of them came over to us where we picketed. Jillian, Cindy, Michelle, Austin and I all took turns running over to Michelle and Austin's apartment to get high. Each of us still had tiny stashes of the blonde Columbian, and by three that afternoon, we were all terrifically buzzed. Cindy ran down to the IGA towards the end of the afternoon and grabbed a couple of pounds of hamburger and a couple of boxes of Hamburger Helper. When we got back to Austin's and Michelle's, dinner was being served, with a couple of loaves of garlic bread and cheap jug wine.

Michelle and Austin had their TV set up in the living room, and somebody else had come over with a cheap little black-and-white set that was put on top of the larger TV. We kicked back to watch the coverage on all three of the Indy stations and both of the stations in Terre Haute. The story ran third or fourth, depending upon the station. Natas had achieved his goal. Each newscast was the same. After a quick shot or two of Jeffries playing guitar, pickets in front of the ads building, and a pan of the students gathered in front of the stage, there was a clip of Farina speaking, then his attorney—without sound, just a voice-over from the reporter explaining the whos whats whens and whys—then a close-up, head shot of Natas and his baby blues stating what the goal of "Students for Academic Freedom" was. Then there'd be one more shot that was supposed to hit at the "heart" of the story. Their shot of Austin picketing caught a classic Jaguar XKE coupe passing by in the background. Very DeForrest.

Wolff dropped by. We chatted. When I was going to leave, he said that he was heading that direction.

"Natas and I have bumped heads ever since we were freshmen," he said as we walked along. It was chilly out, but the wine and the hot food had warmed me considerably. "I should have warned you about him."

"I should have seen it coming," I said. "From the moment those goddamn committees were formed."

"You have to watch the liberales," he said. "People like Jimmy say they're concerned about blah-blah-blah. Then they'll knife you in the back, and use your corpse as a stepping-stone for their advancement."

I nodded. We walked on for a while longer, silent. "What's the next step?" he asked.

"I don't know. I'm out. Cindy's out. We don't have any credibility as individuals now that a named organization has been formed. Thanks to TV, the leadership of that organization has been firmly recognized."

Robert laughed. "You got that right. Jimmy covered all his bases. Once somebody abandons as a goal the purpose of an organization and sets out simply to take it over, things get a bit easier. Once that goal is accomplished, the organization is finished. Just like a rat eating grain in a farmer's silo. Fattens itself up, then shits and pisses on anything it can't eat. Doesn't want to leave anything behind for others."

We were nearing the fraternity. As we came to the end of the walk, we stopped. "No," Robert said, "Everything's over. What is it that Jimmy calls it? 'SAF'? Well—it's dead. Any resistance over Farina's firing, at this point, is dead. Jimmy's gotten onto TV, and that's all he meant to do. So this battle's been fought and lost. But there's still the war out there," he said, gesturing to the east. With that, Robert hunched his shoulders in a "So what?" expression, waved, and turned away.

He was right. Nothing ever happened as a result of the Moratorium. In the next day's Glendale paper, I was quoted as "one of the student leaders." Apparently one of the passersby I had spoken to had been a reporter. So at least I had made a little bit of press.

Chapter 28 - Food

Everything was going down the shitter. No—everything had gone down the shitter. My entire life was a shambles. Everything I had been working so hard to do—and to do well—was fucked.

The thing with Farina was for nought. Natas and his crowd had taken it all over. Their goal was to make TV for a day. Part of what I was doing might have been a product of ego, sure—but the "greater" part, so to speak, had to do with asserting ourselves. The goal wasn't just "academic" freedom, but freedom on a level at which the university—and the alums and peoples' parents and family—had to recognize our moral autonomy. That was all pissed away now, so Jimmy got his three minutes or so on the three Indy and the two Terre Haute channels.

In the process, I had let my grades slip. Slip? That wasn't a fair assessment. Crash? More accurate. I couldn't go to Gleason's class. I couldn't stand the thought of going onto campus, for that matter, so there went the rest of my classes. I think I was aware of the fact of having missed one, then a second, hourly in speech pathology. I was badly in debt. The hash deal had killed me financially. The hundred bucks or so was not exactly a princely sum. But it was a shitload of cash to me. I hadn't the slightest idea of how to replace it. The thought of a part-time job never occurred to me. I had never had to seek employment before. I'd always worked for Adolf and his construction company. I didn't even know how to go about applying for a job. Besides, I was a college student. I wasn't supposed to "work" as such. Jobs were tough to obtain in Glendale, perched, as it was, on the edge of White Trash/Quasi-Appalachia America. A Glendale employer was unlikely to hire a DFU student.

I was hungry all of the time. With the last of the money I had I'd bought two or three huge bags of egg noodles and a hot plate. The noodles were heavy and filled up my stomach so I wasn't so dizzy. Besides, a diet heavy in starch was standard for college students. But in the meals served downstairs or in the dorms, at least other things were served with the starch. I figured that whatever I lost in food value by eating only starch, I would compensate for by taking those vitamins I mentioned earlier. The cramps and shits weren't so noticeable with the starch consumed at the same time as the vitamins. I didn't know if the vitamins worked at that point, but even if taking them gave me a placebo effect, then that was good enough. I needed all of the confidence I could get, no matter the source. The fact of my debt ate away at me. The house treasurer would ask me, from time to time, where the money was that I owed on the last house bill. I would hem and haw and not really give any answers. So in addition to exercising avoidance down on campus, I had to practice it in the frat.

I still could manage to obtain a buck or two in order to get drunk. I became very good at figuring the cheapest means of obtaining a buzz on alcohol. Cheap vodka was always a good avenue of intoxication. I had achieved the state of being able to ignore the awful taste of vodka after only two or three shots. There was also pot. Enough people who owed me buzzes, for all the free buzzes I'd given them in the past, meant I could always cop a pretty good feel for the cosmos.

I withdrew more into my room. The day-glo was omnipresent, omniscient. I would turn on the tunes, and carry myself into my little mental game of being a rock star. What if I had written "Smoke on the Water"? Or any of the other tunes I played. I'd down some more of the vodka. Yeah, I was a rock star, and the name of my band would be The Dendrites.

And I would hitchhike out of this stinking place and write my own songs. And I'd go to the coast—which one didn't matter. And I'd be a star!

Most of all, during that time, I just wanted to sleep. When I was asleep, all the problems seemed to go away, or at the very least get put on hold. I would sleep eight then ten then twelve hours out of the day. I would be in my little cocoon of a room. I think that in intro to psych the previous semester, this condition of reality avoidance through excessive sleep was called neurasthenia.

The tunnel I was wandering into was very dark. Then there was a little pin-prick of light.

Hitch-hiking.

I could thumb my way out of this place. Sure. Why not?

Chapter 29 - Spring Nats

I started to bottom out. Spring Break hit. I always tried to keep out of my mind the thought of going back to Kilkerry and the Farm. With the turmoil in the frat and the brouhaha over Farina added in, it was easy for me to forget about the week that we would have "off." Well, I didn't really have it "off."

Other people made plans that involved fun or relaxation—the ubiquitous trip to Florida—or that, at the very least, involved no work. For me, Spring Break meant traveling to Nationals—"Nats" in our parlance. And because I both (1) wanted to do well and (2) thought we had a decent chance of doing well, I was researching our topic: "Resolved: That all victimless crimes should be legalized." I copied quotes, by hand, onto variously colored 4 x 6 file cards. Each card joined the file that was expanding, divided and color-coded by subject area. Candace and I had met a couple of times at the beginning of the semester to discuss the status of things. Even with all of the other crap that had been going on in my life, I had an affirmative case and a shitload of research done.

DeForrest let out for Spring Break on a Friday. The following Wednesday was the first day of the tournament. We were leaving the day before that for Lexington, Kentucky, the tournament site. Nats ate up our Spring Break. That didn't bother me. I had a plausible excuse for staying away from Kilkerry, although what I needed to do and what I should have done was work for Adolf for a week to get out of debt. But DSR took priority. I stayed at DFU once classes were over. There were a few other students staying on campus: about two dozen foreign students and a half-dozen students from the States who, due to obligations, lack of money for travel or personal choice, had stayed.

The library was not open that weekend, but I had thought of that already. I checked out a sizeable stack of books and carried them back to the fraternity—and by "fraternity," I mean the physical plant. There was no one around to bother me, so I researched during the day. During late afternoons and evenings, I was by myself in the house, drinking, smoking pot and playing the stereo. I'd wander downstairs to watch TV. I had a little money because I'd won an oncampus speech contest. Somebody bought alcohol for me before they'd left.

One evening I sat in my room on one of the cushions tossed on the floor. I was playing "Evergreen, Volume 2," by Linda Ronstadt and the Stone Ponies. The most famous cut from that album was her first hit, "Different Drum." I sat back and watched the shadows from the frames outlining the panes of my window as those shadows had formed on the ceiling. I had the lights out, and I just stared at the shadows as they moved slowly across the cracked plaster ceiling. I hadn't really wanted to stay at the frat during break. What I really wanted to do was find a large woods somewhere and run naked through it. I wanted all the poisons and toxins and negatives in me to be leached out, have the forest soak them all up and break them down so I would be clean and somehow innocent. The semester had taken such a shitty turn, but if I could just run through a woods like that, maybe some ancient spirits of the forests would see me and understand and reach out and help me by magic.

On Monday and Tuesday I was in the library from when it opened at 8 until nearly the time it closed at 5. With so few students around, the place had abbreviated holiday hours. I would take breaks to munch on cheap, bulky starch items, usually bad cake donuts. By Tuesday afternoon, I was done. The affirmative case was tight. Plus I had quotes on nearly every vice imaginable. What I lacked in quote cards, I was confident that I could cover by drawing on personal experience.

On Wednesday morning I took about two minutes to pack a couple of turtle necks, another pair of jeans and my toothbrush, toothpaste and shampoo, plus my flag outfit, and picked up my briefcase and sample case and walked across campus to the PAC to Doc's office. When I was a freshman, the speech department had been housed in an ancient, stucco church across the street from the security police on one street and Sigma Nu. The stained glass windows had even still been there. What had once been the main worship area of the church was used as a theatre. Where Sunday school classes had been held constituted the classrooms. But the administration had viewed the building as being too old, and so a new facility was built. As a result, the "speech department" ceased to exist and, in its place, was the Department of Communication Arts and Sciences. Speech Hall was torn down and, in DeForrest's great tradition, its former site was sodded over. Members of the frat across the street used the site for playing frisbee.

The weather was typical for an Indiana spring—kind of cool and shitty. I mean, it was about mid-50s with overcast sky, no sunshine. As I approached the PAC I saw Doc standing next to one of the university nine-passenger luxury station wagon land yachts. Two guys were loading suitcases and suit bags into the back of the car. They were the other two students going to the tournament. Jerry Danikin was in individual events, participating in extemporaneous speaking. In that event, the participant drew a topic that usually was covered in one of the three "slick-back weeklies"—Time, Newsweek and U.S. News and World Report—and was given about half-an-hour to an hour to prepare a six- to eight-minute long speech. Jerry had won two state championships in that event in high school. Although he was good at that event, he was a shitty debater. He had been my partner at my first college debate tournament, and then a second one later in my freshman year. He didn't like to research. The analysis that he employed was a product of the same process that he used for extemp competitions. Whatever he came up with in a minute or so was what he rode with. He was not very flexible. He still lived in the dorms and was a year ahead of me. I'd met him when I'd come down to visit the campus during second semester of my senior year in high school. My girlfriend at the time—the only great requited love to that point of my life—was from the same high school. In fact, she was on the speech team there, too, and that was how I had met her, at regionals. When I had told her that I was going to go to DeForrest for a weekend visit, she had told me about Jerry, and had even written a note for me to give to him. I showed up at his door on a Friday afternoon. He vaguely remembered me from tournaments, and then I stuck out the note and he took it, smoking a cigarette and soon nodded his head and laughed. The note basically told him to take care of me, and between him and the people at the frat, I got pretty well fucked up that weekend. We'd been friends when I was living in the dorm, but then he had tried to get a position as a CA—Counselor Assistant—and that meant that as being a student supervisor of sorts in the dorm, he got free room and board, so about then was when he distanced himself from me. The other guy was Dean Kropopolos, a freshman. Dean had debated at a couple of tournaments and was basically awful. He wasn't bad at student congress, though, and that was the event he was competing in. He was a big, gangly Greek kid from New York. His father was a vice-president at one of the networks, whose position at the networks was a bit like a corporate game of three-card Monty, from what I could understand. One week he was a vice-president for programming at CBS, the next a vice-president in news for NBC. Dean was extremely obnoxious, probably because (1) his family was rich and (2) he was from New York. But we got along and I had always enjoyed partying with him.

Jerry had driven back from his folks' house near Marion that morning. Dean had flown in the previous evening and stayed in one of the Glendale wonder motels, places that would have been as vacant as the abandoned motels of the 1950s that dotted U.S. 40 a few miles away but for the fact that they were the only motels for miles near Glendale and they jacked their rates to extortionate levels whenever there was a university event. Candace was spending at least part of her break someplace warm and flying into Lexington.

Doc started to get into the driver's seat, but Dean protested, saying he wanted to drive. Doc occasionally had one of us drive, but when that happened it was usually when we were coming home from a tournament. But there was a more important reason for Doc refusing to let Dean drive: Dean was an idiot as a driver. On the way back from a tournament the previous semester, in five brief minutes—that seemed to last forever—he had scared the shit out of everybody on the team. For one thing, he did not believe in stopping at stop signs—he would floor the vehicle and honk the horn as he blew through an intersection. And, whereas the national speed limit of 55 had been set the year before as a means of combating the energy crisis created by the oil companies, Dean viewed 55 m.p.h. as more or less a starting speed for a vehicle. He wasn't happy unless he was cruising along at 80 or 85. Plus, being from New York, Dean wouldn't listen to anybody. Doc had made him pull over and get out of the driver's seat. So now, for the trip to Lexington, Doc politely declined to allow Dean to take control of the car. The drive from Glendale to Lexington was not very long. There's an interstate beltway around Lexington, like there is around most cities, and when we hit that, Doc found the exit for our motel and we were there. It was a cheap place of some sort The cheapness was even in the name—"Budget" or "Savings" or "Low Rent" or "Shlock." It wasn't a Hyatt or even a Ramada. Dean and I were rooming together, Doc and Jerry had another room and, since she was the only female on the trip, Candace would have her own room.

After Doc checked us in and we headed towards our respective rooms Doc handed us each twenty bucks. "This is for food," he said. "Just get receipts."

I'd been down to the nubs, money-wise, and this was a welcome shot. When Dean and I got to our room, I was surprised, because the place looked fucking cheap, and Doc didn't usually scrimp. I walked over to the floor-to-ceiling windows and pulled back a rubberized curtain. We were on the ground level, and I was looking at the grill of somebody's car. As I scanned the parking lot, I saw several vehicles bearing decals on their doors with the names of universities or colleges. So that was it. Doc never stayed in places this cheap unless it was Nats and the place was the tournament hotel.

Dean and I dumped our stuff and ran across the street to a McDonald's and wolfed down some starch and grease. Once we were back to the room, he called room service, and not long afterwards, there was a knock at the door. He'd ordered Heinekens, and the beer was cold and tasted good. We had that one, then another, oblivious to the cost. Hell, we had twenty bucks!

We decided to check out the lobby area. There was a bar down there, so Dean—who was 18—and I walked into the place and were promptly served in a state with the same drinking age—21—as Indiana. I switched to Bud, and when I paid the waitress for my drink, I became conscious of the fact that I had already gone through ten bucks. Dean and I discussed the possibilities as to alcohol. If we continued drinking at the motel, we would run out of money very quickly. However, if we made a beer run now—and I'd seen the neon word "LIQUOR" glowing a few doors down from the motel, behind plate glass windows—we could buy a couple of cases each and have plenty to drink for the next few days. And that's what we did. We trundled down to the liquor store and grabbed two cases of Little Kings—I was pleasantly surprised that they sold them here—each. I felt as if I had an aura surrounding me, because nobody carded me at the liquor store, either. When we got back to the motel, we grabbed ice from the machine down the hall and iced the bottles down in the sink in the bathroom. Then we resumed drinking. This was, after all, our Spring Break. Besides, I'd done all the research I needed to do and the affirmative case was finished and ready for Candace to read the next day. Dean hadn't much to do for student congress, so we sat back, happily, and shot the shit while we consumed cream ale. I knew Doc would go to the airport and pick up Candace in a couple of hours, but until then, I could relax.

Eventually, I pulled out my pipe. Dean turned on the fan in the bathroom, and we took turns going in there and smoking bowls. I was feeling no pain. I was beginning to think about the prospects of another meal. I was down to about three bucks. Yes, Little Kings were that cheap. That was when Doc knocked on the door and came in. The smoke had, by this time, completely dissipated. There were no beers in sight, and why, I don't know. I'd just done the number on my eyes with Visene, and my cigarettes had tasted bad, so I'd just brushed my teeth. So I didn't look fucked up at all or smell of alcohol.

"How are you guys doing?" Doc asked, glancing around the room to make sure we were all squared away. The question was polite but superfluous. I mean, what if we had complained about something?

"Fine, Doc," I replied, sitting down. "I'm all set for tomorrow. Just waiting for you to get Candace so I can hand this stuff off to her."

"Good," he said, and handed me the keys to the car. "You need to pick her up at the airport. Her plane comes in," and he looked at his watch, "in about 45 minutes."

I said the most intelligent thing that came to my mind in that moment, "Huh?"

"I have meetings, and Jerry's being inducted into the speech honorary fraternity."

I thought: Me? Drive a car? Right now? Oh good. As Doc left the room I thought briefly about asking Dean to drive, but I realized I couldn't. Sober he was a dangerous driver and, for some strange reason, I didn't think that being as loaded as he was he would be any more careful behind the wheel. And I couldn't tell Doc why I couldn't drive. He'd be pissed off at me for having gotten loaded to the point that I couldn't perform such a simple task. I walked into the bathroom and looked into the mirror. I could have passed the test of the most paranoid mother. I sighed, said goodbye to Dean, grabbed my jacket and walked out to the car.

The car was a boat. It was huge. I got in, and immediately felt intimidated. I took a few deep breaths, then started the engine. In my brain I went through the first few driving lessons in driver's ed my sophomore year of high school. I adjusted the seat so it was comfortable. I adjusted the mirror inside, then the mirrors on each door. I fastened my seat belt/safety harness. I put the car into gear and backed out of the space, trying to focus on the basic elements of driving. I had only a vague notion of where the airport was. I'd seen a sign for it on our way to the motel. The airport was located in the opposite direction at the time. So I headed that way on the interstate.

I guess I passed the exit for the airport four times before I finally turned onto it. I was talking to myself the whole time. I was paranoid as hell that I'd get busted for drunk driving or having long hair—this was the quasi-South after all, in the days before rednecks had adopted the long hair and weird sideburns, etc., of the hippies. The airport's location was weird. It seemed like I was driving onto a horse farm—white board fence was on either side of me. I'd been on, then off, the interstate. I'd pulled into the same gas station twice for directions. And the whole time I was trying to maintain. When I finally found the place, I got to the short-term parking lot, parked it, took out the keys, made sure they were safely in my pocket, locked the sucker up, and headed into the airport. As I walked into the place through the automatic double doors, Candace was just coming off of the ramp from her plane. We saw each other immediately. As we headed towards the baggage carousel, I handed the car keys to her and explained to her why she was going to drive. She just shook her head and said okay. Once back at the motel, I gave her the affirmative case, and then I crashed.

Our first round the next morning, at 9:00, was against a team from I.U. that wasn't all that great. Second round we hit a team from Vandy that was a little better, but not appreciably. During lunch break, Candace said, "You were right. None of the negative teams want to argue gambling or prostitution. All they want to talk about is drugs."

"Hell, gambling and prostitution are legal in Nevada and easily controlled. Unlike EVIL DRUGS," I said with mock emphasis. It was ironic that half of the people we were debating were druggies, and they couldn't see the simplicity of the arguments for legalizing drugs. Plus, our files were the largest of any of the teams at the tournament, and we didn't have to dip too deeply into those files for our responses. The strategy was simple: in 1AC, Candace argued gambling, prostitution and drugs. Second negative (2N) would cross-ex heavily on drugs, and then that person's partner would hit drugs heavily in 1NC, and pretty much leave prostitution and gambling alone. They were all missing a major point, in addition to the fact that they lacked good evidence—they misunderstood "legalization." What they were arguing was decriminalization. Under decriminalization no one could be busted for sale or possession of drugs, but there would still be a huge black market. There would be no quality controls—so someone buying heroin, for example, could be injecting rat poison or 100% pure uncut smack and, either way, be dead. Organized crime would still be the big player. In other words, most of the harms of drugs being illegal would still be prevalent. Under the status quo, it was far more difficult for a teenager to get a 6-pack than a joint. If legalized, most of the harmful aspects of drugs would disappear. I mean, how many bootleggers and speak easies have there been since Prohibition ended? Anyways, I would get up in 2AC and swat down the 1NC arguments. By rebuttals, the other team would still be reeling. The round was over.

After lunch we killed time huddling in the entrance of one of the buildings as I chain-smoked. We would have gone outside and walked around the campus, but the air was cold and wet, even that far south.

Third round was against Vermont State. Each of the two debaters was male and a hippie. First neg was sort of pudgy with dark hair and a beard. Second neg was sort of thin and clean-shaven. First neg attacked our case just like the others had, except that he made a new point about the Harrison Act requiring users of marijuana to pay a tax each time that a transaction occurred. During cross-ex I asked him if he realized that the Supreme Court had ruled that provision of the Harrison Act unconstitutional because it violated a person's right against self-incrimination.

He looked at me unabashedly. "You mean I don't have to fill out all those forms anymore?"

I smiled. Candace and his partner started chuckling. I didn't see any reaction from the judge, so I went on to other questions.

Vermont State's desks and briefcases were set up so the open briefcases blocked the judge's view of the two debaters. Candace and I sat off to the side. As I grabbed my evidence cards and turned to the podium to give my constructive, the first neg held up a bag of pot so we could see it, but the judge couldn't. I suppressed any reaction and went ahead and gave my speech.

It was easy to tell we'd won that round. The judge thanked us and left quickly. As Candace and I put away our papers and re-filed our cards, the first neg asked us if we partied.

In no time flat we were out of the building and into Lexington traffic to hail a cab. One pulled up and we all jumped in. The cabbie took off, not saying a word when the first neg, Phil, pulled out and fired up a joint. The cabbie just rolled down his window and asked if we could please do the same. Even though there were four of us in the back, the cab was a Checker Marathon, and we had scads of room. We got back to the motel just as the joint died. Bob, the second neg, paid the cabbie while Phil smothered the roach and put it in his wallet. We went up to Dean's and my room and popped open some Little Kings. As we partied, Bob expounded on the history of comic books. He was something of a collector, apparently, and we got into his stories. He said that there was an approval system for comic books. "The industry" had created a watchdog group to give its seal of approval to comic books based upon whether the issue in question was suitable for children. In one comic book, the superhero existed in another dimension. He had a couterpart, an "average human" living in this dimension. When the guy in this dimension summoned the superhero, the superhero replaced the average guy in this dimension and the average guy then went to the superhero's dimension, which was sort of like limbo. The human would sort of hang out there while the superhero fought Evil by using his super powers. The superhero could only do this for a specific number of hours—12 or 24 hours or something like that—before the old switcheroo took place and the human came back to this dimension. Well, apparently, one issue of that comic book was denied the industry's seal of approval . In that issue, the human, who finds limbo to be pretty fucking dull, decides to drop acid right before the switch. After the switch occurs, the acid has really bizarre effects on the superhero over on this side, and he spazzes out, etc. Sounded to me like a pretty cool story line, but the industry didn't think so. The story involved DRUGS as something other than the stereotypical Evil Thing.

After a while, two or three of the Loyola debaters pounded on our door, having finally found us for our typical tournament partying. After that, I remember that people pooled money a couple of different times to make liquor runs. We had one hell of a lot of Little Kings, those little green bottles seeming to be everywhere. Add to all of that some hash that was floating around, and then everyone seemed to have a little bit of pot. We had enough neural toxins in the room for everyone's brain to reach critical mass.

The party grew and prospered into the early evening. It spread to other rooms and the hallway, college debaters whipped up, not into polydrug abuse so much as polydrug enthusiasm. I remember several people, over the course of the evening, asking me why

Dean was such an asshole. At one point, I recall, he was standing in the middle of one of the beds, trying to make some kind of point. I just shrugged at the question and said, "He's from New York." That was enough of an answer. I wandered from room to room for a while, and the more buzzed I got, the more confused I got about which room was mine. Eventually, I got into a game of euchre, a four-handed trump game that was, around the time of the Civil War, the most popular trump game in the United States, and that is still popular in Indiana but doesn't seem to be played anywhere else. The cards were beginning to blur. I glanced over as Dean puked on the sliding glass door. Then things fritzed out.

I awoke in my bed, the first light of day filtering through the curtains and the vomit. I got up and staggered to the bathroom, avoiding what seemed to be hundreds of little green bottles scattered throughout the room. I ran the hot water to max and soaked for a few good minutes. I got out, dried off, and put on my flag outfit. After I yelled at Dean for about the fourteenth time to get dressed, I left the room and bumped into Doc in the hallway. We went to the dining room and had breakfast. There were cops everywhere. I asked Doc what the deal was with all the cops.

"Some kind of convention, I suppose," he replied.

I got a lot of stares from the cops. A few of them laughed. I figured that with my long hair, sideburns and weird clothes, they probably viewed me as The Enemy.

I'd had nothing to eat the previous evening. I was also out of money. That meant that any meals I was going to have would be with Doc so he could pick up the tab. So I ordered a huge breakfast—ham, eggs, hash browns, toast, juice, and a large coke. I wolfed it all down. All that was left were a few smears of grease and a twig of parsley. The cigarette after the meal tasted great. Doc paid the check and we went back upstairs. By some miracle, Dean was up, showered, and dressed. Jerry and Candace were ready, too, so we all grabbed our gear and piled into the wagon.

Candace and I had only two rounds that day, and both of them were in the morning. The first one was against the defending national champions, Northwestern. They were both rude. Candace was in awe. She said that one of them had written two books about debate theory and strategy. I just sat and waited for the judge. I wanted to see what they were going to do that made them so good. I was curious. When the judge came in, I knew that we were in trouble, because he said hi—warmly—to the other team and called them by their first names. Then they introduced us to him. Bad sign. The judge was the coach from Pittsburgh, a circuit school, and they attended all the same tournaments and were good buddies.

Candace did 1AC, but when the second neg got up to cross-ex her, all of his questions related to debate theory. None related to the topic—victimless crimes—that we were supposedly there to debate. First neg got up and introduced a counterplan—the laws against victimless crimes would still remain on the books, they just wouldn't be enforced and, because the negative's counterplan proposed less of a change to the status quo, they maintained the negative presumption and, ergo, they win.

I started laughing. I looked back, though, and saw that the judge was really eating it up. In 2AC I called what they were doing "onanistic." By the time I was into 2AR, and the judge was just fiddling with his pen, his decision made and avoiding eye contact with me, I think that I actually called them "jerkoffs." There was no way we could have won debating that team with that judge. I was pissed, but hey—them's the politics of tournamants, especially Nats.

188

As we made our way to the next round and I grumbled about circuit horseshit debaters, Candace suddenly changed subjects and, with a funny look on her face, asked, "Do you remember very much about last night?"

The sudden change of topics confused me. "Sure," I said, being anything but.

"You do? Do you remember passing out?"

Let's see, I thought. I tried to reconstruct the events of the previous evening. I remembered the playing cards spread out over the table. I remembered getting up from the table after we'd quit playing cards. I shook my head. "Not exactly—no."

She shook her head and smiled. "You did another Loyola. I was playing cards in your room when one of the girls from Washington University came in. She was upset and said that a naked man had passed out in her and her partner's room and he wouldn't get up. He kept mumbling, 'Fuck off,' and 'Get out of my fucking room.' I asked if he had long hair and mutton chop sideburns, and when she said yes, I knew it was you."

I moaned and shook my head.

"Dean and the guys from Loyola and I all went down there to her room, got you back to your room, and then I went over to party with Loyola."

I thought for a moment, and then asked, "How'd you guys get me dressed?"

"We didn't. We had a rough enough time getting you out of the bed and down the hall. Those poor girls wanted to get to sleep."

"You carried me naked down the hall?"

"Yeah. By the arms and the legs. But it was only a couple of doors away. There was a group of cops from that convention walking by and I thought that they were going to choke, they were laughing so hard."

By then we were in the room for the next round, and the team we were debating walked in. It was a team of two females from Butler University. Butler wasn't exactly a rival of ours. We didn't view them as being on our level. Butler was on the north side of Indy, not far away from DeForrest. Most DeForrest students viewed Butler as a place to which a person went if that person: (1) wanted to stay in-state, (2) be snobbish by going to a private school, but (3) didn't have the money or the SAT scores to go to DeForrest. I knew one of the two females from debating against her in high school. She was a year older than I was. I didn't know her partner. Each of them initially smiled and said hello to Candace, but then they turned and looked with hatred at me. I whispered to Candace but she said that no, she was sure the women whose room I crashed in were from Washington and not Butler, and that the two who'd just walked in hadn't been in the hallway the previous night. These two did not like me for my hair and appearance, etc. Or I guess that they didn't like me—period.

The judge that finally came in was the coach of Raleigh College, the all-male school that was DeForrest's arch-rival. Although in sporting events fights usually erupted between the students of the two schools, in debate we got along pretty well. And their coach really liked our approach to debate, so I was glad when he walked in and said hello and sat down. Once he had the names written on the ballot and his legal pad ready, he told us to start.

Candace did her speech. When the second neg cross-ex'd her, we weren't surprised when the entire focus was on drugs. What was different from the other rounds, though, was that the questions were asked in an extremely mocking tone. "People don't have 'bad trips' on LSD?" "What type of music—if you could call it that—did you refer to?" "'The Moody Blues'—where they get these names, I don't know—do they perform music with artistic merit?" I thought I was hearing a younger version of Eva and Adolf.

When the first neg got up, she started right away into the machine gun chatter of a spread. She was trying to toss out 30 or 40 arguments, most of which were bogus. Plus her tone was even snottier than her partner's had been. She attacked drugs not from the standpoint of individual rights vs. harms to the individual from its use, but from the standpoint that drugs engendered ideas and behaviors that are threats to society. She brought up street violence and warfare between nations, the declining belief in Jesus and in the "work ethic." She talked about people with long hair and "filthy jeans" and mocked other aspects of the counterculture as well. Then she drew a parallel central to her and her partner's arguments, a parallel that really taxed the mixing of metaphors. "When Jimi Hendrix, Jim Morrison, and Janis Joplin overdosed, theirs were not the deaths of individuals so much as the tip of a cancerous iceberg of death. Of the death of a portion of our society. Society has a right to control these persons. For their own good, but more importantly for society's good."

In cross-ex, Candace tried to get an admission from the woman that the rights of the individual were important in some way, but the first neg would not do that. Of course, Candace then pointed out the contradiction between that position and the fact that the status quo—what the negative team was supposed to be defending—set individual rights on a fairly high level in the Bill of Rights. Then Candace asked her whether the individuals were a part of society, too, and whether they had rights to form society to their beliefs. The woman stonewalled and time for the cross-ex ran out without her having really answering the question.

I got up and walked around the end of the desk, long hair hanging to my shoulders. I'd kicked off my shoes so my feet were bare. I wore the American flag belt I'd received as a gift from Lane. I felt the eyes of the negative team fix on me, and I could sense their revulsion. The atmosphere in the room was really weird. I felt as though we were debating the Nazis. This was really a debate against The Enemy—that's how they felt, and goddamn it if I didn't agree with them on that. In 2AC I had two overviews. The first was reinforcing the argument that Candace had touched on in cross-ex that there was an inherent contradiction between the negative's burden of defending the status quo and its unilateral attack on human rights. "Nothing could be so basic a right as my right to put into my body whatever I wish. I have sovereignty over my body. Besides, how is a plant—like marijuana— illegal? It has evolved over millions of years, far longer than the government of the State of Mississippi has existed." I could tell I was scoring points because the judge laughed at that one. My second overview was that the "facts" as related by the first neg were largely erroneous. "Hendrix didn't die of an overdose—he choked on his own vomit. Morrison died of a heart attack in a Paris whorehouse. Joplin did die of a heroin overdose—because she didn't know how pure the stuff was. If the affirmative plan had been in place at that time, she would have known the purity of the stuff from the statement on the package. She would not have overdosed. That's the crux of our case—protect the consumer." I tied into that the common misconception, adopted by the negative team, that decriminalization was the same as legalization. Then I was able to refute most of the first neg's arguments through these two overviews. For the rest of the arguments, I made specific responses as necessary. I concluded by saying that the model of the negative team was one of totalitarianism. "Put to its extreme we would have a dictatorship. Sorry—I don't like the idea of watching parades on TV every August 9 celebrating the inauguration of Gerry Ford as armored vehicles pass by in review before an eight-story-high picture of him. Sort of scares me. Vote affirmative."

The first negative had a pained expression on her face as she came up to cross-ex me.

"Are you proud of abusing the American flag like that?" she asked.

Things went downhill from there. She didn't score any points, and I just kept smiling and politely answering questions in the face of her bitchiness.

When second neg got up, her tone was even icier than her partner's had been. She spread, too. She mischaracterized my arguments or ignored them altogether. By the time she was done I was not impressed. I glanced back at the judge and caught the expression on his face and saw that he wasn't all that impressed, either. When she answered my first question, she did it in the exaggerated slowness that one adopts when addressing a young child, someone who is hearing impaired or a person who does not speak English. So for the rest of cross-ex I addressed her in the same manner, as though she were an idiot—but I still kept smiling.

Cross-ex was over, and they did 1NR. Nothing new came up there. Candace did a really good 1AR. She grouped 2NC's arguments and shot them down. Then she pulled affirmative case structure through as well as my extensions. I congratulated her when she sat down. Hell, we were really on top of our game!

The second neg's features were a sort of scarlet, her eyes narrow and filled with a hatred. Her motions were Germanically precise and clipped. She gathered up her flow sheet and evidence cards and marched to the podium. She started 2NR by quoting a right-wing columnist as saying that our society was being destroyed, from within, by the counterculture. She delivered a diatribe against the "longhairs, the punks, the malcontents." Then she started slamming rock and roll music in a way that I thought had died in the late 1950s. She tried to roll through case structure, but her voice was choked with rage. "People like him," she declared, pointing at me. "There will be more of them. Our country will regress. Is this the individualism that our Founding Fathers saw as important? The right to smoke pot. The right to grow long hair. The right to engage in illicit sex." She paused, then, voice shaking, said, "I have a niece and nephew, four and five years old. And I'm scared for them. Anywhere they go out in public, they see these people. Their parents can't shield their eyes from the filth on the covers of magazines. It makes me sick. Ours is a society that needs to go back to simpler times. We need to re-establish the proper morals values and goals. We can only do that by keeping morals laws on the books and enforcing them strictly. Otherwise, we abandon our society to this filth." With that she sat down.

As her ass hit her seat, my bare feet swung high into the air as I vaulted over a desk. I grabbed my legal pad and went for the podium. Yes—this was battle with The Enemy. I was trying to place where I'd encountered this hatred before. Of whom did she remind me? Ah, yes—that was it. The born-agains who dominated Kilkerry, looking haughtily down their noses at everyone. Self-righteous, petty, and mean-spirited—a community of hatred.

I was about to speak, but then I checked myself. I realized that if I spoke now, I'd simply blow up. I needed to focus my thoughts, direct my arguments.

I turned my back to the judge, leaned my forehead against the wall, and rubbed my eyes. What was the right way to reply? Then I had it. I knew what to say. I turned back around and looked straight at the judge.

"You know," I said. "I hate niggers." The judge's eyes bulged. "I hate the way they look. I hate the way they smell. I hate the way they talk. Second Neg talks about the evils of rock and roll. Well—guess where we got it? Niggers. Yeah, I hate them. I don't like to see them on the street. I don't want our children to be around them. No telling what them niggers'll do. They're destroying our culture." I stopped and looked at the judge. "If you buy the negative team's arguments about 'filth' like me, whether to deny liberties to people is a given. The only question then is whom do we define as 'filth'? That depends upon who is doing the defining. Follow their line of reasoning and you'll see that the attitude is the same as the Nazis had. They had an entire list of people they considered to be 'filth,' with a group called 'Jews' heading the list." I moved around in front of the podium. I said that if you deny freedoms to people based upon those peoples' social status, then we all lose. I said that the negative proposes totalitarianism, which was an unarticulated counter-plan in the round—and that, consequently, they had abandoned negative presumption—but that we opposed totalitarianism regardless of its status as an argument. I pulled through our case structure then, and my extensions. I referred to 2NR's comments about the "founding fathers" as being inherently sexist, but also wrong. The "founding fathers" smoked pot, wore their hair long, and—using the examples of Jefferson, Washington, and Franklin— were prolific in their illicit sexual dalliances. I concluded by saying, "Reject the venomous hatred spewed forth by the negative team. Vote affirmative."

The judge smiled and nodded. I knew we had won. I sat down. We did not shake hands with the other team as is custom. The judge and the timekeeper left the room. The other team left the room.

"You did really well," I said to Candace after everyone had gone. We stood and started out and down the hall.

"That's the best round I've ever seen you do," she said.

We caught a cab back to the motel. As I approached our room, I saw the maid's cart parked outside. I remembered what the room had looked—and smelled—like that morning, so I walked slowly past the open doorway and glanced in. Two maids were standing there, hands on hips, staring at the room. I heard one of them mutter, "Oh my god." I continued down the hall and banged on Candace's door. I waited in her room for a while, figuring to give the maids enough time to clean the room. I waited for about an hour. Then I walked back and found the room exactly as I'd left it that morning, complete with vomit on the window. I couldn't blame the maids for not wanting to clean the place. They wanted to clean it up as much as I wanted to live in it. And, since I'd had a hand in its creation and they had not, that was that.

I put my sample case down and started picking up little green bottles, even finding some in unused drawers of the dresser. The vomit had to be sort of peeled off the window, and that task was the only truly gross part of the business. Once that was done, I opened the door and turned on the fan in the bathroom. The air was quite cool, thank you, but at least now it was not so foul-smelling.

After Dean got back, he and I ordered room service. He bought the first round of two Heinekens each. I had money. The previous evening debaters had kicked in on the beer and, because there were so many bottles, I guess the people misjudged how much money was needed. I had a twenty, though, and Dean still had a couple of bucks left from what Doc had given to us. So we turned the TV sound to "radio" and listened to Seargant Pepper on a local station. When we killed that first round, I ordered the next. By the time that our Arab waiter had arrived, Candace had come in with the Vermont State debaters. They had just gone to the liquor store and bought a case. I paid for our round with a twenty. The waiter said he didn't have change, but that he'd be back. After I'd sucked down the two Heinekens, I started drinking from the case at the Vermont State debaters' invitation. After while, I became concerned about my change and called room service and asked for our waiter. About ten minutes later, good old Ahmed appeared.

"Where's my change?" I asked. I was buzzed, but I was polite. I figured the guy had just spaced.

"What change?" he asked, politely.

"The change from the twenty I gave you a while ago."

"Excuse me. You must be mistaken, but you did not give me a twenty."

"We were here," Candace said. "We saw him give you a twenty."

As Ahmed continued denial, I called the front desk, asked for the manager and told the person our room number. Ahmed started to leave but I told him to wait for the manager.

The woman who arrived appeared to be in her mid-fifties. She looked tough as nails. Mean, too.

"What is all this?" she asked as she entered the room.

I explained.

"I've known Ahmed for two years," she stated unequivocally. "His honesty is beyond reproach."

"And I have four witnesses," I replied. "And we're guests here. Are you saying that we're lying?"

I saw her glance around the room in consternation. The maids had probably told her about the condition the room was in only that afternoon. She was wondering if the maids had lied to her. "I just know he wouldn't steal and he wouldn't lie." Ahmed stood by, smiling sheepishly.

An idea dawned on me. "I'm just from a small town, you understand. This place is the big city to me. Any time I go on a trip like this, I always write down the serial numbers of any tens or twenties that I take, just in case something happens, you know?"

Everyone turned and looked at Ahmed, who maintained that sheepish smile as he said, "How else can I make a living here? You weren't tipping."

The assistant manager was pissed, I could tell, and more than a little shocked, but then she said to me, "Is there anything else?"

"I want my change."

She looked around the room again. "Wasn't there a lot of damage to this room?" I could tell that she was looking really hard at the window. Nope—there wasn't any vomit there.

"No," I said, now letting my anger surface. "There was no damage to this room. Jesus Christ! What kind of a place are you running here?"

The assistant manager turned to Ahmed and told him to give me my change. As he did so, she turned on her heel and left the room without another word. I received my change, and then Ahmed was gone, too.

I was really very good after that. We all were, pretty much, partied out from the night before. We got drunk and passed out, but nobody puked on any windows, none of the help tried to steal from us, and nobody dragged my naked body through the lobby of the motel. I considered us to be worthy of being canonized, almost.

The next day was cold, but clear and beautiful. I got up and made it downstairs for a nice, big breakfast with Doc. When I got back upstairs, everyone was ready. Dean didn't even look hung over.

Our first round was easy, against a team from out West someplace. In off-topic, we had seven rounds with no elims, just match of records and ties broken by speaker points. Candace and I knew we were doing well, but we weren't sure just how well. The rounds were power-matched and the team that we'd just hit was good, ergo, we weren't doing too badly. After that round we'd had to go back to our motel. The tournament organizers had run out of classrooms at UK so we had to use the motel rooms of teams competing in the tournament.

In our last round I did even better than I had done in the round against Butler. Our opponents were from the University of Illinois. Their main guy, J.P., was called "Silver Tooth" because of one of his two front teeth was entirely silver. That gave him a somewhat odd appearance, but he was pretty cool and one of the best audience debaters in the country. When he and his partner walked into the room, Candace and I realized we must be doing pretty well. It was awkward setting up our files on one of the double beds.

I was edgy about who the judge would be, but the coach from Hanover College, an Indiana school down near Louisville, walked in. He'd judged me four times and I hadn't lost a ballot from him yet.

As we got into the round, everybody had more and more fun. Usually the negative team would try to blur the affirmative case and confuse the affirmative debaters with a spread. Our affirmative case had eight major points. Those eight points became six in 1NC. In 2AC I boiled them down to four. Silver Tooth took them down to three. By the time that I got up to give 2AR, we were down to two major points.

I got up to do my rebuttal and I tested the TV. It appeared to be anchored well, and of sufficiently substantial weight. I climbed on top of it and sat cross-legged as I went into my speech. "Whatever became of Rousseau's noble savage?" I asked.

By the time I had finished, the judge was smiling. "You all did an excellent job," he said. "This was the best round of debate I've ever judged. Thank you."

That felt good, getting a compliment like that. Of course, now the tournament was over for us. Instead of carefully replacing all of the evidence cards into their proper places in the files, I dumped them into the sample case. All that work had fulfilled its purpose. We were done.

The tournament banquet was held that night. The two debaters from Vermont State, J.P. and his partner, and Candace and I commandeered a table at the back of the huge dining hall. There were two or three conversations going on among us when one of the circuit debaters from U Mass pulled out the only empty chair at our table and said, "Mind?" It really wasn't a question the way he said it and, besides, nobody had a chance to say anything because he sat down so quickly with two full plates of food. He launched into his food just as fast as he could probably speak. And he did speak as he ate, allowing us all a view of each masticated portion as it began its journey through his gastrointestinal tract. He used his napkin—first to blow his nose rather loudly, and then to wipe his mouth. As food flew forth from his lips into space and onto the table and other people, I tried to figure out if there was any correlation between particular parts of speech or particular dipthongs and the cascade of morsels finding their way out of his mouth. When he found out that we went off-topic, he commented that he was in "real debate." Candace smiled at him and he stopped talking. Still smiling, she called him a fucking asshole and told him to move to another table to spew his food on people as he ate. Without saying another word, he grabbed his plate as quickly as he spoke and moved across the room to another table at which it appeared that several circuit debaters and their coaches sat. Why he hadn't sat there in the first place, I can't say.

As it turned out, we had dropped the round to Northwestern, as we had assumed, and the round to Vandy and finished fourth. Candace and I received a nice little trophy. Neither Dean nor Jerry took home any hardware. We didn't party that night, and the next morning, after breakfast, we headed back.

And that was it. Debate was over for the year. Candace and I were on speaking terms again. I was watching Interstate roll by the window. We were headed back to Glendale. I'd been able to escape my problems and crises for a while. The sky was nice and clear on a cool day. Ahead lay the problems.

Chapter 30 - House Dance

Spring house dance popped up on my calendar, right after spring break.

Spring house dance was a big thing for most of the frats, and they all tried to plug it into rush as being one of The Main Events of the year. Ours was no different. In fact, our Spring house dance was The Rose Dance, the same name every chapter of our national fraternity used all across the country—and some parts of Canada—I guess to add some some of bullshit mystique to the Greek letters on the front of the house. All that any of the frats' spring house dances amounted to, though, was a glorified high school prom held at the collegiate level at which alcohol could be consumed in the open. I only went to one prom in high school, and that was my senior year. It wasn't even at my high school. I went to the prom at my girlfriend's high school, and most of our evening was spent indulging our recently-acquired enthusiasm for pot and furtively groping each other in our parked car.

Anyways, Rose Dance always had a "theme." That spring, our social chairmen—plural for some reason that year—hunkered down to come up with some stupendous theme that would go down in our frat's history as one of the best, and stick with us the rest of our lives as one of our cherished college memories. Now, I can't remember what that theme was. I think maybe the social chairmen did one of those numbers of saying that they had a big surprise then kept putting off revealing it and putting off revealing it because they didn't really have an idea, then when the house dance occurred and they did all the work, etc., almost daring anybody to ask them about the theme. Also, each date was to receive—ta da!—a dozen roses! Hence the name for the dance. However, finances were slim, what with so many people having moved out of the fraternity—and by "fraternity," I mean the physical plant—and the impact was sorely felt. What money there was that could be allocated to Rose Dance was barely sufficient to pay for the necessities—a band and booze. We also roasted a hog each year, but everybody figured we would have to bag that little tradition, due to lack of funds.

The alcohol was not really for the night of the dance itself. The house bought kegs for the parties on Thursday and Friday nights leading up to the house dance on Saturday. For the dance itself, there was a ritual to the matter of drinks. Each member of the house would select and prepare a mixed drink for himself and his date. Then everybody would mingle downstairs, cocktail glasses in hand, acquiring the social skills necessary to engage in just such a type of partying over the next four decades of their adult lives: dressed uncomfortably, getting hammered, listening to tunes and thinking about sex. The drinks themselves represented a "best of" list from the Mr. Boston's Bar Guide, a dog-eared copy of which usually made its way around the house each spring: Martinis, Rob Roys, Manhattans, Tequila Sunrises, for the overly-ambitious Harvey Wallbangers, stingers, zombies, White Russians, etc. A few unimaginative types went for whiskey and 7-Up or rum and coke.

That year, I went for the exotic. When I was in high school, one of my teachers had talked about getting fucked up in college on a drink called a Western Rattlesnake. He said three of those would knock a gorilla on its ass—or maybe he meant "guerilla," I'm not sure. I'd never heard of that drink before or since, but the name was sufficiently sinister that I wanted to try it. I wanted a drink that would shnocker me and my date. However, finding the recipe proved to be difficult. I perused two different editions of the Mr. Boston's Bar Guide, both our dog-eared copy and a new copy at the bookstore downtown. No luck. I tried at the library, going through Esquire and other magazines that had pleasure-related articles. I called the guys who wrote the weekly drink column for The Daily DeForrest, but again, no luck. I called each of the six bars in town. By Thursday before house dance, I was about to switch drinks. I figured I'd go back through the bar guides and pick something venomous-sounding. I didn't really want to do that. I mean, I wanted to have a drink so obscure that no one in the house had ever heard of it. Also, I'd really talked up the fact that I was going to have this thermonuclear drink. It would be a loss of face if I failed in finding the goddamn thing. Then somebody mentioned that a SNu worked during the summer as a bartender and that he might know. So I called him, explained who I was and what I was trying to find out, and—bingo! He said sure, he knew what it was. A Western Rattlesnake was a whiskey sour with an ounce of something called drambouie floated on top. The recipe didn't sound all that threatening. In fact, it sounded pretty mundane. But by this point, I'd gone to so much trouble I figured, fuck it.

I called Eastside Liquors and was told that, yes, they carried drambouie. They priced it for me. I had hoarded money from someplace. And I had just enough. Somebody was making a run just then, so I gave them my order and my money, and when they got back, I hid everything in the pile of dirty clothes in my closet.

The kegger we had later that night was almost like any other—until the commandos went out on their raid.

At about 10 I went downstairs for one more mug of beer. The party was dead. Everyone was upstairs, doing the usual by getting wasted in individual rooms. I was ready to crash but had a thirst for one more beer. Suddenly, four darkly-clad persons shot up the stairs. The last one was almost past me, and must have seen that I was wearing a black turtleneck. He hooked me by the arm and I was being dragged up the stairs, through the Informal, and out to Charlie Whitman's van.

"What the fuck's going on!?" I demanded.

"Shut the fuck up!" somebody replied. I recognized Whale Man's voice.

Somebody else shoved a bottle of whiskey at me and said, "We're gonna get some groceries!"

That statement made no sense, although I now recognized that voice as belonging to East. Then I saw the forms of Rudolf and Edwards as they jumped drunkenly into the van. I heard the stairwell door behind me open and then Whale Man was getting into the driver's seat, carrying a longneck bottle of beer in one hand and what looked like—yes, it was. He had a crossbow in the other hand. Crossbows look wicked enough, but this wasn't some William Tell model from antiquity. This looked like it was the product of nuclear engineering. The stock appeared to be made from some synthetic combination of high-impact plastic and a jet-age alloy of titanium, steel and carbon fiber. The "dart" that lay in the groove of the stock wasn't really a "dart." That makes the projectile I saw that night sound innocent. The goddamn thing was a brushed stainless steel missile with metal-like fins. I wouldn't have been surprised if someone had told me there was a radar tracking device situated behind an explosive charge in the highly sharpened tip.

Drunk as I was, it took me all of two seconds to figure out that: (1) they were going for "groceries"—i.e., some type of food—that (2) required a commando-type operation

(3) in the dead of night with (4) a crossbow–i.e., a silent method of killing. I didn't think the guys were going to knock off a cashier at the IGA. Then I remembered that: (5) we needed a hog to roast for Rose Dance, (6) we were short on money and (7) there were hog farms all over the countryside outside Glendale.

Just short of being shoved into the van, I pulled back. I couldn't go along. There were several reasons why. First, although I'm omniverous, I did not want to witness the killing of the source of our meat for Saturday's dinner. I've seen livestock slaughtered, and the activity is a bloody mess. Second, I was sleepy, and I was comfortable with the idea of soon being in my bed. Third—this was a felony the commission of which involved weapons. While felonious conduct per se didn't bother me—activities that related to the chemical substances and my intellectual growth sprang immediately to mind—I did not want to engage in this particular activity. With weapons near, any cops the group might encounter would have legal cause to shoot us. I did not relish the idea of giving Glendale's Finest an opportunity to legally shoot DeForrest students. Fourth, I was confident that there was a possibility that the owners of the hog operation had hired security, and that those people might just shoot back. Finally, Whale Man was so drunk I didn't think that he would outright kill the hog, and I didn't want to see the animal suffer, running around bleeding and squealing with nuclear crossbow missiles popping into it every 30 seconds.

The van pulled out of the parking lot. Then I heard it jar as it crossed the pothole at the end of the eastern half of the driveway. The brakes had been shot in it long ago.

The sun was warm when I awoke the next morning. Light was streaming through my window. If I'd had any Friday classes, I would have cut them. I glanced at the clock and saw that I still had half-an-hour to grab breakfast. Then I remembered I hadn't paid for meals on my housebill. I yawned, got up, put on my robe, or what was left of it, and went down the hall and showered. I walked downstairs then to at least read the paper and have a cup of tea from the complimentary stuff that was always there. No one was in the dining room, although sections of the paper were strewn across the tables there. Then I saw the trail of blood running over the threshhold of the door from the parking lot. The trail went from there, around the corner, through the dining room, and on under the door to the kitchen. I assumed it led to one of the huge refrigerators and ended with the corpse of a field-dressed hog.

I helped in the huge task of building the "moat." Each year for Rose Dance, the frat built a structure consisting of a rectangle 40 feet by 20 feet, made of railroad ties. The ties were stacked about four feet high, with one wall being formed by the little hillside that led from the front yard to the front porch. The thing was then lined with cardboard and garbage bags taped together and—Voila!—we had a "moat." In the meantime, Whale Man and a couple of the other guys were digging a huge hole in the front yard. By late afternoon they had hauled bags of charcoals and a couple of gallons of charcoal starter and gotten everything going. Then I helped as six of us carried a very dead pig, wrapped tightly in burlap, outside to the hole. Then a couple of people took turns filling it over the dead hog. Even though we were on "social probation" because of being turned in for the keg, it was difficult to tell, from observing the activities in the house that weekend, that we were suffering from having been consigned to that status. There was a keg tapped in the basement, and Whale Man and Rudolf were consuming the suds while standing guard over the roasting pig. The hole they had dug was approximately the same dimensions as a human grave, perhaps fitting considering the fact that farmers say that pigs have the greatest intelligence of the barnyard animals and share the most traits with humans. I walked over at one point and said hello. By then they had each reached an astonishing level of intoxication. Whale Man's eyes were bloody red and he said something to me that I couldn't understand, his tongue was so swollen.

I had been hard-pressed to figure out whom I would ask to the dance as my date. Most of the women I knew were either already committed to a relationship or were friends of mine with whom a romantic relationship was not feasible or possible. TV had suggested that I ask Candace, and I told him that was an absurd idea. We were debate partners. Another factor was my predilection for catching a buzz. I wanted to go to the dance with someone who liked to alter her perception of reality or, at the very least, a woman who would not be aghast at the prospect of my smoking a bong or two in front of her. Really, it was not very likely I would encounter a woman who harbored such objections.

There was a woman in the freshman class I had met and with whom I had partied. Carrie Templeton was kind of spacey, but really cute. I'd called her the week before and asked her if she wanted to go to the dance, and she'd said sure. I was pretty upbeat about the whole thing, even though my life was slipping further into the pits each day. There was always the possibility, after all, that I would get laid for the first time in my life. I didn't necessarily think that that would happen, but at least it was a possibility. Aside from that, I was looking forward to a nice party with an attractive woman whom I liked.

Early evening of the important day arrived. I had swept the carpet in my room, and straightened everything so it all looked pretty cool—neon graffiti and all. I showered and then put on a turtleneck with dark corduroy flared bell bottoms. I wore platform shoes, of course.

I walked over to pick up my date. She lived in the Freshman Quad. The night started out well as, three or four steps out of the door to her dorm, she whipped out a joint. So there we were, walking down the street passing a hagel on our way back to the fraternity—and by "fraternity," I mean the physical plant. Carrie looked really cute. She wore a simple dress that looked dynamite on her. I was a bit nervous—I don't think she was nervous at all—but then the joint helped to calm me a bit.

When we got to the house, we walked past the dining room, where the band was setting up at the far end. I thought I saw the word KILKERRY stenciled on the flat black side of an amp.

We got upstairs and I mixed our drinks, pouring liberally from the quart bottle of Jack Daniel's green label, then adding the whiskey sour mix, and proudly topping each with drambouie. Some of the guys in the house bought commemorative glasses for the dance, giving one to their date and keeping one for themselves. I couldn't afford that. Instead, I'd ripped off a couple of glasses from the dining room and hoped nobody would notice, or at least not say anything. I'd never tasted drambouie before. In fact, I didn't know anybody who had. The label on the bottle had a paragraph about the history of drambouie. It originally had been the drink of choice of Bonnie Prince Charlie and had even been made with laudanum.

Carrie took a sip and said, "It's a little sour, but not too bad."

I took a sip. I could taste the whiskey sour mix. Then the Jack provided a tad bit of a bite. The drambouie gave a sort of background, a tartness combined with a hint of chemical, but it was okay.

We walked across the hall to Sid's room and knocked on the door. A muffled voice said to come in, and I opened the door for Carrie.

Sid's date was a woman from Starr whom I vaguely knew. Criminal Phil had been out a couple of times before with his date. She was also from the Chicago suburbs and she and Criminal Phil had known each other in high school. After introductions were made, we sat down. The house bong made its way slowly, from person to person, around the room. When it was my turn, I felt the smoke condense in my lungs. I held back the urge to cough, and eased the smoke out through my mouth. I lifted up my drink and took a long sip, the cold wetness feeling really good on my throat. I noticed that Sid and Criminal Phil and their dates were using the same glassware I had purloined from the dining room. We could feel through the floor as several chords were played and amplified from the band warming up just below us. We used that as a cue to get up and go downstairs.

The dining room lights were still on as the band made their final adjustments. About half of the guys from the house were down there with their dates, a few without. Everybody stood around, ill-at-ease in semiformal attire, wanting to "get on" with the party. I took the opportunity to walk over to one of the band members and asked if they were really from Kilkerry. He acted annoyed. He said yeah, they were from Kilkerry. I said I was, too, and he didn't act too thrilled, until I asked him if he and his bandmates wanted to get high at the end of the first set. That was when he smiled and said sure.

I was nearly at the end of my drink, and saw that Carrie was, too. I took her glass and went upstairs and filed both glasses again. When I got back down to the dining room, nearly everyone from the house was there. I also saw that nearly everyone was using the same glassware for themselves and their dates as were Sid and Criminal Phil and I. The music started and the party officially commenced. The band broke into a Doobie Brothers tune "Listen to the Music." Everyone started dancing. The rheostats had been turned down so the light was dimmed. The music, the lights, our frenetic movements, and of course the alcohol and other drugs—all combined to give us an incredible buzz. The pot and the Western Rattlesnakes were really doing a number on me. I remember bits and pieces of the evening. Going up to my room a couple of times to get high with the members of the band. Refilling our glasses a couple of times. I remember going out to the moat at one point and tossing things into it, just to hear the different tones that different sized and shaped objects made upon impact. And I remember somebody barfing along the side of it but—tastefully— not into the water itself. There were people taking off their semiformal attire and jumping into the goddamn thing. My date seemed to be enjoying herself, and we were definitely getting trashed.

Then—nothing. Rest. Darkness. Followed a considerable time later by the sounds of birds. Then I felt a coolness on my face as a breeze stirred, and felt a grittiness from sleeping in my clothes. I woke up and found myself lying next to Carrie, our clothes fully on, on the dining room tables that had been moved to the patio to make room for the band and the dance floor. I moved slightly and, in so doing, felt as if my head would explode.

I heard her make the small groans of a woman awakening to mild pain. As I gazed at her face, her eyes came suddenly open and she was staring straight at me. She looked confused for only a few moments, then everything seemed to register and I think she figured out where she was.

"Take me home," she said without hesitation, and sat up.

I said sure, and rose to unsteady legs. Fortunately, I was still a bit drunk, so the intoxication helped to mask elements of the pain. We walked the several blocks to her dorm. A car passed us as we walked down Anderson Street. The occupants, a good little Christian family of townies, looked all dressed up in "Sunday best." The father even smiled at me and gave a little wave. We ignored them, as well as every other aspect of the world.

I got Carrie home. I languished in bed the rest of the day, battling the effects of the Western Rattlesnakes.

Chapter 31 - Senior Banquet

Senior Banquet was the last major event of the school year in the house, held right before finals. It sounded very special, as if featuring jackets and ties, a nice meal, and humorous speeches. You get the picture. However, the reality was at great odds with that picture.

Here I was in my sophomore year, battling the demons of depression. But I would not miss Senior Banquet. I hadn't paid for meals at the house, but Senior Banquet rose above such mundane considerations.

At 5:30 on the appointed day, dinner was announced and everyone, except the seniors, filed into the dining room. The few seniors still residing in the house—Whale Man, Jerry Blue, Carson Davidson, a couple of others—were seated at a table covered with a nice table cloth and nice china. Each senior had been served salad, steak, baked potato and roll. Also, out of the house social budget, each senior had been provided with a gallon of the booze of his choice. Everyone else, juniors down, sat at the other tables in the dining room, tables bare except for serving dishes, simple plates and the usual cheap flatware that was used for lunch each day. The serving dishes all held left-overs of the previous couple of days and were heavy in the starch and grease: chicken and dumplings, spaghetti, etc. Between the head table and our own was a trash can, empty but for a clean, plastic bag for a liner.

Somebody tapped a glass to signal the okay and we began to eat. I was really hungry, and, knowing what lay ahead, I started cramming food in as fast as I could.

After a last few minutes of sobriety, we reached the heart of Senior Banquet. Whale Man was the first to signal an underclassman—his old roommate TV—to come up and have a drink with him. That meant TV did a shot of the rot-gut, venomous off-brand of bourbon that Whale Man had located someplace. This was the purpose of the gallon of booze purchased for each Senior, and the purpose of the banquet itself. The seniors themselves, if they were drinking at all, were only drinking beer. The point of the exercise was that each underclassman had at least one shot with each senior. I did a shot of vodka, a shot of sloe gin, two shots of Jack Daniels, a shot of gin, a shot of the rotgut that Whale Man had chosen, then a shot of Johnnie Walker black. Then I went back to the starting point and began another lap. The shots went down quickly, then I did a couple more. In the space of 20 minutes I managed to do 12 or 13 shots. I went back to my chair to rest a moment, and TV sat down beside me.

"I'm completely sober," I told him. "And in 15 minutes, I'll be plastered."

"No shit," he replied.

What we were doing by present-day fraternity standards was outrageous. It was completely inappropriate for members of a frat to do and exemplified the worst of frat house living. Compelling frat members to engage in binge drinking that very easily could have resulted in death due to alcohol toxicity. There. Lip service to the "correct" thing to say. For us, though, it was a challenge.

At some point, Whale Man became evil. He chuckled and pulled a quart bottle out of a paper bag. Then he pulled out what looked like bean dip. The bottle held ouzo, a Greek liquor that tastes like cheap licorice on fire.

I had a cursory knowledge of medical terms. I had acquired it here and there over the years. An emetic is something that induces vomiting. The challenge of eating a big spoonful of jalapeno bean dip followed by a healthy chaser of ouzo was to overcome the overwhelming urge to blow lunch—or, in this case, dinner.

Tom Cleveland was one of the house pre-meds who'd gone nocturnal. He had managed to get a chem lab space assigned to him, and he was taking organic chemistry that semester, so he was always in his lab—especially in the dead of night when no one else was around and he could get a lot done. He worked all night, then interrupted his sleep during the day only to stumble to class and back. He was one of the few pre-meds I thought would genuinely make a good doctor. He was smart and seemed to care more about people than he cared about annual income figures. With his schedule and lifestyle that semester, I'd seen him maybe twice.

TV was the first to accept Whale Man's invitation of ouzo and bean dip. We all cringed as TV ate a big spoonful of dip, then downed the shot. His face flushed red and his eyes watered. I thought he was going to zuke—puke, vomit, blow lunch, boot, yack. Whatever. But he held it back and sat down to cheers.

Then Cleveland, a rather bulky lad, stepped up and grabbed a spoon. He ate the dip and downed the shot. He reacted the same way that had TV—his face flushed bright red and his eyes watered. He promptly walked over to the trash can, lifted it with both arms, stuck his head into it and, to even louder cheers than TV had received, disgorged the contents of his stomach.

Things became fuzzy for me about that time as the alcohol began to take hold. I remember the bean dip and the ouzo and the fact that I didn't puke. I remember a few more shots, then I fast-forward to being on the front lawn trying to kick a soccer ball and landing on my ass. At another point I was back in the dining room. I saw Buchanan throw a Little Kings bottle in a perfect spiral and with such force the neck of the bottle punctured the paneling there and the bottle stuck, unbroken. Chairs were being thrown and people were jumping up and down on tables. I walked out of the dining room. Then I blacked out.

When I awoke, I was on my old mattress in the cold dorm, in which I hadn't slept in a couple of months since I was now sleeping in my room. My head was tilted to one side. A bucket was on the floor next to me. I looked around and saw other casualties. Whale Man came in then to check on everybody, making sure no one vomited in their sleep and choked to death. I mean, we're talking about responsible drinking here, folks.

I got up and trundled to the water fountain in Third New. I think I absorbed about five gallons of water, then went down to my room, suddenly drunk again, and crashed out in my own bed.

The next day the damage reports were in: 3 dining room tables were trashed, 17 chairs were destroyed, and 81 windows had been dusted.

Surprisingly enough, I wasn't badly hungover. Maybe my body had been shocked by how much alcohol it had consumed so quickly.

While I might have been untouched by hangover, though, the depression was still there, ready to nag at me after this brief, too-brief, respite.

Chapter 32 - Frat Wars Continued

There was a day in there that the calendar took the house by surprise. We were scheduled to have a group picture taken. Everybody was cussing about it at dinner, when Edwards stood up and reminded us about it.

Traditionally, there were two pictures. One would be a picture of everyone seated in three, neat little rows in the formal living room. The photo itself was not formal in any sense. We could wear jeans and "neat" T-shirts, etc. The second photo was a humorous sort of thing. People could yuk it up in such a way that, presumably, parents could look at it and think everyone was behaving appropriately. Unfortunately for the Carson camp, the second photo did not take the course it was supposed to take.

Interestingly enough, no one thought to cancel or otherwise bag out on the picture. We gathered in the formal living room at 7:00. No one spoke to or with Carson and his two or three pals still in the house. The photographer called out for everyone to move into position. He was telling jokes and making wise-cracks that probably were funny in the late 1950s. Unfortunately, our sense of humor was a tad bit beyond that.

Once the guy got through the "first" photo and onto the "second" or humorous photo, there were a few twists. Several of us were wearing Greek letter shirts. Just before the taking of the second picture, several of us slapped pieces of electricians tape in front of the Greek letters in the shape of an "X" to signify that we were no longer of the house. In the split-second before the flash fired, Edwards, who was standing behind Carson, dropped his pants and stood directly behind Carson with his dick hanging about a half-inch from the back of Carson's head. Symington pulled out a machete and held it directly over his head as though ready to split Benson's skull, who was sitting right in front of him. Two people mooned the camera, and somebody pulled a gun and pointed it at another one of Carson's buddies and—well, you get the idea. The irony was that neither Carson nor any of his pals were aware of what had transpired until they paid for and received the prints in the mail.

The last thing I really needed to fuck with was the bullshit at the frat.

After the alums of the house corp had "interviewed" everyone, and the day after the photo session, the alums announced by letter that the decision to throw out "the Five" stood, even though most of the people who had supported that effort now lived outside of the frat—and by "fraternity," I mean the physical plant. House corp even said our electing our own officers was not valid. The prospects for staying in the frat were bleak for me.

OIT was out. I didn't want to get busted, and I didn't know how to go about trying to get an apartment. I was really helpless in that regard. Besides, I couldn't cook. I would starve OIT. I considered moving back into the dorms—for all of 30 seconds. I would be assigned a roommate, I would have no privacy, and the food would be lousy. Besides, the new Resident Assistant they had in my old dorm was an asshole. There, also, I ran a bigger risk of getting busted.

So I just hung on, getting wasted at night, along with everybody else, wondering what the fuck to do.

Chapter 33 - The Conversation

The most unpopular person in the fraternity was not any individual member. The most unpopular person in the house was the housebitch. She had turned us in for the keg the weekend of the Loyola walkout. She had met with the members of the housecorp immediately before the Inquisition. She was in tight with the now-former president and his buddies, and made no secret that she wanted them back. We knew she reported all the house goings-on to the housecorp, the national fraternity and the university. We might have provided her with an apartment and a paycheck, but she was doing everything she could to fuck us over.

I believed she might have ESP, that she might have some ancient Hungarian or Slovakian crystal ball hidden in a closet in her apartment. I mean, she stopped eating her meals in the dining room the night a bunch of us had decided to nail her with mashed potatoes and dinner rolls. We had waited for the clack of her gold lame peekaboo pumps on the short staircase outside the dining room, but that echoing resonance never came. She had ordered her meal to be brought up to her apartment instead. We never again saw her in the dining room. A few days later, when several people got the idea of loading up her food with Ex-Lax, she stopped taking her meals from the kitchen altogether. It was kind of late in the school year for her to interview on the housemother circuit of midwestern universities, so her goal was to remain where she was, but with a different bunch of guys—the bunch just departed—living in the house. When we realized her economic considerations, we understood that her survival was geared towards throwing us out of our home.

Everything had reached critical mass on a Friday afternoon—everyone was against us. The key was the university. What the university wanted, the university got. If, as was scheduled for the following Wednesday, the Five were to be moved out, then something had to be done. We did not know what that something was.

Then a miracle occurred.

Four guys in the house had taken it upon themselves to monitor the housemother's movements. They had discovered that she spent a lot of time at the Leisure Inn next to the interstate. She would hit the lounge for cocktails with various of the local farmer-types and, sometimes, repair to a room in the motel.

The next phase of the plan was ballsy. One guy in the house—Carlo Rooter—was an electronics whiz. He had been a techie on about two dozen rock band tours in the West since high school. I have to hand it to Buchanan—he came up with the plan. Then Rooter, with several other guys, executed it: they bugged the housebitch's apartment. They drilled holes through the floors of the rooms directly above her apartment, then popped a couple of holes through the plaster in her living room and two in her bedroom, and even one in her bathroom. Wires fed from the holes up into Buchanan's room where Rooter set up a long, narrow table as a console. There were two Tandberg reel-to-reels connected to the feeds, and two Pioneer cassette decks as back-up. Just as we had been under her "watchful" eye for the past months, she was now a captive of our attentive "ears." When she inserted the key in her door and walked into her living room, "thumbs up" signs were waved at the quality of the sound. The needles jumped across the meters on the mixer just the way Rooter had wanted.

The investigation, such as it was, was very thorough. I wasn't privy to the information until the very end, but the file included photographs, photocopies of motel registers, and logs of the housebitch's comings and goings. The thing really needed at this point, however, was recorded dialogue. There had to be a tape of one of her liaisons: the seedier, the better.

The evening it all came down was an evening Sid and I, as it happened, were tripping. We listened to the Dead, then we adjourned to the front of the house, to sit on the front steps and enjoy the early Spring air.

We started talking about *Easy Rider* for whatever reason, and I started thinking about going out on the road. The hitch hiking mystique was really playing on me.

Then a ten-year-old Cadillac pulled up to the end of the front walk, out next to the curb on the street. Nobody parked way out there if they were visiting someone in the fraternity—and by "fraternity," I mean the physical plant. The car was old enough and beaten-up enough that it could have been the car of a student from I.U. or Purdue. I mean, it wasn't like it was an expensive import or some arcane sports car. And it was a shit-brown color, with spots of oxidized paint, that really made it Upper Appalachia. There were probably two more at home like it, up on cement—pronounced "CEE-ment"—blocks in the driveway. It wasn't even a four-door, but only a two-door. Talk about cheesy. But by god it was a Caddie. An older guy got out, probably in his mid-sixties. His boots clopped on the sidewalk as he made his way towards us. His face was very red and his hands large. He had a rough, mean look. He walked past us without speaking or nodding or making any eye contact, as though we were janitors at a bordello. Or scummy hippies from wealthy families come to ruin the landscape of his pretty hometown.

We got up and went inside just as the heavy door to the housebitch's apartment closed. We ran upstairs, but there was already a crowd spilling out of the doorway to Buchanan's room. Edwards came out and started signaling everyone to move back. In a voice that was a loud whisper, he said, "Go on back to your rooms. If she hears anything going on up here, she'll get suspicious. You know she has ESP when it comes to these things."

He made sense. We still remembered the aborted mashed potato massacre. As I turned to go back to Sid's room, I glanced past Edwards and saw Rooter and Buchanan seated at the long table, headphones on, listening to whatever gross sounds were emanating from the microphones in the ceiling of the apartment below.

Sid put "Yessongs" onto his stereo and we jammed for a while. At the end of the album, somebody banged on the door and said that there was a meeting in the foyer. That was weird, because I'd never heard of a meeting being held there. But Sid and I headed downstairs, and stood with just about everybody else who was still living in the house. Then Rooter, or somebody, turned on the intercom and started playing back the tape that had been recorded only minutes earlier. One line was particularly poignant. In the middle of heavy panting, a hilljack male's voice said, "Suck me, Sonia." The words reverberated throughout the house. A few moments later, the door to the housebitch's apartment opened and the hilljack—his face much redder and one shirt tail of his polyester Western-style shirt, complete with snap buttons—hanging out hustled out of there and through the foyer to mild applause from us. His left hand went to his forehead to wipe off sweat and the gold band on his ring finger caught some light from the bulb hanging from the fake chandelier. The fucker didn't even look at us as he shot through there, then down the walk and out to his car. The tires squealed and the back end fish-tailed a little as he gassed it out of there.

Rooter remixed the tape, working late into the night to improve the quality of the sound and add a little bit of reverberation for effect. Copies were made. The next day Edwards, Buchanan and Jones made an emergency appointment with the dean of students and took a portable cassette deck with them. Apparently the tape, the photographs and the dossier that had been compiled were very convincing. The university switched sides. They were now—reluctantly— in favor of us. They formally recognized our "new" officers. With the university went— reluctantly—the house corp. The national fraternity, lacking the support of the alumni to carry out its actions and the school to stamp its imprimatur, was forced to back off. Two days later, the Five were informed that they would not be evicted. At the house meeting that night, we all voted to terminate the housebitch's contract. By the next week, she had packed her belongings and split in the dead of a very foggy night. The next day we threw a party.

The house wars were now over. We had won. True, the national fraternity and the alumni were not going to send us money, but they hadn't for the last couple of years anyway. But that didn't matter right now. We were free. And all the powers that thought they were above us could go to fucking hell. We had won.

Chapter 34 - Depression

I felt as though I'd hit the end of everything. I was in debt. I'd stopped going to classes and was, by my reckoning, flat-out flunking one of them, the easiest, speech pathology. Everything had fallen apart and I was wondering why I was alive.

I started sleeping a lot again. I would go to bed earlier and earlier—9, then 8—and stay in bed later and later. That seemed to help me. I could shut out the world and not have to fucking hassle with things.

The room was now depressing me. The graffiti seemed more like fading scrawls on adobe walls in an abandoned wartime village than the markings of friends.

I wandered around campus one evening instead of sitting in my room while everyone was downstairs at supper. The start of finals was only three days away, and everyone else was studying, getting in the final cramming to make up for a semester of quasi-lassitude. I walked past the Science Temple and on out to the football stadium. Then I went on, past the stadium, across the practice fields to the hillside looking out over the woods. An evening mist had risen over the trees and turned a shade of gold with the light of the sun.

I thought of all of the problems I was facing. I wanted to talk with someone, but there was no one to whom I could go. My friends were losing patience with me and my seemingly endless problems. I felt like an odd bodkin—that seemed like such a trippy term, an English sort of thing—slightly twisted, ready to crack.

I thought about freshman year just before finals. Things hadn't been so bad then. In fact, everything had seemed so upbeat. Z and Butkus. Brammie and Simos.

Yeah, where was everyone? Well, I knew where Simos was, at least. Up in Maine.

I began to wonder how I would explain everything. The grades were the worst part, and yet, in another way, they seemed so trivial. By flunking I would end up out on my ass, hat-in-hand, going back to Kilkerry to Eva and Adolf. To attend classes at the extension there. Living at "home" with the sewage backed up in the toilet. Working at "the Shop." Just as bad as all that was having to admit to myself that I'd failed at something. That I'd failed at the biggest challenge of my life, that also happened to be my main goal in life. And I'd be back in Kilkerry where everyone would know. And Delores Potter would have a field day gossiping.

I wanted to get out of there. Not just Kilkerry, but DFU, too. I wanted to go someplace.

Then I thought about Brammie coming through, hitch-hiking all over the country, and I thought about his descriptions of travel, and of settling down and living places. He had created a new place in the world for himself. He'd stopped, gotten a job, and started living. When he got bummed out with a place, he moved on. I remembered the stories Lane told of being out on the road, and I thought about the freedom all of it implied. I could go to Maine—I had some vague concept of forests and mountains—or California, the ultimate experience. And I'd go through the West, and Arizona and see the deserts, and the great mountains of that part of the country. I remembered what I'd said to Sid, out there on the front porch. How the sidewalk led to the street, then on to the world.

The idea of hitch-hiking began to take over my mind. I started considering logical choices. California was the home of so much that was radical, and had been the center of the hippie movement, if "movement" was the right word. And Tom Hayden, he of the Chicago Eight, was running for United States Senate out there. California was a long way, but if I got a couple of rides from semi drivers, I could do it. Rides in semis could take me a thousand miles at a clip. Once there, I could work for room and board in the Hayden campaign.

Maine was closer. Besides, I knew no one in California, but I knew someone in Maine—Simos. He lived in a place called Caribou, near an Air Force base. He worked there at the base exchange.

But again, I reflected on the risks and the dangers. My body could be found curled up and bloody in a ditch with my pants around my ankles. Or my body might not be found at all. I would just cease to exist.

I got up and shook off the thought. It was after the dinner hour. I started back to the fraternity—and by "fraternity," I mean the physical plant—but then I thought I'd detour to Starr and see what Cindy and Jillian were up to. I walked into the lobby and asked the receptionist to page one or the other for me. She paged both of them. I walked away from the counter and over to one of the plate glass windows and stared at the foliage. Everything was alive outside. Nearly all the trees had all their leaves. Everything was green and vibrant, and it all seemed to be drawing energy out of me in the process. I heard someone call my name, and I turned to see Cindy standing on the third or fourth step from the bottom, motioning for me to follow her.

"What's up?" I asked as we made our way up the carpeted stairs.

"We're going to Sullivan's. Wanta go?"

"Sure," I said. I had maybe only two dollars, but it was money.

"Good, then I'll let you buy a pitcher. Two pitchers, if you're lucky."

When we walked into the suite, Jillian was sitting cross-legged on the floor, throwing her usual game of solitaire, and chain-smoking. Their suite mate Patricia was sprawled across the arms of one of the drab, gray chairs that were standard issue for the suites in Starr, watching TV on the tiny screen of a black-and-white portable. She had a plump cuteness that I'd never noticed before. She and Jillian both looked up.

"We're waiting on Cassandra," Jillian remarked, then resumed her game.

"Winning?" I asked.

Jillian just grunted.

Cassandra came out a minute or so later, dressed in jeans and a peasant-type top. The look was casual, but she had worked to give it the right nonchalant appearance.

We walked down the stairs. The dorm was the most quiet that I had ever heard it, but that was because everyone—but a few diehards—was studying for finals. We headed out into the mild evening. Starr was on the extreme south end of campus, but it was still about a six block walk to the bars. We took the back streets of the poor neighborhoods in that direction. Kids playing outside some of the houses were oblivious to us. DFU students were not liked in Glendale generally, but especially in the poorer neighborhoods such as these. We were a weird crew moving down the street. Cindy was trudging along in her Earth Shoes. Jillian was clomping along in her clogs, dressed in her ubiquitous fatigues. My appearance was weird any way one looked at it in Glendale, what with being a male and having long hair. Patricia looked like the sorority girl she once had been, rather stylish with a white hat in the Capone-mode, brim turned down.

We got to Sullivan's and he was so glad to see us—business was slow due to finals. He didn't even fake checking our IDs. Once inside, we saw how empty the place was: we were the only customers.

We grabbed a booth and ordered a couple of pitchers. Cindy had brought a deck of cards and started pulling out the right cards for a euchre deck. Patricia didn't know how to play, and I didn't want to play, so Jillian, Cindy and Cassandra played three-hand euchre, which is a really bastardized way of playing.

Patricia and I conversed for a while. I'd never really spoken with her that much. She always seemed to be around, but we just had never conversed. All I knew was that she had a boyfriend who was overseas on some program for the semester, and that she was an English major.

"Did you hear the news?" Jillian asked me as she shuffled the deck for another hand.

"What news?"

"Cindy and I are sub-letting Austin's and Michelle's apartment for the summer."

"Hey, that's great!" I knew that neither Cindy nor Jillian wanted to live at home, even for the three months of summer. Austin was going back to his grandmother's and couldn't afford the rent for the time he and Michelle were away. "What're you gonna do for work?"

Cindy said, "I got a job cleaning rooms at the Glendale Motel. I'll be a chamber maid—ha!"

"I got a job at the Faraway," Jillian said. That was a truck stop about two miles north of town. I'd been in there once, my freshman year, for breakfast. The stares from the hilljacks were bad enough, but the music had been the final touch—country-western. I had a difficult time envisioning Jillian in that environment.

"She's going to be able to continue her anthropological study!" Patricia said, and they all laughed at some inside joke, so I laughed along, too, as though I was in on it, too.

Patricia was cute when she laughed. Some funky-ass song came onto the juke box— I think Cindy had pumped some money into it—and Patricia grabbed my arm and took me to the dance floor, and she pulled her hat off and put it onto my head and we danced. When we got back to the table, we fell into conversation that had seemed, by comparison, only tentative before. Cindy appeared at the table with a round of shots, then Sullivan came by later with another round, on him.

Patricia and I were soon leaning close to one another, talking, then we closed the distance and kissed. Then we kissed again. A slow song started playing, and we got up and danced to it. When we got back to the table, the others were giggling, but they didn't look at us. I tried to sneak a peek down at my pants, concerned that maybe my erection was visible through the fabric of my jeans, but I didn't see anything. I figured they were just laughing at our overt signs of affection.

"Can we go back to your frat?" Patricia asked.

"Sure," I said. "Come on."

We made our way back, holding hands, leaning on one another, and stopping every now and then to kiss passionately, tongues and the whole bit. I suddenly realized—this is it! I am going to lose my virginity!

The frat was quiet when we got there, people buried in their books for finals. We got to my room, and I put on an album, the volume not very high, and sat down beside her on my mattress. She tossed her hat to the side and we immediately became lip-locked again. I unbuttoned her top and pulled it off, then did the same with her bra. Her breasts were very full and voluptuous. Then off came her jeans, then my shirt and jeans were off in a flash, and finally her underwear and we were both naked.

I eased on top of her as she spread her legs. I managed to place my dick right at the place where I thought it was supposed to go and it would not go in. She helped me to try and guide it and—it would not go in. Then she grabbed hold of me and tried to force it and—not only would it not go in, but I became embarrassed and that was that. I lost the erection. I felt it deflate.

We rolled around for a few minutes more. I apologized. She mumbled a few "That's okay" lines, dressed and was gone.

I was dejected. I had had the opportunity, and I had failed!

I just sat there for a while, then I turned off the light and lay back on my mattress, staring at the ceiling lit by the reflected light from the parking lot in back of the frat. I lay like that for a good long while, then sleep overcame me—good friend that it was then—and I was gone.

Chapter 35 - Preparations

The main thing I lacked, in all my railing against material things, was money. I needed that in order to do anything. I was tapped out.

I took inventory of the items of personal property that I had in my room. There was nothing there that was really worth very much. My stereo, perhaps, but only the amp/tuner, and that had been a discontinued model only a couple of years before. The turntable was a piece of shit, the speakers were flimsy and cheap, and the albums were scratched up and shot to hell. I had a little shortwave radio that might fetch a few bucks. I had a tennis racket. That was about it.

I talked Jennings into buying the short-wave for 25 bucks. I found no takers for anything else. Then I remembered my books. Hell, what did it matter? I took several of the books—the only ones I owned, the only ones not on semi-permanent loan from I.U.'s library system—and headed to the bookstore.

As on every college campus, the bookstore charged extortionary prices in a market that was monopoly. If you didn't like the prices—too fucking bad. They bought back my books for a total price of 20 bucks. I lugged the other books back to the fraternity—and by "fraternity," I mean the physical plant—and tried to figure out what all I would need.

My planning was no longer idle daydreaming. I actually was going to hitch hike the fuck out of there. That was it. I'd get the hell away from DFU and the problems there and Eva and Adolph and the Cousin and everything. I would go to one of the coasts—California was appealing to me right then. Work with the United Farm Workers, living in a tent and passing out strike materials. Or I could find a job as a counter person someplace selling bongs in a head shop and sleep on the floor of a rundown apartment. I didn't know.

There were two items that were absolutely necessary for my trip. One was a backpack. This was before the days when college students—and high school students and grade school students, for that matter—used backpacks as a sort of universal method of carrying things. At least at DFU that was the case. The only people who used packs were people who camped. Or hitch hiked. The other thing I needed was something I already had—a sleeping bag. I'd had mine since borrowing it from someone in grade school. It was green, and the exterior fabric was cotton. Not water-proof, not even water-resistant. And there was a bit of a split seam on it.

I'd seen backpacks at the five-and-dime just off the square downtown in Glendale, so I headed down that way, the soles of my water buffalo sandals slapping against my feet with every step.

The dimestore was a G. C. Murphy's. It was as if a chunk of the late 1940s had been ripped out of the web of time and set down in this one spot in south central Indiana. The sign ran the width of the storefront and the lettering was reminiscent of sign lettering in the Old West. The wooden floor creaked as I walked down narrow aisles to the back of the store. There were shelves crammed full of piddly-ass crap. There were also huge display tables, divided into compartments a few inches wide by a few inches long and a few inches deep, filled with even smaller items of piddly-ass crap. At the back of the store were the "packs." The selection was both narrow—they had two models of packs—and cheap. I chose the larger of the two. I thought it might be sturdy enough to last a few days. Maybe. If I wasn't too rough on it. It was five bucks and made of thin canvas.

I took my purchase to the check-out. An old man was in front of me. He turned around and glanced at me. When the customer ahead of him paid and left, he moved up and said hello to the woman at the cash register as if they were old friends. "These young 'uns are all just looking like a bunch of Indians," he said. I read the woman's name tag. "Hi! My Name Is MYRTLE!"

She glanced at me and said, "Yeah, I know. Bathe about as much as Indians, too."

"My grandson's like that," the old man agreed. "Hair down to here and no respect." He looked at the cash register, did some figuring in his head, used all of the fingers of one hand and a couple of the other, then counted out the change Myrtle had given him and pondered whether the change was right.

He finally stepped aside so I could step up and make my purchase. "Seems to me something's gone wrong with this country," he said.

"That'll be five-ten with tax," Myrtle advised me. She did not look up when I handed her the exact amount.

I was seething. I had to say something. "Yeah, old man," I said, turning. "We sure made a huge-ass fucking mistake. That's for sure." At the use of a form the word "fuck" their eyes bulged. "Charlie Manson didn't execute enough of you. But others are gonna come along and finish the fucking job."

I turned and left the store without giving them a chance to reply.

I headed back to campus. As I walked past Downbeat Records, the music store/head shop for the campus, I reflected on the fact that, if I ever came back to this place, it would only be after a very long time. I turned up a back street, by the Fluttering Duck, the coffee house. As I came up the walk between classroom buildings and across the Academic Quad, I felt almost nostalgic about the seeming security of the place, so safe and removed from the real world. Somebody else paid all of the bills, and we enjoyed all of the freedom. There was very little responsibility demanded of us: we merely had to go to classes and take a few tests, write a few papers.

And here I'd fucked all of that up to the point to where this environment was no longer "safe" for me. The pretty lawn of East College and the old brick building itself only represented my failed role in SAF. I shook my head, then realized that, where I was walking, I might run into one of my professors or someone else I knew, so I turned left and hurried over to Austin's and Michelle's. I went up their little, hidden driveway, grown-over by vines and shrubs in late spring foliage. I hopped over the black-and-rust iron railing of their little porch, and knocked on the door. No one answered, and so I knocked again and took in the scene of that porch. I hadn't noticed its look—cut out from some old, European village and transplanted to mid-south Indiana.

Finally, I heard a sound, and it was Austin opening the door.

"Come on in," he said, smiling.

I could tell he was preoccupied.

"What's up?" he asked.

I looked into the living room and said "hi" to Michelle, who sat in one of the old, battered easy chairs. She looked up from the book in her lap. There were notebooks scattered on the floor and on the small coffee table. They were into preparation for finals like everyone else on campus.

"I'm leaving," I said.

"Leaving? Before finals?" Michelle asked.

"Yeah," I said. "I bought a pack already." I lifted up the bag as if asserting a fact or piece of evidence that verified what I was saying. "I already have a sleeping bag."

Austin started laughing. Michelle just looked perplexed.

"Where are you going to go?" Austin asked.

"Maine or California, one or the other."

"There's a lot of difference between those two," Austin said, still grinning.

"I know," I said. "But it's all the same to me—distance. I figured I'd decide tonight which place I'd go to. But I need to ask you a favor."

"Sure, what?"

"Can you give me a lift to the interstate tomorrow morning?"

"Sure," Austin said, without hesitation. "Our first final isn't until day after tomorrow."

"Thanks," I said. We agreed that I'd be over at their place at eight the next morning. I left and plodded on across campus to Starr. I figured I'd say goodbye to Jillian and Cindy. While the woman at the front desk paged them, I sat down to wait. Just then another woman who was in our con law class walked by on her way upstairs. When she saw me she said, "Ready for con law tomorrow?" I'd forgotten that that was my first final and that it was the next morning at nine. I said "Sure." Yeah, right.

Jillian came downstairs and escorted me up to their suite. Cindy and Cassandra were sitting at a cheap card table, playing gin. Patricia was staring at one of her textbooks. They all said hello.

"What's in the bag?" Cindy asked.

"A backpack," I said. "I'm leaving."

"For where?" Jillian asked.

"Maine or California. I haven't decided which one yet. I'm leaving tomorrow morning."

"You're bagging finals?" Jillian asked. She was smiling, like somebody had outdone her. She'd really sloughed off classes all semester. But I was bagging finals. "I don't believe this! Wait'll Farina hears about this."

I hadn't thought about Farina for a long while. Weird how things change so quickly. I pulled out a cigarette as Jillian lit one. She extended a lighter, still going, to Cindy's cigarette. Then, as she extended it to mine, she said, "Third on a match, can't get it up" and they all laughed. I tried to laugh along with them, but my effort was not all that successful.

"Why Maine? Why California?" Cassandra asked.

I shrugged and gave a cursory explanation. After a few more minutes I made my goodbyes and left.

I walked back to the fraternity—and by "fraternity," I mean the physical plant—in the fuzzy light of dusk. The pack was in the bag. The sleeping bag was on the floor of my room. I didn't care about anything now. I just wanted out of there. I would miss some of the people.

My packing was quick, but then again, I wasn't taking very much along. Two pairs of jeans, three shirts, some vitamins, toiletries, sandals. I picked several books to take along, and that was a challenge. I had one survival manual, Steal This Book. Even though I hadn't all that much stuff, the pack was full. I tied the sleeping bag to the pack. It looked like the stuff that David Carradine carried in Kung Fu.

Sid and TV came into my room, and I told them what I was doing. They both stared at me and the pack. Then TV started laughing, and Sid joined him. I had to explain again that I didn't know where I was going to go and that I wanted to decide that night. TV pulled out a road atlas and we looked at it for a while. The two-page lay-out at the front showed the entire interstate system. We traced the possible ways to California. There were two possible routes to Maine—one across the tops of Ohio and Pennsylvania, and the other across the border at Detroit/Windsor, through Canada, then across the border back into the States at Maine. Even having looked at the maps, I still hadn't decided. The goodbyes were awkward, but they agreed not to tell anyone I was leaving until after I'd gone.

I called Candace and by the time I walked over to her sorority, she was waiting there in the foyer. We walked over to the city park a couple of blocks away and found a stone ledge of some sort to sit on. She pulled out a joint.

"I've been saving this up for a special occasion," she said. With the first hit, I knew it was rolled from some of the now-infamous blonde Columbian.

I told her what I was going to do. Her reaction was a combination of curiosity and admiration. I was going out there and doing something we'd only read or about which we had heard second-hand. I was leaving the pristine security of our campus and risking my neck out there on the nation's highways.

"Aren't you afraid?" she asked.

"Yeah, but it's something that I have to do."

"But you could be killed, or raped."

"I'll be all right," I said. "I'll be careful."

We hugged, then I walked her back to her sorority. By the time I got back to my room, it was dark. I lay down on my bed and stared at the graffiti-laden ceiling. I dozed off that way.

The future was almost here.

Chapter 36 - Taking Off

I got up, showered, dressed, and grabbed my gear early, before anybody else in the frat was up. I even managed to grab a couple of Emma's enemas, and chewed on them as I walked over to Austin's and Michelle's.

My gear wasn't too heavy, and only a little cumbersome.

I wore an Indiana University sweatshirt. I figured it would show that I was a college student. That, I thought, would count in my favor. It also said something of where I was from, without being too vague. I mean, if somebody in California saw "DeForrest," even if they knew where the school was they might have to think a couple of seconds and, if they were going 55 or faster, those couple of seconds could cost me a ride.

Austin and Michelle were up and showered, but they weren't quite ready by the time I got there.

"Figured where you're going to go?" Michelle asked.

I realized just then that I hadn't, and said so. "I was thinking about other things," I explained. Austin laughed at this.

"Well—where are you going to go?" she asked.

I still couldn't decide. But "hitch hiking to California" as a phrase had such a ring to it. Right out of one of the shows about hippies I'd seen as a kid. The whole mystique was right there—hitch hiking to California. I had no idea what would be waiting for me there. I doubted that there was any kind of welcoming committee standing by for every person who entered the state by thumb and looked a certain way. But the idea of going out there seemed like such a major league thing to do, the apotheosis of all I had thought about and all I wanted to try to be. Anyways, I just sat down and waited for Michelle and Austin to get ready.

We walked outside to Austin's 1968 Chevy Impala station wagon. The shocks were shot so the thing sort of shimmied going down the highway. The paint was oxidized with a few places showing heavy rust. It had gotten us to and from a lot of places, though. I got into the back seat and set my pack down on the seat beside me. Austin fired up the engine and, with a cloud of bluish-black exhaust and a hearty hi-ho Silver, we backed out of the driveway. We were off the campus in a minute, then we turned onto the state highway, cruised past the bars and onward toward the interstate.

I was silent, but Austin was chattering away, speculating as to what the campus reaction would be about what I was doing. Really, I didn't expect there to be any "campus reaction." I'd sunk from sight on campus. I was a ghost, walking around occasionally but not being seen. I'd be forgotten in a few months. Oh, next year, or the year after that, a senior would tell a story to a couple of freshmen about the weird guy with the long hair who'd bagged finals to thumb to California or Maine—I still hadn't decided—but my name would be forgotten. And soon, with the matriculation of one more class out and one more class into the university, that mention would be eroded slowly and even the occasional story would stop.

The nine miles were covered quickly. We crossed the four lanes of U.S. 40 and descended the steep grade. Ahead, past the flat fields, was the interstate.

"Decided yet?" Michelle asked.

"No," I said. I was trying to decide how to decide. California or Maine. Either represented a scary trip. I'd never hitch hiked before, and here I was looking at departure for one coast or the other in just a few moments. I thought about what Lane had said. West you had to worry about cops in Missouri, Oklahoma, Texas and Arizona. Those were four states that covered quite a few miles. East, I was faced with cops who were pricks in Ohio, Pennsylvania, New York, Connecticut, Massachusetts and Maine. Of these, the cops of Ohio, New York and Connecticut were supposed to be real shitheads. But the distances weren't as great—and, for some weird reason, dealing with an asshole cop who had an Eastern accent seemed preferable to dealing with one who spoke in a drawl. But then again, the idea of going to California was so strong.

We pulled up to the ramps for the interstate. Both Austin and Michelle were watching me. I'd been observing the traffic as we approached the ramps. The traffic was much heavier going east. Hardly any cars at all were going west.

That decided it. Out of practical considerations, I was going to Maine.

I told them of my decision, and we got out of the car. I hugged each of them as we stood there on the berm at the side of the road. They got back into the car and sat there for a few moments. I turned around and waved, as they sat there watching me trudge along. A few moments later I heard their tires crunching in the gravel as they pulled out and did a U-turn, heading back for campus.

I saw the sign on the access ramp: "NO HITCHHIKERS, PEDESTRIANS OR NON-MOTORIZED TRAFFIC." I thought about the risk of walking up onto the interstate itself and standing on the emergency lane. No cop would hassle me for that, I thought. But then I realized that, yes, there were a lot of cops who were assholes and who would do just that. I didn't want to end my trip after only a few minutes and get thrown into the county jail in beautiful Glendale, only a few blocks from campus.

So I stood there on the access ramp, not able to take advantage of the rather heavy flow of eastbound traffic up above on the interstate itself. I was rather self-conscious standing there. But at least it was beautiful day, the sun shining from clear blue skies.

The first car came along and, bundle at my feet, I lifted my right hand and stuck out my thumb. The car passed me. I took off my sunglasses. I thought that maybe they gave a slightly sinister tint to my appearance. I started to pull out a cigarette, but then thought better of it. I didn't want to blow a ride just because the driver didn't smoke. I could deal with not smoking for a while if it meant I could get some distance. But, novice that I was, I did not have any immediate luck, even with all of the measures I had taken.

After 20 minutes, I began to have second thoughts. The walk back to campus was only about nine miles, and I could make that in two hours, without having to hitch hike.

Another car went by, then another. The occupants of a third car looked to me to be in their thirties or thereabouts. They looked at me scornfully as they rolled by, and I heard the loud click of the automatic door locks.

I had money, so I could buy some pot and beer and get plastered. I could give some bullshit excuse to my profs about why I'd missed finals. Of course, by now a lot of people knew I'd taken off. I'd have to face that embarrassment. I'd made a dramatic gesture in taking off like this, and then I would have come back so quickly the drama would seem fraudulent.

A car was northbound on the state highway. It slowed. It had its signal on for the exit. I saw that it was a government vehicle, a sedan. It was the dark weird government bureaucratic blue of the Air Force cars that I'd seen at and around Grissom Air Force Base, just north of the Farm. I stuck out my thumb and heard the engine hum down as the driver took his foot off the gas. The car passed me, but eased over and onto the berm. I picked up my pack and ran the 20 or 30 yards to where the car finally had stopped. I was unsure of the etiquette involved at this point. Like—what to do with my pack? Instead of opening both the front and back doors and maybe alarming the driver, I just opened the front door, tossed my pack onto the floor in front of the passenger's seat, and squeezed my feet and legs in around it.

The driver introduced himself as we took off. I glanced over and it took a few seconds to register. Initially, his shirt looked just like an open-collar, light blue shirt of a businessman. Then I saw the stripes on the sleeve—several of them. I'd always wondered why the Air Force people had so many goddamn stripes. I wasn't going to ask him now, though, and possibly offend him, and then end up standing at the side of the road so soon after finally getting a ride.

It was ironic that I'd gotten a ride with someone in the military—and the Air Force at that. I'd seen Air Force people all my life, because of our proximity to what had been Bunker Hill, then later Grissom Air Force base. Then again, I was reminded of the stories I'd heard from friends of mine my freshman year who'd run over to Champaign-Urbana for a weekend of partying at the University of Illinois. They'd come back laughing about the military personnel from nearby Chanute Air Force Base. The "fly boys" would travel into Champaign on weekends to try and score with the "college chicks." However, the "fly boys" found it difficult to make any connections with the U of I women. Women on college campuses in 1975, for the most part, wanted nothing to do with military types. The haircuts of the "fly boys," short and closely cropped by our standards, caused the guys to stick out a mile away. So the Air Force guys bought wigs. Long-haired wigs—probably women's wigs. And the guys would hit on the college women in disguise. Of course, the guys still had the problem of overcoming cultural barriers. Between the backward patter, the polyester clothes, and the obviously synthetic shoulder-length hair, they were pretty obvious. So they still didn't get laid.

No one I knew liked anyone or anything about the military. Austin had applied for, and received, conscientious objector status in the draft. I had applied for it, going so far as to be listed officially as having requested the proper forms. But I'd done so from my campus address and when the local draft board had mailed the forms to me, they were sent to the Farm. Eva, as usual, had opened my mail instead of forwarding it to me. I was in class that day, oddly enough, and a harried assistant dean had come to that classroom and called me out. Once I was in the hallway, he informed me that there was a family emergency. I went quickly to a pay phone. I had no idea what was up. When I had called the number at the Farm, Eva answered on about one-tenth of a ring and accepted the charges. Then she immediately informed me that "no one in this family is a coward." That gave me a chuckle. I mean, the Cousin had done the ultimate dodge to the war—avoiding the draft AND suing for damages. Adolf had been 4-F during World War II. An adult white male of fairly average intelligence living in the States during WWII could make a financial killing. And Adolf had. Well, back to me. Eva burned the forms necessary for me to apply for CO status. I imagined that that was quite a little bonfire. The Selective Service made application for CO status a bureaucratic nightmare, with about 90 million forms to fill out. I called my local draft board, told them I had not received the forms, and could they please mail them to me at my campus address. They had. There was no way, however, that I was going to spend all that time with all that paperwork. So I had written a truncated note to the draft board, explaining that I could not kill for the United States and that I did not believe they could tell me what I really felt about that. Their response—again sent to the Farm—was that I had provided insufficient evidence to them to substantiate my claim of CO status, and so I was ruled 1-A. Not like I was going to get drafted or anything. Saigon had fallen and it didn't look as though the US was going to get into a war in the next few years, so I was safe. But then, irony, here I was getting a ride from an Air Force non-com. Way to start the trip.

"How far ya going?" he asked.

"Maine."

"Long ways to go," he said, appreciating the distance.

Then I remembered where it was up there I was going. "Yeah. Going to visit a buddy. He's getting married. Going to the wedding. His dad's at Loring Air Force Base."

The guy looked at me questioningly, then said, "No shit." He was about 28 or 30. Of course his hair was closely cropped, and his uniform was neatly pressed and creased. But there seemed to be something about the way the wrinkles formed around his eyes that made me think twice about my innate prejudice against the military. I pulled out my sunglasses, since he was wearing shades, too.

"Pilot's glasses?" he asked as I put the case away in a little side pocket on the pack.

"Yeah," I said. I was really proud of those shades. They were the best I'd ever owned, and I told him just that. "I got them at an army surplus store," I added, deciding not to try and bullshit the guy about having been in the military or anything. I figured if I tried to bullshit him, about two or three questions into it he'd nail me. I mean, what was the point anyway? I had the ride.

"Where you from?" he asked.

"DeForrest."

"Fine school," he said, and I nodded because that was usually what people said. "I'm just driving up from I.U. I'm a recruiter."

I held my breath—shit. I didn't need to here a sales spiel for the military.

"Wild town," he said. "Nice bars. Pretty girls," he added, with a grin. Suddenly I felt sorry for him. He seemed like a nice guy. I wondered if he had a wig packed away in the trunk. "I'm driving over to Indianapolis now. To Indiana Central. I can give you a ride as far as I-465 on the west side."

"Thanks."

"How you going up to Maine?"

"Well," I said. "I figured I'd shoot up to I80/90 and take that across to the coast, then shoot up I95 from Boston."

He nodded. "Thought about Canada?"

"What do you mean?"

"You could take I-69 up to Michigan, then go over to Detroit, cross into Canada there at Windsor. Then go across to Maine from there. The scenery's prettier. Besides, hitch-hiking is legal up there. And the cops aren't assholes."

It was strange hearing a guy in a uniform badmouth other guys in uniform. But what he said made sense. We traveled the rest of the way shooting the shit about things in general. He dropped me off at the big interchange just south of Weir Cook Airport, where I-70 intersects I-465, about eight o'clock relative to Indianapolis's north-south axis. I thanked him, and I felt as though perhaps I hadn't made a friend, but that I had at least communicated with another human being. He pulled away, leaving me there to wait for my next ride.

That interchange is big and busy. Indiana has more interstates than any other State, and the amount of traffic where I stood was great. Plus I was on the interstate proper—there were no ramps there. What I was doing was illegal in the first place, but to be standing where I was standing was inviting trouble from cops. I glanced at the sky, and saw that it was clouding over. Then a car came by me and skidded to a stop on the berm. I ran for it and jumped in.

The guy was in his mid-20s and needed a shave. He explained to me that he was only going a couple of stops north on 465, but that was fine by me. Any bit helped.

He dropped me off and I again waited for a ride, this time on an access ramp, pointing my thumb for northbound traffic. The air was slightly damp and cool with the feel that rain is imminent. Then a carload of high school girls stopped and gave me a ride two more exits up. A salesman was my next ride. He was going to Chicago "to sell shit, goddamn it." But his age—about 60—and the year and condition of his car—about a 1966 and oxidized/rusty—told me that he was, maybe, not much of a salesman. He let me off at the interchange where I-65 goes northwest from I-465 and Indy. Again, I wasn't on a ramp, and as soon as he let me out I saw a state cop go by in one of the southbound lanes. I saw the cop look at me, see me. I panicked. Hell, I wasn't even past Indy yet. So I grabbed my stuff and jumped over the fence there, heading generally east and north, where I knew there was a set of on-off ramps.

I was in an orchard. The trees were lined neatly, and spaced evenly, and the grass was freshly cut. I heard a low rumble, and saw that the sky was darkening. I walked more quickly. I did not want to be caught in the fucking rain.

I walked through stands of different trees, then shrubs. The place was a nursery. I was paranoid as I passed behind a house. What the hell would the occupants think if they saw me walking by there, carrying a pack and strolling through their back yard? I walked even more quickly, almost going at a trot, until I was on the road that passed in front of the house, and a hundred yards down it, besides. I made it to the access ramp, a little out of breath. I'd barely gotten my thumb out when a semi rolled to a stop past me and I ran to the passenger's side of the cab.

I hefted the strap of the pack onto my shoulder, put my foot on the bottom step of the chrome ladder, grabbed the chrome rail, and pulled myself up. I opened the door and slid in. I'd never been in a semi.

"How far ya goin'?" the guy asked in a twangy voice loud enough to be heard over the traffic and the noise from his engine.

"Maine," I replied.

He grinned, and the truck jumped as he put it into gear and gunned it back onto the traveled surface of the ramp. "Shee-it! You got a ways to go!"

"Yeah," I said, feeling pretty good. I was beginning to get the hang of this hitch-hiking business.

"I got a load of beer I just took on. Taking it to Fort Wayne. That okay?"

"Sure is!" I replied, my voice just as loud. Fort Wayne was quite a ways north— over 100 miles. I wouldn't have to go two and three exits at a time to cover the distance. That was a big relief.

"I'm from Jasper," he said. "Name's Don. Been driving five or six years now." Jasper was in the southern part of the state. I looked at him, and he didn't seem old enough to have driven for that long of a time. "Just got this rig last year."

It was what they called a "cab-over"—a box-shaped tractor in which the cab, or seating area, was over the engine with the front of the tractor being flat. There was a housing between us, from under which came the muffled roar of the big engine. Behind us was a rebel flag, and it hung from curtain hooks.

"Got a sleeper back there so I can catch a few winks when I have to. Own your own rig, you gotta drive a lotta hours. More than you report in the log. These motherfuckers ain't cheap to maintain."

We headed East on I-465, and passed the exit for the highway north to Kilkerry. It struck me that I'd always taken that way back to what had been home, but that it wouldn't ever be that again. I was not saddened by that prospect. Don downshifted a few minutes later and we were heading onto the ramp for I-69, where it departs I-465 at about 1:30 on the map. We merged into traffic, and I noticed that the smaller vehicles made way for us.

He picked up a microphone I had not noticed, and then reached down next to his right leg. It was then that I saw the top of the CB radio there, apparently bracketed to the side of the engine housing.

"Breaker, breaker," he said. "This is the Woodman, looking for a smokie report. Just coming onto I-69. Come on." He released the transmit button on the mike. I was surprised that he could make out the words from the unit, over the noise in the cab. But then I found out that if I concentrated, I could even make out what the other people on the airwaves were saying.

"Got us some smoke up around Marion," came a reply. "I'm just coming south from up there. Other than that it's clear all the way to Michigan."

"Thank you. Over."

Don looked over at me and said, "You get high?"

I didn't know what to say. Was he trying to entrap me? This shit about smokies, then pot, confused me. Finally, I said, "Yeah, sure."

"Then reach back into the denim jacket there on the mattress," he said. "In the left front pocket is a vial."

As I parted the curtain and reached for the jacket, I asked him about the chatter on the CB, and what it meant. He laughed.

"We call cops 'Smokie' out here, 'cause most of the troopers wear those Smokie the Bear hats. If there aren't any cops out on the road, that means that I can crank up the speed a little more. If they're out there, though, I slow it down so's I don't get a ticket."

I found the vial, then sat back in my seat, the vial in hand. I recognized the container as being one of those waterproof things for hunting and camping and fishing. It was of heavy, dark brown plastic, and the top screwed off. Inside it were half a dozen huge joints rolled out of dark brown paper, and I extracted one. He took the vial and stuffed it under the seat, then tossed a butane lighter to me. I politely handed that back and took out my cheap, imitation Zippo. I lit up the joint and took a big hit.

I started to hand it over to him, but he waved me off. "Great weed," he said. "Go ahead and hang onto it a couple of minutes. It's a pain in the ass trying to pass it acrosst this console."

I took several hits, but I wasn't very impressed with the quality. I didn't say anything, though, because I didn't want to insult him. He seemed like a nice enough guy, and, besides, I was getting my longest ride of the trip so far. Fifteen minutes later, I was mildly buzzed.

"How ya gonna go to Maine?" he asked.

"I-80/90 across," I explained. That had to be the best route, I thought.

"Pigs in Ohio and New York are a bitch," he observed, matter-of-factly. I was surprised to hear a trucker—a member of a group of flag-waving rednecks—refer to cops as "pigs."

"I've heard that," I said.

"Yeah. Plus those motherfuckers on the East Coast are fucking crazy. Some would sooner kill you as look at you. Especially if you're hitch-hiking." I nodded. Yes, danger was a concept looming always in the back of my mind. "If I was you, I'd take I-69 up to Michigan, then shoot over to Detroit. Cross over there and thumb through Canada."

I was surprised that I'd heard this same advice twice now. I told him that, then added, "I guess that it's legal to thumb in Canada."

"Yeah. Buddy of mine did it a couple of years ago. You sign in at the border. They got a couple of forms you gotta fill out. You're officially designated a hitch-hiker, for a designated number of days, with a permit and everything. Cops don't hassle you that way. Cops ain't assholes up there, neither. And you don't have near as many nuts up there as you get down here."

I mulled over the possibilities. Canada. A different country. The thought was intriguing. Not only that, it sounded like it was the smartest way to go. I asked Don how far it was from Fort Wayne to Detroit. He told me, then he smiled—happy, I guess, to think that I'd taken his suggestion seriously.

We traveled on, occasionally talking. Once in a while, he'd get onto the radio for a Smokie report and shoot the shit with other truckers. But there were no cops out, and we made good time to Fort Wayne. The miles peeled off as we crossed the flat expanses of mid-north Indiana, the fields freshly planted, punctuated by the occasional subdivisions, and the farmhouses spread out, and the exit ramps every 15 or 20 miles, with the gas stations and fast food places having sprung up every other one or so. There were several exits for Fort Wayne. Don pulled off at the first one. As I gathered up my pack, he wished me luck. I jumped down and watched as the rig pulled away.

Yeah, I'd go through Canada. Why the fuck not?

I waited for a few cars to go past, then crossed the road to stand by the side of the on ramp. I stood there for 20 minutes or so without any luck. Finally, an old Ford rolled by me and stopped. As I jogged after it, the passenger's side door opened, and I jumped in.

For the first time on this trip, I felt creepy. The guy was in his mid-50s and his hair was slicked down with some sort of smelly shit. He was decked out in polyesters, and he had a manner that made him seem like one of the churchgoers in the area around the Farm, like somebody who was in the choir and even went to church on Wednesday evenings. He seemed perverse. He said hello, and asked me where I was going. I told him, but he gave no reaction. He just drove up the ramp and onto the interstate.

There were others smells in the car, smells other than the shit in his hair. I couldn't place them, and that fact merely added to my feelings of discomfort.

The ride was short. He was only going a few exits up, he said. But we were quickly out of the Fort Wayne area, and the distances between exits increased greatly. Still, the time in that car seemed to drag, and the guy made only a few comments. At first I tried to make conversation, but I soon gave up. Finally, he slowed for an exit and pulled off of the interstate. I was ready to jump out of the vehicle, even as it moved, if I had to, if he made any sort of move that was threatening. I had the feeling that this guy was some sort of pervert—no, I had more than just a feeling. I was sure of it. Maybe he was a killer, too. He'd try to take me to his home and feed me rat killer in a drink. Or drive down a backroad to a narrow lane in a woods at the end of which would be a clearing. Yeah, I had to be ready to jump out. But before we reached any point where I would have to jump, just off the ramp of the interstate he brought the car to a halt and wished me luck. I thanked him for the ride. As I stood there at the side of the road, once more waiting, I thought that I had been rash in judging the guy. Sure, maybe he was a pervert. Or, maybe, he was just a weird little guy who was socially retarded. Whatever the case, he'd given me a ride without any harm coming to me, and that had to constitute the basis for my judging the integrity of people at this point. I was, after all, hitch hiking across the country.

The sky up here was clear. It was now late afternoon. The exit was way out in the middle of nowhere. The onramp was cut into a hillside that was covered with the same type of short plant. Even this early in the year and this far north, the plants had a deep green color.

There was hardly any traffic. The place was dead. The few cars that appeared passed by me, their occupants either scowling at me or averting their eyes. Finally I lit a cigarette, and kicked my toe into the dirt. I figured I'd come about two hundred miles. I was just shy of the toll road that ran east and west across the top of the state. I'd been keeping an eye on the mileage signs as to what I was near. I felt good about my progress and, if I got hung up here for a while, then hey, I figured that's the way it goes sometimes.

I heard the engine of a semi down-shifting and slowing, and then I saw it turning onto the ramp, heading towards me. The driver seemed confused at first, but then he stopped so the passenger's door was directly in front of me. The tractor and trailer were tricked out in the logo and colors of a trucking company unlike Don's truck, which bore only the decals of the Federal and State licenses and tax permits he was required to carry. This semi was old, with a hood in front and rounded fenders. Behind the seats was the back wall of the cab—there was no space back there for much of anything. There was only a window.

The driver looked short and smallish, and he was older, maybe in his fifties. His gestures were jerky, and he was glancing into his mirrors, then ahead to the highway. "I could get fired for this," he said. "Company says we ain't s'posed to take on no hitch-hikers." "As I slammed the door shut behind me, he said, "Insurance rates go way up. Some other driver from the company sees you in this cab with me and I get reported, that's it."

"Sorry," I said, and started to say something else, what, I don't know, but he cut me off.

"Where ya going?"

"Maine."

I could as easily have said "Timbuktu" or "next exit" and his reaction would have been the same. "I'm goin' to Detroit. Terminal there on the south side."

"That's okay," I said. "I'm going to Windsor."

He looked at me suspiciously. "Thought you said you were goin' to Maine."

"I did. I am. But I'm going to cut across Canada from here."

He huffed sarcastically. "Well, good luck. We're gonna get to Detroit at dark. How ya gonna get to Windsor?"

"Walk, I guess."

He looked at me sharply. "Not bein' a white boy in Detroit, you're not. Not and makin' it to Windsor alive." He paused, and looked quickly between me and the road several times. "Where you from, anyway?"

"Kilkerry."

"Jesus Christ. Mighta figured. Farm kid." He chuckled and said nothing more, entertaining himself with his own little joke, or pictures of him getting fired for having given me a ride, and then me getting flailed by a mob of black people angry over the fact that a white hitch-hiker walked through their neighborhood after dark.

We rode on. As we got closer to Detroit, we swept under huge bridges that spanned the interstate. I'd never been that close to the damn things before, and when we approached the first one, I flinched and nearly ducked, thinking that the cab was going to slam into the beams of the bridge. But we passed under it smoothly, and I tried to relax. That was tough, though, with the driver as tensed up as he was.

We turned off the interstate and onto an access road. I followed the driver's instructions and crouched in my seat. When he turned into the entrance to the terminal, I jumped out and slammed the door without a word.

I hadn't spent any money up to this point, and I realized that, indeed, Detroit could be the place of my death. The sun had just dipped below the horizon, but there was still light enough to see. There was a phone booth a couple of hundred yards away, its lights already on. I walked to it. It was next to a phone pole at the entrance of a parking lot for a gas station. Fortunately—and surprisingly enough—there was a telephone directory in the phone booth, pages filthy and dog-eared, but I could still find the number for a cab company. I told the dispatcher that I didn't know the names of any roads, but I knew the exit number, and that I was a couple of hundred yards away from the truck terminal at a gas station. Finally, the dispatcher figured out where I was and said a cab would be there in 15 minutes.

The back road got a lot of traffic from the truck terminal. There was an industrial grit in everything around me. Its smell was a mixture of creosote and diesel exhaust and rust, and a couple of kinds of mildew. A couple of cars drove by, but for the first time that day, my thumb wasn't out. My anxiety eased, but only a little. In a few minutes, I'd be entering a foreign country, and I didn't know what to expect.

I saw the cab pull onto the access road and make its way towards me, its headlights on. I waved and stood from the railing which I'd been leaning on. When the driver stopped in front of me, I opened the back door, tossed in my pack, and followed it.

"Where to?" he asked. He was about 45 or so, and his sideburns were cut really long, like a parody on a country western singer. There was a license attached to the dashboard, and I glanced at it and saw that his name.

"Canada," I replied, thinking that that sounded weird, to tell a cabbie that your destination was another country. He looked at me like I was weird, but then I explained about going to Maine and everything. He turned around and looked at me, then at the pack. He grinned.

"Maine? That's pretty far to go." I agreed with him on that. He shook his head and pulled the lever on the meter so it started up. "Ever been to Detroit before?"

"No. Never."

"Rough town. You were right to take a cab across it."

I was paranoid about the fare. Every time the numbers on the meter rolled over, I felt a little sick. That meant I had that much less money to travel all the way to Maine. Then, once we got into the city proper, I didn't feel so bad about having sprung for the luxury of the cab.

We were on a "main" thoroughfare of some sort. The buildings lining the street were all commercial, and even though the day was slightly past dusk, all were closed with huge steel accordion gates protecting doors and plate glass windows. On some of the buildings the plate glass on the street-level floors was gone—broken or removed, I didn't know—and in its place was plywood or, in some cases, concrete block. Some of the buildings had second floors and some even had third floors, and the windows of some of these upper floors were lit up, and I guessed people lived up there. The buildings were filthy with the soot or other residue of industry that had fallen from the air and attached itself to everything. The streets were dirty as well, with trash strewn on sidewalks and in the streets. People were walking about. I glimpsed rows of houses but few lights.

"See what I mean?" Wayne finally asked, as though reading my thoughts.

"Yeah."

"I wanta move outta here. Go to Florida. Or someplace out of the country, ya know?" He was talking to me, and making eye contact with me in his rearview mirror. "This country is just too nuts these days. Too many controls. Too much government. They control everything that we do."

Of course what he was saying was at the heart of my beliefs about government, but I wasn't really listening. I was only taking part in the conversation mechanically. My mind was on the passing squalor. The squalor hadn't stopped. It was going on and on and on. It was as though the decay was infinite. I was looking at a world cast off by industry: drained of people, spoiled by pollution, and abandoned to poverty.

Finally, we swung through some gates and I saw a bridge, lined with huge sodium vapor lights.

"They'll wave us through on the other side," Wayne advised me.

I saw the U.S. Customs sign, and I glanced at the meter. The fare was only six bucks. I was relieved.

We crossed the bridge, and I tried to glance down to see water, but all I saw was blackness. Then I looked ahead and saw Canada. It seemed to be cleaner than the U.S. side. I eased back in my seat, then remembered I had a fare to pay, so I reached for my wallet. Wayne must have caught what I was doing.

"Hold off on paying me until we're sure everything's okay. No sense jumping the gun."

"Yeah, okay," I said.

We pulled to a stop beside a small building. I grabbed my pack and got out. I walked into the building and up to a small counter. The gentleman behind the counter looked at me politely and smiled. He was wearing what looked like a Mr. Ranger uniform, but it wasn't starched or laden with any accoutrements of false authority.

"May I help you?" he asked politely.

"Yes. I'm an American and I'm hitch-hiking to the State of Maine and I wanted to get there by going through Canada."

"Certainly," he said, smiling. He reached to a shelf behind where he was standing and grabbed a huge ledger book. He set it down on the counter and leaned back as he opened it, it was so big. The thing looked as though it had been there for decades, and as I paged through it I saw columns and columns of writing—names, I thought. The names of thousands of hitch-hikiers who had come into Canada right here. Man, I thought, I was about to get a lot of stress off my shoulders! I'd be legal hitch-hiking to Maine! No more furtive looks around for cop cars. Shee-it!

He asked my name, Social Security Number, date of birth, purpose for entering Canada. For purpose, I said, "Hitch-hiking to the State of Maine by way of Canada."

He looked up from the page and smiled. "Perfectly legal here. We issue permits for that sort of travel. Only a couple of questions more. How many days do you plan to be in Canada?"

I was beginning to feel confident now. These people were so polite. The room was so neat and clean. This was all turning out to be okay.

"Three days. Four at most," I replied.

He nodded with understanding. "And how much money do you have with you?"

Money? I didn't know what that had to do with anything, so I answered the question honestly. "About thirty-five dollars."

He slammed the book shut. "Sorry, but we cannot admit you to Canada," he informed me, the smile now suddenly stiff and formal. "You must have at least thirty dollars for each day you will be in Canada. We're tired of young Americans living off Canadian welfare."

He carried the book back to its place on the shelf, set it down with a thud, then sat down at his desk. I felt Wayne tugging at my shoulder, and we left.

Fuck! I was really pissed. The guy had seemed so polite, but then the lecture on Canadian law had made me feel like scum.When I got into the cab, I looked at the meter. The little lecture had cost me another three bucks. Not only that, but I would have to take the cab back across Detroit. There went at least half of my money.

Wayne seemed to be reading my thoughts. As he put the cab into gear, he asked, "You only have thirty-five bucks?"

"Yeah, almost to the penny."

"We can work something out on the fare. I won't hit you for the full amount."

"Thanks," I said, thinking about my situation. "I don't know what to do now."

"You have an alternate route?"

"What I was going to do originally, I80-90 across."

"Then do that. I can drop you off on the south side of Detroit. I75 runs straight down to Toledo. You can hit 80/90 there and go across that way."

"Yeah," I said, my mood improving. "That's what I'll do."

I guess Wayne assumed we'd be waved on through by the U.S. Customs people, but as we approached the complex of structures on the U.S. side, a man in a uniform was holding one hand up and pointing to a parking area to the side with his other hand.

"What the hell?" Wayne muttered, following the man's directions. He glanced at me in the rearview mirror. "You're not wanted or anything, or trying to smuggle drugs?"

"No," I said incredulously. "I'm a college student."

He parked the cab where the uniformed man indicated. We got out, and I grabbed my pack.

"Into the shed," the officer said to me, and I walked through the doorway and into the tiny structure.

"Open the trunk," another uniform ordered Wayne. I heard him protesting as he did what he was told.

"Please spread the contents of your pack on the floor," still another uniform said to me. And another one after that asked me questions related to my identity as I did so, including how long had I been out of the country.

The uniforms seemed to sneer when they saw the titles of the books I was carrying. I figured, hey—fuck 'em. I only wished I'd had a book titled How to Snuff Customs Cops. Then they saw the vitamins I was carrying, and they really went ape shit. One guy grabbed a heavy catalogue I recognized as the Physicians Desk Reference. He checked my pills against the glossy photographs and shook his head with each one. Then he grabbed a couple of really thick three-ring binders that looked to contain more photographs of pills.

"Those are all vitamins," I finally explained. "The B-complex are the yellow ones. They're good for energy. The big white ones are vitamin C, for good health. The capsules are vitamin A. I take those for my eyes." I might as well have said nothing at all, though, because they weren't paying any attention to me.

One uniform was playing with a computer, punching things into it and waiting for responses. I saw him hit one button as though his motion constituted the finale, and I saw his expression drop as he read the screen. "He's clean as far as I can tell," he said, in a voice that betrayed his disappointment.

"They're vitamins," the guy with the binders said finally, as though no one had ever thought of that or mentioned the possibility before.

Wayne came in just then, fuming he was so pissed off.

"They wave us through one way," he said to me, but really meant it for the assholes in uniform. "We don't even get into the other country. But they want to disassemble my car." He saw the vitamins resting on the counter and his expression changed. "What the fuck are those?"

"Vitamins," I replied, then gestured to the guy who'd been sitting at the computer. "Just ask him." He just scowled. "They all say that I'm 'clean.'"

"Can we go then?" Wayne asked one of the uniforms, and the guy just shrugged.

As we walked out and towards the cab, I said, "I guess it was my hair."

"Yeah, like you don't have a right to grow it any length you want."

We got into the cab and I glanced at the meter. It had hit twenty-five and change. Wayne shut it off. "I'll get you to the south side. Just pay me six bucks and we'll call it even."

We got off of the bridge and went a different direction through the fair city of Detroit. I fished six bucks out of my wallet, handed it to him and thanked him profusely.

"This country is so screwed up," he said, taking the money and tossing it onto the seat next to him. "Fuck Florida. I want to go to another country. New Zealand, maybe. I have a good piece of change saved up. I could do it." We were on an expressway now. I saw a sign for I-75 South. He followed that. "I'll get you far enough south so you'll be out of the main area of the city. Try not to get shot. I'll let you out where there'll be traffic."

We drove on like that for a couple of minutes, him thinking about a new life in New Zealand, me thinking about yet another change of direction in my journey. He took an off-ramp and pointed to where I should stand. He wished me luck on my trip to Maine. I wished him luck on getting to New Zealand or wherever the fuck it was he wanted to go. Then he pulled away.

I tried to figure out what I had to do. South to Toledo. East across I-80/90 like I'd originally "planned." Man, this whole Canada thing had been a fiasco. Fuck, this entire life seemed like a fiasco. Once again, I thought of the prospects of admitting defeat and going back to Kilkerry. And that's where I would end up. Flunked out of DeForrest. Living at the Farm with Eva and Adolf and the Cousin. I cursed myself over everything.

A big, newish Cadillac pulled up while I was in the depths of my self-chastisement. It startled me when it pulled up. It was a convertible, with the top up. I heard somebody yell to jump in, and I did.

The driver looked to be in his mid-30s, although I could have been wrong. His hair was a reddish-blonde and curly—long in that socially-acceptable way, like the guy in the Winston ads. He had a cigarette between his fingers and squinted as he looked at me. The lines on his face were well-established. As he floored the car and we took off, I smelled the whiskey, then saw the half-empty pint bottle wedged between his leg and the seat.

"How ya doin'?" he asked as we shot down the highway. He didn't wait for an answer. "Where ya goin'?"

"Maine," I replied, reaching around for the seat belt. But I couldn't find it. Either it had been removed or it had disappeared inside the seat from lack of use.

"Whooee! Maine! That's a hell of a long ways to go from here!"

"Better believe it," I commented as he grabbed the bottle, undid the cap, and took a swig. He offered it to me but I shook my head.

"You had supper yet?" he asked.

"No," I replied. I realized then that I hadn't eaten since morning. But the thought of food hadn't crossed my mind.

"My old lady and I are cooking out," he said. "This is her car. Well, really, it's her husband's car. He's a trucker. He's away a lot and doesn't take care of her like she needs to be." He began rambling then about love. No, about—Love. What it means, how important it is, and the car rocketed down the road, and things blurred by as we passed them and his voice slurred. His window was down and his left arm hung out of it as he seemed to steer with his right hand.

It was then that I noticed that his clothes were expensive. Harris tweed jacket. Slacks that looked comfortable and were obviously of a good cut. I glanced down at his feet and could make out a pair of top-siders. The guy looked preppie as hell, but there was a sort of wrinkled look about him.

He'd now gotten to describing how he'd met his girlfriend. Something about his father's company and a party. She worked there, apparently. How they'd arranged for a date. " . . . never thought she'd meet me. But hell, we went out after that. Went over to Windsor, couple of places I know. Had some kicks, you know? Hell of a woman. Really good. Hey!" He said, suddenly thinking of some great idea. "She'd love to meet you! You oughtta come to dinner with us!"

I declined. I could not imagine a situation more uncomfortable: being invited as a guest to her house by her drunken lover to have dinner on the grill while her husband was away. And her husband was a trucker who probably carried a gun. But this guy would not take "no" for an answer.

"We're almost there," he said. "But we need another steak!"

He had gotten off the interstate after only one exit. We were now entering a small town. He slowed, then turned abruptly into the parking lot of a grocery store. He lurched out of the car.

"I'll be right back!" he nearly yelled, then staggered into the place, leaving me in the car.

I noticed two middle-aged women coming out of the store. They stared at him as he walked by them. One looked in my direction and, when she saw the car, she elbowed her friend who also looked my way. They crossed the parking lot, talking with one another heatedly and tossing hateful looks at me. Oh good, I thought. The town gossips have connected the husband's car with the drunken boyfriend and some friend of the boyfriend who's a hippie. Whatever discretion had cloaked the budding romance between this guy and the trucker's wife was gone. The affair would be common knowledge within the small town within the hour. The news would get to the husband one way or another. At least I'd be gone from this place before then.

I could see him through the plate glass windows as he stood at the cash register, fumbling with the bills in his wallet. He suddenly smiled as he apparently found the correct denomination and handed it to the checkout girl. A couple of people were in line behind him, and they were watching him, their faces expressionless. As he walked out of the store with the piece of meat, wrapped in butcher paper, people kept their eyes on him and followed his path from store to Cadillac. Their expressions changed. Ah yes. He was found out. His fate was sealed. He was oblivious to all this, though, and I don't think he would have listened to me if I had tried to explain it.

He got into the car and said, "Okay! Steaks!" and started the car. We pulled out of there, the tires squealing as he turned onto the street and hit the gas, followed by the hateful gazes of all those people back there.

We drove through town. Then, about a half-mile outside of the town limits, on a flat stretch of highway, he turned into the gravel drive of a one-story house. It was stone up to about six feet, and the rest of its walls, all the way up to the eaves, was red brick. The house looked expensive and nice, but there was an unkempt appearance to it.

The guy got out, grabbing steak and whiskey, and staggered cheerfully to the door, humming all the way. I lagged behind him. When the door opened, the first things I saw were her eyes. Even through the dusk I could see the anger there.

"Where the fuck have you been!?" she spat out, then glanced over at me, long hair over my shoulders, blue jeans, pack. "What's this!?"

"He's a buddy I picked up," he replied, trying to calm her down with his jovial tone. "Gonna join us."

"Is he a hitch hiker?"

Before my "buddy" could do any more damage, I said, "Yes, and all I want to do is get back to the interstate for a ride." I made as if I was glancing at my watch. "I'm behind schedule as it is."

"Did you drive through town?" She asked him, ignoring me now that she knew I posed no threat by actually wanting to come inside her house and stay for dinner.

"No. No," he replied unconvincingly. "But fuck all those people anyway. They can't take a joke."

"I want you to get him," she said, indicating me, "down to the interstate. Then I want you back here."

He was whipped. He nodded drunkenly, and turned back to the car. "Come on," he mumbled to me. She glared at us all the way to the car, and even as we backed out of the driveway.

He put the car into drive and we started down the road. He grabbed the bottle again and took a big swig of whiskey.

"Fuckin' women," he said. "All a buncha fuckin' bitches. Get bent outta shape for nothin'." He lit a cigarette. "I'll tell ya," he said, and glanced over at me. I only wished he would keep his eyes on the road. "I don't care about her. Don't care about her a lick. I'm gonna get outta this place. Go someplace new. You got the right idea. Hitch-hike. Get away from where you are." He paused and took another drink.

We finally got out to a complex of ramps, where he slowed and let me out. As he pulled away it was impossible not to notice that he was not going back to her house. He was going on to someplace else, maybe his own home if he had one, maybe a bar, maybe a dead-end road where he could drink in peace and pass out. I shook my head.

I looked up at a sign that said "Rockwood." I did not know exactly where I was. I knew I was someplace south of Detroit and north of Toledo. The interstate was down below from where I stood. I walked to a section of the on-ramp and toosed my stuff onto the ground. I was tired, but then again I wasn't.

I was charged up in a way I'd never felt before. Here I was, a couple of hundred miles from home, out hitch hiking. Being thrown out of a country. Meeting weird people. And only that morning, I'd awakened in the frat.

The traffic was sparse. The few cars that passed ignored me as I stood there with my thumb out. Down on the interstate there was a steady flow of cars, even though it was getting onto nine o'clock. But I didn't want to risk getting arrested. I sat down on a rail. For the first time that day, I began to think about the problems I'd left behind. The scene with Patricia was the most immediate. I felt very lonely out here next to the interstate.

A cop car was going by on the road that went through the interchange. There were two cops in it. I could barely see their forms but I knew they had to be watching me from the way the car slowed suddenly. They went on but I was paranoid. I cursed them and tried to will a car to appear, one that would stop and give me a ride and get me away from this place. That didn't happen, though.

My thoughts drifted back to Patricia. Her breasts had been so big and she was so cute. The hat really set things off, too. I was aching with loneliness and a lifetime of pent-up horniness. I was now starting to get tired, too.

Traffic was absolutely dead. I wasn't going to get a ride here. I saw headlights from down the road then. I was hopeful for a couple of seconds that maybe this was a ride. Then I saw the bubble gum machine on the roof of the vehicle. The cops were coming by to check me out again. They slowed once more, this time lingering still longer to observe me before going on.

Aristotle always put things in threes, it seemed—well, except for the proper number of acts in a play. I had a gut feeling that if the cops came by a third time, and I was still standing here at this same place on the on-ramp, that they would bust me on whatever charge they felt was appropriate, if only to combat the boredom.

Down below where I stood, maybe 30 yards down the hillside, was a small stand of trees. Grass grew tall around the bases of the thin oaks and maples. I grabbed my pack and loped down the hillside. I tossed it into a space between the trees, then followed. Once inside, I pulled way back in, then untied the sleeping bag from the pack and spread it on the ground. I went back to where I'd come in between the trees and pumped up the brush there so it didn't look as though anyone had walked through there. Then I moved the sleeping bag a few feet so it wouldn't be in the line of the cops' sight on the off chance that they shined a light down here.

I crawled into the sleeping bag, my clothes still on, and placed my head on the pack. The traffic on the interstate was intermittent and very close. I had trouble getting to sleep.

I was facing uphill and I saw the cop car stop. It sat there for a few minutes. At first I was really scared the cops would get out, walk around, and either figure out where I'd gone or follow my footsteps in the dew to this copse of trees. But that didn't happen. They simply went on and continued their patrol of Rockwood, Michigan, or whatever the fuck this place was. The exciting point of their evening—"Dispatch—we got a hitch hiker out here!"—was now over.

It took me a while to get to sleep. The traffic soon began to fade, though. Finally, I dropped off into a dreamless sleep, oblivious to everything around me.

Chapter 37 - Day Two

I woke up when it was still what I've heard described as "false dawn." The sun had not yet broken over the horizon, but it was no longer completely dark. It was just a sort of grayish light. I knew where I was immediately. I also immediately sensed that I should get my ass moving for fear of the cops.

I was surprised to see, as I rolled up my sleeping bag and tied it to the pack, that the traffic on the interstate was heavier now, before dawn, than it had been the previous evening. I zipped open the side pocket of the pack and brushed out my hair, a couple of twigs coming out as I did so. As I watched the traffic though, I saw that most of it was northbound.

I weighed my options. Either I could stand here and, possibly, be arrested by the same cops as those who passed me last night, or I could take my chances across the interstate, actually on the highway, and go north an exit or two, then turn and go south. I glanced at my watch. I had been there for nine-and-a-half hours.

I grabbed my stuff and walked out of the trees. I waited for traffic to pass, then crossed the lanes quickly. I got to the far side of the northbound lanes and stuck out my thumb. I wasn't there 40 seconds before a car zipped out of traffic and came to a stop a few yards behind me.

The guy was middle-aged and had a styrofoam cup of coffee balanced on the dashboard. Once I was in the car, he hit the gas and we were off.

"Where ya going?" he asked with a very pronounced, almost eastern, accent that I recognized as native Michigan.

"Maine," I said.

"That's a long ways," he observed. "Goin' up through Canada?"

"No," I said, and then briefly explained last night's events and why I was now headed north.

"Good thinking," he said. "Never get a southbound ride down there. Not if you stay on the ramps. And the cops around here don't like to see hitchers on the roadway proper."

"Why so much traffic going north?" I asked.

"Ford. That's where I work. All the people around you right now work days. Heading in. I'll drop you at the place you wanta be for a southbound drive. If I can, I'll tell one of my buddies from graveyard shift, just getting off, to give you a lift. He lives pretty far south."

"What's graveyard?"

"Oh, nickname for the shift that comes in 11 p.m. to 7 a.m. It's real dead during that time. Gets to feeling really weird along about three-thirty, four o'clock." He seemed to shiver a little, remembering.

I saw the factory a short time before we took the off-ramp. I thanked the guy as I got out. Waved. He wished me luck.

The only reason that I had missed the goddamn thing the night before was the route that the drunk had taken off the interstate, because the factory was huge—the largest I'd ever seen. Corrugated steel walls covered with a brownish layer of soot rose tens of stories on the square structure. It looked as if it should be quite small because of its shape. Things that square and squat are short. But things as tall as it should rise thin and straight. On the roof, also made of corrugated steel, was the Ford logo. Traffic was heavy, especially going in. As the sun rose, the building took on a golden hue, reflecting sunlight off soot.

I wasn't standing there for very long. A brand new LTD, sticker still in the window, pulled up next to me and stopped. He said he was from down near the Ohio line and that, sure, he could give me a lift that far. He wanted to know where I was going, and I told him. Wanted to know where I was from, why I was hitching, the whole bit. It felt good to talk, riding along for a ways after having been stuck for so long in Rockwood. I wasn't a coffee drinker, but I didn't refuse when he poured me a cup out of his thermos, the top of the thing acting as my cup. It was hot but tasted good, and it woke me up.

He told me we were getting close to his exit.

"There's a truck stop there," he said. "You can use the bathroom to clean up. Maybe get a ride from a trucker."

I thanked him, even shook hands, as I got out.

I walked up an embankment, then started across the huge expanse of asphalt parking lot. There were 40 or 50 semis at the stop, at least, sitting there with engines running while drivers were inside eating. The smell of diesel fumes enveloped everything, gone for only a second or two with the shift of breeze. The asphalt was blotched with huge spots of soaked-in oil and grease. Trash and discarded cigarette butts were everywhere.

With all the trucks around here, I figured I could get one ride, but as I walked in I saw three or four hitch hikers lined up against the wall of the entry way, holding their signs. They all appeared to be roughly my age, but they made no eye contact with me. Apparently they were not traveling together, as each of their signs stated a different destination. They didn't seem to be going anywhere, only staying here, standing in this truck stop, so my spirits fell a bit. With all the trucks here, one would have assumed that rides would be easy to get.

To the left was a gift shop and the place to pay for diesel fuel and gas. To the right was a restaurant. I went in and took a booth. One middle-aged waitress eyed me suspiciously, then nudged a younger one who came out from behind the counter, a bit nervous.

"Excuse me," she said. "But you can't sit here unless you plan to eat something."

I was a bit embarrassed, because of her statement by itself, but also because two or three other people nearby were listening.

"I intend to eat," I said politely.

"I mean," she said, hesitating. "I mean, you do have money, don't you?"

I could feel my face turning red. "I have money," I replied curtly. I was still polite. "I would appreciate a menu, though."

The waitress persisted. "I mean," she said, "I have to see the money. We have hitch hikers in here all the time who'll order food and eat it, then leave or ask to wash dishes."

I was ready to stand up, tell her to piss off, and walk out. I really wanted to, I was so angry. But I was hungry. And I felt sorry for her. She hadn't formulated or initiated this policy. Reluctantly I reached for my wallet and flipped out a five. I held it up for her to see. I felt as though someone had asked me to drop my pants, right there in the little greasy spoon, and conducted some kind of intimate examination. She seemed confused. I mean, this wasn't supposed to happen. She glanced back at the older waitress who seemed mollified and nodded, and the younger one reached over to the wait station and grabbed a menu. She exhaled heavily in relief.

I looked over the menu. I was happy to see that the prices were cheap. I ordered a good, solid breakfast—ham, eggs, hash browns, whole wheat toast, and a large coke.

"A coke?" she asked as she took my menu. "That's a funny thing to drink with breakfast."

I shrugged and smiled. "When I was a kid, my aunt and uncle never let me have cokes with breakfast but they always let the Cousin have them. Now that I'm old enough to order on my own, I have cokes with breakfast."

She smiled.

As she turned away, I asked her, "Can I leave my things here and use the restroom?"

She seemed to hesitate again, but then said, glancing over her shoulder and noticing that her superior was absent, "Sure. Right back around the corner in the entryway. I'll watch your stuff."

She placed the order, and I grabbed my kit bag and towel from my pack.

As I started past the other hitch hikers, one of them, a ratty-looking individual who appeared to have not bathed in a considerable period of time, said, "Hey, buddy, spare some money?"

"No," I said, and tried to continue on, but he stepped out and somewhat blocked my path.

"I saw you order in there," he said. "I'm hungry. I want to eat but I can't. I'm broke."

He was skinny, but taller than me. He had the same type of build as hundreds of other hilljacks I'd seen. I was scared now—scared of standing here, and scared of what might happen if I went to the restroom. But I'd noticed the fairly heavy traffic of truckers in and out of the restroom. And I wasn't going to allow myself to be robbed by someone with an I.Q. of an ashtray and the hygiene of somebody from the hills.

"No," I repeated, and walked on past him and into the restroom.

When I went through the door, I sensed someone behind me. I glanced up at the mirrors, and the guy who was coming in looked like one of the truckers.

"I saw that shit in the diner," he said. "And I guessed that that guy out there just now saw your money. You wanta get cleaned up, you go ahead. I'll watch your back."

I thanked him and, rapidly, and as thoroughly as possible, brushed my teeth and combed my hair. After I'd begun, the other hitch hiker had eased into the room. I saw him in the mirror. But the trucker had moved behind me and looked at the other hitchhiker with a menacing expression, and the guy had slunk back out.

Once I got done, I thanked the guy, and he said, "No problem." I ignored the other hitch hiker as I walked past.

My hair was wet but, even though I'd had to wash it in the sink, the feeling of washing some of the grit from my scalp had been wonderful. My hair was brushed, and it smelled of soap, and my teeth were minus the moss that had seemed to have grown on them during the night. Breakfast was just being put on my table as I sat down. I thanked the waitress and grabbed a piece of toast. I glanced up, and the guy who had tried to shake me down was staring straight at me. I glanced over at another table and saw that someone had abandoned a newspaper. I got up and grabbed it. When I sat down in the booth, I sat in the place opposite where I'd been, and moved everything around accordingly. I ate my breakfast in peace as I read the paper. I was so acclimated to the reporting of Indiana local events and the right-wing slant of the Indianapolis Star that it was always strange to read a newspaper of another city. But there I was, reading the Detroit Free Press, and enjoying my ham and eggs. I ate every scrap and crumb on those plates, then leaned back and smoked a cigarette. Cigarettes hadn't been tasting all that good lately, perhaps because I'd cut back so much in my consumption. But this one tasted just fine. When I finished I picked up my check and pack and walked to the cash register. The older waitress handled the money. With other customers I'd heard her ask if everything was all right and wish them a good day. She said nothing to me. She took my money and the check, made change, and shoved it at me across the glass top of the counter.

I lifted the pack, and the girl who'd waited on me wished me a good day, and I thanked her and wished her the same. When I walked through the entry way, the guy who'd tried to shake me down just glowered at me, but he said nothing and made no move toward me. So I ignored him again and headed out into the morning.

I walked the quarter-mile or so to the on-ramp and set down my pack. Now that I was away from the terminal and the trucks, I took in a deep breath. Even next to the highway, the air smelled clean and fresh.

I hadn't stood there long when an old Lincoln pulled up. It was about a 1964, long and low, and black. The paint wasn't oxidized, but it certainly could have used a good wax job. It was a four-door model with suicide doors. The outside handle for the back doors was at the front of the door and the outside handle for the front door was at the back of the door. As I came running up to the car, I saw there was a couple in front, a man driving and a woman riding shotgun, so I grabbed the handle of the back door, passenger's side, and jumped in. The car had the faint smell of exhaust that the interiors of old cars sometimes have. The interior was a bit drab, but there were no cuts or holes that I could see in the leather upholstery. The driver introduced himself as Ken and his wife as Laura. They looked to be in their late twenties and kind of hip. We took off into traffic.

"Where you headed?" Ken asked.

"Maine," I replied.

"Wow!" Laura said. Ken just nodded and said, "80/90 across, and 95 from Boston up."

Sounded good to me, so I nodded.

Ken's was a rather acerbic personality. After explaining that they could get me to the west side of Toledo, just short of 80/90, he told me about his days of "thumbing." He launched into regaling both me and Laura with tales of journeys to Arizona and Florida. He asked me why I was on the on-ramp, and not down on the interstate where the main traffic was, didn't wait for a reply, answered the question himself, and then commented, "Fuck the police," all in a heavy accent that I'd always identified as northern Ohio.

The traffic narrowed, and soon we were crawling along in a single lane of traffic several miles long, traffic barricades of orange and white, little yellow strobes atop them, on both sides of us. As he spoke, I got the picture of the two. He seemed very domineering and authoritative. She seemed shy and reserved. He was something of an asshole. I wondered why women were attracted to his type.

Then I thought about DeForrest, for some weird reason. It seemed to be so far away. So long ago. But it was only yesterday, about 24 hours ago, that I'd left.

Soon traffic cleared up, and Ken said, "This is our exit up here. It looks like traffic's pretty good. You shouldn't have any problem getting a ride."

I agreed and thanked them. He let me out at the bottom of the ramp so I could wait on the interstate itself. But I just waited until the Lincoln had turned right off the ramp and disappeared down the road before I hoofed it up the ramp. I had no intention of getting busted.

The area must have been quite a ways from downtown Toledo, because it was desolate. Of course, I had no idea how big Toledo was. I hadn't waited very long when an old Ford Maverick rolled past me and stopped. I was getting pretty good at the drill of picking up the pack and running after whatever vehicle was my ride. I saw only a driver in the car. When I got up to the side, I saw that a girl in her late teens was the driver. I thanked her and got in. We took off, but not onto the interstate. She did a U-turn and started down the road above.

"You're wanting 80\90 East, right?" she asked, after introducing herself as "Tonya." I nodded. "I'll take you through a lot of the crap, around some of the bad sections, onto the other side of Toledo. You'll have a straight shot that way."

I wasn't sure what to make of that, but I thanked her anyway.

She was a bit heavyset and had a moderately severe case of acne. She started talking about parties. Then she asked me questions, changing the course of her talk without giving much thought to it. We were soon passing through an industrial area. Warehouses, and huge lots fenced in by chain-link in which sat various types of equipment, surrounded by stands of weeds, made up the scenery. There were a couple of factories.

She wanted to know if I was really from Indiana, as if a Hoosier in Ohio was a rare visitor. I told her that I was a lifelong Hoosier, born and bred.

"Do people party over there? I mean, pot and everything?"

That seemed like an odd question, but I said that, yes, a great many people partied.

She launched into tales of parties that she and her friends had thrown. She tossed in descriptions of people using LSD and vaguely hinted that she had tried it herself. As she talked, I watched her and wondered if she was as lonely as she seemed. Her moves and her voice were so nervous, and she talked so rapidly, that I thought, perhaps, she had been cloistered somewhere for a long time, without being able to talk to another human being and that she was making up for lost time upon whomever she encountered. I thought she seemed to be like me. I felt it was odd to get a ride from a female, and thought about the risks she was taking by giving a ride to a stranger—a hitch hiker at that—in order to enjoy some sort of company.

We were rolling down narrow back streets with small homes, some neat, some rather grubby. I saw no signs for, or of, the interstate.

"So, where you goin?" she asked me.

"Maine," I replied, watching the passing scenery with a bit of concern.

"Wow, that's a long ways," she said. Then hardly missing a beat, she asked, "Ever think about settling down in a town like Toledo?"

Now I was a little concerned about where she was driving both the car and the conversation.

"I don't know anyone here," I said politely.

"You know me." Her voice was the most sincere any human voice could be. She really meant it. Now I really felt sorry for her in her loneliness. I also felt concern for my personal situation here in her car.

"How far is the interstate?" I asked.

"Oh, just about a mile or so," she replied, and concentrated on her driving.

Her eyes were cute, and she was an intelligent person for all of her bravado.

I wondered what it would be like—to say, "Yes, I think I'll stay here in Toledo"— living with Tonya from Toledo—in an apartment at the top of a slum dwelling in a grubby neighborhood—each of us working and coming home at night to our apartment, a tiny shelter—the world, a great stormy thing around us. By the time I realized that this had been an opportunity for me to get laid for the first time ever and this very day, I'd pondered enough negatives that the prospect was not tempting. I had enough emotional detritus for one person. I didn't want to take on that of another person, as extensive or more so than my own, as well.

I was broken from my reverie by the car coming to a stop. The on-ramp seemed to have been sliced out of the neighborhood of old, asphalt-shingled houses.

"Here you are," she said, a hint of sadness in her voice and in her eyes, too, as she turned to me.

"Thanks," I said, grabbed my pack, and got out of the car.

As she pulled away, I saw her wave, staring into the rearview mirror, and I waved, then turned my attention to traffic.

Traffic on the interstate was heavy, but not on my on-ramp. Still, my luck held. I was there only 15 minutes when a plain, no-frills, Plymouth pulled up, and the passenger door opened.

The woman was big and double-chinned and greeted me warmly.

"How far you headed?" she asked.

"Just here on 80/90, then east."

"Darling," she said, "this is the by-pass. It ain't the toll road." We started down the ramp. "I can get you there, though. Not far out of my way."

I thanked her for that.

"Lord says to help people all we can," she commented.

I wanted to groan, but I didn't. That was where I recognized the smile. Corners of eyes and mouth tight. A smug countenance. A condescending attitude. A born-again Christian. Oh good.

She introduced herself as a minister in some off-brand church: Lamb's Holy Book Chapel Mission, Lighthouse of the Lord, or something like that—a name the acronym of which would form a sentence all by itself.

"You born again?" she asked as I slipped on my shades.

"No," I said, taking them off again in order to clean the lenses. "I'm an atheist."

I already knew what her response would be. These people never change. They're only offended when you seem to waffle or when you blaspheme.

"Well, praise the Lord, another sinner," she said. She started to custom-make an explanation of her "Lord" that would appeal to me. They all do that. It always made me wonder about them. If their world view is so good and all-encompassing, why do they feel compelled to beat other people over the head to accept it? She continued, talking about the blind being able to see and the lame being able to walk, all that happy horseshit. I was just glad to have a ride.

She had tuned her pitch perfectly.

"You know, I respect you for your views," she said.

I thanked her.

"But, would you do me a favor?"

"What?"

"Just say, 'Yes.'"

I looked at her sharply. "I don't agree to something without knowing what it is."

"You'll never regret this."

"What is it?" I asked.

"Pray to Jesus to come into your life as your personal Savior," she said, automatically.

"No," I said, pissed off, but holding my anger in check. She had a lot of nerve, telling me that she respected my opinion. Then, of all things, trying to "trick" me into salvation. Oh, like that'd be eternal.

She was nonplussed. We rolled to a stop at a huge cloverleaf.

"Have a nice day, and may Jesus be with you," she said.

I looked back at her, the corners of her mouth curled up in that grin. I saw a cruelty there, suddenly. I realized that I always had seen that smile on the faces of people who were not just "saved" but also leaders of the flock. Fake grins laced with cruelty.

I got out of the car. Something, some rule, prevented me from telling her to kiss my ass. It was a rule of hitch hiking, maybe. You don't flip off someone who's just given you a ride.

She pulled away and I looked up the cloverleaf, the long, curving drive that led to the toll booth area. Ahead I could see a sign in bold letters that left no doubt in the mind: "HITCH HIKING ON THE TOLL ROAD IS A MISDEMEANOR PUNISHABLE BY 180 DAYS IN JAIL AND A $150.00 FINE." That meant no thumbing on the highway, itself. And that was why, every 20 yards or so on the curve, stood a hitchhiker. The place nearest me was open, and without batting an eye, I grabbed it, just as someone from up top seemed to be moving to come down and try to take it.

I groaned. This would be a long wait.

Cars passed by. Traffic was fairly heavy. I had a lot of competition for the rides available; but, when I glanced up at the other hitch hikers, I was struck by how scummy most of them looked. Then I thought about how scummy I looked. I rationalized that I'd bathed that morning, or at least I'd tried to.

I realized again how far away my problems seemed—how little I'd thought about them since I'd gotten out and started my trip.

My sunglasses were on, but I figured, fuck it. I was going to be out there a long time, anyways, and the sun was getting bright. Then a Porsche zipped right up in front of me and stopped. The driver was a male, young—25 or so, and he appeared to be hip: sideburns, longish hair. The car was a 914 like Merriman's and the top was off. He yelled, "Which way?"

I said, "East!"

He said, "You're in luck! Hop in!"

I grabbed my bag and tossed it in. As we drove up the incline, the other hitch hikers looked sullen. Some looked downright pissed off. So many of them were old and weathered.

Hell, I'd taken a ride, though, after some of them had been out there all morning, maybe all night and part of yesterday.

"How far you goin'?" he asked. His voice was raised slightly to be heard over the engine and the wind.

"Maine!"

"What part?"

"Caribou!"

"You going to Loring?"

I was a bit surprised. He slowed down and took a toll ticket from the machine, then gunned the car again. We zipped past cars and trucks as they merged from eight to about three lanes.

"You been up there?"

"My cousin was based up there a couple of years ago. Real pretty country."

"Mind if I smoke?" I asked.

"Cigarettes?"

"Yeah."

"No, go right ahead. Smoke's no problem in this buggy."

He seemed to have a very sober, analytical way of expressing himself as we talked, tearing down the interstate in his sports car. He was a rock promoter, he told me, and he drove a lot of miles.

"One thing you don't want to do," he said, "is spend any time at all in Ohio or New York. Cops in both places are flaming, fucking pricks. Connecticut's not much better."

"How should I avoid states?" I asked, rather perplexed. I watched the ash of my cigarette automatically disappear after each puff, the wind sucking it out into space.

He reached beside his seat and pulled out a map. He steered with one hand while he folded back the pages. It was a small book in a plastic cover, a road atlas of the entire United States.

"I'm going as far as Cleveland," he said, stabbing his finger at another general map of the country's interstate system. "That'll get you halfway across Ohio, a little more. You wanta split off there and take 80 to the New York line. Get up to 84. Then, across Connecticut. Shoot up to Springfield, Massachusetts, on 91, then the toll road to Boston. That means you only got this little bit in New York. And stay off the Massachusetts Toll Road. The cops have to bust hitch hikers, and it's an automatic stay in jail."

He folded the map and put it back, wedged between his door and his seat.

"Once you're in Boston, shoot up 95 and it'll take you just shy of Caribou."

I thanked him. My route was finally planned out for me.

"A lot of people were hitching back there," he said after a few minutes' silence.

"Yeah," I said. "I was afraid I wasn't gonna get a ride. Thanks."

"Hey, you wouldn't have had any problem. Somebody would give you a lift before they would those guys."

"Why's that?" I asked.

He glanced at me a couple of times, then put his full focus on the road. "You're a college student. Freshman or sophomore. Sophomore, right?"

"How'd you know that?" I asked, weirded out just a bit.

"College is written all over you the same way the joint's written all over them."

"Huh?"

"Jail—prison," he said, and fished a package of gum out of his pocket. He offered me a piece, and I took it. Doublemint always went well with menthol cigarettes.

"Those guys back there have all done time. Some of the younger ones might not have done it yet, but it's their destiny. You can read it."

We continued sailing along, making good time. It was now getting close to noon.

The speed limit was 55, and he didn't vary much from that. He left the car in fifth gear, and we tooled along. The sun got even higher in the sky. He asked me what I was "into," and I started to try to explain the World as I understood it. That the World turned on an axis made up of equal parts hatred and greed and bullshit, but that hope somehow was there. How Jefferson Starship had sung on their album "Dragonfly" that, come the summer of '75, there was going to be a lot of change. That the Weather Underground had just come out with a pamphlet called "Prairie Fire," and that it spelled out a lot of events that were going to take place. He listened with a bemused look on his face. I was into these theories, and they came pouring out of me. I hadn't put them together like this before. It felt good.

The drive to Cleveland was just over a hundred miles. The time, like the miles, went quickly.

"Good luck," he said, as we approached the exit. "Hope you get good rides. I remember hitching to California when I was in school. Fucking bummer one place. Waited about 10 hours."

"I've already done that once," I said.

We went through the toll booths, and after he'd paid, he pulled over to the shoulder. I got out and grabbed my pack and waved as he pulled away.

I jogged over to the other side of the pavement and had hardly positioned myself when a semi came to a halt right there. It happened so suddenly I thought that maybe he was having mechanical problems, but after a few moments the passenger door opened, and he shouted to come on up.

I now had enough experience getting into a semi that I simply tossed my pack over one shoulder, grabbed the rail and shot up the steps. It was another cab-over without any company markings. The absence of markings meant the guy was an independent.

He was in his 40s. Of about average height and weight, maybe a little paunchy. He had on a plaid shirt, was balding on top, and the hair he did have was dark and cut short.

"Which way ya headed!?" he hollered as I stuck my head in.

"East!"

"Then you're in luck! Hop in!"

I glanced back at the trailer. It was a flat trailer, not enclosed at all, and he had nothing on it.

I swung my pack onto the floor, and landed in the seat, slamming the door behind me. He cranked up the engine and we lurched forward. I was getting into semi rides. It was weird being so high up, looking down on the world, then looking eye-to-eye with people in other trucks.

He geared down as we pulled up to the toll booth and took a card. Then, he cranked up again, and we merged through the traffic.

"Sam!" he yelled, by way of introducing himself.

I yelled and introduced myself.

"How far ya headed?" he asked. When I told him, he said, "Well, I can get you as far as State College, Pennsylvania. That's about half-way across the state. Get there after dark."

"That's a good long ways!" I said appreciatively.

"Yeah, but I have to get off the interstate for a couple of hours north of Pittsburgh. Onloading fire brick."

234

I nodded. Distance versus hours. Space versus time.

"If you want to," he said, "I can let you out when I get off the interstate. But, if you'd like, I can use some help onloading those bricks. You can ride there with me. Help onloading, then I'll buy you dinner."

That sounded like space and food versus very little time.

"Sure!" I said, grinning. "I don't have that much money, and anything like that is a help."

I wondered for a moment what I'd gotten myself into, but then I looked at him, and I felt okay.

He grabbed his CB microphone and called for a Smokie report. A voice immediately came back. There were, apparently, a lot of cops out.

"That's one thing about Ohio," he said, pointing to his speedometer. "The cops here will ticket you for one mile per hour over if you're a trucker. They derive a lot of revenue that way." He shook his head, then pointed up ahead. "Right behind the overpass up there. Watch."

As we passed the concrete supports, I glanced over and saw the cop car sitting there.

"Do all the trucks have CBs?" I asked.

"Yeah," he replied. "Couldn't do a profitable business without them. Time's money. It's a cliche, but it's true."

He started telling me, then, how long he'd been a trucker. Started in the early 1960s. Managed to save and buy his own rig, even when his wife was having three children. "It's tough," he observed. "I spend so much time on the road. I mean, I love my family a lot, but I have to provide for them. And I do make good money at this."

He asked me about myself, my life. I had the feeling of freedom, then—I could tell him anything. He had no idea who I was. I wasn't pinned down by any knowledge that he had of my past. And, after today, I'd never see him again. That fact, and the fact that I was trying to get away from what had happened back at DeForrest, made me want to lie like a rug. But no lies came readily to mind. And he seemed to be extending a trust to me. So I tried to explain what I thought about life. The thing I'd been discussing in the Porsche. But in a different way. This wasn't political at all. It was about people and getting along. I hadn't done so consciously, but I guess I was adapting to my audience. What I said wasn't any less sincere. And it was helping me. I'd been down for so long, and here I was finally coming "up." Everything was coming out as a positive. Even the stuff about revolution was hopeful: the side of right would eventually win.

Sam nodded during the whole thing, agreeing with what I said at every turn. We gunned down I-80 and passed by Youngstown. "Wish more people would think like that," Sam said. "Too much fighting. Too much hatred. And life's too short."

He picked up the microphone then and asked for a Smokie report for Pennsylvania.

"You got the Brickman here," he began, using his handle for the first time, and then asked for the status of cops on the Pennsylvania Turnpike.

"Haven't you heard, Brickman?" a voice came back. "It's a holiday in good old PA. The prison guards are on strike, and all the state troopers are covering the prisons. There's Smoke only two places—going into and coming out of the good Commonwealth of Pennsylvania. You can put the pedal to the metal. Come on!"

This conversation took place before the Burt Reynolds movies made talk over the CB seem trite and laden with the cliches of lower-class white people. So what would later become passe.

Sam laughed. "This here is the Brickman. Are you pulling my leg?"

Another voice came back. "No, Brickman. This here's Redbird, and he's telling you the truth. I'm just crossing the line right now and waving 'bye to PA. Made it across 80 at 80. Over."

"I know Redbird," Sam said, replacing the mike. "He wouldn't kid around. Damn!"

When he said, "Damn!" I realized it was the first time I'd heard him cuss. I was a bit surprised at that, being around a trucker who didn't swear. But then I figured, so what?

We came to the Ohio toll booths, and Sam paid the money. We crossed the state line and stopped to pick up a new ticket and, sure enough, there was a Pennsylvania state trooper sitting in his car, parked on the median. He seemed bored, or maybe he had reached that state of apathy that follows extreme frustration. Whatever. He just watched the traffic going by. When we were about a half-mile past him, two trucks zoomed by us, and Sam slammed the pedal to the floor. The drone of the engine jumped to a roar, and we rapidly picked up speed. I glanced over at the speedometer and saw the needle pointing to 80.

"We'll make good time now!" Sam hollered. "But only for a while. We get off the interstate about 25 miles from here."

"Yeah," I said. "But unless the strike is settled this afternoon, we'll have the same situation when we get back on."

He laughed. "Yeah! I wish it was always like this!"

We cruised along. All the traffic was roaring, except for a few cars, the drivers of which either hadn't figured out what was going on, or didn't want to run fast. We soon came to the turn-off, and Sam directed the rig onto the exit and down the ramp. He paid the toll again, then turned onto a two-lane highway. As we picked up speed, I saw a diner and thought of food. It was now well past two, and I hadn't eaten since shortly after dawn. The meal Sam had promised would taste good, no matter what it was.

"We're going way back into the hills," he explained. "A little town offa the main highway. Offa any highway, for that matter," he laughed. "The place is so remote it's only got a combination gas station/grocery/general store there. That's it."

We rolled along for a while and encountered very little traffic. The cars that were on the road were all headed the other way, as if the last persons who lived here were leaving. There were few houses. The trees were gorgeous and rose high above the road. After while, Sam downshifted, then downshifted again, and we turned onto a side road. The terrain before had been hilly, but nothing compared to this road. It was just tar on gravel, and it wound through trees, over a small bridge, then girded a hillside. I looked down to my right, and a small river snaked along, about a hundred feet down.

"Coming out," Sam said, "we're gonna really have a load on. You'll be on the hill side of the cab. If the road gives way, you're gonna have to be ready to jump." I shot him a sharp glance. "Not that I think we got any worries, mind you. Just, well, prudence dictates that we be prepared for the worst."

I chuckled then and shook my head and looked back down at the river. We soon began descending and my ears began popping. The grade was very steep, and the engine strained against something. Sam saw the quizzical look on my face.

"That's the jake gear," he said. "It kicks in to slow us down as we go downhill."

I nodded and looked back out the window. There were trees between the road and the river now, and I caught glimpses of the river through branches, from time to time. Finally, when we were about 15 or 20 yards above the river, we broke out into a little valley. The road moved away from the river, and we approached a little hamlet. Little kids and a couple of dogs were playing outside houses that were sided with tar paper. Smoke

236

curled up from the chimneys on a couple of the houses. The only structure of any size was ahead on the right. It was the brick factory.

Sam pulled the truck onto a gravel parking area and swung the rig around, then backed it up to a loading dock. He'd been here before, probably many times, and when the truck nudged slightly as it touched the dock, Sam shut off the engine and jumped out. I got out, too, and walked around the front of the truck. Sam was talking to a man who'd appeared on the dock.

The sun had crested long before. The color it splashed against the hillsides around us made everything much greener. It was a beautiful little valley, and yet desolate. I wondered what it would be like to live here. Even TV would be hard to receive, so civilization's in-roads would be limited to the weekly deliveries at the hamlet's store, and visitors to the brick factory, like us.

Sam walked toward me, and I saw the man he'd been talking to walk back inside.

"He's gonna get the forklift and onload us," Sam said, and at that moment I heard an engine start up in the factory. "This won't take very long. Come on."

With that he jumped up onto the flat trailer and went to the front of it, to the wall that formed just behind the cab. At its base were several long rolls of material, secured by big heavy rubber bands with hooks on the ends. Sam grabbed the rolls and tossed them onto the ground. Underneath where they had lain were even more of the rubber bands.

The forklift brought the first load of bricks out of the factory. The man's head was darting around, checking the way the load was riding, watching where the wheels were going, and making sure everything cleared the doorway. The drop from the loading dock to the ground was a good five feet. He could have been killed, or at least badly maimed, if he fucked up. The bricks were on a square wooden framework called a pallet. The bricks were stacked up about four feet high and formed a pale yellow cube. I recognized them as the brick linings of fireplaces. Each pallet probably weighed a ton or so. The forklift lurched as he drove it off the dock and onto the trailer. He took it all the way to the front of the trailer, then his hands hit some levers, the fork assembly tipped forward, and he backed out from under the load.

"Here," Sam called to me, handing me a corner of one of the rubberized canvas sheets. "Crawl across the trailer with this. Go in front of those bricks."

By now the forklift was hitting the ass end of the trailer with another load. The guy was just that quick. The pallet was in place by the time my feet hit the ground on the other side. Sam took charge and the sheet was over the two loads of brick with a quick flip of his arms. He moved along the sides of the trailer using the rubber bands to lash down the sheet. When the fourth, and last, pallet was on, I crawled across the trailer with another sheet in my hand, and soon that was in place.

"You wouldn't believe how these bricks pick up moisture," Sam explained as he made the last corner secure. "I'll be right back," he said, and hopped up onto the loading dock, disappearing in the huge doorway.

I walked over to the loading dock and looked into the place. There were no workers to be seen. I figured the man on the forklift had to be the owner. Maybe the operation was so small people only worked here part-time. I walked back around to the front of the truck and looked around the valley. The smell of the river was in the air. The trees were beautiful. This was an excellent place to be, and a good day for living. I realized I hadn't felt like this in a long time. I heard footsteps across the gravel and turned to see Sam walking to the truck, folding a piece of paper. He stuffed it into his shirt pocket as he stood at the side of the truck.

"Let's head out," he said to me and gestured toward the truck.

I got in, and he fired up the engine. We eased away from the loading dock. The truck felt a lot heavier. The engine strained as Sam hit the accelerator. We swung onto the road and headed out.

"Remember what I said," Sam told me. "The road up ahead doesn't have that great a base to it. With as much weight as we got on, I just don't trust it."

"So be ready to jump?"

"Uh huh."

"How many times have you driven out of here with a load like this?"

Sam shrugged. "Fifty or sixty." He saw my reaction. "Yeah, I know. Doesn't make sense. But I'm the only driver that'll make this run. Everybody else thinks it's too dangerous."

"But why do you do it?" I asked.

"The factory's about the only means of income back there. Factory's only open part-time. Employs about 40. If nobody picks up these bricks, the whole place shuts down. Don't get me wrong—it's not charity. I make decent bucks doing it."

He let it go at that. We started up the grade. The engine was getting louder as we made our way up the hill. I was aware now of how narrow the road was. The road did look fragile, as if it could collapse under the weight of the truck. We moved slowly. I saw my knuckles white, on the door handle, and realized I'd placed my hand there without thinking. But we finally reached the crest of the hill, and then we turned onto the state highway. We were back in the real world. It was only when we turned into the gravel parking lot of the diner we'd passed earlier that I realized again how hungry I was.

"Time for me to pay up," Sam said, smiling.

We climbed out of the truck and he left the engine running.

The diner was a relic, an antique from the 1950s. The booths were upholstered in vinyl that was pinkish with weird textured designs. Each table had a little selector for music, with rows of lettered and numbered buttons, all hooked into the main juke box just inside the door. There was a counter, and behind it was the grill. There was an old Hamilton Beach mixer for malts, and a weird, stainless steel assembly of cans of Campbell soups lined up on the shelves. The walls were paneled in pine and bore a slight coat of grease and dust. The place smelled of good food. At least it smelled good to me just then. There were only a couple of other customers in the place. A single cook stood at the grill, his apron dirty, his T-shirted belly bloated. Only one waitress was on duty. She was in her 40s and came over to us immediately, glasses of ice water already poured.

She seemed to know Sam, but not by name. His was a face she'd seen often, but a person to whom she had not been introduced. She had menus and gave those to us. Sam said "Coffee?" and I shook my head. She came back with a pot and filled Sam's cup. "What'll you fellas be having today?" she asked politely.

Sam looked at me and waited.

"Uh, I'll have a cheeseburger, plain, and fries," I said.

"Wait a minute," Sam said. "We made a deal. You help me with the truck, and I buy you dinner. What you ordered is just a snack."

"Okay," I said and flipped open a menu. I was incredibly hungry. "I'll have ham steak, corn, mashed potatoes, and a large coke." I handed the menu to the waitress.

"And put a piece of apple pie on that, too," he told her. Then he ordered.

As she walked away, I said, "I really didn't do that much."

238

He waved me off as though what I was saying was irrelevant. Then he launched into stories about driving.

"Drove down to Tennessee," he began. "Oh, this musta been about '63 or '64. Had a trailer full of corn. Grain corn, already shucked. Went off the highway, down back roads, way into the woods. Came up to the place I was supposed to go to. Little hut there next to a dirt path no wider'n a car. Had a gate across it, and a sign on the gate said, 'Keep Out.' I stopped the truck and a guy come outa that shack. Not a smile, not a frown on his face. Just this blank look like, and he's got a shotgun. Told me to stay put. Then a pickup truck come bouncing down that lane. Three more guys get out. Two have shotguns. The other one comes to the truck and says for me to get out, that he'll take charge of the truck for now. I was just a kid, not much older'n you. Didn't know if I was dead or what. So I just did as I was told. They opened the gate, and I could hear that son of a bitch take it straight up that mountain. He was gone for a while. When he came back, that trailer was empty. Not a kernel left in it. Not a speck of corn there. Fella paid me cash money for the load. Right like that. Reaches into his overalls and pulls out a bankroll. Peels the bills right off."

"What were they doing?" I asked. "Running stills?"

He nodded. "Used to be a lot of that down there. Don't see much of it anymore, really. More often you see guys moving drugs around. They hide it in with their loads. I've seem 'em bust trucks at weighing stations. A guy's got his rig between two others, he's real vulnerable. Can't go anywhere. They got him."

The waitress soon came out with the food, and I scarfed mine down with hardly a thought. It filled me, and I felt very happy to be fed. After I'd finished the pie, I stifled a huge belch, then lit a cigarette. I stretched. The day had gone very well, indeed.

Sam paid the waitress and tipped her, and we got into the truck. Back on the interstate traffic was moving just as fast as before. We joined a line of other semis. Sam found them on the CB and heard them talking about coming through. We'd slowed down a bit, then caught onto the tail as they'd gone by. Now we were really close to the back of the truck in front of us, no more than 10 or 15 feet. I glanced over at the speedometer and saw that needle was holding steadily at 85.

We were moving over hills and through valleys. The landscape was all rolling woods, a deep green. Mists had begun to hang there in the fading light of dusk, and the air coming in my open window was loud, but cool and moist. We were covering a lot of miles very quickly.

Soon it was dark, and the headlights of Sam's semi shone against the metal doors of the truck ahead of us. We rode a long way in silence, Sam only occasionally got onto the CB to ask for information.

After while, he said, "You gonna try to get a ride when I let you out—keep on going tonight?"

"Maybe. I don't know. I'm kinda tired."

"Lots of woods around State College," he said. "You can get some sack time. Relax a little."

"Yeah," I agreed, "but, I'd like to get as many miles behind me as I possibly can."

"Let me see what I can do," Sam said and picked up the mike. "Breaker, breaker. This is the Brickman. Anybody out there got ears on? Over."

A couple of choices came back in reply, and Sam said, "I got a college kid here. A hitch hiker. Going to see a buddy in Maine. I'm getting off at State College. Anybody able to help him? Over."

There was static for a few moments, then one guy, and another after him, explained that their companies didn't allow hitch hikers in their trucks. One guy came onto the radio, his voice laced with a thick, southern accent. "I can give him a ride, Brickman. Come on."

"Who is this? Over," Sam said.

"This is Johnny Reb," the guy said. I placed him at about 50. "From the way I hear ya, I'm about a mile from your back door, heading east. Over."

"Where ya going?" Sam asked and glanced over and nodded at me.

"I gotta go to Brooklyn, right there in that Big Apple," the guy said. "But, hey, this kid ain't one of them hipper dippers, is he?"

I shrugged. To hell with it, "I'll camp out, Sam," I said. "Forget it."

"Thanks anyway," Sam said, and then signed off. "It's really not far now," Sam said, and a few minutes later, we were rolling off the interstate. He pulled off the highway there onto the asphalt shoulder. We shook hands.

"Lotta places around here to camp out. Then you can get a fresh start in the morning." He wished me luck, and I thanked him. Then I climbed down from the cab and tossed my pack at my feet. The semi disappeared into the night.

I stood there, trying to decide what to do, when a car came pulling up right there. An electric window on the passenger's side rolled down. A girl was driving and leaned across to talk to me.

"Hitching?" she asked.

"Yeah."

"Need a ride? I'm going to State."

"Sure," I said. I figured that, if nothing else, there was a college there, and I would perhaps find some place to crash. I vaguely remembered a guy from the house having transferred to Penn State at the end of the previous year. Besides, the girl was kind of cute. Hey! I thought. Maybe this was it—that epochal sexual encounter!

We took off, and she started talking quickly, her words clipped and her gestures somewhat angular, as though she was trying to exercise too much control over them. "This is my mother's car. She'd die if she knew I'd picked up a hitch hiker. Home right now watching TV, no doubt. Her life is scheduled around the TV."

Her accent was definitely eastern, with broad "a" sounds. She was short and lively, and her eyes were big and heavily lashed. But something just wasn't right about her.

The state highway led into the town, and soon we were entering the campus. There were bookstores and bars, and the usual student ghetto housing—old and rotting houses with hibachis on the porches and 10-speed bikes chained to the columns.

She finally said her name, Susan. We parked on a side street.

"If you've never been here before, you'll have to see the Wall," she told me.

The streets were crowded with students, most of them in varying states of inebriation. It was a Friday night, and at first I thought maybe that was the reason for the craziness. But there was something more to the weirdness. One guy started pissing in the street, and no one did a thing about it. A couple was making out passionately in a doorway, the guy's shirt off and the girl's blouse partly unbuttoned. This was all craziness.

"What's going on?" I asked Susan.

She shrugged. "Just that it's Friday night."

I shook my head. It didn't make any sense, unless these people were a lot fucking loonier than people any place else that I'd ever seen.

"Want to get some beer?" she asked, and I said, "Sure."

I was thirsty and I hadn't had a beer since I'd started out on this trip.

We went into a package store. I looked over the strange brands. It was always nice to be in a place a long way from home, because there were always so many different local beers. This was the biggest change in variety I'd encountered. Of course, there were the national brands, but there were also all the brands from the east coast—Schaeffer, Rheingold, Genessee Cream Ale. I grabbed a six-pack, bottles, of Rolling Rock and paid for it. I glanced at Susan as we stood at the cash register. Something just wasn't right.

"Come on," she said as we exited the store. "We can unroll your sleeping bag and sit on the grass behind the Wall."

The Wall turned out to be a low, brick wall standing at the heart of campus. Behind it was an expanse of lawn. Hundreds of students were there, all partying. I couldn't figure out why. I mean, there was no stereo system or anything. But everyone seemed to be having a good time, so I figured, "What the fuck?"

Susan and I found a bare area of grass, and I unrolled my sleeping bag. We both plopped down and opened beers. I looked around at the students, watching for any clues to the craziness.

Finally, it happened. A guy not 20 feet from us pulled out some papers and torched them, and everyone cheered. He hollered out a letter and some numbers.

I got it, now. This wasn't just Friday. This was the end of finals. Susan must have sensed something. She said, "What is it?"

I said. "Oh, nothing. Just watching the people."

"Yeah," she said. "Things get really crazy on weekends. Been that way since I was a kid."

A townie? "You're from 'round here?"

"Yeah," she said. "Bellefonte. About eight or nine miles. Borrowed Mom's car to drive in here." I sat back and sipped some beer, and she rattled on in her hypered way. About her friends in Bellefonte. What a cool place that was. How her friends were all into drugs. "Especially acid," she said. "Doing it all the time. Did it during school. A bunch of us almost got kicked out." Bellefonte was not a large town, she said, but she and her friends did a lot of drugs, nonetheless, and so they were well known to the local police. "Cops say 'Hi' to us all the time. Always looking at our eyes and trying to guess what drugs we're doing."

I sat back and opened another beer. The liquid was cold and wet and foamy, and it tasted very good. I was also very tired, and sitting down like this had given my body a glimpse of rest. My body wanted more. She rattled on. I wondered about what was happening back at DeForrest right now; if anybody missed me. I looked around at the students here, and everything seemed to contrast with the staid, small-town atmosphere at DeForrest.

I looked back at Susan, and she was talking even more rapidly. I wondered what was wrong. Maybe she was paranoid about losing my attention. Well, she had. So, I tried to concentrate.

"...the hospital, really. That's why I was there. Everything always seemed so— different. People's eyes, especially, just seemed—rimmed. Set off from the rest of their faces. Their eyes weren't part of their body."

"Hospital?" I asked.

She nodded. "Yeah. Mental hospital. I've been there for the last four months, one week, three days. I'd know the hours and minutes, but I was out cold when they took me in." She looked at me warily, then fear entered her eyes. "You're not going to just walk away from me now, are you?"

"No," I said. I was a little paranoid when I heard the tone in her voice. It combined fear with a sort of pleading—and an unspoken threat. Like I'd better not go away. She didn't seem very satisfied with my answer and leaned back on the sleeping bag. I noticed I was drinking the beer far more rapidly than she was.

"What do you want to do?" she asked, surveying the crowd around us.

"I know a guy who transferred here from the school I go to. Maybe I can crash there."

"You can crash with me," she said, almost too eagerly, hyper-eagerly.

"I thought you said you live with your folks," I said.

"Mother," she said abruptly. "I said that I live with my mother. I never said anything about a father."

I nodded. The subject of "father" must be taboo. Her eyes seemed "rimmed" just then. I emptied another beer, put the empty into the soggy bag, and grabbed the next.

"I thought maybe we could find a place to camp," she said, sounding as if I'd hurt her feelings. Then she began to warm to the idea. "Out in the woods. There's bunches of places. Really."

"That's not a bad idea," I said, and she smiled at the compliment. "But if I can find Tom, I'll be indoors, and I can clean up."

I saw a pay phone about 20 yards away and ambled over. I picked up the telephone directory, attached by cable to the frame of the booth (yes, miracle of miracles, the phone book was still there) and found Tom's number. I called, but there was no answer after eight or ten rings. I went back to where Susan was sitting. I picked up my beer and noticed she was pouting. She brightened noticeably when I told her that Tom wasn't home. She wanted to leave for a place in the woods right then.

"No," I said. "I have to try at least a couple more times."

We continued to watch the crowd and, off the cuff, I said, "So, you haven't really gone to Penn State as a student, then?" I almost bit my tongue as I realized that question would probably get her pissed off.

She shook her head. "I've been around the university all of my life. Known a lot of students. Hung around. Dated some college boys. That sort of thing. But I've never taken any classes."

I got up and walked over to the phone booth and called again. Again, I got no answer.

When I got back to our place there on the ground, she asked, "Do you get high?"

"Yeah," I said off-handedly and lit a cigarette. I was down to three in that pack with another pack in the side zipper of the knapsack. But I wasn't smoking nearly as much. And the smokes did not taste all that good. Still, it was something to do with my hands.

"I know a guy in Bellefonte who has some pot. We could get a joint offa him and get high."

"I don't think so," I said. "I just wanta find this friend of mine and get some sleep."

Her eyes began to water, and she began to blurt out that I must hate her. The words were fast and the tone was low, but it was unmistakable that she was distraught, even if someone had been watching from 20 yards away, they could have seen something weird in her expression..

I tried to calm her down. I explained that I did not hate her. Man, she was a real pro at this game, because I soon was in her mother's car, headed with her to Bellefonte to find the guy with the hooter, even though that was the last thing in the world I wanted to do. All I wanted was to get away from her. She was back into her manic phase as we sped along toward Bellefonte. Talking about her friends and how cool they were. The drive seemed longer than it really was, because I wasn't sure if part of her problem consisted of feelings of suicidal impulses. As we drove along, I wondered if she was going to drive the car into a concrete abutment.

Bellefonte was a small town at the very center of which was a park, with a low wall that fronted on the main street. I was feeling pretty happy from the beer. The kids who milled about and who were lined up at the drinking fountain built into the stone of the wall were different from the people at State. They seemed, some of them, a bit rougher, dressed a bit shabbily. Of course, I was a good one to talk about the ways other people were dressed, but I felt as if I was in the middle of a group of people from Kilkkerry.

Susan darted around talking with people, dragging me by the hand. I had had enough presence of mind to grab my pack and sleeping bag from her car, parked a block away, in case she tried to ditch me. The people she spoke to did so with an effort at tolerance. They always would glance over at me with that look of, "Who the fuck are you?" I did not feel exactly welcome. I looked across the street and saw a cop watching us. Oh good, I thought, she's making a dope deal and I'm standing here with my pack, exuding the image of HITCH HIKER! Fuck worrying about getting busted for vagrancy. This could be felony-drugs. Finally she walked back to where I'd taken up a place to stand.

"A guy I know's gonna meet us here tomorrow at noon."

"Huh?"

"Come on," she said, grabbing me by the arm and moving me back in the direction of the car. "I'll get us to a place where we can camp out. And we'll meet him tomorrow."

"What about your mother's car?" I asked.

"She won't miss it."

I tried to think of some way of getting away from Susan. I was on her turf here. All I wanted was to be back at Penn State. I knew, however, that that was out of the question. We rolled out of town and onto the state highway. I tried to remember how we went, once we were off the highway, but she took so many turns all I had was a general sense of direction. She was talking the whole time. Some weird talk about her drug connections, and about how she "knew people." I didn't know her meaning, and I had the feeling she didn't know either. A nice beer buzz was interrupted and I had been moved Christ knows how many miles away from what might have been a soft couch and a hot shower, all by this woman who was driving me out into the countryside and the darkness, and on top of that, she'd told me of her recent release from a mental hospital. For all the weird bullshit she'd laid on me so far, I didn't think the part about the mental hospital was bullshit, not in the least. I saw some of my own patterns of behavior over the past few months in what she was doing. Maybe that's why I wasn't fully scared. That and the beers and an exhaustion was beginning to take hold. I was confused, maybe, but not scared.

She pulled over to the side of the road. It was a tar and gravel surface out in the middle of the woods. She stopped her monologue and, smiling, said, "Get out here."

Fortunately, I grabbed my pack and sleeping bag, then got out. She reached across and closed the door, locking it with the door lock button on her side, and then she took off.

I watched the taillights fade. I had no idea where the fuck I was. I only knew there were woods around me. There were lights in the distance, the bluish-white lights up on poles (what people in my area called dusk-to-dawn lights), dotting the hills. Other than that, there were trees and woods around me.

I figured that right now was as good a time as any to sleep. I stumbled into the tree line and unzipped my fly. I stood there in complete darkness, pissing and trying to make sure I didn't piss on my self. Once finished, I turned and stumbled several yards in the other direction, roughly parallel with the road. I felt the ground with my feet, then bent down and prodded with my hands. Satisfied that I'd found a good spot, I rolled out the sleeping bag, took off my shoes, put my dirty socks into the side of the pack, grabbed a clean pair, then laid back, the pack as my pillow. I was out like a light.

Chapter 38 - Day Three

I was vaguely aware of light. That awareness began to ease me into the day. But then the vicious barking of a dog exploded just a few feet from my head. I sat up like a shot, turned, and found myself about eight feet from a snarling, barking, fanged German Shepard. In one motion, my shoes were on, my sleeping bag was rolled up and tied to my pack, and I was moving out of those woods.

I looked over my shoulder as I hit the road and saw that I'd been a few feet away from where the tree line broke at somebody's back yard. An old man had called the dog, and the dog went trotting to the back steps. I heard the man saying, "Whatsa matter, huh?" in a light voice to the pet and saw poochie wagging his tail. "Fuck it," I figured. "I'm up. I'm moving. Welcome to a new day."

For some reason, I had the feeling I was moving in the right direction."That" direction. "That" direction was, generally, back toward Bellefonte and, from there, to the interstate nearby. I began walking, and walking. The day was going to be warm. I looked at my watch and saw that it was after nine in the morning. I was surprised that I'd slept so late.

Something snapped, and there was a sharp tug at my shoulder. I stopped and pulled my pack off. One of the two straps had broken on the cheap, goddamn thing. That was of no major importance, really. I could carry it on one goddamn strap. Then I realized that if the thing was so cheap that one of two straps broke under this weight, it was only a matter of time before the other one did, as well. So I bent down and examined it. The threads on the good strap were loose, and I could see that there were only four of them. I grabbed the end of the strap that had broken and tied it in a knot around the entire area from which it had separated. This actually made a very strong single strap of the two original ones. But, when I lifted it, I could feel its edge biting into my shoulder. As I walked, I had to shift the pack every so often. The strap was trying, with each step, to bite a groove into my skin wherever the strap came to rest.

So I walked, the pack slung over my shoulder, down this long fucking road. Houses were few up here and widely separated. They were white board, with bottled gas tanks standing outside. Once in a while a dog would bark at me. I began singing to myself. The songs were all from Jefferson Airplane. That's why that road and that album always will join in my memory. "It's No Secret," with Marty Balin's voice "jumping up and down." Then, "Today." The twangs, and their echoes. The chords that seemed so primitive even then, compared with what the studios were turning out in 1975. I sang the songs on the first side, in order, then flipped the album in my mind, and sang the songs on the second side. Then I replayed the first side again. Then, the second. The music helped me catch the rhythm for my walk. My strides were long, and the workout felt good. I hadn't walked this long, this big a stretch, the entire trip. I was sweating a bit, but not too much. And, I was hungry, but the hunger hadn't begun to gnaw at me. The road was fairly level, too. It had a slight roll, here and there, but, for the most part, it paralleled a valley I was sure was on the other side of the trees to my right.

It was nearly eleven when the road began to slope downwards. The trees began to thin and, sure enough, to my right was the valley and, in the distance, a small town. My pace increased. If I had not reached Bellefonte, I would find out where I was and go for the interstate accordingly.

I heard tires on the road's surface, approaching me from behind, and, automatically, I turned and held out my thumb. I was surprised the guy stopped. I ran up to the passenger's side and got in. The guy was in his mid-thirties and asked me where I was going. When I said "Bellefonte," he grunted and continued in the same direction. "Not all that far," he added, then said nothing the rest of the trip.

He let me out on the main drag right where Susan and I had been the night before. A cop was directing traffic. He smiled at me and nodded when I sat down on the low wall there. I was thirsty from the beer the night before and long walk of the morning. I began to walk toward the water fountain, but then I glanced across the street and saw a drug store. It was of the old type, and I could barely see the details of a soda fountain. I knew I had to have an iced drink, a coke or something. That was all there was to it. I crossed the street and went in. The lady behind the counter was in her sixties. I expected to get the "oh, no, not another hippie" look from her but, instead, she smiled and asked what she could get for me. While she fixed a large coke to go, I looked around the store. It was crammed full of all sorts of crap. I thought that, maybe, it hadn't changed in a couple of decades. It felt comfortable.

I paid for the drink and noted how low I was getting on money. I went back across the street and sat down again on the wall.

The cop smiled at me again, and I smiled back. The coke tasted really good and wet. I looked up the street and followed it away from the way I had come. It rose up a really steep hill. It was the steepest hill I had ever seen in an inhabited place. And, amazingly, the road clung to it. I could imagine what the road was like during a bad winter. Cars could not make their way up that steep of a grade, of that I was sure. Then I thought of what it would be like to ride a ten-speed down the damn thing. Maxing out at terminal velocity at the bottom. Man, that would be a fast ride.

I finished my coke, walked to a trash can, and tossed the cup away. As I did so, my legs already were stiffening from the walk earlier. I thought about Susan and the rendezvous at noon she would allegedly keep. I realized how stupid it would be to wait for her; although, if she did show up, her paranoia at seeing me here would be worth the wait. I figured I'd walked at least eight miles and lost two or three hours because of her. But then I thought about the morning and how good it felt, and I thought, "Well, fuck it."

I called over to the cop and asked him which way to the interstate. He pointed away from the hill and said, "Three or four miles." I thanked him, shouldered my pack, and started.

The town thinned and, on the road towards the interstate, the buildings so close together gave way to the fast-food joints and small businesses that seem to form on the highways leading out of small towns.

Traffic was light, but I chanced it and held out my thumb. An elderly couple in an LTD gave me a ride to the interstate and, in a brief narrative, told me about how their grandson had just gotten back from hitch hiking to California. They let me off at the combination on-ramp\off-ramp, the two lanes separated by a metal barrier. I thanked them.

An old man was walking past me, a pack slung over his shoulder. He asked me for a cigarette.

"See that hot rod over there?" he said, pointing across the way to a souped-up Chevelle, about a '69, pulling into a McDonald's. "The boy's a sailor going back to his ship. Got me acrosst to here real fast. You going east?" I nodded. "This is where I get off. But be sure to ride with him. Fast. And he's a nice kid." He waved at me as he walked away. "Thanks for the smoke." I watched him walk down the road, away from Bellefonte.

I hadn't long to wait. The Chevelle tooled out of the drive-through. The driver fishtailed it coming out of the drive, gunned it between there and where I stood, and screamed to a stop right in front of me. The red enamel paint job was so shiny it reflected the clouds in the sky, and the fat tires were mounted on Cragar chrome wheels. I opened the door. The guy was in "civvies" and looked to be only about 17 or so.

"Going east?" he yelled.

"Yeah."

"Hop in."

I was barely into my seat when he floored the sucker and we shot up that ramp.

"Where ya going?" he asked.

"Maine."

"From Indiana?" he asked incredulously, looking at my shirt. I nodded. "Jesus. You're traveling pretty far." He laughed. "I'm from Illinois. Heading back to my ship in Jersey. I was running late, but, shit, at this rate, I'll get there, no problems."

I glanced at the speedometer as it passed 100 mph, then came fitfully to rest at 110. I explained to him about the prison guards' strike. Why it was that no state cops were out.

"I knew it had to be something," he said, as though it really made no difference. Running late as he was, he probably would have gone just as fast, cops or no cops.

"You get high?" he asked, his voice loud to be heard over the engine and the wind whipping in the windows.

I shrugged, then nodded. I figured, "Why not? I mean, I have a late start on the day, anyways. I'm not going to get to Maine today. I might as well enjoy myself."

We rolled up our windows and he pulled out a pipe, a butane lighter, and a film canister with some hash in it. "This is pretty good shit," he said as he loaded the bowl. He loaded it pretty full, too, and after we'd killed it, I felt a decent buzz.

He punched in an eight-track tape and cranked the volume. He stowed all the stuff under the seat, and put on his shades. I leaned back and watched the landscape blur by. I'd made Pennsylvania in five rides—two, if you only counted the ones on the interstate, the ones that really mattered. And this ride was going in world's record time.

The music was like I'd never heard before. Rock. Pretty hard rock, in fact. High vocals with a cynical curve to them. I asked him what this was.

"White Witch is the name of the group!" he hollered, turning down the volume for a moment. "Pretty fucking good, huh?"

I said, "Sure," and he cranked the vol again. I looked over at the speedometer just to make sure, and we were still at 110.

We rode that way, just as fast and loud and neither of us talking, all the way to just a few miles shy of the Pennsylvania-New Jersey state line. I explained to him that I needed to get off at the highway that ran along the river there. He hollered, "Okay" and pulled the car over when we got there, and I jumped out. He burned rubber as he pulled away.

I was very hungry. There was a truck stop down an embankment and across the state highway that I had to take. I hopped over the storm fence and walked a couple of

246

hundred yards to the main building. I made a bee-line for the restroom. I locked myself in a stall, my pack and sleeping bag wedged between my knee and the wall, and took the biggest shit of my life. Once I was done, I went over to the sinks and washed and brushed my hair, brushed my teeth, washed my face and changed socks. I felt like a new person.

I sat down in a booth after I'd grabbed a newspaper from one of the vending machines. With so many trucks parked outside, I was surprised to see so few people in the place. But I really didn't care. I'd turned pretty mellow by now and, besides, the day was getting very beautiful. Sun streamed in the plate-glass windows that ran, floor-to-ceiling, something like 20 feet up.

The waitress came and set down a menu. When I looked up at her, I was struck by how beautiful she was. Her hair was long and straight and black, and she wore a bandanna. She smiled when she said, "Coffee?" I shook my head and said, "Tea." She nodded and walked away.

I looked over the menu for the most food, volume-wise, that I could get for the buck. The words "Roast Beef Manhattan" stared up at me, and that was my pick. When she came back I ordered that, and a large coke to go with it. I watched her as she walked back to the kitchen. She looked over her shoulder and caught me watching her and winked.

I had only glanced at the paper when she came to the booth and sat opposite me.

"Where you going?" she asked, a whimsical smile on her face.

"Maine," I said, putting down my paper and smiling back.

"You from Indiana?" she asked, gesturing toward my shirt with a nod of her head.

"Yes, I am. Started out from there—geez, day before yesterday," I replied.

"I had two friends who hitched all over," she told me. "Florida, across to California, up to Oregon."

I guessed her age as about my own, maybe a little younger. Her eyes were dark.

"I always wanted to do that," she continued. "I mean, travel."

"It's dangerous to thumb."

"Oh, yeah," she said. "I know that. Especially for a woman. Shit. I'd never do that." She was very rational, I could tell that. But she still dreamed. "I mean I want to travel. Well, get the fuck out of here, anyway." She chuckled.

We talked for a while. She was just out of high school and had taken this job in order to move from her parents' house. She wanted to go to school, she said.

"But my parents never went beyond...hell, my mother quit at ninth grade, and Dad after his junior year. They're against education, period, but especially for a 'girl.' We're supposed to do the usual crap. Stay in the kitchen. Barefoot. Have babies. Yeah!" She shook her head in an exaggerated way, and I had to laugh.

"I've noticed there are plenty of state schools in Pennsylvania," I told her. "You can try for financial aid. All that good stuff."

"Yeah, I know," she said. "I applied to a couple of places. Been accepted. Just waiting for word on the money. Christ, but I want fucking out of here."

A counter bell rang twice and she got up, saying, "Your order, sir," in a tone of mock courtesy. When she came back, she sat down again and we continued to talk. I wished I was staying here. She was so marvelous. Intelligent and strong and pretty. As she described "life around here" and what she wanted to do, especially in the way of going to school, I thought about DeForrest. She would have jumped at that opportunity, and here I had pissed it away. But there were reasons, I told myself, good reasons. Besides, ever since I'd gotten away from there, DeForrest had begun to fade. It wasn't pressing in on me.

I quickly was finished with my meal. I'd been so famished I'd practically inhaled the goddamn thing. I'd listened to her, perhaps, now and then, nodding or interjecting some sort of sound of agreement. As soon as I'd finished, she scooped up the plate and utensils and took them to a bus tub. She gave me the check and said, "Don't worry about a tip. I know your money's gotta be tight. It's about to rain, so you'd better get moving."

I glanced out the windows, and she was right. While I'd sat there, mesmerized by her, the sky had clouded over, filling the huge ceiling-to-floor panes with darkness. I thanked her and grabbed my stuff and the check. When I paid at the register, she took my money, squeezed my hand, gave me a wink and wished me luck.

I walked out of the place in a fog. I still could smell her perfume as I headed through the diesel fumes and across the oil-stained parking lot. I looked over my shoulder a couple of times, but I couldn't see her.

I got to the state highway, then lit up a cigarette. The clouds were moving fast, and the breeze had picked up. I wondered if I'd get a ride at all. If all else failed, I realized, I could go back there and talk with her. Then I realized that she hadn't even told me her name. Shit!

An old delivery truck pulled up. It was a step-van, the kind bakeries use. Tall and box-like and old, it had been re-painted and done over. Instead of metal doors, this vehicle had a wooden door from an old house. The door was weather-beaten and what little paint that was on it had been there for some time. The huge, square pane of glass in its top half gave the driver enough visibility for dealing with traffic.

I turned the knob—an odd feeling for the door to a vehicle—and the door swung open. I climbed the first couple of steps and closed the door behind me.

The driver was in his early 20s, and his hair fell well past his shoulders. He smiled, and we shook hands. I turned and looked behind the thin curtain of beads that hung from behind the only seat and saw that he'd made up the back like an apartment.

"Name's Randy," he said. "How far ya going?"

"Maine," I said, "but, I want to take this state road up to I-84 and across."

"No sweat on that," he said. He glanced at the sweatshirt. "You really from Indiana?"

"Yeah," I said, leaning against what passed as a dashboard, my back to oncoming traffic.

"That's a long ways," he said, shaking his head. "You get high?"

"Yeah, sure," I said. Oh hell, I thought, why the fuck not? I'd gotten high a couple of times so far. I'd found that something about the stress and tension of being out here, of hanging my ass on the line, prevented the buzz from gripping hold of me too hard. It just cut me some slack was all. Let me relax a little bit.

He lit up a joint and passed it to me. He explained that he was into environmental issues. I nodded and went along with him. Hell, I agreed with anyone who did that.

He interrupted me with a knowing chuckle.

"That's not what I mean," he said.

"Huh?"

"Ever read anything by Edward Abbey?" I told him that I hadn't. So he told me about Abbey. He'd written several books, and among them was *The Monkey Wrench Gang*. Abbey always had been an environmentalist with a bit of a "mean" streak in him. He didn't like to let the "powers that be" rape the land and move on. He believed that people should fight back. "*The Monkey Wrench Gang* is about that," he said. "These people get fed up with the way things are run. They chain-saw down advertising signs for fun. Pour sugar into the fuel tanks of earth-moving equipment. That's kind of what I do."

248

"You just travel around and do that?" I asked, handing him what was left of a roach, which had burnt out. He nodded in response to my question, took the roach, and placed it in a film canister. "How do you manage to support yourself?"

"Odd jobs. I'm a finish carpenter, and there's always work around for people with skill. Sometimes I go on welfare when I have to. But, really, my lifestyle isn't very expensive. I mean, this van is my home, and it doesn't cost much to maintain. I do all the maintenance on it myself. Gas isn't too bad. I carry enough dried food back there for a few weeks. I mean, I'm a vegetarian, so that helps." He chuckled again.

He seemed very happy as he described where he'd been in Pennsylvania. A housing development was going in someplace, and he and several others had met there and sugared gas tanks and "spiked" trees.

"We drive spikes into the trees they're going to harvest for lumber; when they cut them up at the sawmill, the blades of the saws will hit the spikes and break." He went on and on like that. We rode together up the state highway, past pretty, tree-laden hills. I got the sense that I was riding with a person of those woods who was trying as best he might to defend them.

As we neared 84, I thanked him for the ride and explained that I'd be getting out there.

"Just be careful," he said. "New York cops are pricks, but the cops in Connecticut are fucking pigs."

"Thanks, I appreciate that."

"No, I mean," he said in emphasis, "if a Connecticut cop stops you, you might get beaten up just for the fuck of it. If they start that, cover the back of your head and your kidneys." He tried to demonstrate while steering the van with his right knee. Placing both hands on the wheel again, he added, "Curl up in a ball, and you"ll protect your crotch that way. Please, be careful of those fuckers."

I thanked him again and hopped out of the van. I walked a short ways up the on-ramp, then turned and waved to him. He waved back and gunned the engine, then he was gone.

It was late afternoon. I was fed, but I was tired and buzzed, too. I could have used a nap. But there wasn't any place to take one and, besides, I had to travel. Traffic was light. The sky had cleared up again, and the sun began to warm. The air was very humid. My bag sat on the ground at my feet. I lit the first cigarette I'd had since after my meal. A light breeze carried the smoke away gently. I had no idea how far I'd traveled, but I knew it was a long ways—from west central Indiana to the Pennsylvania-New York state line. Not too shabby.

Only a few cars passed me. There was no animosity in the looks I got—when I did get looks from them—from the occupants. I caught glances. Curiosity. Simple recognition of my presence.

I glanced at my watch. I'd been standing there for 20 minutes. This was about the longest wait for a ride since that fucking little place in Michigan. I reached into my pocket and pulled out another cigarette and lit it. I felt lonely all of a sudden. Here I was, a single entity, standing next to the highway, the interstate. To the people driving by me, I had no name. I was just a hitch hiker. But I was special. I was to me, anyway. I had friends, a past, interests. I thought of the girl in the truck stop a while ago. I'd been special to her. Yes, a hitch hiker, but someone to whom she could tell her hopes.

But then I wondered about that. After all, she wasn't telling me those things because of who I was as an individual. Me, soon-to-be former college student. A kid who still had his virginity intact. A debater who read a lot. A person who'd painted day-glo graffiti on the walls and ceiling of his room and let his friends do the same. No, she'd confided in the Hitchhiker. I played a role in that regard.

Now, I was terribly lonely. I wanted to go back. But to what? All the crap that had been going on there? The debts. And now, having bagged finals, I had flunked out, too. I couldn't go back there. I'd catch so much shit from people.

I lit another cigarette. It was the first time in quite a while I'd chained like that, lighting one off of the other. I wished I was in love, and that a woman loved me in return. Then I thought, oh great, try to shove responsibility for my own existence onto another human being. That makes a lot of sense. But again, I thought, what's wrong with being in love and loving someone in return? Nothing, I countered, so long as the love is genuine and you're not just placing someone in a role. Not like what had happened already today to me.

I chuckled as I flipped away the cigarette. Deep thoughts or not, right or wrong, I was certainly high.

A medium-sized Ford pulled up, and the passenger's side door swung open. I jumped in. The guy was on his way to work. We pulled onto the interstate, then we crossed the Delaware River. I was now in New York. The course I'd plotted gave me the shortest trip possible across this state. The guy told me he was only going a few stops. He wasn't talkative after that. But hell, he was giving me a ride, so who cared? I hadn't forgotten about Rockwood, Michigan. If I had to one- and two-exit hop my way across New York, then that was fine with me. So long as I got across the state without getting fucking arrested.

As we pulled off the exit, I saw National Guard personnel signaling members of a convoy. The personnel were at the top of the exit we were taking, and they waved at us as we passed them. I returned the wave, although my ride didn't. He let me out at the bottom of the ramp. I thanked him, and he grunted in reply.

I walked up the on-ramp about 20 yards and stood there. The afternoon sun was low in the sky, and I felt very warm.

The rides had become so goddamn slow! I stood there for 15 minutes with absolutely no cars having driven past. I could see why people from New York always seemed like such assholes. I'd only been here for less than an hour and I was impatient, frustrated, and sweating. To top it all off, I was almost out of cigarettes. The only vehicles going through the goddamn intersection at all were from the National Guard.

Up on the interstate, of course, things were different. Traffic wasn't heavy, but it was steady and moving in a good flow. I debated going up there. I'd avoided everything but the ramps to this point in order to avoid any hassles with the cops. But now I was getting pissed off. In New York, of all places, the one place in which I did not want to be stuck, there was every possibility in the world that I would be standing out here for hours. Of course, if I stood up on the interstate, the cops would nail me right there. Then I remembered Rockwood. The cops cruising by so many times. Having to hide in the little stand of trees. Sleeping next to the ditch. Hell, I could get arrested if I stood here for very much longer. Besides, I thought, as I looked up the ramp at the National Guard people up there, I could tell the cops, if they pulled over to question me, that, somehow, I was with those guys. Yeah, right. Hair down past my shoulders and all and I'm with the National Guard. Sure. Like I wasn't stoned.

I walked back up the off-ramp and said, "Hi" to the National Guard people. Three or four of them were directing trucks of a convoy off the interstate and down the ramp. I stood a short distance past them. There was still a shoulder there, so a car could pull over for me.

Almost immediately a state cop car went by. I couldn't tell if he'd seen me or not, but I said, "Fuck!" under my breath. Cars continued to go by, and my skin wasn't so much exuding sweat as crawling in agony. Another state cop went by, and now I was sure I'd get busted. My mind went back to Rockwood and the first two passes by the cops there. Third time's a charm. I had a bad feeling it would be here, too. I'd never been in jail and didn't want that experience now.

A red Ford pick-up truck pulled onto the shoulder just past me and stopped. I picked up my pack and ran, jumped in, and we were off. Man, I was never so happy in all my life. His name was Chuck. I never thought about the possibility of there being rednecks in the East. But here he was, driving a red pick-up truck, complete with rifle rack and the sliding back window for when the camper shell was on the bed. He was about 40, and his mutton-chop sideburns were full and long and a shade darker than his blond hair.

"How far ya headed?" he asked as he lit up a cigarette.

I glanced over my shoulder and, gratefully, watched the National Guard people disappear, along with that fucking exit, as we descended the crest of the bridge. Turning back around, I said, "Maine."

This response no longer seemed to bring surprise from people. "Where ya from?" he asked.

"Indiana."

"Whoo-ee," he said. "Long ways to be thumbing."

"A few miles."

"Well, I'm going to a race track just the other side of Hartford. Is it on your route?"

I instantly remembered the cities along the way I'd traced in the Porsche—what, only yesterday?

"It sure is," I told him.

"Then we're all set." He smiled and we moved right along. The truck was a three-quarter ton, and the shift was on the floor with a long stick instead of on the column. The engine had to be pretty good size, considering the truck's cargo capacity, but I had the idea that, maybe, it was even more souped-up than the usual three-quarter ton.

"What kinda horses ya gonna watch?" I asked.

He looked at me a moment, as if he hadn't heard right, and then he started laughing. "Horsepower, maybe, but not horses. Gonna watch the midgets race tonight."

A gear head.

"You live in New York?"

"No, not too far from the track. But, I had to deliver some parts to a guy in Port Jervis. I own a parts store, and we handle a lot of special parts for race cars. Not Indy-type." His eyes grew a little wide. "Oh, hey, I mean, you're from Indiana. You're probably used to seeing all them big boys. But I just sell to the small fry. You know, guys who race figure-8? I sell them Bondo mainly. The things I do get into are modifieds and midgets. A few sprints. I sell regular parts, too. But, when I get an order for parts like these is when I deliver as far as I just did." He paused. "So, ever been to the '500'?"

I shook my head. "Just listened to it on the radio." People in Kilkerry took it for granted.

Chuck seemed genuinely disappointed. "Shit. You live that close and you've never seen it?" All I did was shrug. "That's one thing I've always wanted to see, is the '500.'

Watch it every year out here on TV. Have a party for it. Yep. Tomorrow we'll have plenty of food and beer and kick back all day to watch it."

I stopped and looked at him. "The '500's' on TV.?"

"Yeah. Why? Oh." He smiled. "It's blacked out where you're from. No wonder. Shit, I've seen more '500's' than a guy from Indiana." He got a chuckle out of that, and it didn't piss me off. I mean, it was good-natured. All I knew was that a major event, the "500," held only 50 miles from where I lived, and something I didn't think that anybody saw on TV, was broadcast live for all the rest of the World. It was as if Indiana was rendered blind for a few hours every year, closing her eyes and turning her head while the World peered inside of her. I'd forgotten that it was tomorrow. That fact had just blown my mind.

We were moving along at a pretty good clip, between 65 and 70. We held steady, but then Chuck would talk and we'd either slow down or speed up. New York was moving by us so fast, that the approach of the state line a half-mile or so in front of us took me by surprise. But we passed over it, and New York and the paranoia I'd felt there were now behind me. But as soon as we were across the line, I heard the engine rev down.

"Gotta watch our speed here," Chuck said. "These state fuckers are bastards."

"Worse than New York?"

He made a grimace as if he'd caught whiff of a bad smell. "New York cops are not bad. Don't give them any lip, they leave you alone. These Connecticut fuckers have a hard-on for the world. They'll fuck with you if they're bored and nothing's going on. Ask them a question, they'll run you in." He watched my expression. Maybe he thought I believed he was exaggerating. "Let me show you," he said, to prove a point. "Watch. Just up ahead. See that overpass? The clump of trees just beyond it. Look back in there as we go by."

We went through the overpass. When we shot past the trees, I looked back in. There was a little driveway, around which trees had been planted. A cop sat back there, his radar gun up on the dash.

"Reminds you of bass sitting back in the weeds, waiting for little fish to go by," Chuck said. "They got them places all along the interstate. Hit people like crazy. And they're assholes, too. One thing you don't want to do in this state is stand up on the interstate like you were back there in New York. Standing on the ramp's bad enough, but these guys'll bust you, beat the living shit out of you, then charge you with resisting arrest."

He shook his head, then asked me what I was going to do in Maine. I explained that I had a buddy up there. It seemed like a good idea to add that I was going up there to his wedding. I mean, I wasn't sure of when the date was, but it sounded like a plausible reason for this long trek, rather than to say to this guy Chuck that I'd freaked out with life in general and school in particular and that I wanted to get the fuck out of there.

"Must be a pretty good buddy," Chuck observed appreciatively.

We rode on. Chuck told me about some of the race cars he'd owned, some he'd built, and some he'd worked on. We came to Hartford. The interstate went through and over the outlying areas. Then it plunged right through downtown. It was a city with a great skyline, and I'd never before looked at a city in quite that way before. The older buildings were probably called "skyscrapers" when they were first built 50 or 60 years before in imitation of the buildings of New York. But, while the old buildings were quite short next to their new kin, there was an elegance to the brick and stone that the newer structures lacked. Yet all of the buildings stood together, making up one mass, glowing in the slanted rays as the sun began to set.

We were soon out of Hartford, and Chuck told me that his exit was a few miles ahead.

"Not a lot of traffic there," he said. "But you can take the state road there. Go across east. It kinda meanders, but you'll hit 86. Really, I shoulda let you off back there, cause you'll save time on 86. It angles more across and up to Massachusetts."

It made sense to me. So we rolled off of the interstate and headed east a couple of miles. A small billboard, hand-painted, the paint beginning to peel, pointed and said, "Speedway." It gave information about the times and types of the Saturday night races. I got out. Chuck wished me luck and drove off.

It was now getting dark, and the air was turning a bit chilly. I'd long since run out of cigarettes. The place in New York had not been lively. This place was dead. I was on a state highway, a "side road," in the dark, in a sparsely populated area with no traffic. My outlook was getting dismal again. I didn't even wait to get pissed off. I picked up my stuff and walked back in the direction I'd come. My legs were stiff from the morning's long march, but soon they were loosening up. Hell, I had no choice. Even if I'd pulled something, I had to get out of there. It was as if I could sense the eyes of the fucking cops, seeing infrared, in the darkness all around me. The paranoia was back, and it was worse than it had been in New York. I was fed up with this whole business. I just wanted to get across the next state line.

The real pain wasn't in my legs, but in my shoulder. The single modified strap that was carrying all of the weight of my pack was scraping into whichever shoulder I had it around. My right shoulder had borne the load the greater number of times. I stopped under a road light and dropped the pack to the ground, then drew back my sweatshirt so I could see the sore area. A red welt had raised up there. I was glad I hadn't had to carry the goddamn pack more often since the walk that morning. All I'd done, basically, was ride. So, I put the strap over my left shoulder and held it with my left hand, making a cushion as I did so.

It was a couple of miles to the interstate but, finally, I was there. Even though this place wasn't very far outside of Hartford, it still seemed pretty desolate. I said, "fuck it," and walked up the ramp. I took my place at the side of the interstate, figuring if the cops busted me, I'd get a place to sleep for the night. But a car stopped, and I got a ride with a businessman who was going to Springfield, Massachusetts. In miles, that wasn't very far. It did, however, get me the fuck out of Connecticut. Made that state in two rides. I chuckled as we went by the last clump of trees, behind which sat a cop.

The businessman wasn't necessarily drunk. But, I could smell booze, and he certainly wasn't very talkative. I really didn't care. I was happy to be moving. What I did care about was where he dropped me off. I wanted to get to an on-ramp for the Massachusetts Turnpike. He let me out on a single-lane elevated ramp. I mean, I was four stories up in the air with traffic going by me at 60 miles per and only about a three-foot "shoulder" area in which to stand. Traffic wasn't all that heavy—hell, it was getting onto nine o-clock—but, it was fast enough and the ramp was narrow enough that I didn't want to move.

I stood there for about five minutes, and then a Cadillac slammed on its brakes and stopped just past me. I was in that car in two seconds, and we were moving again.

"What the fuck d'you think you're doing out there, boy?" the driver asked. He was black and into the Superfly look—white hat with a wide brim, rings on the fingers of the hand on the wheel. The woman in the passenger's side was white and very attractive. Her perfume filled the car. His tone was abrupt, but not unfriendly.

I explained about my last ride and how I was trying to get to the Massachusetts Turnpike. That my destination was Maine.

"We're only going two stops up here, and then I can come back around for you. Get you further along. Right now I gotta get my lady to a party. Ya know?"

I nodded as she giggled. He smiled at her, and from the motion of his shoulder, I think that he squeezed her hand, or he squeezed something. The look that passed between them wasn't one of love. Not like any I'd seen before. Except, maybe, the love of a dog for its master. She seemed happy for his attention.

"I wouldn't normally pick up hitch hikers," he said as we rolled to a stop. "But I thought you coulda been killed out there. And, you seem like a nice kid. Once I take care of my lady's business, I'll be back around. If you're still here, I'll give you a ride."

I thanked him, dutifully, and got out. The car pulled away. I hadn't noticed that the rear window was made over with the same material as the body of the car so only a small diamond-shaped cut-out remained.

I was there only a few moments, and a VW microbus pulled up. The side doors opened, and I jumped in. Two guys were up front. Another was in back of me. They all had long hair. The back was nearly full of musical equipment—amps painted flat black, mike stands, guitar cases.

"How ya doing?" the driver asked. I said, "Okay." The guy in the passenger's seat asked me where I was headed, and I said, "Maine."

"Man," he said to the other two. "This must be the first of the season."

The guy next to me said, "A lot of people thumb up to Maine in the summer. You're the first one this year we've given a lift to that's going there."

"Going across to 95?" the driver asked.

When I said, "Yes," the guy in the passenger's seat said, "Don't get on the fucking turnpike. Massachusetts cops are pretty cool, mostly. But, they don't like hitch hikers up on that fucking turnpike."

"Yeah," the driver said. "You stay on the ramps, you'll be okay."

There was a pause, then I asked, "You guys musicians? I mean, it's kind of difficult to miss."

They laughed a little, and the guy beside me said, "Yeah, we just did a gig last night, and we're picking up our stuff."

"What kind of music do you play?"

He shrugged. "Rock and roll."

The other two broke out in laughter, and he joined them. I didn't see the joke, but I guessed it was a joke of long standing between them.

"Old rock and roll," the driver said, looking back at me in the mirror.

I remembered that morning (was it only that morning?) walking along that road in Pennsylvania, humming and singing the songs of JA to myself. I told them about that.

The driver said, "Nobody listens to that stuff anymore." The comment wasn't meant as a put-down. It was just an observation. But there was a finality to it.

The guy next to me said, "Apparently, there are people who are still listening to JA."

"Yeah," the driver said. "Like there are still people running around doing LSD."

I interrupted at that point with a couple of comments about the acid we had done that year. The three of them looked at me like I'd come from another planet or stepped out of a time machine. Then the driver took the next exit, and I was dropped off at Palmer, Massachusetts.

254

It was now close to 11 at night, and I was standing next to the approach lanes for a toll booth just outside a small town in Massachusetts. I was exhausted. But I was so exhausted all I wanted to do was press on. Get to Maine. Goddamn it, I was in Massachusetts. I was all the way to the East fucking Coast! I didn't know how many miles I'd gone, but I knew they were quite a few. I wanted to get more behind me.

There was absolutely no traffic there. Between 11 p.m. and 1 a.m., two cars got onto the Massachusetts Turnpike at Palmer. I happened to glance up the hillside. I don't know how I missed it, but there was a billboard with the Tampax logo, billing Palmer as "The Tampon Capital of the World." Having sat there for so long at that point, I could get a feel for why the place promoted itself that way. It had absorbed all of my energy. I was becoming too tired to even think.

The toll booth was only 20 yards or so away. Every once in a while, the guy there would glance my way, and I would glance over at him. But, although we were close enough to each other to speak without raising our voices, neither of us initiated a conversation. I sat down on the guardrail. My head was dropping to my chest every five minutes or so. I realized if I was going to get any sleep, now would be the best time for it. I looked over my shoulder and saw that the slope behind me was heavily wooded. I checked the guy at the toll booth. His feet were propped up on the counter and he was reading a book. A thermos of coffee was next to his propped-up feet. I could see steam rising from the cup. He had a cigarette, too, and I realized I hadn't had one of those in several hours. But his back was to me, so I grabbed my pack, swung my feet over the guard rail, and moved as quietly as I could down the hillside. I didn't know why, exactly, but I had the feeling I didn't want the toll booth guy to know where I was: incipient paranoia. I kept checking over my shoulder, and when I could see no details beyond the trunks and branches and leaves of the trees, I figured that no one with a flashlight could see me from the roadway, so I was safe. I spread out my sleeping bag and kicked off my shoes. I climbed inside, again using my pack for a pillow. Almost immediately a swarm of mosquitoes descended upon me. I figured I was near a drainage ditch. I withdrew completely into the sleeping bag, pulling the opening closed behind me. It was hot that way, and more than a little stuffy, but I was so tired I didn't care. Somehow, I fell asleep, the central dynamics of that sleep being rest, and an effort to keep the fucking flap shut.

Chapter 39 - Day Four

It wasn't so much that I woke up, as I refused to fight mosquitoes anymore. I quickly got up, rolled up my sleeping bag, secured it to the pack, and moved up the hillside.

I peeked through the branches toward the toll booth. The guy was still seated there in the same position, as if he hadn't moved in the four hours or so since I jumped over the rail. I jumped back over and took the same position I had earlier. It took him about five minutes to glance my way, but when he did, I saw surprise on his face. Yes, you are in the "Twilight Zone."

I knew I had to be smelly from all of the sweat from the morning, the afternoon, and lying in that goddamn sleeping bag for the last four hours. I felt pretty raunchy. I wanted to wash up, change clothes, the whole bit.

There was a gas station about 50 yards or so away, back at the corner of the approach to the toll booths and the road that ran into the town. It had been closed ever since I'd been there. But I wondered if the bathroom was unlocked. If it was, then I could clean up in there.

Again, I had the feeling that I didn't want the toll booth guy to know what I was doing, but I had to cross 50 yards or so of pavement. I didn't want to do so furtively, as if I were breaking into the place or something. I figured the best way to go over there would be in a calm, unhurried walk, not looking back for any reaction from the guy. If I made it, fine. If I didn't, well, I tried. Besides, all that I was going to do was wash up.

The door to the men's bathroom was unlocked. As I went in, I shot a glance at the toll booth, and the guy still had his feet up, reading. It didn't look as if he'd seen anything.

I stripped down and used one of my washcloths, fully lathered up with soap to wash all over. Armpits, crotch, legs—the first time I'd "bathed" in three days. I knew the job I was doing was inadequate, as compared to a regular shower, but it was better than smelling like a goat. The real pain was trying to wash my hair in the tiny sink. It took a while, and I hit my head on the faucet a couple of times and had to ignore, only fractions of an inch from my face, the filthy porcelain and the crud that was ground into the glaze by hundreds of travelers before me. But, finally, my scalp tingled, and I could smell the scent of the shampoo instead of hair oil. I even shaved and put on clean clothes. The I.U. sweatshirt was pretty rank at this point. I had another one, a blue one, and I put that on. Once I'd brushed my teeth and secured my gear, feeling completely renewed, I turned off the light and walked out of the bathroom.

There, about ten feet from the doorway with its headlights shining right on me, was a cop car. I sort of froze for a second, then I figured I might as well talk with him. At the very worst, I was going to jail anyway. I might as well make every effort in the meantime to bullshit my way out of that trip.

"Morning, officer," I said, ambling over to the driver's side. He was by himself. No partner. I didn't know what that meant. He was younger. About 30 or so. He looked intelligent. My hopes began to rise.

"That gas station's closed," he said, his voice sounding very reasonable, and very thick with an East Coast accent.

"I know," I answered, reaching for my wallet. I thought I'd stay a little ahead of things. Make everything more efficient. Pull out my I.D. before he asked. "But the restroom was open. I had to clean up."

He took the I.D. and looked at my wet hair. I was thankful that I didn't have a blow dryer along. He looked at the I.D.—I.D.s, rather. I'd given him both my Indiana driver's license and my DeForrest student I.D. Work into that cliche: "College student hitch hiking."

"Where you headed?" he asked.

"Maine. Loring Air Force Base."

He looked at the wet hair hanging past my shoulders. "You're not in the Air Force."

"No, but a buddy of mine is. He's getting married tomorrow." And there was an element of urgency to it all. He was getting married tomorrow.

The cop looked over at the toll booth and waved. The guy was watching us and returned the wave.

"You been here quite a time," the cop observed. I knew now how the cop had known to come there.

"Yeah," I admitted. "But I'm stuck here, officer. Everybody I've talked with has said not to thumb on the turnpike. Or else I would."

"No," he agreed, handing back my I.D. "You don't want to do that. The state police will arrest you."

"Well," I reasoned, "I'm stuck here, then." In the Tampon Capital of the World, I didn't add.

"Traffic won't pick up here until 10 or 11 this morning," the cop said. "You're not going to get any rides until then."

I knew he meant the traffic at this spot. I just shrugged and looked bewildered. I didn't know what he was trying to tell me.

He jerked his thumb toward the passenger's side and said, "Get in." I didn't let him hear me, but as I walked around the front of the car, I said, "Shit." It had finally happened. I was busted. I tossed my stuff onto the floor there in front and climbed in.

"I'll tell you what," he said, backing up, and turning the car around. "I'll give you a ride out of town on U.S. 20. There's not a hell of a lot of traffic this time of day. But, it's a straight shot into Boston. And, I can almost guarantee you'll get a ride." Huh? A cop giving me a ride to a better spot from which to thumb? This was too odd. I liked Massachusetts all of a sudden. He asked me about where I was from. What the area was like. How long I'd been thumbing this trip. From the tone of his voice and his questions, I could tell he assumed this was all old hat for me. I didn't disabuse him of that notion.

As we cruised through the modest "downtown," I thought I'd caught a glimpse of pot plants growing in someone's yard. Oh, well, this place was so cool nothing would surprise me.

There in the darkness on the eastern edge of town, he let me out. As he did a 180 and pulled away, I wondered how the fuck I was going to get a ride. It seemed dead as shit. I mean, at least near the toll booth there were lights. But not five minutes later, headlights appeared from town. A Ford Pinto stopped next to me and I got in.

The guy was short and fat and bald. And he had the most complex radio equipment I've ever seen in my life built into his console there. That was how I got the ride. I could imagine the cop radioing, "Anybody out there wanta get a hitch hiker out of my hair?" The guy was more intent on listening to the radio than on talking with me. So, I rode ten miles or so. U.S. 20 was a straight shot to Boston. Just like U.S. 40, it was one of those old highways rendered obsolete by the interstate system. Every now and then we passed what once were prospering, family-owned motels, now gone to seed, or converted to apartments.

As the sky began to brighten, he pulled over and let me out. Just gave me a mild wave of good luck. Didn't say a word. Then turned a 180 on the deserted highway and headed back to Palmer.

I looked around. Sure. Maybe I wasn't next to that goddamn exit any more, but this was a good deal worse, it appeared to me. The main traffic was on the turnpike. This was out in the middle of nowhere. I was at the crossroads of an obsolete U.S. highway and a narrow, two-lane state highway.

The sky got brighter. A Triumph Spitfire rolled up to the stop sign. When the driver saw me standing there with my thumb out, he beeped the horn twice. I grabbed my stuff, ran across the road and got in, jamming the pack into the crammed floor space and my body into the bucket seat.

We took off, and he introduced himself as Gil. He said I was lucky, because there was no traffic on this road. Especially on Sundays. I told him what the cop had done and said. He just listened and nodded.

"Where you going?" he asked. Again, I noticed, the accent was thick. When I told him, he automatically asked where I was from. When I said, "Indiana," he said, "Shit. That's one hell of a long ways." After a few moments, he said, "You must be taking 95 out of Boston north, huh?" I nodded. "Well, I can get you to Boston, no problem." He turned onto another interstate, 86, for a couple of miles. We got to the turnpike and he got a card from the person in the booth, and then we were off again.

The sun had now broken the horizon and I could tell the day was going to be beautiful. Gil switched on the radio. The radio wasn't a regular AM-FM, but a shortwave. We listened to the BBC as we cut along the turnpike. There was very little traffic. The top of the little convertible was up, but our windows were both down, and the air felt cool and good as it whipped in. We rode like that all the way to Boston, where we ran into I-95. This was my way north. Gil swung off the interstate and through the toll area. After he paid, I told him to let me off somewhere near the interstate, if he could. I needed to hit a store. A few minutes later, I was standing on the on-ramp to I-95, smoking my first cigarette in quite a while. That rush of nicotine felt good. I only had time to smoke that one, and then a carload of high school girls—they told me that it was senior week and that they had had an all-nighter—gave me a lift two exits. I got out and walked up the on-ramp. I only stood there a few minutes when a college kid in a VW bug game me a lift for a couple more exits.

I was moving around Boston at a pretty good clip. I smoked another cigarette and waited. I was confident now. Things were going well. The car was a white 240Z. The driver braked and pulled onto the shoulder. Before I caught up to the car, the driver was out and opening the hatchback. The back area was crammed with all sorts of stuff. He was going on vacation. He grabbed my pack and pressed it into the mass of things back there, as though joining one small piece of clay to a much larger mass of the stuff. He introduced himself as Steve, and we shook hands. By the time we got into the car, I hadn't seen the left side of his face and head.

We took off fast. There was a weird-looking box on his dashboard. It was black, had a green and a yellow light, neither of which was on, a level meter of some sort, and a couple of switches. A wire ran from the back of the thing down to where the cigarette lighter had been.

"You do cocaine?" Steve more or less yelled over the engine and the noise whipping in the open windows.

A guy who had sat behind me the previous semester did it and sold it, and a couple of guys I knew had tried it, but not gotten off. I'd never done it, because I'd heard that if you got to like it, you would really like it to the exclusion of all else. Right now, though, I was on the interstate, going to Maine.

"Sure," I replied, wondering, with the wind as strong as it was, how he was going to cut the delicate stuff into a line, like I'd watched people do before.

He pulled out a metal cylinder, about three inches long, with a finish of stainless steel. There were two openings. Steve demonstrated how to use the thing by putting his nose to one of the openings, pressing a button and sniffing. He handed it to me, proffering the other end. I imitated what he'd done, and coke shot up first one nostril, then the other. I was struck by its medicinal flavor. I handed the thing back to him and sniffed a few times, trying to get all the powder out of my nostrils.

"How far ya going?" he asked. The accent was there, but not as pronounced.

"Maine," I said, now quite used to the drill.

"Whereabouts in Maine?"

"Caribou," I said. "I'm going to see a buddy at Loring Air Force Base." I was trying to detect any change in metabolism or perception that the cocaine had caused. So far, I could detect neither.

"You're in luck," he said. "I'm going about a hundred miles south of there. I'm going to Medway."

I'd never heard of Medway before, but I was happy to hear I'd be within a hundred miles. Shit! This was going to be one hell of a long ride, my longest of the trip.

He began pawing cassettes piled in the recessed area of the console. He finally selected one and put it in. He had to crank the volume so we could hear the music over the noise.

"You from Indiana?" he asked.

"Yeah."

"How long ago'd you leave?"

"Three days ago," I said, not bothering to add that it seemed like three years.

"I been out there a few times to the '500.' You know, they're running it today." I told him that, yeah, I knew that. "Went out there when I owned the motorcycle shop." At that, I looked at him and thought, yeah, sounds plausible. "Mainly sold weird foreign makes. Nortons, Triumphs, BSAs, BMWs. Attracted clientele with a lot of money and weird tastes. Boston's like that. So we were all gear heads and made the '500' for a few years. You ever go?" I told him no. Then he went on to describe how his business in cycles had boomed, then he'd finally sold out for a "nice chunk of change." He cranked up the stereo even louder. The guitar was amazingly fast. At the end of the long solo, he turned it back down.

"You going on vacation up there?" I asked him.

"No," he said, lighting a cigarette. That seemed like a good idea, so I reached for my smokes and pulled one out. "I own a cabin up there. On a little lake about 20 miles from anywhere. Out in the woods. I take off like this every few weeks for a few days at a time. Capitalism's a great system if you can manipulate it."

This last part sounded rather odd. But, if what he said was true, he'd been able to do just that.

By now, we were off the beltway around Boston and heading straight up 95 to Maine. Riding along, I saw three or four other hitch hikers, one here, one there, etc., with packs and holding cardboard signs on which, in various inks and writing styles, was always the word, "Maine."

"A lot of people heading up there," I commented.

"Yeah," Steve agreed. "It's great up there. I've been going there since I was a kid. Owned this cabin now for a little over four years. Bought it at an estate sale. Doctor and his wife. Doctor died and the wife had always hated it. Bid went real low, but she wanted to get rid of it, so it was mine for...a...song." Each of the last three words was pronounced distinctly, followed by a pause. He described the lake, and the way the water looked at dawn. How sometimes a moose would come out then, and swim out into the water. What it was like to see one munching on grasses at the shore line, knee-deep in water, its reflection showing. It seemed that the word "moose" should be capitalized. The animal was so majestic as to deserve that.

We were flying along. When I glanced at the speedometer, I saw that the needle was holding at 85. I didn't say anything. That was part of the etiquette. If someone gives you a ride, you don't criticize that person's driving. Besides, he seemed to be in control. The main concern I had was that we would get stopped and searched, and the cops would find the cocaine. But, I was only a hitch hiker, right? Still, at that speed, 30 miles per hour over the limit, it was certainly possible we could get stopped. We entered New Hampshire and sped on. Steve was talking about the miles we would cover and how I'd lucked out on this ride when the yellow light on the black box came on and a loud buzz started from it. In a split second, Steve hit the brakes and the car lurched from 85 to 60.

He looked at me and saw my expression. "Radar detector," he told me, indicating the box. "Ever seen one?" I shook my head. "Better than a CB. See?" As we topped the crest in the highway, we could see the cop parked on the crossover of the median. I glanced at the box and saw that the green light was now on. As we passed the cop, I saw that he was already looking behind us at the crest, his radar gun pointed and ready for the first car going over the limit. About a mile down the road, the light went out, Steve floored the Z, and we were back up to 85.

"This is worth every penny I paid for it," he said, tapping the box. "We can make really good time this way." I nodded in agreement. Hell, we'd be covering the distance in no time. We were moving along at a nice goddamn clip.

He asked me about my trip and how I'd chosen my route. I went through the whole thing. Canada. Walking in Pennsylvania and my strap breaking. The New York, Ohio and Connecticut cops, and that one cop in Palmer, Massachusetts.

"How'd you decide on Maine?"

I explained about how the flow of traffic going east had been heavier than that going west, and he seemed to get a kick out of that.

We passed from New Hampshire into Maine. The names of the places were all strange and Indian. Kennebunk and Nashua and Chebeague Island. Or old and European like Portsmouth and Dover and Rochester and Portland. As we passed the exit for Lewiston, I remembered from when I was a kid that Muhammed Ali (then called Cassius Clay) had beaten Sonny Liston there, and it was for the title. I asked Steve if that was correct, and he said, "Yes"; and, it struck me as odd that two black men would come to such a remote place in the Northwoods to fight for the world heavyweight championship as the World listened on radio.

We'd ridden for a while, not talking. I asked Steve what it was like to be retired at such a young age.

"Oh, I'm not retired."

"No?"

"Huh-uh," he said, looking mildly surprised. "I'm a hair stylist."

With his rough demeanor and biker background, the fact of his being a hair-stylist seemed a bit incongruous. Also, the old prejudices, the ways of prejudging people, seemed to bob to the surface. Hair-stylists were always gay. Right? Sure.

He talked for a bit about his shop. How well business was doing. How many people he had working for him. "That's how I met my old lady," he added. "Came in one day and I was doing her hair. And all I could think of was how fucking gorgeous she looked."

So much for the prejudices, I concluded.

He went on to say he hadn't seen her for a couple of days. She had preceded him to the cabin. He was looking forward to being with her.

"You hungry at all?" he asked.

Frankly, I was starved. I hadn't had anything to eat since the previous day at the truck stop. My belly was empty, and it was letting me know it. I told him, "Yeah."

"Augusta's just ahead," he said. Of course, we saw the "golden arches" from quite a way off. Steve guided the Z off the interstate, turned right, and we were right in the parking lot of the place. It had been quite a while since I'd walked, so my legs were very stiff as I got out of the car. It took a few moments to stretch them and get adjusted to standing on the earth. Steve got out of the car and stretched, too. Then, he turned to look at me, and I saw the earring.

It was hanging about an inch-and-a-half from the lobe of his left ear. Seeing it shook me for a moment. I'd never seen a male wearing an earring before. Steve was saying something, but I wasn't listening, and it took some effort to concentrate on what he was saying but, by then, he'd finished speaking, and we headed on into the Greasy Mac's. It was the usual, mass marketed, corporate environment.

I ordered three cheeseburgers, plain, and a large order of fries, and a large coke. I was hungry. When the girl rang up my food, Steve stepped up and said, "These are together." He ordered, and then, as the girl got our food, said to me,"You'll need your money. Hell, you're not far from where you're going, but every little bit helps."

I thanked him. When the food came, we sat at one of the cramped tables in the usual uncomfortable, high-impact, garish green-and-yellow swivel chairs. I wolfed down my burgers and fries. The coke helped to replace fluids I'd sweated out the night before. The food had met a need as profound as any I had ever felt. When I was finished, I pulled out a Vantage menthol and lit up. I felt great as the nicotine rushed into my bloodstream, and I experienced the modest hyperventilation of that first drag.

Steve was talking about jobs on the East Coast and, in particular, in Maine. Apparently, the outlook wasn't all that good. While I was in school, we had discussed recession as an academic subject. I had referred to it as a possible cause for my "Revolution." Now I realized that it had never been a reality to me.

"What can you do?" Steve asked.

"Do?" I said. "I can do a lot of things. I've worked construction before."

"What trade?" he asked.

I exhaled a huge cloud of smoke and thought back to the previous summer and how much I'd hated that job. "I was a laborer," I finally said.

"Shit, you'll be lucky to find work," Steve replied.

"But I had 1410 S.A.T.s," I wanted to say. I'd placed at DSR-TKA nationals in debate. I had been the organizer and leader of demonstrations that shut down my prestigious, liberal arts school. But all that I could say was, "I'm smart. I can learn."

"I can tell that," Steve replied. "There are a lot of people out there who are smart. A lot who may be smarter. With all sorts of work experience. And they're out of work. What do you think that means for you?"

It had been my assumption that one simply got a job. It was handed to you as you left college. I was one of the intellectual crowd. We were wanted for our brains. People would hire us on that basis. But now, a guy whom I was coming to respect was advising me that it was a different world out there. We tossed our trash into a waste bin, all nice and made of polished fake wood, and went out to the car. Steve drove out of the parking lot and into the gas station next door. I thought about employment as a gas station attendant. But I realized all of the pumps were self-serve and that only one attendant was needed. We were only a few feet from the booth he sat in, and he reminded me of any other person, similarly employed. That realization—that I might end up on one of those high metal stools in a gas shack like that—gave me a start. Then I thought about the frequency places like this were robbed. I remembered a joke I'd heard: what's the difference between a male convenience store worker and a female convenience store worker? When they find the corpse of the male convenience store worker, its pants are usually still up. I rejected "Gas Station Attendant" as a vocation. Steve paid for the gas, got a receipt, and then jumped back into the car. We were off and rolling onto the interstate again, soon back up to high speed.

Steve began describing Maine and explained about the flies. "Little black fuckers I've never seen anyplace else," he said, blasting some coke and handing the charger to me. "They bite you, and you get these little, hard welts that hurt like a fucking bitch. The goddamn things are really bad in the late summer."

He pointed to the sides of the interstate, pines now growing tall and thick on either side of us.

"See those alleyways they cut through there?" And, as we sailed along, I saw that a swath of trees had been cut out, about a hundred yards long and maybe twenty yards wide, back into the woods. It was covered with grass and formed a little meadow. "You'll see those every couple of miles. When we pass them, look back in. You might see a deer. Maybe even a moose."

The rest of the ride to Medway, I kept my attention to the forests on the sides of the interstate. I never saw any animals except small birds, but the exercise kept me alert.

"The weather up here's weird, too," he continued. "You can be in one of these valleys between two small mountains. On one mountain, the sun is shining and over it, the sky is clear. Across the valley, you can't see the other mountain for the rain clouds. And that storm will not cross the valley. Weird."

After while, he pulled out a joint and didn't even bother to ask me if I got high. It was good pot, with the earthy flavor to it, and I caught a good buzz from it. Then, he cranked up the volume again.

"Roy Buchanan!" he hollered, obviously getting into the music. The finger work on the guitar was very fast, about the fastest that I'd ever heard. There was a rush to it. "The best guitarist alive!" he shouted again, and then beat the steering wheel in rhythm to the music.

We rode on that way, shooting the shit and grooving on the buzz. Finally, we got to his exit. He wished me luck as I got out of the car. He took off, and I stood there. If other places at which I'd tried to thumb rides had been desolate, this place made those other places look like hubs of activity. The exit was surrounded by forest, and there were no gas stations or fast-food places or truck stops. There was nothing here but forest and the exit sign.

I looked at the late afternoon sky. There were still about three hours of daylight left. But, if my guess about the traffic here was correct, I'd be those three hours and maybe more waiting for a rare car to stop and give me a lift. I looked around at the trees and thought that, at the very least, I'd have plenty of places to choose a campsite from. No ditches for me tonight. I was still scratching mosquito bites from the night before. A couple were scratched raw. Then I thought about the black flies Steve had described. He'd said they were at their worst in August because of the heat. I hoped it was still too early for them.

I saw the car in the distance before I heard it. It was a Ford, about ten years old, with the over-and-under headlights. It began slowing long before it got close to me, and the driver stopped the car so the passenger's door was right in front of me. I knew the distance left to Caribou was quite a trek. I hoped this ride would get me there. He was in his late teens or early 20s, and his hair was closely cropped. I saw that his eyes behind the pilot's sunglasses were red. He asked me where I was going. When I told him Loring, he said, "Hell, I'm based there." His accent was Midwestern.

Yes, my luck had held. This would be the last leg of the journey. I'd made it, or so it appeared.

"You really from Indiana?" he asked. After I'd said yes, "Shit" was all he could mutter.

We drove along, at slightly less than the speed limit. He said nothing for the longest time. We passed several exits, then we neared Houlton.

"Interstate ends at Houlton," he said. "Two lane all the way up from there. You'll be able to see Canada from the base. Hey, why you going to fucking Loring? It's about as far out in the boonies as you'd wanta be."

I told him I had a buddy there. Simos. He was getting married and I was going to the wedding. I kept everything as vague as possible because at this point, I really didn't care.

"Does your buddy party?" he asked. When I said that he did, the guy asked me what Simos' real name was. I said it, but the guy shook his head. "Huh-uh. Don't recognize it. I mean, I'm the biggest dealer on the base and I ain't never heard of him. What's his rank?"

I explained that Simos was a civilian working on the base, but this only confused the guy. He said, "Do you party?" When I said yes, he pulled a joint out of the pack of cigarettes in his pocket, fired it up, and split it with me as we passed the small towns that dotted the two-lane road.

I'd seen a "60 Minutes" segment on U.S. 1 when I was a kid. Morley Safer had described how U.S. 1 ran from Key West, all the way up the East Coast to Maine and the Canadian border. That's the highway I was on now. No national TV specials or segments or anything were ever done about highways in Indiana, even if Indiana billed itself as the "Crossroads of America." Here I was on the old principal highway of the East.

The East had always represented intellectualism to me. People wore black turtlenecks and sat cross-legged listening to bleak poetry or folk music and discussing the various meanings of existence. This appealed to me also because I was coming to believe in a subjective basis for reality. Around Boston, I'd seen a glimpse of that in the people I saw, maybe; but, for the most part, I hadn't. And up here, in northern Maine, what I saw was completely different from my prior conception of the East.

The area North of Houlton along U.S. 1 looked more impoverished than I thought places on the Northern Eastern seaboard could be. The hills and forests began to flatten and thin a bit, so the backdrop was not as pretty as that I had seen further south. The houses were nearly all wooden framed, and most were badly in need of paint. The yards all had the cold moist look of early spring, the scattered toys, old washing machines, and discarded paper bags and bottles giving the impression that the glacier of winter had receded and left its shit all over the place. Cars were up on cement blocks in driveways and lanes, reminding me of Kilkerry and Kentucky.

I had never known that people in Maine grew potatoes, but now signs everywhere made me suddenly aware of that fact. After while, I realized the wooden structures next to some of the houses were structures used to store the potato harvest.

We passed through Presque Isle, I guess one of the larger cities in the area. The guy told me it was the only place with an airport. I don't know why he said that. He hadn't said anything for quite a while. We traveled the remaining miles to Caribou. As we approached the town, I was a bit disappointed. From the town's name and geographical location, I had imagined that the place would be cut from an episode of "Sergeant Preston and the Northwest Mounted Police." Unfortunately, there were no saloons with dog sleds parked outside, or long, wide streets lined with log structures. Caribou was no different from the countryside south of it. The downtown area was of narrow streets with wooden and brick structures intermingled.

The driver asked me where I wanted to be let out, and I asked him what the drinking age was in Maine. When he said, "18," I asked him to let me out at a bar near the base. The bar he took me to was only yards from one of the entrance gates to the base. It was called the Pioneer, and only half a dozen or cars were parked outside. The driver was too stoned to say anything when I got out of the car. He simply pulled away after I got out.

In the entrance was a pay phone. I reached into my wallet and extracted the slip of paper, from between the seven wrinkled dollar bills I had remaining that bore Simos's telephone number. I reached into my pocket and felt the few coins there. I tried Simos's number. No one was home.

Oh, well. I figured that, maybe, since it was Sunday, he might be out someplace. I tried to ignore any other possibilities.

I picked up my pack, pushed the inner door open, and entered the bar. The interior was done in dark wood with a Western motif. The dim light came primarily from the long lights hanging low over the three or four pool tables.

There were about a dozen other customers in the place, and one bartender. I was happy to see the place was open. I'd assumed that the eastern states were more advanced than Indiana.

I was tired. "Exhausted" is actually more accurate. Here I was, One Thousand, Five Hundred and Fifty Miles from home, all on the strength of my thumb. I expected a band to be there, all brass instruments and flags and streamers, banners welcoming the transcontinental traveler. Of course, the pool players hardly looked up, nobody seated at the bar turned around, and the bartender simply looked up, wiped her hands on a towel, and appraised me in such a way as to determine whether to ask me for I.D. I must have looked at least 18, because she didn't card me.

I took a seat at the bar and dropped my pack at my feet. I ordered a pitcher of Rolling Rock "with one glass" and leaned back.

I was finally "here." My destination. But, so what? The bartender set everything down and said, "Two dollars," and I paid her. I poured a glass and drank it. The beer was cold and foamy and tasted really damn good.

What would I do now? Brammie had had a job up here for a while. Maybe jobs weren't hard to find. I could work at something mindless and make enough to rent an apartment. Something with a balcony. Buy some furniture. Then I thought about my stereo and my albums back at the fraternity, half a continent away. All the things I had worked a (short) lifetime to accumulate. Well, I hadn't actually "worked" for them, I realized, but they were mine nonetheless. I finished another glass of beer, then walked back out to use the phone. Again, all I got was a continuous ringing at the other end. Where could he be? I should have called before I started up here.

I went back to the bar, and one of the pool players asked if he could have part of my pitcher. I said, "No" in such a tone as to imply, "Who the fuck do you think you are?" As scrawny as I was, the trip must have done something to me. Enhanced my looks or something. He was bigger than me, but he backed the fuck off.

The beer tasted very, very good as I downed one more glass, then another. I killed that pitcher and signalled the bartender. I paid two more dollars and continued drinking, as I did the math in my head. Twelve ounces to a beer, 64 ounces to a pitcher. That meant there were five and one-third beers per pitcher. I had enough for sixteen beers at this rate. Sure, I would catch a buzz.

I used the phone again, this time watching my things at the bar. Again, no one answered.

I was getting worried now, the drunker I got. What if Simos's wedding had been that day? This was a Sunday, after all. Sundays were popular for such events. Or, maybe he'd gotten married the day before. If that was the case, he and his bride were on their honeymoon, and I knew nobody up here except, on a passing basis and with no name, a guy who claimed to be the biggest drug dealer on the base.

I remembered one of the books I had with me—*Steal this Book*. I reached down for my pack and, in so doing, very nearly spilled my pitcher. I swore to myself to be more careful. I turned to page 77. Abbie explained there how to fake telephone credit card numbers. I had listened to a guy a couple of weeks before at the Union Building make a credit card call. I'd remembered his number and written it down. I wasn't going to use his actual number. I couldn't do that. Even though he was probably an alum, and he looked very affluent, that would be ripping off an individual, and I couldn't do that. But I could rip off the phone company. There was nothing morally wrong about that, after all.

I figured out the letter in the guy's credit card sequence that correlated with a number in a specific spot later in the sequence. I created a fake number from that, then turned to use the phone, but the pool player was already on it.

I relaxed and drank some more beer. I sighed. This was all so hopeless. All this distance, and for what?

The guy finished his call and left.Great. If the phone company sicced their phone cops on the place, and came storming into the bar, their automatic weapons at the ready, shouting for the perpetrator to identify himself, I'd say, "I cannot tell a lie. It was him." And I'd give them the description of that mother fucking son of a bitch who'd tried to mooch my beer.

I dialed the operator and gave her the number of the fraternity, told her it was a credit card call, then gave her my fake credit card number. She thanked me and dialed it all right through. I heard a ringing on the other end, and somebody answered. It was Ridgeway.

"Hey, Ridgeway. What's happening?"

He muttered my name, then asked, "Where the fuck are you?"

"Maine."

"Fuckin' A, he's in Maine!" he said as though speaking to someone else, although I knew that he wasn't. It was just a habit he had. "What ya doing up there?"

"Drinking some Rolling Rock out of the tap."

"Oh, great," he said. "We don't even have anyplace open on Sundays, and you're drinking the beer from the glass-lined tanks at Old Latrobe in a fucking bar."

"How're finals?"

"Eh, the usual. Hey, TV's been wanting to talk with ya."

"Yeah, that's why I called."

"Let me page him."

I was put on hold. The whole time I crossed my fingers, hoping I wouldn't be disconnected or that, worse, the operator would run a check of credit card numbers and figure out what the fuck was going on.

There was a click on the line, followed by TV's voice.

"Hello?" he said.

"Hey, TV, what's up?"

"Where are you?"

I told him and he started laughing. "You're the big mystery on campus. Your and my con law prof asked where you were at the start of the final. I said California, and Cindy said Maine. He was all confused."

I laughed at that.

"Eva and Adolf are gong ape-shit, too."

"What?"

"Yeah, they were down here yesterday. They were about this far from calling the cops until I told them you'd hitch hiked out of here. You'd better call them, 'cause they're giving the guys here in the house all sorts of grief."

"Okay," I said.

"How is it up there? What's it like?"

"Like Northern Appalachia," I said. "But some of the scenery is fucking beautiful."

"How were your rides?"

I didn't know how to answer that question. The only proper way would be to go back over the whole trip. Instead, I just said, "Okay." We talked for a minute or two longer, and then I hung up.

I went back to the bar and sat down. An old man had taken a stool a couple down from me. The salt and pepper stubble on his face was grown out of neglect, not as any statement of fashion. He wore a sock cap over hair that needed washing. I could smell hair oil from where I sat, along with a musty smell I associated with the need for a bath. Of course, the smell could've been from me, but I didn't think so. His lips protruded in a kind of flat pucker. Then I saw why—they fit the beer mug he was drinking from perfectly.

I wondered if I would end up like that. A broken old bum living an alcoholic existence. That thought scared me. I'd never before considered failing at life. When I was a kid, I'd always thought about being President of the United States. That dream had changed. The notion of success had not. The past few months had twisted me around. I was sure that by now I'd flunked out of school. What was next? Unemployment? Life in the slums?

I got up and went to the bathroom. On my way back to my seat, I detoured to the phone and tried Simos again. Again, no one answered.

I was beginning to feel a healthy buzz. I finished this, my second pitcher, and ordered a third. I hadn't much money left for anything else. One dollar bill and some loose change. Just barely two dollars. Enough for a fourth and, no doubt, final pitcher.

I concluded the worst now. Simos was on his honeymoon. I would have to camp out tonight and figure out what to do tomorrow. Shit. I'd looked forward to sleeping on a couch or floor or anything except the hard earth. And, I badly wanted to take a shower and wear clean clothes.

When the thought struck me, I laughed harshly to, then at, myself. I thought about what a fucking incompetent idiot I was. I'd traveled all the way to Maine, only to find that the person I'd come here to see wasn't at home. Cool. What a fuck-up I was.

The beer tasted so good. I decided that I'd go ahead and buy that fourth pitcher, even if it meant being broke tomorrow. So fucking what? I'd come up with some money for food somehow.

I went out to the telephone one last time. I told myself that this would be the last time that I'd try to reach him, although I knew that was not true. I'd keep trying until I passed out.

There were three, then four rings. I was about to hang up after the fifth, when somebody picked it up. I immediately recognized Simos' voice.

266

"Simos!"

He must have recognized my voice because he called me by name and asked if it was me..

"It sure is."

"How you doing?"

"I'm fine," I said. "I'm sitting in a bar on a Sunday afternoon. Figured I'd give you a call and see how you're doing."

"You got I.D.s?" he asked.

"Nope."

"Come on, nobody would mistake you for being 21."

He was definitely right about that. "I'm in a state where they serve to 18."

"No, shit?" he said. But I don't think he suspected anything.

"Yeah, the name of the bar is the Pioneer."

"We got a place named that up here."

"Funny," I said, "I'm right next to an Air Force base."

There was a pause. "What's the name of the base?"

"Loring."

"Shit!" he exclaimed. "You're up here?"

"Yeah."

"When'd you get in?"

"About an hour ago."

"Look, I'll . . . Shit!" He was laughing, and I was, too. I knew I'd sleep on a couch tonight or, at the very least, a dry floor. I knew I'd have some food. And, maybe, just maybe, Simos would know of any available employment opportunities. "Look, I just got married last Saturday..."

"Yeah, I thought that that was coming up," I said.

"We just walked in from our honeymoon."

"No shit!" I said. It didn't dawn on me that this fact might endanger my staying there. Apparently, that thought didn't dawn upon Simos, either.

"My wife and I will be right there."

"Okay."

I walked back to the bar elated. I'd trusted to luck and luck had been with me. I killed the glass of beer on the counter and filled it with what remained in the pitcher. I even celebrated by lighting up one of my last cigarettes.

The wait wasn't long. The door of the bar opened and Simos came in, as big as ever, followed by a short but cute girl. He gave me a bear hug, then introduced me to his wife. We exchanged nods and "hellos"; then all of us went to a table and sat down, Simos buying another pitcher and grabbing two more glasses.

He wanted to know how everyone was doing. By "everyone," he meant all the people who'd been freshmen with us when we'd lived in the dorm. I did as best as I could, but it was difficult. People had either moved to a frat, gotten an apartment OIT, or transferred out. Very few had stayed at the dorm. Even though the campus was small, the social structure at DeForrest was so compartmentalized that effort was required to associate with people outside one's "living unit."

Simos was genuinely pleased by this. He'd been a four-sport athlete in high school. He only had part of the jock mentality. I mean, he was a goof-off and expected all things to be given to him, but he wasn't a mean asshole about it. His father was in the Air Force and probably couldn't have sprung for the tuition at DeForrest, but Simos had received a scholarship. We'd spent freshman year getting wasted with each other among the same set of friends. We bummed money, beers, cigs, and pot off each other. And, through the combined efforts of his first and second semesters, Simos had flunked out, and, hence, lost his scholarship. Now, sitting here in an off-base bar in Maine, Simos was trying to recapture the feeling of those days. Once or twice I tried to ask him about what he did up here, but he simply said, "Stock clerk at the base exchange," and continued his questions. We reached the inevitable point where we swapped stories from freshman year. I grabbed another pitcher, thus blowing the last money that I had on the Earth. When we were close to the bottom of that pitcher, Simos finally broached the subject I should have raised initially.

"Need a place to stay?" he asked.

"Yeah," I replied. "If I could use your couch for a day or two, I'd really appreciate it."

"Honey?" Simos asked, turning to his wife.

She looked very young, but I didn't realize just how young she was until after, when Simos told me that she'd turned 17 a week before the wedding. She was still in that daze caused by love, and she grinned throughout the entire conversation that Simos and I had had. I was someone from his past. The talk had confirmed much of what he'd said. Sure, it was only about a nine-month period of his life. He'd only appeared up here a year before. It was nice to have confirmation of details.

"Sure," she said smiling, but in a meek tone. "Brammie stayed up here for two or three months. There's no problem."

We stopped at a liquor store and Simos bought a 12-pack and some cigs. His wife asked me if I'd eaten. I told her no, but what I really wanted to do was take a shower. She laughed and said that would be no problem.

They lived in an apartment in an old, wooden-framed house. There were two other apartments in the place, all intertwined within one another, one occupying the space forfeited by the other two. The living room, kitchen, and bathroom were on the first floor, and the bedroom, apparently, was up a short flight of wooden stairs. I tossed my pack in the living room on the floor. As I pulled out the shampoo and other items I'd need, I glanced at the wallpaper and the furniture and the old carpet. Everything looked as if it had been purchased at the same store as the items in Austin and Michelle's apartment.

I carried clean clothes into the bathroom with me, along with my toiletries, and closed the door. The shower was a recently-installed affair on the bathtub. I turned the water on hot, took off my clothes, then eased under the spray. It felt great. I lathered up my hair with shampoo, then let the soap work into my scalp. I worked soap over my body. By the time I was ready to rinse off, I must've looked like a snowman or something. I felt clean, though. After I'd dried off, I looked at the tub and saw the incredible ring I'd left. I found a scouring pad under the sink and cleaned the tub. Then I dressed, brushed my teeth, ran my big hand brush through my hair, and made my way, barefoot, out of the bathroom.

Simos handed me a beer, and I let out a huge sigh.

"Man, I feel human," I said.

They both laughed. Simos was at the stove frying something. Plates with slices of bread lay on the counter. "Hope you like fried bologna," he said, using his fork to flip slices of the meat out of the skillet and onto the plates.

"Love it," I lied. I hated bologna. The Cousin used to have bologna "on white" with mustard and wash it down with iced tea. For breakfast. Every goddamn day. I hated the shit. But, I was in no position to argue.

We sat down at an old table and ate our sandwiches. Simos and his wife didn't say a word to each other, they just grinned. Once in a while Simos would say something to me, but it was always a perfunctory comment or question. "How's the sandwich?"or "Need a beer?" Once the meal was finished, he told his wife that he and I were going to find Brian and have a few beers. She seemed a little disappointed, but she didn't say anything. So, Simos grabbed his coat and we went out to his car and took off.

"Where'd you meet her?" I asked.

"Party. She was with a buddy of mine's girlfriend. I didn't realize she was still in high school 'til two days later." He grinned at the last comment and rolled his eyes. "So, what're you doing up here?" Simos asked.

I shrugged and began to tell him parts of what had happened in the last couple of months. He was nodding his head. He understood in a general way until I talked about Brammie hitch hiking all over the country. Simos got into that. Brammie was his best buddy from high school.

I asked him then about work, and he started shaking his head.

"Didn't Brammie tell you? That's why he left. No jobs up here. I mean, I got the job I got because of Dad. Not because there's a lot of work available."

"There's none available?"

"Nope. It's a high unemployment rate around here. Short 'Help Wanted' section in the paper."

I tried my best to hide my disappointment. The disappointment still showed, of course. And, Simos was a good buddy, but he didn't quite know what to say.

We pulled into a liquor store and Simos asked me what I smoked. He came out with an eight-pack and a couple of packs of smokes. We booked over to a house that was like so many of the others I'd seen between here and Houlton. The front porch seemed to melt into the gravel of the driveway-parking area. What must have been a yard was nearly all mud littered with toys, trash and empty beer cans. An old, overstuffed couch was being weathered on the front porch. And, there were several pairs of boots next to the front door. Simos honked his horn several times, not bothering to get out of the car. About 30 seconds later, the front door opened, and a guy emerged, pulling on his coat. He came to my side of the car, so I opened the door, then leaned forward, grabbing the back of my seat so that he could get in. Simos wasted no time getting out of there.

"She pitch a bitch?" Simos asked, and his buddy grinned and shook his head.

"You wouldn't believe it, but we're getting the system down, Simos. You and me. No phone call. Just those beeps. I have my coat on and I'm half-way out the door before she can react. By the time I get home, I'm so loaded, it doesn't matter."

I assumed that he was talking about escaping home before enduring the wrath of his mother. Simos introduced us. Brian worked with Simos at the base.

We drove just a few miles and then pulled onto a huge expanse of dirt and gravel. We were on a bluff fringed by pine trees. Below us two rivers came together in a fork and formed a new one. The sun was setting over mountains in the distance, and there was some haze on the horizon. Simos handed each of us a beer and, leaning against the hood of the car, we shared the joint that he pulled out and fired up.

I listenened to Brian complaining, apparently about the woman whose clutches he'd just escaped. After a few minutes I realized he hadn't been talking about his mother. He was bitching about his wife. He did so vehemently and energetically: a participant, a warring nation in the "global marital conflict." Simos sat there, nodding his head. I knew the broader question was escaping him. Simos was a nice guy, but not terribly deep. The peripheral things were registering with him. The arguments. The insults. The strategic ploys to enable his escape from the house. He was storing these vicarious experiences away for later use against the girl he'd just married who was sitting at home while he partied with his buddies. Up here where there were no jobs and the landscape looked like a Life photo spread about Appalachia and its poverty. Here, of course, on the bluff over the river the scenery was beautiful. But, something was wrong. I couldn't do it. I couldn't say up here. Well, at least I doubted it.

It was weird to have traveled 1,550 miles for this. I killed a couple more beers. The shower and bologna had revived me. But, the extra beers and the pot had worn me down again. My eyelids were getting very heavy.

Simos looked over at me and interrupted Brian's monologue to point out my condition.

"He used to do that at DeForrest," Simos said. "You could count on this guy passing out by 9 every night." He laughed, and I grinned at that. Brian just nodded a little. He didn't see the humor, and Brian definitely did not understand an interruption of his pissing and moaning about his marital strife.

I gathered up the cans the other two had dropped on the ground. I said I didn't want us to screw up nature. Brian made a cryptic comment about how people had screwed up nature anyway. I had the feeling he didn't like me. Simos wasn't taking sides in the matter, but I knew it was only a matter of time.

We headed back to town.

"Hey!" Simos said to me, "I don't have to work tomorrow and I'll be damned if I'm going to crash yet."

"I can dig that," Brian agreed. I could tell how much he was savoring his freedom from "the nest."

"You've already seen one of our bars up here. But, we'll take you to one that's fun."

They both laughed as I merely looked on from the back seat. The sky was dark now and beginning to drop rain. The air was chilly, too. My hands trembled a little as I lit a cigarette.

We pulled into the parking lot of the place and had to take a spot near the back, there were so many cars. Inside, nearly every black naugahyde chair was taken. But, miraculously, we found an empty cabaret table with three chairs near the wall and took it. Simos bought a pitcher. The place was really unremarkable. There was no dance floor. I didn't even see a juke box. There were no pinball machines of any sort. The place was just a big room with a bar running the length of the wall on one side, a bunch of small circular tables with black naugahyde chairs, and a big-screen TV. The word "lounge" seemed to fit the place perfectly.

Brian seemed happy to launch into the tales of his marital strife once again. Simos occasionally grimaced or shook his head. I looked at the decorations behind the bar. There was an American flag there. That was never a good sign in a bar in the 70s. I glanced out the picture window at the vehicles in the parking lot. There were as many or more pick-up trucks than cars. I looked back at the patrons of the establishment.

The East had always represented so many things to me. And, I was now in the East. I had expected to encounter "intellectuals"—people discussing books and art and thought and history. I guess I'd expected a superheated version of the talks we used to have at Neal's and Sullivan's. But, this place—not just this bar, but what I'd seen of Maine—held none of that. The place reminded me of fucking Kilkerry At that realization, I leaned back in my chair, the drone of Brian's complaints combining with the noises of the barroom talk as a white noise. I sat there stunned. Four days and 1,550 fucking miles for this?

There was another sound that caught my attention, and I looked up at the TV. The station was showing a replay of the "500." I couldn't believe it! Something from home! The shots were scenes that were familiar to me, even though I'd never been to the race. We always had to wait a week or so for the local stations to show the race "in its entirety."

I looked at Simos. He'd dropped out after one year. And now he had a job as a stock clerk. And, maybe that's what I would end up doing one day. I didn't know. But, if I did, I wouldn't do it here.

I decided, in that moment, to go back to Indiana.

We finished the pitcher and left the bar. Brian now talked about how filthy his wife was. After we'd dropped him off we drove back to Simos'. His wife had spread a blanket on the couch and left a pillow there. All the lights were out except for one in the stairwell. We said goodnight and he crept up the stairs.

I undressed and lay down, exhausted from the day, and more than a little fucked up. I started to doze off immediately, but then I heard the creakings of the floorboards above me as Simos crossed the floor, then the sounds of springs as he crawled into bed. It was distracting, but stopped, and I started to doze again, when another sound started. It was rhythmic and soon involved the springs and the floorboards and little giggles and moans.

I'd never heard people actually fucking before. I'd never done it, certainly. And, while I went to an X-rated flick at a drive-in with a bunch of guys in the dorm freshman year, I'd never actually seen it done, either. Now, it was going on only a few feet above my head.

I just grunted and rolled over. In only a few seconds, I was sound asleep.

Chapter 40 - A Day Spent In Maine

When I awoke, Simos's wife was already in the kitchen cleaning up from the night before. I don't know how long she'd been there, because my sleep had been very deep, a blackness, a total void. I had had no thoughts or dreams. My body and brain were happy. There was none of that gritty feeling in the linings of my eyeballs. My muscles were sore, especially in my legs, from all of the walking I'd done. But on a day-to-day basis I was always walking and running, so the soreness wasn't all that bad. I pulled on my jeans while I was still under the covers, then pulled on my shirt. The toilet flushed. Simos had beaten me to the bathroom.

He was scratching his head and yawning when he came out. He just said, "Morning," as I passed him on my way in. I performed my morning ritual of shower/shave/brush teeth in World's record time.

When I came out, Simos said, "Come on, we gotta go to the store and cash a check."

He was already pulling on his jacket, and I followed him out to his car.

"Whaddya gonna do?" he asked as we headed down the road.

"Go back to Indiana. Probably tomorrow." I sensed a sigh of relief rise from him. "Where's the closest airport?"

"Closest airport?"

"Yeah, I figured I'd call Adolf and have him wire me a ticket so I can fly back." I said it matter-of-factly, having figured out the details the night before. That figuring had taken all of three seconds.

"Fly back?" Simos asked, now laughing. "You're the only person I know who'd hitch hike half-way across the country, then fly back."

I shrugged. "Answer my fucking question. Where's the nearest fucking airport?"

Still smiling, Simos said, "Presque Isle. It's about 15 miles south of here."

"Yeah, I know where Presque Isle is," I said. "I passed through it."

"Oh yeah. So when're you going?"

"I don't know. I gotta call Adolf. See what's shaking. Gotta call the airport, too, and see when the flights go out. I'll do that when we get back to the apartment."

"We don't have a phone," Simos advised.

I looked at him curiously. "Where was I calling you yesterday?"

"Think about it—the base is a few miles away. I could see the bar from the window I was standing at. That's my parents' place."

"Oh," I said, slumping down into the seat.

The grocery was called Dairyland or something like that. It was the missing link in the evolutionary chain between Mom-and-Pop groceries and the modern convenience store. Simos cashed his check, then got some change from the woman behind the counter. He gave me the change so I could make my calls.

The first one I made, to Presque Isle Airport, fortunately wasn't long distance. The person there told me that only one flight the next day left for a major city: the 10:30 a.m. flight on Eastern Boston.

I took a deep breath and looked at the telephone, then I glanced around. I was outside the electric in/out doors of the store and the air had a chill to it. This phone call signaled a defeat for me. I'd come all this way—for what? Once the call was made, I could never double back. I took another deep breath and fed the coins into the slot. The operator came on and I gave her the information necessary to make a collect call.

Adolf's voice came on at the other end, and he sounded startled when the operator asked him if he would accept the charges. He said yes, and I said hello.

He asked me where I was.

"Maine," I replied.

I knew he was in the kitchen then, because I could hear him fumbling around with all the crap that was on a safe he and Eva kept in the kitchen, next to the dinner table. He was grabbing the Rand-McNally atlas that was always kept there for some reason.

"Whereabouts in Maine?" he asked.

"Okay," I said. "See the part of Maine that's at the top of the state but too big to fit on the page, so they stick it into a box in the corner?"

"Yeah."

"I'm there," I said, visualizing every map I'd ever seen of Maine.

"What's the name of the town?" he asked, a bit surprised.

"Caribou," I answered.

"Pretty far north," he observed. I think his reaction was to the name of the town and not its location on the map.

"Yeah, I'm looking at Canada on two sides of me right now."

"Well—what do you want to do?" His tone was wary.

"I want to fly back to Indiana."

"Why?"

I wanted to say because that's where I live, but I knew saying something like that would only invoke some smartass comment. Instead, I said, "I want to take my finals. I have incompletes to make up." That was bullshit. I had no way of knowing if any of my profs would let me make up the exams I had missed. But it sounded plausible.

"We talked with the dean. He said that you're probably going to flunk out."

They had talked to the dean already? Whoa! "I don't know how he could say that," I said. "He would have had to talk with my profs, and I'm telling you that they gave me incompletes." It sounded plausible. Then I decided to embellish it a bit. "Besides—why would I jeapordize losing payment of my tuition by the trust?"

There was a pause, and I thought for just a moment that he was going to quote my profs—unlikely, I figured, since he would have done so already had he actually spoken with them—or, far more likely, that he would quote the trust officer as saying that I was fucked. Instead, he said, "Where's the nearest airport?"

"Presque Isle," I replied.

"What?"

I spelled it for him, then told him to look at the map, that it was only 15 miles south of Caribou. I gave him the scoop, too, on the flights out of there and everything.

"No flights today?" he asked.

I wasn't going to tell him it had taken me three and a half days to thumb up here and I'd be damned if I was going to leave that quickly—I wanted to stay at least for a day. Instead I said, "My ride can't get me there until tomorrow morning."

"All right," Adolf said. "We'll have a ticket waiting for you at Presque Isle tomorrow morning. But"—and he said this last bit with special emphasis—"we'll have a long talk when you get back."

Other persons having custody of a recent post-adolescent might have reacted differently. Eva and Adolf might have reacted differently under different circumstances. There was a snag someplace. I figured it had to be something to do with the trust. Whatever the reason, Adolf did not say the thing I feared that he might: "You hitch hiked up there—you want back, you hitch hike that way, too"—or a reasonable facsimile.

Simos came out of the store just then with all of the fixings for breakfast, and I told him about my conversation with Adolf. Simos was even more relieved, I think, that I'd actually called Indiana to arrange to do what I'd only talked about.

"Do you think you can drive me to the airport tomorrow morning?" I asked as we pulled up in front of the house.

"Sure, no problem," he said, and we went on in.

His wife fixed eggs and toast and something else. I ate everything, even though the eggs were really runny and the toast had a funny taste to it. She was still so very young, and I didn't want to hurt her feelings. She had a solemn expression. She had undertaken the role of housemaker, and she was damn well going to do it. I can't say that it was out of her love for Simos—I mean, maybe it was, because I can't read minds and maybe her thoughts spun around him as she put her hands to the tasks of making food. I got the feeling, though, that it was for herself that she was doing this. That she had defined herself in this way and was bearing down to learn all the skills necessary for her role. For some reason, I was a little sad with this realization, but I also felt proud for her.

About half-way through the meal, Simos pushed his plate away. From the tone of his voice, I could tell he'd held back the commentary, but could do so no longer.

"I can't eat these eggs," he said. He shoved the plate toward me. "You can have them."

I saw her face flush in embarrassment and anger. I quickly grabbed the plate and said, "Yeah sure. I like these eggs fine." But then I've always liked my eggs a little runny.

Maybe I risk salmonella and all that. I was convinced that something plastic had fallen down into the toaster and melted, imparting the terrible flavor to the toast. But the eggs were okay. My actions were meaningless, however. Simos had leveled an insult at his wife and the cooking she had worked on so hard. She got up and quickly left the room. We listened to her feet clomping up the stairs and then across the floor above us. There was a moment's silence, then her body crashed onto the mattress and erupted in the squeakings of box springs.

Simos rolled his eyes in disdain and cast a sideways look at me seeking my commiseration. He exuded a deep sigh, then slowly pushed out his chair, stood, and left the room. His feet were soft on the stairs, and I heard a mild press of box springs as he sat down on the bed.

I was uncomfortable. I had never before had to sit through other persons' domestic disputes. At least not when I was an adult. The few times that, as a child, I had witnessed arguments between parents of friends of mine, I was a captive audience and the spats were over quickly. Maybe those parents knew Eva's reputation as the evil spreader of gossip and did not want my little ears to pick up things that would be repeated to her later, then amplified over the neighborhood. Right now I felt like an intruder. Although I could not hear the words, I could hear, through the plaster and lath of the old ceiling, the soft tones of Simos's voice and the faint, choked sobs of his wife. I felt sorry for her. She really had tried.

Then I thought of Brian, Simos's friend, and I wondered what effect that guy had had on Simos. I knew then this marriage would not last. I also understood, in that moment, how little Simos and I had in common, now that we were no longer classmates. And I wanted to go back to school.

I finished the last bit of egg left, then went to the sink and rinsed the plate. I pulled out one of my last two cigarettes. The meal hadn't been all that big, but cigs were meant to be smoked after meals.

Simos came down the stairs about a half-hour later. He was not happy.

"Come on," he said, putting on his jacket and ignoring the dishes on the table. "Let's go."

He said nothing as we drove. Simos had always been a "happy-go-lucky" kind of guy. I mean, that's the only phrase that described him adequately. But his face bore an expression that I'd never seen there before. Simos was hunched over the wheel, grim-faced and chewing on the butt end of his unlit cigarette as we negotiated the narrow streets of Caribou. Of course, we went to Brian's, and the same scene as the day before played out. I let Brian into the backseat and we pulled away.

I wish I could relate fully the events of the balance of my only full day in the State of Maine, but I cannot. We got drunk. I remember that. Brian had some money and we went back to the lounge where we'd been drinking the night before. There was always at least one, sometimes two, pitchers on the table at all times. The place had a good crowd for a Monday, but then I realized a couple of things—that this was a holiday, and that the sign in the window read, "Open at 6," which meant that this was the haven for the people in the town who were really into their booze. I kicked back and stared at the scenery outside the huge windows while Simos joined Brian in bitching and moaning about marriage. Soon we were doing shots, and I pounded as heavily as I could. I wanted to be brain dead by the time we got back to the apartment. I could pass out then and not worry about anything except getting up tomorrow.

I only have a vague recollection of staggering towards the couch, catching an angry look from Simos's wife, and crashing out. My sleep was deep and, again mercifully, without dreams.

Chapter 41 - Flight Back

Something was weird about my metabolism when I woke up. Even though I had consumed massive quantities of alcohol the previous two days, I was not hungover.

There was a musty smell to the cushion of the couch. I sat up. No one else was up, and the sun had barely risen. I shot into the bathroom and cleaned up as quickly as I could. When I came out, Simos was sitting on the couch. He went into the bathroom and brushed his teeth. By the time that he was done, I was packed and standing next to the front door. He smiled and grabbed his jacket, and headed out with me, easing the door shut as we left. We got into his car and took off.

"Next stop, Presque Isle," I said.

"No," Simos said. "I gotta get to work. Besides, someone's pissed off enough as it is. She didn't even want me to give you a lift to the highway. I work with her old man, so she'll know what time I get to work. She'd shoot me if I broke my word to her."

I stared at him for a few moments. After all of the harsh talk he and Brian had shared the previous two days, all the avowals of women being their servants, and "running my own home," I was surprised he was doing this.

He glanced at me and said, by way of rationalization, "You've hitch hiked 1,500, miles to get up here. Fifteen miles to Presque Isle isn't gonna kill you."

We were coming to the highway I'd taken into town only two days before. Traffic was brisk as everyone drove to their jobs at the end of the three-day weekend. We pulled onto the gravel shoulder.

"Good luck," he said.

"Got two bucks I can borrow?" I asked. "I got 13 cents on me, is all I have."

"Nope," Simos said. I didn't believe him, but then I figured, fuck it.

"Thanks," I said, and got out of the car. As he pulled away I was sure I'd never see him again. I paused, watching the car as it headed north. I stuck out my thumb and went south.

A 1964 Impala Super Sport, red with a white rag top, pulled over. I ran after it and jumped in. The driver introduced herself. She looked to be almost 30, an age I viewed, at that time, as being ancient. She seemed to be really hip, though, wearing jeans and a tie-dyed blouse, and driving with a mug of coffee perched on the dashboard. She held it in place as she floored the car and got us into traffic. She cranked an 8-track, and I glanced down at the player and saw that it was Janis Joplin's "Pearl." She left me off downtown and pointed in the general direction of the airport.

"About a mile-and-a-half," she yelled over the music. I slammed the door, then waved as she took off.

I assumed there was little point in trying to thumb the short distance to the airport, so I walked. The air was fresh and cool, and, besides, I wanted to enjoy these last minutes I would spend in Maine.

The airport was spread out, and I spotted a parking lot next to a building with a lot of windows. Arrows pointed in that direction to "TERMINAL." The pack strap was biting into my shoulder again, and I was happy I would get to deposit the goddamn thing into the hold of whatever plane was taking me out of here.

As I approached the building, I saw that most of the dozen or so cars were privately-owned, probably cars of employees and passengers, with a couple of rentals—one from Hertz and the other from National—tossed into the mix underneath signs bearing the logos of their respective companies. The terminal was tiny. Only one plane, a commuter type with the name and colors of Bar Harbor Airways, was parked on the other side of the building. Next to hangars and about 100 yards away were smaller planes, the single-engine jobs of weekend fliers.

I walked through the double automatic doors. To my left was a corralled area of seats, access to which could be gained only by passage through a metal detector, next to which sat an older man in a dark blue blazer and gray slacks. He wore a badge on the left breast pocket of his jacket. He looked bored, slumped over a bit in a scratched-up folding chair. Straight ahead was the counter for Bar Harbor Airways. The rental car companies simply had telephones the colors of their respective company's logo sitting on the counters. Brochures for those who wished to learn more about the rental of GM cars or Chryslers or what have you, were readily available for perusal. Behind the Bar Harbor counter, a neatly-uniformed, attractive woman did paperwork beneath a huge board of the arrival and departure times of the dozen or so flights that passed through here.

To my right was the longest counter of all. Above it was the blue and gray logo of Eastern Airlines. The man there was staring intensely at paperwork. A teletype machine behind him began chattering, then spat out paper. He turned to the machine, and waited for it to stop. Then he tore the paper off and brought it back to the counter where he'd been before, and seemed to be comparing it with something else in front of him.

I walked up to him and said, "Excuse me."

He looked up and regarded me with suspicion. "What?" he asked harshly.

"I'm here to catch the Eastern flight to Boston and . . ."

"No you're not," he said abruptly. I think he was reacting to my appearance—hair to my shoulders, sweatshirt clean but ratty, faded jeans, a ridiculous growth of five or six days on my chin, and tennis shoes that looked as if they had, indeed, been walked in for fifteen hundred miles. In short, I looked like Maynard G. Krebs, the beatnik character, played by the guy who played Gilligan, on the old "Dobie Gillis" show. "You won't be on that plane because it's booked up," he practically spat at me, then went back to his paperwork.

"Excuse me," I said. "My uncle will be wiring a ticket for me from Indiana." I could visualize the bus station in downtown Kilkerry, that was home to the travel agency. I told the guy behind the counter my name and that the ticket would be wired for me. "I'll be sitting right over there," I added, then pointed to the plastic chairs about ten feet away, that were the only places to sit outside the corralled area behind the security gate.

The guy glared at me. "I don't think I made myself clear. That flight is a 727. A small jet. We have it filled with people going to Boston. This is the first flight after the holiday weekend. You will not get a seat, so I suggest you loiter someplace else."

I shrugged and walked over to the chairs, sitting in one and setting my pack on the other. I didn't want this prick to triumph over me. Besides that, I didn't want to get stranded in Presque Isle with 13 cents to my name and no place to go for another 24 hours. I leaned back in the chair and stared at the ceiling. The 10 or 12 people milling around in the security area didn't seem enough to fill a jet. I figured that the plane had to hold 80 or 90 at least. The counter guy had to be acting out of spite, telling me the plane was full.

At about 9:30 I heard airbrakes and looked up to see a tour bus pulling into the parking lot. I reached for my pack and pulled out a book as the first people got out. The print on the side of the bus, just next to the door of the thing, gave its capacity as being 43. And I really believe 43 people got off of that bus. The plane was in-bound from Nova Scotia. That meant that there would be people already on board. I began to feel uneasy. Maybe the fucking thing was booked up.

At about 9:45, two or three cars pulled into the parking lot, almost at once. Their occupants got out and came into the terminal. I thought maybe some of them were there to see off family or friends, but I was wrong. They were all passengers and stood in line at the counter, checking baggage and getting boarding passes before going through the metal detector. One of the people was an Air Force officer. I saw what I'd heard Adolf call "scrambled eggs" on the visor of the guy's hat, signifying that his rank was at least that of a full colonel.

I was sure, now, that I would have to scrounge for a place to sleep, and would either starve or forage for food. That was when the teletype kicked into life again.

I had avoided looking at the counter guy for a while, but just then I did. He looked at the machine with annoyance, and then he glanced up and our eyes met. I smiled just then. He ripped off the paper, and stood there for what must have been a full minute reading the fucking thing. Then he walked to the counter, ripped some border material away from the pages, stamped them, and placed everything into what looked like an Eastern Airlines ticket envelope. Then he grabbed a microphone. The tinny speakers of the terminal carried his voice as he announced my name and requested that I come to the Eastern Airlines ticket counter.

What a dick! I was nearly laughing. He handed the ticket to me, then I swung my pack up to be tossed onto the plane as luggage. He processed it and tossed it onto a cart. I went through the metal detector. The air marshal gave me a surly look. I was the only hippie who'd gone through his security checkpoint this part of the day, and maybe he thought he might have a real, bona fide terrorist on his hands. But the only metal I had in my pockets consisted of three pennies and a dime, even my keys were in the pack, and the machine was set to skip change, so I sailed through.

The corralled area was crowded now. There were no spare seats. I was, by far, the youngest person waiting to board. The Air Force guy was probably next youngest, and he looked to be at least mid-40s. Everyone else was retirement age or older. I didn't know if the people up here shipped off their old people in the spring.

Everybody started turning to look out the windows and across the airfield to where a jet was landing. I saw the Eastern Airlines logo and colors and figured it was our flight. The plane flared, for just a moment, then puffs of smoke appeared where the tires impacted the pavement and the plane was down. A few people began to crowd toward the only "gate" in the terminal. We would board the old-fashioned way—using one of those stairways-on-wheels. The Eastern logo was painted brightly on each side of it, the handrails were stainless, and two ground people were waiting to roll the thing up to the plane's door. The guys wore headphones, but no wires came out of the things. They're called "mouse ears" and kill the noise from the jet engines.

As the plane taxied toward the terminal, its engine made a constant whine with a dull underbeat to it. The plane bounced as it crossed the asphalt, and its wings shook with each such motion. I "joined" the line that had seemed to form around me. People were shoving against each other. I thought the effort was not only rude, but futile. We were all going to get off the ground at the same time and our seats were assigned.

The engines whirred down as the plane came to a stop, its shape filling the great panes of glass of the windows. One man in the ground crew chocked the wheels of the plane while the other fellow wheeled the stairs to the door immediately behind the cockpit. The surly bastard from the ticket counter came around the corralled area and walked up to the podium. "Flight"—whatever number it was—"from Presque Isle to Boston will now be boarding at gate one." The guy went on narrating the pertinent regulations regarding smoking on the flight and that passengers with impairments should board now, etc.

One of the stewardesses—they were still "stewardesses" back then—opened the door of the plane as the stairs were wheeled to a stop. Two or three people walked past her, off the plane and down the stairs, having reached their destination. Then the people in line seemed to crush against each other. I was surprised that, as old as this crowd seemed to be, no one in a wheel chair needed to be helped aboard first. In fact, I was surprised that I didn't recognize any of these "seniors" from play in the National Hockey League. They were mean and physical.

As I got my turn at the counterman, toward the end of the line of passengers, I said, smiling, "Looks like someone took off with your 'Gate Two.'" He just glowered at me and ripped my ticket apart at the dotted line and stamped and stapled and shoved the whole thing back at me.

I climbed the steps. The threshhold of the doorway marked my entrance into the stainless steel of the galley/foyer of the plane. To my left, the door of the cockpit was open. The crew members were checking their equipment and chatting. No one was muttering "Oh my god," or, the worst thing you can hear the member of a crew on an airliner say— "Oh shit"—because that's the last phrase anybody usually hears on the cockpit recorder when one of the planes goes down. I thought about when I was a kid and Adolf had taken me on a flight. I was about 10 and was the only kid on a chartered airliner full of construction contractors. I got to go up to the cockpit then and watch the pilots while they operated the aircraft and sipped champagne.

The first compartment after the foyer was the short one, of three or four rows, two wide leather seats to each side, that made up the first-class section. There were only three or four passengers there but, even though we were still on the ground, there was one stewardess assigned only to them, and she had their drinks full and items of snack foods in front of them. I thought that it would be nice if there had been a mistake and I had been placed in that section. Bummer.

It took a couple of minutes for me to get to my seat. The people ahead of me were all trying to get their stuff put away in the overhead compartments. I only had my book to worry about, a paperback copy of Inside the Third Reich by Albert Speer. I had purloined it someplace along the way and felt that reading it now, on my way back to the Farm and life with Eva and Adolf and the Cousin, would be a good re-orientation to that environment.

My seat was next to the window. It also was next to the Air Force guy. All that I could think of was those guys from Chanute who had to wear the long-haired wigs in order to hit on the college girls at the U of I. He smiled and nodded to me, moved his legs aside so I could shimmy into my seat. I sat down and immediately buckled in. As soon as I had done so, I heard the door of the plane slam shut.

We got moving pretty quickly. The senior stewardess got onto the intercom. She thanked us for flying Eastern—as though anybody flying out of Presque Isle to Boston had a choice—gave us details of the flight—estimated time of arrival, maximum altitude that we would reach, weather "conditions" in Boston—then began telling us about our seat belts, oxygen equipment, escape routes from the plane, and that our seat cushions could be used "as flotation devices in the unlikely event that that should prove necessary." I noticed that she didn't say "crash," or "ditch in the ocean," or any similar metaphor or adjective. Then she wished us a pleasant flight.

My stomach was beginning to growl. I had hoped breakfast would be served. If it had been, it would be included in the price of the ticket, so I could eat. Unfortunately, the flight was so short I realized there was no way that we could be served. The Air Force guy turned to me and introduced himself as Colonel Somebody. It was written, white letters etched into black plastic, on a standard military issue name plate above the left breast-pocket on his powder-blue uniform shirt. He offered his hand and I shook it, then I leaned back and tried to look bored as he tried to strike up a conversation. In a couple of minutes I no longer had to try to look bored. I was bored. Or at least not hiding any longer my disdain for conversation with him. He was talking about engine nacelles and different aircraft he'd flown that had crashed.

Right. I hadn't mentioned this fact until now, but I was—am, still—scared shitless of flying. Maybe it was seeing those guys in the cockpit sipping champagne when I was 10. Or reading about airliners flipping over and impacting with the Earth and nearly the speed of sound. On the two or three occasions when I was a kid and got onto a plane, I could always see the headline in the local paper in Kilkerry—"Local Youth Claimed in Air Crash." But I hadn't been on a plane in years. So this guy was really being considerate, telling me about air crash disasters he'd investigated or witnessed or nearly been "claimed" in. It got me to looking around, now, trying to imagine what would happen in the event of an in-flight disaster, like another plane hitting us. I'd seen a movie like that one time, where Dana Andrews is flying a small plane and has a heart attack and his plane collides with an airliner. I could imagine bodies flying around the cabin and becoming nearly stuck to the ceiling of the cabin as gravity pressed them into it. Small items would fly about. Then I thought how weird it was, to get onto a plane and not realize until too late that your fellow passengers are the people you're going to die with.

The plane turned into the wind. Then the pilot shoved the throttles to the max, the engines blew into a roar, and we began that roll. We rolled slowly, at first, the wings jiggling, the fuselage bumping a bit. There was a point where the speed forced the craft into a sort of gracefulness. The bumps were hardly noticeable. Then the front of the cabin rotated up and, a moment later, the plane cleared the ground and the landing gear came up with a "thump." I looked out the window and watched as Maine fell away.

The stewardess came by and asked us what we would like to drink. I ordered a Scotch and soda, and she didn't bat an eye as she started to prepare it. I thought I'd scammed my way into getting served underage. But then she told me the drink was a dollar and a quarter. Only the soft drinks were free. So I just had a 7-Up. I couldn't even eat the airline peanuts that were offered free. When I was little and all through adolescence, Eva had forbidden me from eating peanuts, or nuts of any kind, saying I could choke to death on them.

We came out across the Atlantic Ocean, and I looked down at the dark blue mass, waves catching the sun and sparkling up to me even at this altitude. I looked for boats or ships, but I couldn't see any wakes.

We began our descent to Boston. I had to switch planes there for a flight to D.C., then on to Indy. Weird flight plan, I thought. But hey—at least I was getting back. Yeah, right.

We touched down and taxied to the terminal. The ramps hung like the legs of spiders from the squat, fat terminal complex, extending to the planes, attaching themselves, then sucking out the passengers. The flight from Presque Isle was going on to Miami. Most of the people were staying on board. Probably retirees who shuttled between vacation resorts, pummeling each other in lines in airports while in transit. Maybe they had some sort of league set up for it. I don't know. I stood up and walked down the aisle. I knew I had an hour-and-a-half to kill, but I was paranoid as fucking hell about getting to my gate. I did not want to get stranded in Boston's airport with only 13 cents on me.

I got out of the plane and walked up the "jetway" into the terminal. Big TV screens carried the information on arrivals and departures. This was all a new experience for me. I hadn't flown since I was a kid. My only recent experiences with airports lay in going to Indy to meet guys coming back from breaks. I pulled out my ticket packet and looked for my flight number. I was switching airlines, I saw, which was weird. Because I would be on a different airline, I had to go to a different "concourse" of the terminal. As I made my way down long, wide hallways, I passed at least two huge tanks holding lobsters for sale to travelers. They were all advertised as "Fresh Maine Lobsters." I chuckled to myself. All I'd had to eat in Maine was McDonald's, fired bologna, and some eggs. I guessed the delicacies would wait for a later time, when I was a touring rock star with the Dendrites, or maybe when I was some kind of revolutionary on the lam.

I found my gate and checked in with the ticket person. He smiled—big switch from the guy in Presque Isle—and flipped through my packet and stamped a couple of things. I thanked him and went to sit in the waiting area. There was a smoking section. I really wanted to have a cigarette. A woman sat down five or six seats away. She was attractive and had a worldly sort of look about her—a look as if she was sophisticated and intelligent, that she'd been through and around a lot of bullshit, and knew pretty much what to expect from the World. I sat there trying to read, but torn between hunger and nicotine jonesing, it was pretty diffcult. Then she pulled out and lit up a cigarette—Vantage menthols, my brand. She glanced up a couple of times and once caught me looking at her. She seemed annoyed, and went back to reading her magazine and smoking.

I didn't know what to do. I didn't want to beg in an airport. Bumming cigarettes from friends was one thing. This was different. And how could I do that? It would sound staged—she already had me pegged, no doubt, as some sort of lecher. Finally, I got up and walked toward her. She immediately looked up and watched me guardedly as I crossed toward her.

"Excuse me," I said. She said nothing but simply shot me a suspicious and angry look. "I'm a college student. I just hitch hiked halfway across the country. I was wired a ticket to fly back to Indiana. I'll be back there in just a couple of hours. But I have only 13 cents to my name, I am going through nicotine withdrawls, and you smoke my brand of cigarettes. Is there any way that I could bum one off you?"

Her looks softened. She glanced up and down my skinny frame. She picked up the pack and shook a couple of cigarettes out. "Go ahead," she said, "take a couple. I know how it is. I hitch hiked Europe one summer."

I thanked her and took a couple. She invited me to join her. She offered me a light, and as I drew in the first of the smoke, my head became dizzy from the nicotine rush. We sat there talking for the rest of my lay-over. She was interested in my stories of hitch hiking, where I went to school, and how I'd decided to do what I had done. She drew out every fact from me that she could. She wasn't simply a good listener—she was almost like an investigator, squeezing me for every detail. She seemed intrigued that I had hitch hiked out, but that I was flying back. As we talked, the waiting area around us filled with passengers. They called the flight about 20 minutes before take-off, and we continued to sit and talk as the flight boarded. I noticed that several of the men who were taking the flight were glancing over at her and letting their gazes linger. Like I said, she was attractive, but not in a way that really appealed to me. Her looks were those of a model—high cheek bones, very striking features. I felt flattered, though, by the fact that she was spending her time with, and giving her attention, to me. By now I was on the seventh or eighth cigarette from her, and she had broken open a fresh pack. Finally, when they announced the last call for boarding, we snuffed out our cigarettes and walked over to the gate. She pressed three or four more smokes into my hand and wished me a good flight. When we boarded, she took a seat in first-class. I walked on back to steerage, found my window seat, and squeezed by the old woman who was sitting on the aisle. As I buckled in, I realized that in all of our conversation, the only detail about her I'd learned was that she had hitch hiked Europe after college, and that she was getting off of the plane in D.C. I leaned back in my seat, happy for having met her—actually, she never even told me her name—and certainly happy for the cigarettes.

The flight to D.C. was uneventful. I suffered my usual phobic reactions on take-off and landing, knuckles white and gripping the armrests of my seat. We were on the ground for maybe 20 minutes. The old woman next to me got up and was replaced by a portly businessman. Neither spoke to me at all. The businessman slept through take-off and most of the flight.

As we neared Indianapolis, I grew more pensive. I dreaded being greeted by whomever it would be. I figured Eva would be there. She would not be alone. I didn't know if it would be Adolf or the Cousin. Whoever it was, the welcome I would receive would not be "happy." They would be smug and condescending. I looked down on the fields and roads and highways and wished I was someplace else. On a tour plane with my rock band. Yeah, sure. Writing a new song on the piano I first would have to learn to play.

As though summoned by a wake-up call in his head, the businessman's eyes opened about 15 minutes out from Indianapolis. We began our descent long before I became aware of it, of course. I mean, there's a slight tilt forward that's difficult to detect. But finally the stewardess came onto the intercom and advised us that we were ten minutes from arrival. She told us the weather conditions in Indy and thanked us for flying Delta.

Until now, nothing about Indiana had been real since I had left it nearly a week ago. It didn't exist anywhere except on a map, or at the end of a phone line. Living on the interstates, sleeping in ditches or wherever else I could, and trying to get to Maine had been my only reality. I'd chosen the wrong direction at the interstate that first day. I definitely should not have gone east to Maine. That had all turned out wrong. Then I'd made a call and—Boom!—my ticket was wired to me. I flew in a few hours the distance it had taken three-and-a-half days for me to cover by thumbing. I was in a giant tube traveling at excessive speeds through the skies to another place. Hey!!!!—Maybe this vehicle was just like Austin's station wagon I had ridden in to the David Bowie concert! But no. I wasn't on acid right now, and this was all too real.

I hadn't the least idea of what to say. I always tried to play-act in my mind the scenes of personal drama I anticipated facing. I would practice lines. I would discard some, re-write others. Then I would imagine someone saying something different, and I would try to anticipate. But I'd done none of that for my "homecoming" to Indiana. The confrontation lay only a few minutes ahead.

The sun was out and, except for a few little bumps, the flight was smooth. As the plane made its final approach, I looked down and saw where I-70 hooks up to I-465 on the west side of Indy, where I'd thumbed only six days ago. I leaned back in my seat for the mild shock of touchdown. The stewardess advised us to stay in our seats until the aircraft had come to a complete stop, what the weather was like, thank you for flying Delta, etc.

The plane took a while to taxi to the terminal. The Indianapolis Airport—Weir Cook was its name, for a Hoosier aviator of the 1920s—had really expanded since I was a kid. We used to drive down to Indy to drop off or pick up Adolf on one of his business trips. The interstate hadn't been built yet, so we had to follow a circuitous route of back roads, streets, and narrow, two-lane highways. The airport itself had been tiny. The terminal was small and flat with an observation deck on the roof. Nearly all of the aircraft were propeller-driven. "Jets" were an exotic development. There were no metal detectors. The whole thing was very innocent.

Now the Indy airport was a sprawl, with giant 747s landing regularly, and the whine of jet engines a constant. There were a couple of "concourses" in the terminal. The city had even attached the word "International" on the name of the airport. The vehicular ground traffic came by way of several interstates.

The plane eased up to the huge arm reaching out to it. There was a bump as the aircraft and arm joined, then another couple of similar sounds as the crew opened the door. People around me were getting up and moving. I was amazed that the businessman next to me could fall asleep so quickly then, at the end of the flight, waken and be ready to move, particularly with the rapid movements he now displayed. He was nearly to the curtains of the first-class section before any of the other passengers had set foot in the aisle. I was definitely in no hurry, though. While I was glad to leave Maine, I knew I was about to walk into some serious shit. I was the last passenger out. The stewardess smiled at me as I exited. She wished me a good day.

I immediately saw Eva as I came out of the jetway and into the terminal. She was next to the velveteen rope used to separate passengers from other people. I walked straight toward her and had no expression on my face. As I neared her I could see the crevice of wrinkles at the corners of her mouth—deep things that had been formed by decades of anger and hate—tighten; as though the crevices held a neural toxin that would kill on contact. She didn't say a word, and neither did I, as we walked down the concourse. But then I saw a newsstand.

"Do you have a couple of bucks?" I asked. She gave a malevolent sound of disgust, sort of like a snort, but more vile. Then I added, "I need a pack of cigarettes."

"You can wait," she said, and I knew from that how pissed off she was. The one vice she understood was smoking. If I was broke at school and I needed money for books or paper or shoes, that was a waste and I had no common sense. But if I said that I needed cigarettes, I could count on a carton of my brand being mailed to me immediately.

We went to the baggage claim area. She stood back as I went to the big carousel spun. I didn't have to wait long for my battered cheap backpack/sleeping bag. I grabbed the one good strap and carried it at arm's length. I didn't know if I had far to walk but I was damned if I would put that fucker over my shoulder one more time.

Eva accompanied me out of the terminal and, who was sitting there in the driver's seat of the big Buick there at the curb, but my favorite person in all the Universe—the Cousin! He was biting down on some sort of thin, filtered cigar stuck into the corner of his mouth. I sort of recognized the silhouette he intended to strike, then I had it. George Peppard had made that sort of visage famous in his role as the insurance fraud investigator "Banacek," coming to you weekly on whichever network. I opened the back door and tossed in my pack, then plopped into the seat next to it and slammed the door. The Cousin just sort of shook his head and, once Eva was in place in the shotgun seat, we took off.

As we got onto the interstate, I felt my stomach growl again. But then I remembered the cigarettes the woman had given me in the terminal in D.C., and I pulled one out, flipped open the ashtray in the armrest next to me in the backseat. As soon as I lit up, I felt thankful for the nicotine coursing through my system.

"You're going to Glendale tomorrow," Eva said in a very clipped voice.

I'd never really notice before how her face bent naturally into a frown like that. Sort of like Norma Desmond's expression in Sunset Boulevard, this garish, lipsticked evil look. I looked away, and saw the billboards alongside the interstate, advertising various airlines. But why would they advertise in the direction going away from the airport? Shouldn't they be advertising in the other direction, trying to catch people going to the airport? I guess I didn't see the point, but that shows how much I really wanted to listen to Eva.

"We paid the money you owed to the fraternity," she said, solemnly. Oh fuck, I thought. This is going to get nasty. Her words were stated in a sharp, accusing voice. The venom seeped from the corners of her mouth and into her words. She turned slightly, a look of disgust still there, yep, yessirree Bob. What a great fucking time this was proving to be. "We just want to know what it was for."

Well now, there it was, right out onto the table—or into the air-conditioned comfort of one of the truly great interstate monster cars ever designed, the 1975 Buick Electra Limited, with a 455 four-barrel under the hood and seats made of leather and as big as a good-sized living room. How could I explain about the hash that had been ripped off me? Yeah, right, like—See, dear Auntie, there were these drugs that I was dealing so that I could cach a buzz more cheaply—fiscal responsibility and all that, okay—and these two guys I met in a bar weren't hip to the thing I was saying about revolution and all they knew was that they were partying with some affluent white kid in a fraternity and he had all this hashish and they figured they'd rip off what they could, even though it was from the Kid here, and I'd borrowed against my house bill for the hashish and I haven't eaten on a regular basis since February and my stomach is growling right fucking now because I haven't really eaten anything except these weird eggs yesterday morning and fried bologna the day before.

Possibly a bad tact. How about explaining the debt by way of another vice? "I lost the money getting too deep into poker." No, I was too good a card player. She would never believe me. I tried hard to think of some other vice. "It wasn't my fault, it was this urge I had."

But, of course, I did not say any of this. I simply sat there, staring straight ahead for a minute or so, puffing once or twice on my cigarette and hoping this conversation, and this ride, would soon end.

"It was a girl, wasn't it?" Eva asked.

I was confused by the question. Why would I spend that much money on a—Whoa!!! I looked at her again. She was remaining calm. And, bad driver though the Cousin was, he was maintaining good control over the car. Eva meant that she thought that the money had been meant to pay for—an abortion!!

Well, that was one I hadn't thought. I was, after all, still a virgin, even after having nearly lost that particular station in life so recently with Patricia. Huh! An abortion! As if I'd do that—get a woman pregnant, pay for an abortion, then leave the state. Right. Eva must think that I am really some kind of nice guy. I inhaled deeply on the cigarette, and peered at Eva through squinted eyes and the smoke. What alternative did I really have? Tell her the truth? Yeah, sure, right. Sorry, but—no. Eva and Adolf could be far more tolerant of an abortion than they could of a kid smoking drugs and getting ripped off in that pursuit. Besides, this was a ready-made, all-in-one solution/explanation for the trip to Maine, the debt at the fraternity, the whole nine yards. The truth was far too complex to explain. Eva and Adolf and the Cousin had thought this all out in a much more simplistic and smutty way.

THEN IT HIT ME!

The Big Realization! Eva was a Roman Catholic and abortion was a mortal sin! In her mind, I had enabled the taking of an unborn human life. She had aided in that by paying for the debt to the fraternity that had supposedly been rung up paying for the dirty deed. Even though that set of events had never occurred, in the context of the Holy Roman Church, it didn't matter. One could sin in word, deed, and thought.

I thought, "Cool." What I said was, "Yeah." And she turned around and sighed in disgust, and I was off the hook. She still had to deal with Jesus or the Mother Mary or the Holy Ghost or one of the saints she prayed to, and she'd probably be told by one of the molesting priests in the parish to put so much money in the poor box, but so fucking what? I was off the hook! Besides, I felt as if I had just racked up a major score against the big lead that she had over me in a lifetime of registering enmity. I had just racked her with a Mortal Sin. I was happy. I smiled and held a greater appreciation for the beauty of the passing countryside. The World was good in some ways. Sure, as an atheist, I knew that there wasn't a Hell she would go to. I didn't—don't—believe that the Big Guy in the sky exists. But, in her mind, she was potentially fucked for Eternity. She'd do a lot of work on the rosary to dodge this one.

We rode on in silence for a while. I was surprised that the Cousin hadn't said anything, but I figured it was only a matter of time before he got in a few digs. I insisted that we stop at the World's Largest Dairy Queen. Eva forked over a couple of bucks. I got three hot dogs, a large order of fries, and a vanilla coke. I wolfed everything down, then lit up my next to last cigarette. Except for the huge belch I managed to produce a few minutes later, the rest of the 50-mile trip passed in silence. I'd be back in Glendale tomorrow. Shit, one week was all I'd lasted. Sort of like Steve McQueen in *The Great Escape* being tossed into the cooler at the Stalag for a few days after a short taste of freedom. I would go back and some people would laugh at me.

We turned into the drive, and I was truck by how little things had changed. To the right, in the small valley that looped around the hill, was the pond. To the left, in another valley, was the front field. The hills were plush with the foliage of hundreds of trees and bushes and grasses and other ground cover. Perched on the hill itself, white pillars shining in the afternoon sun, was the house, about a quarter-mile, up the winding gravel driveway. As we drove up the lane, I thought about my single greatest accomplishment as a 10-year-old: learning to ride a bike, then managing to peddle one all the way up the hill without having to stop.

Once the car was parked—and the Cousin had not said anything for the entire trip now—I got out of the car and started for the house. Then I heard the yelping of a dog and looked over and saw a doghouse next to the Upper Barn, the barn at the top of the hill next to the Japanese House. The dog was a short-haired bird dog. It looked like a Weimerauner—a German breed of dog, one we'd had, like I said before, when I was a little kid. I tossed my pack over in front of one of the doors of the Japanese House, and walked over to the dog, which wasn't much more than a pup. She was really happy when I knelt down and let her lick my face. I petted her and tried to hold her. She was chained around the neck, and the chain ran to the doghouse, and I could tell no one paid her much attention.

"Her name is Muffin," Eva said. "I just bought her last week."

I already felt sorry for the dog. Then I thought about how much more sunshine and fresh air she got than the Cousin's dog down in the basement. I cringed realizing I was actually back here, and I hugged the dog and she stopped struggling. She just stood there loving the attention and wagging her stub of a tail. Finally, I walked across the expanse of driveway and went inside the house. I went upstairs to the room I shared with the Cousin and lay down on my bed. Oh boy, I thought, tonight's supper—yes, we lived in the country, so the evening meal was called "supper"—ought to be something special. But it turned out to be anti-climactic. No one said anything to me. I had the eerie feeling I did not exist. The Cousin's silence, I knew, was temporary. Eventually he would erupt. That time had not yet arrived, though, and, once I was done with my meal, I got up from the table and went outside to savor my last cigarette.

This summer would be too weird, I thought. The previous summer I'd set up my stereo in a cramped space next to my bed and listened to headphones. I wanted to minimize my contact with the others. I went over and petted the dog some more. Then a thought struck me. I decided to check out the Japanese House. This time I would look at it, not for the books and albums I could find, but as a refuge.

It was musty in there, and smelled of old fertilizer that had been stored there years before. I finished my cigarette and went back inside the house. I read the Speer book. It was weird how Speer described going to dinner parties hosted by Hitler. The dishes were all vegetarian—I'm sure it was not out of any humanitarian impulses that the German dictator felt. Maybe they were made out of real vegetarians. Hitler at random would make fun of people, even as they sat there at table. I mean, what could they do? He was frying people for the fact that they simply existed. Bumping someone off for displeasing him at a dinner party was not out of the question. I read until I crashed. Tomorrow I would return to Glendale.